Public Finance in Canada:
Selected Readings

Public Finance in Canada: Selected Readings

edited by

A. J. Robinson
James Cutt

Methuen

Toronto   London   Sydney   Wellington

Public Finance in Canada:
Selected Readings

Published in Toronto by Methuen Publications
(A Division of the Carswell Co. Ltd.)
and in London by Methuen & Co Ltd

Library of Congress Catalog Card Number 68-8672

SBN 416 99530 6/44

Printed and bound in Canada

Contents

Preface   *ix*

Chapter One
The Objectives of Economic Policy

1   Sources of Value-Judgements and Bias   2
T. W. Hutchison

2   The Objectives of Economic Policy   7
E. S. Kirschen & Associates

3   Is Economic Welfare Synonymous with   12
Total Welfare? *A. C. Pigou*

4   The Economists' Objectives for Budget Policy   14
A. J. Robinson

5   Economic Goals for Canada to the 1970's   17
Economic Council of Canada

6   Widely Accepted National Objectives for Canada   20
Royal Commission on Taxation

7   The Unfairness of an "Equitable" Tax System   23
F. Low-Beer

8   The Concept of "Equity" in the Carter Report   27
A. J. Robinson

9   Why Growth Should *Not* be a Policy Objective   30
E. J. Mishan

10   The Concept of a "Trade-Off"   33
R. G. Bodkin, E. P. Bond, G. L. Reuber, and T. R. Robinson

11   The Trade-Off Between Inflation and Unemployment   34
Economic Council of Canada

12   The Conflict between Economic Growth and Equity   37
Royal Commission on Taxation

13   Equity and Growth *James Cutt*   38

14   The "Faddiness" of Economic Objectives *H. G. Johnson*   44

Chapter Two
Government Expenditures

15   An Economic Theory of Democracy   50
Anthony Downs

16   Governments Maximize their own Interest   53
Albert Breton

17   Decision-Making by Official Commission   57
W. Irwin Gillespie

18   The Orthodox Model of Majority Rule   60
     James M. Buchanan and Gordon Tullock
19   The Programme and Performance Budget   74
     UN Department of Economic and Social Affairs
20   The Benefit-Cost Analysis Approach   77
     to Project Evaluation
     W. R. D. Sewell, J. Davis, A. D. Scott and D. W. Ross
21   Problems of Differential Measurability in Benefit-   83
     Cost Analysis *Anthony Downs*

Chapter Three
Federal-Provincial Relations

22   Federal Government Defined *Kenneth C. Wheare*   88
23   The Constitutional Basis of Public Expenditure   90
     in Canada *B. U. Ratchford*
24   The Rowell-Sirois Views on Canadian Tax Policy   103
     J. Sirois, J. W. Dafoe, R. A. Mackay and H. F. Angus
25   The Carter Views on Canadian Tax Policy *K. L. Carter,*   107
     A. E. Beauvais, S. M. Milne, J. H. Perry, D. G. Grant and
     C. E. S. Walls
26   The Objectives of Canadian Federation: 109
     A Federal View *Mitchell Sharp*
27   A Provincial View of Federation *John Robarts*   111
28   The Inseparability of Cultural and Financial Autonomy   113
     in a Federation *Daniel Johnson*
29   Conditional and Unconditional Grants in Theory   116
     Anthony D. Scott
30   The Principles of Federal Finance and the   123
     Canadian Case *R. Dehem and J. N. Wolfe*
31   The Fiscal Equity Principle   132
     John F. Graham
32   The Economics Component of Canadian Federalism   143
     David M. Nowlan
33   Revenue Sharing Between Federal and   156
     Provincial Governments *A. J. Robinson*

Chapter Four
Taxation in Canada

34   Other Principles of Taxation   161
     Ontario Committee on Taxation
35   The Incidence of the Total Tax Structure   167
     W. I. Gillespie
36   An Overview of Tax Revenue in Canada   173
     Canadian Tax Foundation

37	The National Revenue Structure *Canadian Tax Foundation*	175
38	Provincial Tax Revenue *Canadian Tax Foundation*	183
39	The Canadian Concept of Income *J. Harvey Perry*	192
40	A Comprehensive Definition of Income *Royal Commission on Taxation*	195
41	Capital Gains: To Tax or Not To Tax *Ronald Robertson*	198
42	The Taxation of Capital Gains *Royal Commission on Taxation*	202
43	Capital Gains *J. Harvey Perry*	203
44	Statistical Comparisons — Personal Income Taxes *M. Bryden*	205
45	Criteria Governing the Selection of a Rate Schedule *Royal Commission on Taxation*	208
46	The Family Unit *Royal Commission on Taxation*	212
47	Income Averaging *Royal Commission on Taxation*	213
48	Alternative Approaches to Integration *J. R. Petrie*	217
49	Corporation Income Taxation *Royal Commission on Taxation*	220
50	Estate and Gift Taxation *Royal Commission on Taxation*	223
51	The Taxation of Wealth *Ontario Committee on Taxation*	225
52	History of Sales Tax in Canada *Ontario Committee on Taxation*	228
53	Sales Tax and Equity *Ontario Committee on Taxation*	229
54	Economic Effects of Sales Taxes *Ontario Committee on Taxation*	232
55	The Inclusion of Services in the Tax Base I *Ontario Committee on Taxation*	235
56	The Inclusion of Services in the Tax Base II *Saskatchewan Royal Commission on Taxation*	238
57	Merits of the Retail Tax *J. F. Due*	240
58	A Federal Sales Tax *Royal Commission on Taxation*	241
59	Cumulative Turnover Tax *Royal Commission on Taxation*	243
60	Value-Added and Single Stage Taxes: A Comparison *Royal Commission on Taxation*	245
61	A Value-Added Tax for Canada? *R. M. Malt*	247

62   The Selective Employment Tax in Britain   250
     James Cutt
63   Negative Income Taxation *C. Green*   254

Chapter Five
Municipal Finance

64   A Pure Theory of Local Expenditures   262
     Charles M. Tiebout
65   The Organization of Metropolitan Governments   271
     George F. Break
66   Financial Implications of Urban Growth   277
     Economic Council of Canada

Chapter Six
Fiscal Policy for Stabilization and Growth

67   Fiscal Policy for Stability   290
     Royal Commission on Taxation
68   The Time Lags of Fiscal Policy *R. M. Will*   305
69   The Theory of Fiscal Policy from the Point   317
     of View of the Province *C. L. Barber*
70   Taxation for Stabilization *S. Surrey*   323
71   Fiscal Policy for Growth   329
     Royal Commission on Taxation

Bibliography   348

Index   353

Preface

These readings have been selected to complement a standard textbook in Public Finance. The practice in Canadian universities is to use one of the many "foreign" textbooks, most of which are satisfactory at the undergraduate level. Our book of readings will not be a substitute for any of these textbooks, but will provide additional discussion of the theoretical and practical problems of Public Finance in a Canadian context. We also refer the student to the excellent descriptive material and statistical analyses of Canadian government finance brought out regularly by the Canadian Tax Foundation, especially *The National Finances, Provincial Finances* and the *Local Finance* series.

Another purpose of our book is to introduce topics which are currently being discussed in economic journals and articles, or as questions of public policy, but on which insufficient material is available to permit their inclusion in the standard economics textbooks. A book of readings can present a sufficient variety of viewpoints to indicate what the main issues are, without the editors pronouncing the last word. For example, we have included a number of authoritative statements on policy objectives without attempting to steer the reader to a "correct" view, and we have included material on the new approaches to public expenditures and municipal finance which do not yet occupy much textbook space.

There are two possible approaches in introducing a book of this kind. The first would examine at length the nature of the subject covered and would offer in the Preface extensive editorial comment on the extracts included. The second approach would briefly introduce the subject matter, leaving detailed editorial comment on each section to the appropriate place in the text. We have adopted the second approach.

One of the features of Canadian public discussion is the interest aroused by economic issues. This is not unusual, since the forces that shaped modern Canada have been economic — the market for furs; the demand for waterways and railways to market Canadian products; the national policy to develop Canadian manufacturing; the imperial connection, which increased the security of Canadian export markets as well as providing raw materials for the mother country; and even Confederation itself, which established a vast continental market for Canadian manufacturers. The major issues in modern public policy — the exchange rate, wage parity with the United States, poverty and the distribution of income, foreign investment in Canadian industries, the status of Quebec — are also mainly economic issues, some of which have political overtones.

There is, then, no lack of economic policy issues for discussion in Canadian economics classes, and these questions are foremost in the minds of today's politically sensitive students. But there is a deficiency of conveniently accessible material to provide a sound basis for discussion. This book of readings, it is hoped, will remedy this fault. The principles of economic analysis used in Canada are not different from those used in the rest of the world, but generally they do not take on real meaning for students until they are applied to concrete issues. This is particularly true in a policy-oriented course such as Public Finance, where it is the conflict between economic theory and institutional constraints that gives rise to many important issues.

The first chapter raises the question, so important in a period when the Canadian government is assuming a larger role in the economy, of what government policy ought to be aiming at. What are the objectives of government policy; how are these objectives decided and by whom; whom do they benefit; which objectives should have priority? Since there are no absolute answers to these questions, the solutions adopted by the community will not be constant. The pieces we have selected show the nature of the problems involved and indicate the solutions that the modern Canadian community has found acceptable.

The second chapter goes on to discuss the vehicle by which these objectives are translated into policy measures, examining the theory of economic policy formulation in a democratic society, and some of the techniques of economic decision-making in government.

Economic decision-making in the context of Canadian federal government is the theme of Chapter Three. The extracts deal with both the theoretical background of federalism and the Canadian experience of federal governments.

Chapter Four examines the general field of taxation. The federal and provincial tax systems in Canada have not developed in accordance with any overall tax philosophy but rather in response to the requirements of particular situations. The resulting lack of coherence and consistency at the federal level has been analyzed at length in the Carter Commission Report; and the McLeod, Belanger and Smith Reports have examined the tax systems of Saskatchewan, Quebec and Ontario respectively. This chapter brings together significant material from the earlier literature in the study of taxation and from these recent Commission reports.

In Chapter Five, some of the work is introduced which has resulted in the recognition of municipal economics as a branch of public finance in its own right. This development owes much to the growing urbanization of western economies, and the growth of cities whose policies encompass most of the main areas in public finance and whose budgets rival in size those of the territories in which they are located.

Chapter Six examines the role of fiscal — tax and expenditure — policy in Canada with respect to the policy objectives of stabilization and economic growth. Although attention is primarily directed to federal fiscal policy, the chapter includes one extract which examines the feasibility and usefulness of a provincial role in stabilization policy.

We would like to acknowledge the generous help we have received from colleagues in our own and other universities, who have given us the benefit of their views on the need for a volume such as this. We express our gratitude to all the authors and publishers who granted us permission to reproduce their work. Special mention should be made of the Queen's Printer and the Canadian Tax Foundation for their generosity in this regard. Finally, our sincere thanks to the staff of Methuen Publications not only for their constructive support in the preparation of the book, but also for their contagious enthusiasm and energy in getting it published.

York University   A.J.R.

Toronto   J.C.

July 1968

Chapter One
The Objectives
of Economic Policy

Within the last generation or so, the demands upon modern governments for expenditures on war and defence, on the maintenance of full employment, on the provision of education and social welfare, and on assistance to underdeveloped countries, all without curtailing private consumption and investment, have made governments acutely aware of the meaning of scarcity of resources in the economist's sense, and of the consequences of attempting to satisfy too many objectives with limited national resources. The usual consequences of these demands have been inflation and deficits in the balance of payments. Experience has brought the concept of opportunity cost within the purview of policy makers: they have realized that mere adoption of a policy objective provides no resources with which to achieve it, and in fact a decision to provide the resources to achieve one policy objective may *ipso facto* be a decision to withdraw resources from programs set up to achieve other objectives. When government is a relatively large sector of the economy, as it is in modern economies (in Canada expenditure of all governments, excluding intergovernmental transfers, is about one third of gross national product), lack of restraint in the public sector could disrupt the total economy. To preserve order in the economy, governments must therefore establish some mechanism to decide which objectives are to be achieved and to what extent. Then the first question to be decided is: what are the objectives of the community? Since there will be a multiplicity of objectives, the order of priority must be decided. The community may have major and minor objectives, and a low level of achievement of the latter may be less disturbing than a low level of achievement of the former. Once the weighting of the various objectives is completed, policy makers will decide how taxation and public expenditures will be used to achieve them.

This chapter deals with the weighting of objectives in public policy. The selection and ranking of policy objectives involves value judgments, which is why it cannot be carried out completely within the ethically neutral science of economics. Yet as Walter Heller, Chairman of the Council of Economic Advisers under Presidents Kennedy and Johnson, has noted, value judgments are inescapable in the making of economic policy; moreover, "value judgments are desirable, for to say anything of importance in the policy process requires such judgments". The following papers show how value judgments underlie economic objectives, but that nevertheless modern

1

communities can agree on a set of economic objectives. In the remainder of the chapter, the problems of reconciling conflicting objectives and generally arranging objectives in a manner that enables them to be handled within the usual budgetary framework are discussed.

How Value Judgments enter into Policy Decisions

The following extract shows how value judgments enter into all economic discussion. The first type of value judgment, which the author calls "pre-scientific", is one that economics shares with all the sciences. It involves the selection of the scholarly rules of the game, including methods of procedure, criteria of scientific method, the choice of concepts and definitions, and the selection of certain problems for study and the rejection of others. The second type of value judgment, one in which we are more interested, concerns the way in which ethical or political values affect the nature of policy objectives adopted and the means chosen to achieve those objectives.

1   Sources of Value-judgments and Bias*

T. W. Hutchison

It seems clear that if the economist confined himself strictly to 'scientific prognoses', on the basis of 'well-tested and corroborated' scientific laws, he would be able to offer very little genuinely useful advice — though not absolutely none. But as regards most important realistic policy-issues, the scope of his advice would be extremely limited or negligible, unless he resorted to judgments and hunches on which different experts will often not agree, and which are inevitably liable, especially in the field of economic policy, to ideological prejudice or bias. To expect or suggest that in the vast majority of *realistic* policy issues an economist can or should 'demonstrate' the economic gains of one policy as compared with another — like the proof of a geometrical theorem, beyond all reasonable disagreement — is to indulge in intellectual delusion.[1] To state that

---

*Reprinted by permission of author and publisher from T. W. Hutchison, *'Positive' Economics and Policy Objectives*, Allen & Unwin, London, 1964.

[1]"It cannot be stated too emphatically that no economist of any standing in this country has alleged, much less demonstrated, that significant economic gains would accrue to this country on entering the Common Market." E. J. Mishan, *The Times*, October 2, 1962. We are not concerned with what economists ("of any satnding" or otherwise) *alleged* on this issue, but with the epistemological misconception of suggesting, even as a remote practical possibility, that any conclusions about economic gains or losses could be *"demonstrated"* — either from Britain entering or from her staying out of the Common Market.

there are significant economic gains from adopting one policy rather than another, one has to make predictions as to what the effects of the different policies will be. Logical, mathematical or geometrical 'demonstration' *may* illuminatingly analyse or elaborate a prediction when made. But in the majority of realistic cases it is the quality of the judgment in predicting or forecasting which is essential.[2]

The question arises then as to how far the economist's judgment or hunch is 'better', or more often 'right', than the non-economist's, with regard to economic predictions or forecasts; and how far he is entitled to claim or assume some measure of 'expert' authority for predictions in which subjective judgments are or may be present in differing degrees.

There are many different kinds of economic, or politico-economic, predictions or forecasts, and with regard to some, the sceptical conclusion that 'anybody's' guess will be as good as the economist's is less justified than with regard to others — though economists can probably be found predicting with equal cheerfulness in both kinds of cases . . . . [Paul A.] Samuelson has claimed that though economists 'cannot forecast well . . . they forecast the economy better than any other group thus far discovered. Empirical statisticians, clairvoyants, down-to-earth businessmen, hunch-players — all these turn out to have a worse "batting average" than government, academic and business economists' — though not, it seems, very much worse.[3] No one is better qualified to assert such a generalization than Samuelson, though it is not clear on how much systematic evidence he bases it, and it obviously holds only for some economists and not for all. Moreover, it should be noted that Samuelson's claim might be taken simply, or

---

[2]*Cf.* the classic pronouncement by Sir James Fitzjames Stephen: "The one talent which is worth all other talents put together in human affairs is the talent of judging right upon imperfect materials, the talent if you please of guessing right. It is a talent which no rules will ever teach and which even experience does not always give. It often co-exists with a good deal of slowness and dullness and with a very slight poser of expression. All that can be said about it is, that to see things as they are, without exaggeration or passion, is essential to it; but how can we see things as they are? Simply by opening our eyes and looking with whatever power we may have. All really important matters are decided, not by a process of argument worked out from adequate premises to a necessary conclusion, but by making a wise choice between several possible views." *Liberty, Equality, Fraternity*, 2nd ed., 1874, p. 352, quoted by A. S. Ashton, *Lloyds Bank Review*, October 1962, p. 30. Stephen's recipe of "simply . . . opening our eyes" may seem a little *simpliste*. But he is surely right that the "batting averages" are not likely to be very high of the ideologue (with his "passion") or the geometrician concentrating on processes of argument "from adequate premises to a necessary conclusion". Unfortunately, so much economic education concentrates exclusively on these logical or geometrical processes as "the one thing necessary", to the neglect of developing at least an awareness of the need for judgment — which itself may not be so completely unteachable as Stephen suggests.

[3]P. A. Samuelson, *Problems of the American Economy*, Stamp Memorial Lecture 1961, 1962, p. 23. I. M. D. Little holds that it 'cannot be taken for granted' that 'economists are better at forecasting, and better at judging the economic consequences of alternative policies, than are administrators or bankers', but that their training does give them certain advantages. 'The Economist in Whitehall', *Lloyds Bank Review*, April 1957, p. 35.

mainly, as covering, say, the forecasting of next year's G.N.P. for the United States, and not many other sorts of prediction (e.g. with regard to the economic effects of Britain joining the Common Market) which economists attempt.

Anyhow, a considerable complication regarding predictions in the social and economic field arises from the interaction of observer and observed, or the influence of the prediction on the predicted event — the 'Oedipus effect' as Popper calls it. It is as though meteorologists had to forecast the weather in conditions where private and/or governmental rain-making (as well as counter rain-making) agencies could, and did, frequently and effectively operate. But it has been shown that however much 'Oedipus' effects may complicate prediction they do not make it impossible, or render it, in the social field, completely different in principle from prediction in the natural sciences.[4] The problem, rather, which we are centrally concerned with here would be presented by a situation where some meteorologists were passionately interested financially and otherwise in outdoor activities, while others were passionately committed to indoor activities, and where these ideological prejudices and presuppositions affected their weather forecasts.

We conclude that because scientific 'prognosis' on the basis of 'well-tested and corroborated scientific laws' has, at any rate for the time being, a limited range, insufficient to support the wide policy ambitions of people and government, much or most social and economic prediction *has* to consist of forecasting on the basis of hunch, judgment, guesswork and insufficiently tested generalizations, which may well be shaped by subjective optimism and pessimism stemming from political and ideological presuppositions. It does, however, seem reasonable to expect that one be given as clear indications as may be practicable as to how far the different elements — empirical generalizations, tendencies, hunches and 'guess-timates' — on which different predictions are based, consist of well-tested and corroborated laws and their initial conditions, on which a consensus exists, and how far they are untested and subjective, and therefore specially liable to bias. As we have already noted, we have the authority for the view that 'economic studies are not to be limited to matters which are amenable to strictly scientific treatment'.

He went on:

"Those conclusions, whether in detail or in general, which are based on individual judgments as to the relative desirability or different social aims or as to matters of fact which lie beyond the scope of any individual's special studies, should be clearly distinguished from those which claim to have been reached by scientific method."[5]

We would simply add that the conclusions 'based on individual judgments', which should be clearly distinguished from those claimed 'to have been reached by scientific method', should also include forecasts and predictions other than what we have called 'prognoses' firmly based on acknowledged scientific laws

---

[4]K. R. Popper, *The Poverty of Historicism*, paperback edition, Harper, New York, 1961, pp. 12-17; and E. Grunberg and F. Modigliani, 'Predictability of Social Events', *Journal of Political Economy*, December 1954, p. 465.

[5]*Industry and Trade*, 1919, p. 676.

and generalizations; and should also include . . . attitudes to risk — of preference, aversion or neutrality — which are inevitably subjective.

The uncertainty and subjectivity of predictions and forecasts in economics leave a wide scope for the possible workings of bias and 'prejudice'. To some extent, and in no pejorative sense, a kind of prejudice may be inevitable in venturing a prediction as a basis for a policy recommendation. Just as, in Keynes's phrase, 'animal spirits', or 'a spontaneous urge to action rather than inaction', rather than reasonable calculation alone, is the basis of 'most, probably, of our decisions to do something positive, the full consequences of which will be drawn out over many days to come',[6] so a kind of intellectual high spirits prompting one to say something rather than nothing are the basis for some, if not many, kinds of predictions and forecasts. As Hazlitt said in his *Paragraphs on Prejudice*: 'Without the aid of prejudice and custom, I should not be able to find my way across the room; nor know how to conduct myself in any circumstances, nor know what to feel in any relation to life. Reason may play the critic, and correct certain errors afterwards, but if we were to wait for its formal and absolute decisions in the shifting and multifarious combinations of human affairs, the world would stand still. Even men of science, after they have gone over the proofs a number of times, abridge the process, and *jump at a conclusion*.'[7]

There is nothing wrong in stating one's 'prejudices' provided one makes it quite clear that that is what they are, not trying to pass them off as scientific conclusions with claims to what Popper has called 'the authority of objective truth'.[8]

The problems of bias, and the detection and neutralization of its devious workings, are more difficult than those of value-judgments. There is a strong initial drive and propensity to bias in the ideological prejudices and 'visions' with which economic problems are approached, and which often shape initial hypotheses about economic behavior. When the scientific testing process gets started, the practicable tests are often inadequate, or too inconclusive, to promote consensus. Testing may narrow the range of hypotheses, but still leave a number of sharply conflicting competitors in the field, and, where tests fail to 'select', bias or prejudice (mostly more or less political), is free to, and often does, take over.

Though the biased 'selection' or use of persuasive value-loaded terminology and concepts has been prominent throughout much of the history of economic thought, this infringement of scientific procedure or criteria does not seem today to be more than a minor controversial nuisance *among economists*, and infringements are usually not difficult to detect and neutralize.

It is in historical evidence, causal explanations, and in predictions, particularly when a high degree of uncertainty is inevitable, as is most often the case, that selection by political bias, rather than by scientific criteria, becomes serious.

---

[6] J. M. Keynes, *The General Theory of Employment Interest and Money*, Harcourt, New York, 1936, p. 161.

[7] Quoted by Krsto Cviic, *The Listener*, December 13, 1962, p. 1008.

[8] *Conjectures and Refutations*, Basic Books, New York, 1963, p. 375.

Though it may not be difficult for the critical economist to detect it in the works of the more blatant propagandists and ideologues who write about economics and economic policy, it may, also, not be easy to tell just where it ends and some genuine positive insight may be beginning. When the propagandist element in one's own or other people's writings is not deliberate, the difficulties of detection may obviously be very great, especially when the evidence that would constitute an adequate test is not obtainable.

Moreover, bias may and does operate not only when policy proposals and objectives are under discussion but at the general theoretical level, for example with regard to short and long period treatment, theories of interest, and even of value, which may be shaped by ideological prejudices or political predilections for or against 'capitalism' or 'socialism', free markets or state regulation. In fact, . . . subjectivity and bias operate almost as pervasively in general theorizing as in policy discussions and decisions. Certainly, in the case of policy discussions, the pressure of prejudice is likely to be more acute, and the pretext of the need for rapid decision and action on uncertain evidence more effective. Indeed, when particular policy proposals, and the predictions involved, are being debated, flatly contradictory empirical generalization may be asserted as valid (e.g. with regard to the presence of economies of scale in a larger European market).

Furthermore, in acting or in recommending action on uncertain predictions, a kind of value-judgment as to risk-attitudes is inevitably involved. Orthodox analysis of consumers' or policy choices in terms of certainties has encouraged too facile a separation of normative and positive. Though we are not prepared completely to agree with Churchman 'that knowledge and value are "inseparable" concepts',[9] they are intertwined much more deeply than may be realized by those who have concentrated on the choices between certainties.

Finally, the much more complex and often conflicting nature of policy objectives, discussed by economists and aimed at by governments in the last decade or two, has logically required, but has not been matched by, much more complex and precise value-judgments in the discussion of policies. For, apart from the inevitable 'preliminary' value-judgments and 'proposals' regarding choices of problems and criteria, it is policy objectives, in the broadest sense, that bias and value-judgments, latent or explicit, are mainly about. When it is reasonably, if optimistically, demanded that political value-judgments should be made clear and explicit, it is as clear and full statements, as reasonably possible, of policy-preferences, or reasonably full evaluations of different policy objectives, that are required.

---

[9]*Prediction and Optimal Decision*, Prentice-Hall, Englewood Cliffs, N.J., 1961, p. 187.

The range of economic objectives

Of the set of all possible policy objectives, economic objectives would form a subset. This would usually be taken to mean objectives which are in principle measurable in money terms. The achievement of economic objectives could be measured by the increase in national income, or the improvement in per capita income either of the whole society or of a group within the society, such as the aged.

It would be possible for a group of economists to draw up a list of such economic objectives. There would probably be agreement on which of the possible objectives should be comprised within the subset "economic objectives", though they may not agree completely on the order of priority in which they should be achieved. The following piece is an attempt by an international group of nine economists belonging to eight different countries to produce a set of precisely defined economic objectives.

2   The Objectives of Economic Policy*

E. S. Kirschen and Associates

The dividing lines which this analysis of economic policy requires, between aims, objectives, instruments and measures, are necessarily somewhat arbitrary — as are all such divisions between means and ends. In producing our classification of objectives, we tried to find the one which was most useful in showing up the important differences in the policies of our nine countries [i.e. Belgium, France, Germany, Italy, Luxembourg, Netherlands, Norway, United Kingdom and United States]. The classification has been derived partly from the analysis of actual economic policy in these countries, and it takes into account the objectives which the various Governments themselves have stated from time to time. It also uses the various systematisations which have been prepared by other economists.

A short list of the objectives is given below, together with a short description of the components, where appropriate. The list is followed by a discussion of the extent to which they can in fact be quantified . . . . To keep our analysis as near as possible to actual experience, we have tried to use in the list phrases which were in fact commonly employed to describe the objectives; this means that sometimes the objective is defined in terms of the state which it is hoped to reach (full employment), and sometimes in terms of the direction in which it is hoped to move (improvement in the balance of payments) . . . .

*Reprinted by permission of authors and publisher from E. S. Kirschen, J. Benard, H. Besters, F. Blackaby, O. Eckstein, J. Faaland, F. Hartog, L. Morissens. E. Tosco, *Economic Policy in Our Time*, Vol. I, North-Holland Publishing Company, Amsterdam, 1964.

OBJECTIVE

SHORT DESCRIPTION

Mainly Short-Term

1. Full employment

This includes both the short-term objective of reducing cyclical unemployment and the long-term objective of reducing structural and frictional unemployment.

2. Price stability

This has also been mainly a short-term objective (though some countries by the end of the period were beginning to regard it more as a long-term problem).

3. Improvement in the balance of payments

This includes both the short-term need to protect the gold and foreign exchange reserves and long-term objectives, such as a structural change in the proportion of exports or imports in national expenditure.

Mainly Long-Term (Structural)

MAJOR

4. Expansion of production

This is concerned with the long-term promotion of economic growth.

5. Improvement in the allocation of factors of production

This objective comprises
(a) Promotion of internal competition
(b) Promotion of coordination
(c) Increase in the mobility of labour within countries
(d) Increase in the mobility of capital within countries
(e) Promotion of the international division of labour.

6. Satisfaction of collective needs

Collective needs are grouped under the following heads:
(a) General administration
(b) Defense
(c) International affairs
(d) Education, culture and science
(e) Public health

7. Improvement in the distribution of income and wealth

This is concerned both with direct changes in the distribution of income (brought about, for instance, by taxation) and also with changes brought about indirectly — for example, by social security systems. It includes any deliberate changes in either direction towards or away from greater equality. It also includes the redistribution of wealth — by death duties, for example — as well as of income.

8. Protection and priorities to particular regions or industries

This includes both the protection given to a particular industry which may be threatened by home or foreign competition, and the industrial or regional priorities arising, for example, from a national plan.

MINOR

9. Improvement in the pattern of private consumption

This includes any changes which the Government wishes to bring about in the pattern of personal consumption. The Government may wish in some instances to prevent consumers from buying what they would like to buy, (deterring them from buying alcohol, for example), and in other instances it may wish to make it easier for them to do so (by consumer advisory services, for instance).

10. Security of supply

This is concerned with the safe-guarding of essential supplies.

11. Improvement in the size or structure of the population

Government intervention in matters of emigration, immigration or the birthrate is included here.

12. Reduction in working hours

This includes both the reduction of the working week and any increase in statutory holidays.

We kept the number of objectives as small as possible, subject to two conditions. First, it had to be possible to subsume all measures of economic policy under the heading of one or other of the various objectives. Secondly, if we found that very different sets of policies were aiming at one broad objective, then we subdivided the objective. For instance, we thought the promotion of competition should be kept separate from the promotion of coordination — although they can both be grouped together under the general objective of the improvement in the allocation of factors of production. They need to be kept separate because we want to know the relative importance of each in the economic policies of different countries.

The objectives are divided into two groups: mainly short-term and mainly long-term. This is because it is of interest to examine separately the various methods used in the different countries to counteract short-term cyclical fluctuations, and the methods used to pursue longer-term economic policies. However, all the short-term objectives have long-term aspects as well. For instance, the objective of maintaining full employment was most commonly a short-term cyclical problem; but Governments have also had long-term full employment objectives, of reducing structural unemployment, for example. The longer-term objectives are divided into major and minor ones . . . . This systematisation may make Government policies appear to have been much more logical than in fact they were, . . . [but] our standard list of objectives could not possibly include all the various economic objectives which may have been in the mind of some particular Minister in one or other of the nine countries at some time. At various times some people have elevated to the rank of objectives such things as the balanced budget, the reduction of the national debt, or the preservation of a particular exchange rate . . . .

The objectives are not, of course, independent of each other. Some are complementary — when the achievement of one helps the achievement of another; some conflict . . . .

When the word improvement is used, this only implies that the change that was intended was an improvement in the judgment of the Government which took the measures, and nothing more. An improvement in income distribution, for example, is not necessarily a move towards greater equality. It could be the opposite.

Quantification of Objectives

When Governments pursued these various objectives, how far did they have specific figures, or quantities, in mind? The answer varies according to the objectives.

For some of them, most Governments did have some figure or figures in mind, which acted as a kind of 'norm' in their thinking about the objective. This 'norm' was something accepted in a general kind of way, not only by the Government but usually also by the opposition parties and impartial observers. For instance, in the United Kingdom any Government would have been seriously worried if unemployment rose above 3 per cent, or if an annual rise in prices was much above 4 - 5 per cent; and to the extent that these figures were exceeded, it was generally agreed in the country that the Government had failed to achieve full employment and price stability.

Most Governments probably had some explicit norm of some kind in mind (which varied between countries, and within countries at different times) for six out of the twelve objectives: for full employment, for price stability, for the improvement in the balance of payments, for the expansion of production, for the reduction in working hours, and also — to some extent at least — for the improvement in the distribution of income and wealth; for many Governments had either a minimum wage or a minimum scale of national assistance, and this was the main part of their policy for the redistribution of incomes.

For the other objectives (and also in some countries for those just mentioned) there was generally speaking no 'norm' in the sense that there was a generally agreed figure for the desirable range of values for that objective. In these cases, the measures actually taken can be considered as an indication of the quantification of objectives implicit in the minds of the policy-makers. For most of these objectives Governments did in fact come to some quantitative decisions about relative priorities — they decided, for instance, how much they were going to spend in fact on roads or hospitals; or perhaps they decided — in the field of improvement in the pattern of private consumption — how much they would like to increase milk consumption or to reduce alcohol consumption.

The Relation Between Economic and Non-Economic Policy Objectives

A list of possible community objectives may include some objectives that are incompatible with others. If two were "either-or" objectives, so that realization of one completely ruled out realization of the other, the community would have to choose between the two; but such choices would be rare. Most possible objectives would be realizable to a greater or to a lesser degree, so that trade-offs among objectives would be possible. For example, in an industry in which there are technical economies of scale in production, economic efficiency may call for a small number of firms or a monopoly, whereas freedom of consumer choice calls for a large number of firms. In such a situation, policy makers may devise a solution that keeps the number of firms small enough to obtain a reasonable degree of technical efficiency (though less than maximum efficiency), but large enough to allow consumers a meaningful choice (but not an infinitely large number of alternative sellers). We will assume that the set of operationally possible community objectives that enter into community decision making are either independent of one another, or are alternatives realizable to a greater or lesser degree and thus susceptible to trade-offs. All economic objectives are ultimately alternatives in this sense, since economics deals with scarce resources that have alternative uses and the realization of an economic objective involves the utilization of resources that could have been used to further the realization of some other objective or objectives.

One possibility of conflict that comes to mind is between economic and non-economic policy objectives. The following extract represents the widely-held view among economists that policies to improve economic welfare will not usually conflict with general welfare and that the two normally move in the same direction, though not necessarily in the same ratio. The author's argument is that there is a presumption that a policy that improves (or harms) economic welfare would have the same kind of effect on total welfare, especially where the non-economic effects are small.

3   Is Economic Welfare Synonymous With Total Welfare?*

A. C. Pigou

It [is] plain that any rigid inference from effects on economic welfare to effects on total welfare is out of the question. In some fields the divergence between the two effects will be insignificant, but in others it will be very wide. Nevertheless, I submit that, in the absence of special knowledge, there is room for a judgment of probability. When we have ascertained the effect of any cause on economic welfare, we may, unless, of course, there is specific evidence to the contrary, regard this effect as probably equivalent in direction, though not in magnitude, to the effect on total welfare; and, when we have ascertained that the effect of one cause is more favourable than that of another cause to economic welfare, we may, on the same terms, conclude that the effect of this cause on total welfare is probably more favourable. In short, there is a presumption — what Edgeworth calls an "unverified probability" — that qualitative conclusions about the effect of an economic cause upon economic welfare will hold good also of the effect on total welfare. This presumption is especially strong where experience suggests that the non-economic effects produced are likely to be small. But, in all circumstances the burden of proof lies upon those who hold that the presumption should be overruled.

The above result suggests *prima facie* that economic science, when it shall have come to full development, is likely to furnish a powerful guide to practice. Against this suggestion there remains, however, one considerable obstacle. When the conclusion set out in the preceding section is admitted to be valid, a question may still be raised as to its practical utility. Granted, it may be said, that the effects produced by economic causes upon economic welfare are probably, in some measure, representative of those produced on total welfare, we have really gained nothing. For the effects produced upon economic welfare itself cannot, the argument runs, be ascertained beforehand by those partial and limited investigations which alone fall within the scope of economic science. The reason for this is that the effects upon economic welfare produced by any economic cause are likely to be modified by the non-economic conditions, which, in one form or another, are always present, but which economic science is not adapted to investigate. The difficulty is stated very clearly by J. S. Mill in his *Logic*. The study of a *part* of things, he points out, cannot in any circumstances be expected to yield more than approximate results: "Whatever affects, in an appreciable degree, any one element of the social state, affects through it all the other elements. . . . We can never either understand in theory or command in practice the condition of a society in any one respect, without taking into

---

*Reprinted by permission of publisher from A. C. Pigou, *Economics of Welfare*, Macmillan, London and Toronto, 1952.

consideration its condition in all other respects. There is no social phenomenon which is not more or less influenced by every other part of the condition of the same society, and, therefore, by every cause which is influencing any other of the contemporaneous social phenomena."[1] In other words, the effects of economic causes are certain to be partially dependent on non-economic circumstances, in' such wise that the same cause will produce somewhat different economic effects according to the general character of, say, the political or religious conditions that prevail. So far as this kind of dependence exists, it is obvious that causal propositions in economics can only be laid down subject to the condition that things outside the economic sphere either remain constant or, at least, do not vary beyond certain defined limits. Does this condition destroy the practical utility of our science? I hold that, among nations with a stable general culture, like those inhabiting Western Europe, the condition is fulfilled nearly enough to render the results reached by economic inquiry reasonably good approximations to truth. This is the view taken by Mill. While fully recognising "the paramount ascendancy which the general state of civilisation and social progress in any given society must exercise over all the partial and subordinate phenomena," he concludes that the portion of social phenomena, in which the immediately determining causes are principally those that act through the desire for wealth, "do *mainly* depend, at least in the first resort, on one class of circumstances only". He adds that, "even when other circumstances interfere, the ascertainment of the effect due to the one class of circumstances alone is a sufficiently intricate and difficult business to make it expedient to perform it once for all, and then allow for the effect of the modifying circumstances; especially as certain fixed combinations of the former are apt to recur often, in conjunction with ever-varying circumstances of the latter class."[2] I have nothing to add to this statement. If it is accepted, the difficulty discussed in this section need no longer give us pause. It is not necessarily impracticable to ascertain by means of economic science the approximate effects of economic causes upon economic welfare. The bridge that has been built in earlier sections between economic welfare and total welfare need not, therefore, rust unused.

Simplification of Policy Objectives

The range of possible economic policy objectives is wide, but the simultaneous achievement of a multiplicity of objectives would present a political and administrative problem of enormous complexity. In practice, the policy problem may be simplified by concentrating upon a comparatively small number of objectives of great importance. The following selections indicate the three problems of major importance to economists, and two official statements of the policy objectives that ought to be pursued by Canada.

---

[1]*Logic*, ii. p. 488.
[2]*Logic*, ii. pp. 490-491.

4   The Economists' Objectives for Budget Policy*

A. J. Robinson

In public policy, there are a number of objectives, and emphasis on any particular objective may vary from time to time. Adam Smith in his *Inquiry into the Nature and Causes of the Wealth of Nations* was preoccupied with economic growth, but the later classical economists such as Ricardo and Mill, Marx, and the marginalists including Clark and Marshall, were more concerned with distribution of the national product than with increasing its size. In the 1930's, persistent unemployment turned the attention of economists towards the objective of economic stability.

In recent years, the emphasis in public policy has turned back towards the objective of economic growth. This is partly because the domination of international organizations by newly independent underdeveloped nations has brought their problems to world attention, and a stream of statistics and reports from United Nations' agencies has measured and analyzed the economics of growth. But economic growth has also emerged as a policy for the developed countries, partly because of anxiety about defence, expenditures upon which would reduce standards of living unless the national product were increased; but also because elimination of mass unemployment has brought to the fore the problem of long-term labour productivity, and it has become recognized that there are limits to redistribution as a means of raising the standard of living of the bulk of the people.

From the point of view of tax policy, the adoption of economic growth as a policy objective for governments may mean some consideration of the extent to which tax policy for growth is consistent with tax policy to achieve other objectives. If a tax policy designed to increase the rate of economic growth conflicts with tax policies to achieve other objectives, then the government will need to consider the relative order of importance of the various objectives. Moreover, a failure to recognize the possibility of a conflict among objectives may lead to fruitless disputation at the level of policy formulation, and a disappointing degree of achievement of all objectives at the level of policy implementation.

It is not the purpose of this article to attempt a judgment as to which of the various possible objectives of tax policy is to be preferred — this is a judgment that must be made at the political level — but to point out that the issues arising in the formulation of tax policy would be clearer if discussed in the light of these objectives. Actually the desirableness or otherwise of a particular tax will depend upon the objective toward which it is intended to contribute, and tax measures that may be right for one objective may be wrong for another.

*Reprinted by permission of publisher from "Tax Policy for Growth: Reconciliation with Other Objectives", *Canadian Tax Journal*, Vol. XII, No. 4, July-August 1964.

It might therefore facilitate discussion if the main alternative tax objectives could be stated . . . .

Public Policy Objectives

A society may set many objectives for public policy, but . . . the three objectives which seem to have been frequently adopted by governments in recent years [are]: first, economic growth; second, stabilization, the maintenance of full employment with stable prices; and third, a more equitable distribution of income.

Economic Growth

Acceleration of the rate of growth of the national product may require the transfer of resources out of current consumption and into the production of new output-creating industrial capacity. From the viewpoint of government tax policy, this would call for measures to discourage private expenditure upon consumption and to stimulate expenditure upon new plant and other investment goods.

Success in achieving the growth objective may of course have favourable effects upon the achievement of other objectives. Without any change in income distribution, an increase in the rate of growth of real per capita income would benefit all groups in society, and if one assumed generally downward sloping marginal utility of income schedules, in most cases it would increase economic welfare more in lower income groups than in higher income groups. In addition, for a relatively advanced country such as [Canada] there would be the effect of the long swing noted by Kuznets, namely that income inequality tends to narrow in the later phases of economic growth.

Economic Stability

Policy for full employment without inflation will vary at different points in the business cycle. When aggregate demand falls and unemployment appears, government policy would be directed towards stimulating private expenditure both upon investment and consumption and discouraging saving (hoarding). Once full employment is reached, policy should be directed towards restraining inflationary price increases, and this may involve using tax policy to reduce private expenditures on both investment and consumption, and to encourage saving.

Equity

Application of the equity criterion to taxation requires value judgments as to what the desirable state of income distribution should be. It is not proposed to discuss here the various issues involved, but merely to state two propositions which it is believed are more or less widely accepted, namely that a more equal distribution of income than the present distribution is desirable; and that, other things being equal, a tax structure that was progressive as a whole would be preferred on equity grounds to a proportional or regressive tax rate structure.

Canadian Economic Objectives

In discussing the policy objectives of a specific community, the question arises as to which objectives will be selected as *the* objectives, what is the order of priority in which they should be achieved, and which are expendable in the event of a crisis (such as a war or a galloping inflation). Who determines the answers to these questions, and how does the general public participate in the selection and ranking of objectives (if it does)? This is the problem of decision making in a democratic society to be discussed in the next section. At this point, we can examine statements of official objectives for the Canadian economy made by bodies set up by the Government of Canada.

The Economic Council's Economic Goals for Canada

The Economic Council of Canada was established in 1963, by Act of Federal Parliament, with duties "to advise and recommend to the Minister (President of the Privy Council for Canada) how Canada can achieve the highest possible levels of employment and efficient production in order that the country may enjoy a high and consistent rate of economic growth and that all Canadians may share in rising living standards; . . . conduct such studies, inquiries and other undertakings as may be necessary with respect [thereto] . . . , and . . . report to, advise or make recommendations to the Minister with respect thereto, as the circumstances require". In addition, the Council is required under its Act to assume the duties of the former National Productivity Council having to do with "promoting and expediting advances in efficiency of production in all sectors of the economy, [particularly] . . . the development of improved production and distribution methods, . . . improved management techniques, the maintenance of good human relations in industry, the use of training programmes at all levels of industry, and . . . retraining programs to meet changing manpower requirements, the extension of industrial research programs in plants and industries . . . , the dissemination of technical information . . .".[1]

The Economic Council interprets this as a direction to study and advise upon the medium and long-term development of the Canadian economy in relation to the attainment of the following economic and social goals:

    i)   full employment
    ii)   a high rate of economic growth
    iii)   reasonable stability of prices
    iv)   a viable balance of payments, and
    v)   an equitable distribution of rising incomes.

The Economic Council publishes an annual review of progress towards its goals. The following extract sets out the Council's definition of its goals as presented in its most recent statement (Fourth Review, 1967).

---

[1]From *Canada Year Book*, 1963-1964.

5   Economic Goals for Canada to the 1970's*

The Economic Council of Canada

Full Employment

We believe that, over the medium term future, economic policies should be actively directed towards achieving a target of a 97 per cent rate of employment (or a rate of unemployment of not more than 3 per cent). This objective has important implications for other objectives — such as the maintenance of reasonable price stability and a viable balance-of-payments position — and an effective combination of policies will be required to achieve these various objectives in a consistent fashion.

Certain features of this employment target deserve special emphasis. First, we do not regard this to be an ultimate or satisfactory goal for all time. We would hope that with sustained improvement in our economic performance it may eventually become realistic to aim for an even better performance in the level of employment. Second, the 97 per cent employment objective, whose attainment is to be worked for over the medium term future, is intended to be an *average annual rate*, which allows for seasonal variations. Third, the target rate is a *national average*, within which there will be some regional variation. Fourth, the rate is intended to reflect a goal for a year of high business activity; short-term movements away from the target could occur at some stages of the business cycle, but persistent deviations would suggest a short-fall from the target. Fifth, the employment target should not encompass any sizeable element of either long-duration unemployment of individuals or of long-duration unemployment in areas where special measures are required to deal with the problems of structural unemployment. Finally, to be realistic, this target necessarily implies favourable international economic conditions — in particular, a high level of employment in the United States.

Economic Growth

Economic growth is usually measured in terms of long-term rates of increase in the volume of a country's total output, or its per capita output (a rough measure of improvements in the standard of living). Another concept is that of output in relation to the manpower required to produce it (a measure of advances in productivity). This is a concept which we emphasize.[1]

Taking all factors together, we conclude that actual physical output of the Canadian economy should grow by an average annual rate of 5 per cent per year in 1965-70 to attain potential output by the end of this decade. For 1970-

---

*Reprinted by permission from *Fourth Annual Review, The Canadian Economy from the 1960's to the 1970's*, Queen's Printer, Ottawa, 1967.

[1]*First Annual Review, Economic Goals for Canada to 1970*, Queen's Printer, Ottawa, 1964, p. 12.

75, when the labour force will grow somewhat more slowly, an average annual rate of growth of 4¾ per cent is an appropriate objective.

Reasonable Price Stability

The goal of reasonable price stability was formulated in the following terms in our *First Annual Review*:

> The goal of reasonable price and cost stability is one which is extremely difficult to define. In terms of our preceding discussion of the important role of prices in our economy, and because of the need for flexibility in the pattern of relative prices, we do not believe that a rigid structure of constant prices is a desirable or feasible objective. These flexible price adjustments in response to changes in underlying demand and supply conditions in our market economy should result in some year-to-year variability in over-all prices. However, we would regard persistent and rapid price increases as inappropriate and dangerous. After careful consideration, we have assumed that if annual average rates of changes in prices and costs to 1970 can be contained the limits of [1.4 per cent and 2.0 per cent], this would represent the attainment of a satisfactory degree of price and cost stability . . . .

We still believe that this is an appropriate goal over the medium-term future.

A Viable Balance of Payments

We emphasize that the balance-of-payments objective should be not merely the maintenance of a flow of total international receipts adequate to cover the country's international payments, but also some strengthening of Canada's international economic position. In line with these requirements, as well as the high potential rates of increase in employment, income and output, we concluded in our *First Annual Review* that, even under favourable international conditions for expanding Canadian exports, the current account payments deficit (and accompanying net capital inflow) at potential output in 1970 would be of the order of $1.5 to $2.0 billion . . . . After a careful reappraisal, we have concluded that this goal was appropriately formulated in these terms and is still relevant.

Equitable Distribution of Rising Incomes

The goal of an equitable distribution of rising incomes is another very complex matter, defying simple formulation. Much of our earlier work in this field was concerned with the identification, measurement and analysis of regional disparities, a long-standing Canadian problem.

[The legislation establishing the Council refers to the broad goals of a high and consistent rate of economic growth and a sharing by all Canadians in rising living standards. Regional participation in rising living standards is obviously an important aspect of this latter goal, and our terms of reference specifically direct us "to study how national economic policies can best foster the balanced economic development of all areas of Canada" . . . . The problem of integration and balance, in the sense of assuring an appropriate participation on the part of each region in the over-all process of national economic development, has long been an elusive goal and a continuing concern of the people of Canada . . . .

Our concept of regionally balanced economic development can now be outlined. There are, we suggest, two main, interrelated considerations involved in moving towards a better regional balance. The first is the importance of reducing the relative disparities in average levels of income as they presently exist among the regions . . . . The second consideration is the need to assure that each region contributes to total national output, and to the sustained, long-run growth of that output, on the basis of the fullest and mose efficient use of the human and material resources available to the region . . . .

The narrowing of income disparities, and the achievement of this result consistently with our other basic economic and social objectives, remains one of the most difficult issues confronting the country as a whole.][2] However, income distribution has many other important facets which need attention. We need more information about the distribution of income among individuals, families and various occupational groups. Why do some groups receive little benefit from the general rise in incomes and living standards? What elements lie behind the vicious circle of poverty that still traps far too many of our citizens? Some of the problems here may range far beyond the realm of economic studies. Yet these difficult matters will have to be understood and faced if appropriate policies are to be devised to achieve this goal.

The Carter Commission's Economic Goals for Canada

On September 25, 1962, the Federal Government appointed a Royal Commission under the chairmanship of Mr. Kenneth LeM. Carter, "to inquire into and report upon the incidence and effects of taxation imposed by Parliament . . . upon the operation of the national economy, the conduct of business, the organization of industry and the positions of individuals". In Volume 2 of the Commission's Report, "The Use of the Tax System to Achieve Economic and Social Objectives", the Commissioners found that in order to appraise the existing tax system and suggest improvements they needed to know what the community's objectives were. The following statement sets out what the Commission considered to be a widely accepted set of national objectives.

---

[2]From *Second Annual Review, Towards Sustained and Balanced Economic Growth,* Queen's Printer, Ottawa, 1965.

6   Widely Accepted National Objectives for Canada *

The Royal Commission on Taxation

We believe that four fundamental objectives on which the Canadian people agree are:

1. To maximize the current and future output of goods and services desired by Canadians.
2. To ensure that this flow of goods and services is distributed equitably among individuals or groups.
3. To protect the liberties and rights of individuals through the preservation of representative, responsible government and maintenance of the rule of law.
4. To maintain and strengthen the Canadian federation.

To Maximize the Growth of Output

. . . we believe that the tax system should be used, in conjunction with the other instruments, to achieve the following specific goals under this general objective:

(a) Maintenance of full and continuous utilization of Canadian resources through policies designed to maintain an adequate demand for Canadian output.

(b) Maximization of the rate of increase in the productivity of all Canadian resources assuming full employment is achieved. . . .

(c) Prevention of wide or prolonged fluctuations in the general level of prices, and at the same time maintenance of the flexibility of individual prices in the economy.

The Equitable Distribution of Output

The government can change the distribution of the flow of goods and services among individuals and groups of individuals, by imposing higher taxes on some than on others, by making larger transfers of purchasing power to some individuals or groups than to others, and by providing public goods and services that benefit some more than others.

In our opinion there is a consensus among Canadians that the tax expenditure mechanism (including transfers) is equitable when it increases the flow of goods and services to those who, because they have little economic power relative to others, or because they have particularly heavy responsibilities or obligations, would otherwise not be able to maintain a decent standard of living . . . . Our principal concern is that the allocation of taxes, given the existing transfer

*Reprinted by permission from the Royal Commission on Taxation, *Report*, Vol. II, "The Use of the Tax System to Achieve Economic and Social Objectives". Queen's Printer, Ottawa, 1966.

mechanism and public expenditures, should be such as to achieve an equitable distribution of the flow of goods and services among Canadians.

The Protection of the Liberties and Rights of the Individual

In a democracy such as Canada, restrictions on the liberties of individuals are accepted primarily because those who make the laws are representatives of, and responsible to, the public. The legislative process ensures that the laws serve the public good. Maintaining and strengthening this democratic process is a fundamental general objective.

The Strengthening of Federal-Provincial Relations

[Strengthening of the federation] requires realization of the following goals:

(a) the maintenance of the autonomy of the provinces within the agreed division of powers and responsibilities between the federal and provincial governments.

(b) The development of a flexible tax system that can adjust to the changing needs and aspirations of the people and the provinces in which they live.

(c) The transfer of resources, through the federal government, from rich to poor provinces, so that the residents of the latter can, if they choose, enjoy minimum standards of public service without undue tax burdens.

(d) The undivided control of the instruments needed to maintain the stability and growth of the economy if dispersal would reduce control over Canada's collective economic destiny.

(e) The acceptance of the proposition that the fiscal relationships among all the governments will require continuous re-examination, re-negotiation and adjustment.

Priority of Objectives

The list of objectives that has been compiled is an extremely ambitious one, and we are under no illusion that all of these desirable ends can be easily achieved. We realize that some of the objectives are in conflict, in the sense that movement towards one goal means that others might be achieved less adequately. Simultaneous realization of all the goals in some degree will constitute success if, as we hope, our choices as to the appropriate compromises adequately reflect the consensus of informed Canadians . . . . We assign a higher priority to the objective of equity than to all the others . . . . We are convinced that unless this objective is achieved to a high degree all other achievements are of little account.

The Choice and Ranking of Objectives

When a government decides on a list of policy objectives, two types of disagreement may arise. The first is opposition to a particular objective because it is in itself unacceptable. Some people would argue that no national objectives are acceptable because in a democratic society only individual or group objectives are appropriate. The individual is sovereign, and it is proper only for individuals and groups to seek to maximize welfare — their own welfare. Nevertheless democratic societies do agree on a number of meaningful objectives, such as preservation of law and order, the guarding of freedom of expression and freedom of choice, the reduction of social tensions, the defense of the country from outside attack and the raising of the standard of living of the population. We can therefore assume that our society is able to agree upon some public objectives (the process of formulating objectives in a democratic society will be examined in a later chapter).

There will be general agreement on some objectives which should and should not be pursued by society. There will also be objectives on which disagreement will exist; for example, those set out in (a) below.

The most common type of disagreement arises where all the objectives are considered desirable but there are differences as to their urgency. For example, probably everyone is against inflation, but an anti-inflationary policy would be considered more urgent by fixed income receivers than by skilled workers and businessmen whose wages and profits are more flexible in an upward direction. This may be a question of the order in which objectives should be ranked — whether, for example, control of prices should be given priority over the maintenance of full employment. However, while the complete achievement of one objective may be incompatible with the complete achievement of another, it may be possible to reach some compromise, represented by a trade-off between the conflicting objectives. The first selection in (b) below explains the nature of a trade-off, and subsequent selections deal with trade-offs made between conflicting objectives in the area of public policy.

(a) Critiques of major economic policy objectives

The Elusiveness of Equity as a Policy Objective

The two Canadian statements of policy objectives include equity as one objective that it is believed Canadians agree upon. The Economic Council's concept of equity, however, is rather a special one — namely, an equitable distribution of national income among the governments of the federation rather than among individuals (a question which is treated at greater length in Chapter Six). The Carter Commission on Taxation sets up equity between individuals as a policy objective; this attempt to add flesh to the bare bones of a theoretical concept is analyzed critically in the following extracts.

7   The Unfairness of an "Equitable" Tax System*

Francis Low-Beer

"Equity" is generally used in two different senses in the *Report* [of the Royal Commission on Taxation]: in a broad sense of what is just and fair, and in a narrow sense of what tends to redistribute wealth in the direction of the poor. It is not always possible to discern which sense is intended. This ambiguity in the *meaning* of equity is to be distinguished from the *criterion* adopted by the *Report* as to whether equity has been achieved. That criterion is provided by the application of the principle of discretionary economic power discussed below. It is difficult to judge the adequacy of a test unless we are clear about what we are testing. Yet for all the weight placed by the *Report* on this concept it is left woefully vague.

Equity finds its residual place in the *Report* in the catalogue of objectives set out above. What meaning is to be attributed to the sentence: (a) "We believe that fundamental objectives on which the Canadian people agree are . . . to ensure that this flow of goods and services is distributed equitably among individuals or groups."?

The Commission did not mean by this sentence merely to state that each Canadian would deem equitable some scheme of distribution of which he personally approved. Some objective standard of equitable distribution must therefore be assumed. But as the manner of distribution of goods and services is the characteristic that distinguishes economic systems one from the other, it is only meaningful to speak of equitable distribution in the context of a specific economic system. Beliefs in particular schemes of equitable distribution therefore relate to beliefs in particular economic systems. It is to be observed that unless all Canadians believe in the same very particular economic system (indeed as it turns out in the very system which would result from the implementation of the *Report*) the above sentence which is the repository of the equity objective is either false or meaningless.

There is a further appeal to the common belief of Canadians on what is equitable at pages 10 and 11 of Volume 2: (b) "in our opinion there is a consensus among Canadians that the tax-expenditure mechanism (including transfers) is equitable when it increases the flow of goods and services to those whom . . . would otherwise not be able to maintain a decent standard of living." As most known tax systems do increase the flow of goods and services to the under-privileged, it would follow that such systems would all be equitable. Surely what is in issue is the *degree* and manner of the increase, on which a consensus would be surprising.

The problem of degree is also involved in the next passage: "We believe that in order to achieve a more equitable distribution of output, the tax system should be consistent with the following objectives:"

*Reprinted by permission of author and publisher from Francis Low-Beer, "Carter's Logic", *Canadian Tax Journal*, Vol. XV, No. 5, September-October 1967.

The concept of a *more* equitable distribution is now introduced. One wonders what a most equitable distribution would involve. Does the Commission countenance the possibility that a *most* equitable future system will displace the tax structure now recommended . . .?

The same difficulty of degree underlies the series of passages dealing with progressiveness in taxation on pages 19 and 20 of Volume I.

The *Report* attempts to justify progressive taxation on its principle of discretionary economic power. It is said that because expenses for necessities absorb a much larger proportion of the annual additions to the economic power of those with low income than of the wealthy, these increases to total economic power be taxed at progressive rates. But the statement then made points rather the other way: "The wealthy man's necessities are the poor man's luxuries; with a rising income what was once a luxury becomes a necessity." If this is true, a progressive tax rate based on the principle of discretionary disposable income would be inequitable rather than equitable.

The problem is twofold. The first is whether we are committed to equalization; and if so, to determine the degree of equalization to be effected by the tax system and the degree of progressiveness of rates. It is not helpful to suggest that this second perennial problem can be solved (and the answer justified) by the touchstone of theory.

What the Commission has done in these passages is to try to fuse its two senses of equity together through the purported consensus of the Canadian people. It has tried to anchor its concept of equity in the general will. But no consensus on particular schemes of distribution and particular rates of progression has been demonstrated, which is the matter in issue.

The *Report* then summarizes the measures it recommends which constitute the criterion of equity that has already been referred to: "Equity has two dimensions. Horizontal equity requires that individuals and families in *similar circumstances* bear the same taxes. Vertical equity requires that those in *different circumstances* bear *appropriately different taxes*."

It adopts the well worn concepts of horizontal and vertical equity. But in determining whether horizontal and vertical equity have been achieved everything hangs on *what* circumstances are to be taken into account in determining similarity or difference. The *Report* tells us there can be no objective criteria for determining what these circumstances are and we are simply given what the Commission believes to be fair. Therefore, as the recommendations of the *Report* depend upon the principle of equity, and as the application of that principle depends on a criterion for selecting certain circumstances to determine whether horizontal and vertical equity have been achieved, and as that criterion depends on the belief of the Commission as to what is fair, so do the recommendations. No relation is demonstrated between this belief and statements (a) and (b) above.

It would seem that there are other ways of achieving horizontal and vertical equity by fastening on circumstances other than those isolated as relevant by the Commission. Indeed, all western tax systems known to the writer (except the one recommended by the Commission) assume certain circumstances as to the source of the gain as relevant in determining whether horizontal equity has been achieved. Furthermore, there is a remarkable uniformity among these tax systems as to the sorts of circumstances which are deemed relevant. Distinctions are made between circumstances which result in gains by reason of income, by reason of accretion to capital and by reason of death benefits and gifts. Making such distinctions does not necessarily mean that such gains will not attract tax but it does recognize the differences in equity that require different tax treatment. Implicit in these distinctions is a distinction beween the creation of assets, the increase in value of existing assets and the transfer of assets (a receipt of assets resulting in a reciprocal loss to another). It may be that these distinctions which at present underlie our manner of achieving horizontal and vertical equity are ill founded, but the *Report* has advanced few cogent reasons for believing so.

Perhaps the Commission is driven to its "a dollar is a dollar is a dollar" position by a misconception about the relation of equity and generality. On page 11 of Volume 2 the *Report* states that tax concessions to particular industries and for particular kinds of income are always inequitable.

Usually, just the opposite is true. Concessions and exceptions are enacted into the law because there is recognition that justice can be done only by taking certain cases out of the general rule. In this context, equity and justice are interchangeable, and both concepts subsumed under public policy. When any system of law (including a tax system) is first enacted, one must perforce deal in broad generalities, but as the public's sense of justice is sharpened by experience, irregularities in the area covered by the general law become apparent which require particular treatment to mould the rules to our feel for the facts. Laws become more complex and sophisticated; put another way, concessions and exceptions creep in. For example, it may become apparent that certain sorts of capital gain are very much like our present concept of income and should be taxed. But at a yet deeper level, distinct sorts of capital gain emerge which we may recognize as involving different equities. There is the capital gain of the speculator, the capital gain of the entrepreneur and the capital gain due to inflation. The tax system that does not reflect these differences is to that extent insensitive and inequitable. Differentiation is the mark of the developed organism.

Furthermore, the legal criterion of justice and the aesthetic and administrative criterion of simplicity are distinct desiderata, not functions of each other. Given the complexity of the social fabric, it is tempting to formulate a rule that the justice of a legal system, when enacted, varies inversely with its simplicity. Justice is messy. For reasons of administrative convenience and comprehensibility, distinctions may need to be jettisoned, not for equity, but in spite of equity. Although there is no reason to believe that present exceptions in our tax law were inequitable when they were introduced, the equities then present may now have vanished. If so, the exceptions should be removed or consolidated. This is an essential part of the process of reform. When the Commission re-examines the wisdom of providing special treatment to banking, insurance, oil and mining companies it is performing a vital task. But that task is quite separate from constructing a new tax system. It would be wrong to seek the *equitable* answer to the problems raised by such special cases by looking only to "first principles" when possibly a dozen apply. It is unlikely that the answer can be found by wielding theory and letting the chips fall where they may; better to place each chip according to the total public policy considerations bearing on each condition to be treated, and then examine the pattern.

Lastly, it is delusive to sacrifice the present system (or other possible systems that might be put forward) on the altar of elegance because it is wrong to suppose such elegance will endure. The inevitable process of incrustation and dismemberment will begin and the structure will become corroded by exceptions. So again, if the *Report* depends on equity, and if equity depends on a unity of certain general rules, the *Report* will by its own verdict stand unjustified a few years hence.

The reader must form his own opinion as to whether the recommended system is in fact elegant. But one of the elements he might consider is symmetry. One would think that no criterion would lend itself better to symmetrical application than that of change in the economic power of the taxpayer. The simplicity and finality of the criterion is set out on page 9 of Volume 1: "We are completely persuaded that taxes should be allocated according to the changes in the economic power of individuals and families . . . . Nor do we believe it matters whether the increase in economic power was expected or unexpected, whether it was a unique or recurrent event, whether the man suffered to get the increase in economic power or it fell in his lap without effort."

But the *Report* does not allocate taxes according to changes in economic power. A dollar is a dollar is a dollar when it increases economic power but not when it decreases it. For the decrease in the economic power of the tax unit, if that decrease results from gifts or gifts on death, is not deductible. Apparently, whereas the source and kind of increase does not matter, the source and kind of decrease to the economic power of a tax unit does matter. On page 465 of Volume 3 it is said: "The only deductions we recommend are expenses which are reasonably related to the earning of income, and certain special types of deductions such as charitable donations within specified limits. *Inter-vivos* gifts are a voluntary exercise of the donor's economic power. They are personal expenditures that should be treated in exactly the same way as personal consumption expenditures. Neither *inter-vivos* gifts nor testamentary gifts are related to the earning of the donor's income".

Why should "earning" suddenly become relevant at this point or, indeed, any examination into the hows and whys of a decrease in economic power? Do we not see the discarded concept of income lurking in the background waiting to take over the action at a convenient time? For there seems no clearer case of decrease in the economic power of a tax unit than the disposition of that power without a corresponding receipt, as on an *inter-vivos* gift or gift on death. The only other justification for this apparent inconsistency is a statement appearing on page 465 of Volume 3 that the giving of a gift is a form of consumption, and therefore is not to be eligible as a decrease in economic power. The meaning of "consumption" used in that sense is not the meaning of "consumption" otherwise used by the Commission in the *Report*. For example, it is not the concept of consumption which underlies the treatment of intermediaries where it is said that corporations cannot consume; for it is clear that corporations can give gifts and otherwise dispose of assets. Conversely, the money paid by a merchant for his goods is not deemed consumed. It is counter-intuitive to think of the unilateral transfer of assets as consumption. If such a transfer is denied a deduction on the grounds that it is consumption, the concept of consumption becomes central, for the incidence of taxation can then be regulated by shifting the incidence of what is deemed consumed. Thus are recalcitrant cases made to fit the procrustean bed of theory.

8   The Concept of "Equity" in the Carter Report *

A. J. Robinson

In its recommendations for change in the Canadian tax structure, the Carter Commission emphasized strongly its belief that equity, above all, should dominate the Canadian tax system, and references to the desirability of equity and the present lack of it are scattered throughout the Report.

What does the Carter Commission mean by "equity"? At this point we run into difficulties because the Commission does not define the term. The nearest it comes to a definition is the statement that "equity has two dimensions. Horizontal equity requires that individuals and families in similar circumstances bear the same taxes. Vertical equity requires that those in different circumstances bear appropriately different taxes". Does the present system meet these criteria? The Commission's belief is that "the present system does not afford fair treatment for all Canadians. People in essentially similar circumstances do not bear the same taxes. People in essentially different circumstances do not bear appropriately different tax burdens".

This is as far as the Carter Commission goes in defining equity, but a new concept is introduced, "discretionary economic power", in terms of which the Commission feels that equity can be defined — equity prevails when all individuals pay the same proportion of their discretionary economic power in taxation. Discretionary economic power is defined as total economic power, "the power to command goods and services for personal use, whether the power is exercised or not", minus the amount needed to maintain an appropriate standard of living. Economic power in the Carter sense comprises consumption plus gifts plus changes in the value of assets that could be transformed directly into

*From *Canada's Tax Structure and Economic Goals*, York University, Toronto, 1967.

consumption goods. This comes close to income in the sense in which it is ordinarily understood (including capital gains[1] on an annual basis), since income can only be spent on consumption, given away or invested (savings normally being the same as investment to the individual).

From economic power is deducted an amount sufficient to pay for the necessities of life. This amount is not constant but varies with income, but not proportionally, except at the lower end of the income scale, where it varies inversely with income. The residual is discretionary economic power, and equity in the tax system will be achieved when individuals and families pay taxes that are a constant proportion of their discretionary power. It will be noted that the smaller is the allowance for "necessities", the closer this scheme comes to a proportional income tax, another example of the Commission's "withdrawal from the idea of severe progressivity, in line with the less egalitarian philosophy of the current age".

Is that all there is to the equity problem? Can the problem of equity in taxation, which has worried tax theorists from Edgeworth, Bastable and Pigou to the present, be disposed of by the addition of "discretionary economic power" to our vocabulary? Despite the claim of the Commission that its recommendations give "primacy of place" to the achievement of equity, its treatment of equity has in fact been very shallow. The problems of equity in taxation and in public policy generally are real problems, and are not to be disposed of by coining new phrases. In particular, the Carter Commission seems to have been confused between equity in the sense of fair and reasonable taxes, which is a matter pretty well confined to the tax system itself, and equity in the sense of an equitable distribution of the national income, which is not limited to taxation but also includes government expenditures and government policies such as protection and regulation of industry and monetary policy.

In considering equity in a tax system, the most obvious problem is measurement. In deciding whether the tax system needs more or less equity, some criterion is needed to determine how much exists at present, and to decide how much further to go. Such measurement is possible for other goals in taxation. The efficiency of a tax system could be measured by the administrative cost per dollar of tax revenue, or some similar measure. The effect of taxes upon growth could be measured by observing the changes in the growth of national income associated with changes in taxation, holding all other factors constant, a task which is within the capabilities of modern econometrics. The effect of taxes upon

---

[1]It is well known that because capital gains receive more favourable tax treatment than salary income, many business men convert income received as remuneration for services rendered from salary into capital gains. In an economic sense these capital gains are part of income, and should be treated as income. Such capital gains should be distinguished in principle from appreciation of capital proper. which is not income in the sense of remuneration for services rendered, and for which there may be strong arguments for taxing differently from income. Given the natural and quite rational propensity of individuals to evade taxation (legally) if they can, the devising of a tax law that will separate the two kinds of capital gain is very difficult, as is evident in the cumbersome proposals of the Carter Commission. This article is concerned only with the economic problems, and will leave legal problems to the lawyers.

unemployment and price stability present no conceptual difficulties, and could be handled by modern econometric techniques. But how could one measure equity in a tax system?

The answer of course is that equity in taxation is relative, and involves a subjective judgment as to what is fair and just, which in turn is a judgment about whether a particular state of affairs conforms to tacit but generally-accepted rules of business and society. It has no necessary relationship to income distribution, and is not enshrined in any particular form of tax or rate of taxation. For example, an average tax rate of 20 per cent on one man's income of $10,000 would be equitable if everyone else with the same income paid 20 per cent, but it would be inequitable if others with the same income paid 10 per cent, and the same would apply to any other tax rate. Taxes that unequivocally penalize individual effort and thrift, both regarded as virtues in our society, relative to laziness and dissipation, would be regarded as inequitable by most people. It may be inequitable for a wife's salary to be a tax-deductible expense if she works for another man's firm but not if she performs identical work for her husband. It may be inequitable when of two men living away from home, one claims a tax deduction of more than $5,000 a year as living costs, while the other is refused a similar claim of $4.00 a day for a short period. It may be inequitable to tax a man on profits that he might have received for his work if he had sold it, but which he gave to someone as a gift. Many of these problems of equity in taxation are dealt with in the Courts. What the community accepts as equitable may change from time to time; a tax system that no one objects to on equity grounds in a period of full employment and high incomes may become intolerable when employment and incomes are falling.

This concept of equity, which applies to the tax system *per se*, must be distinguished from the application of the equity principle by the government sector, of which taxation is only one aspect. Equity in this sense involves the ancient principle of redistribution, the rationale of which is that under the market system, based upon the remuneration of people according to the value of their productivities in production, those in occupations of low productivity will receive too little to live at what the community has decided is the minimum acceptable level. It is recognized that the raw judgment of the market is sometimes too harsh for our humanitarian principles to tolerate, and it is one of the duties of the state to ameliorate its worst excesses. This can be done without unduly interfering with the market system by a transfer of income from the more successful beneficiaries of that system. Given the decision of the community, this, after all, is the only source of funds.

Taxation and redistribution are used in our society to remove inequities due to the rigors of the market. They are also used to remove inequities due to the imperfections of the market. In the market system, the marginal productivity principle determines income, but this will not be equitable if some people are unable to enter the highly productive (and therefore well paid) occupations. For example, the children of wealthy families in our society have more opportunities to enter well-paid occupations than children of the poor. Government expenditures to subsidize the advanced education of less-privileged people so that those with ability will not be disqualified from entering highly-paid occupations may therefore be justified on equity grounds. Government expenditures to equalize opportunity and in other ways to offset imbalances in the market system are justifiable on equity grounds.

To achieve equity in the sense of a reduction in income inequality is one of the major objectives of modern government. The two principal instruments are taxation and expenditures, and it is the combination of the two that determines the net effect on equity. Whether any particular set of tax measures improves or impairs equity will depend upon how the government spends the revenues collected. A set of tax measures that would improve equity given one set of government expenditures would have a different effect on equity for all other possible sets of expenditures. For example, a steeply progressive tax schedule combined with expenditures that benefit the well-to-do (highways, power boat facilities, airport construction, subsidies to cultural activities) could be less equitable than a moderately progressive tax schedule combined with expenditures that benefit lower-income groups (public hospitals, low rent housing, services to the aged and indigent).

It must be concluded that it is presumptuous of the Carter Commission to claim that their tax proposals are equitable in any meaningful sense without specifying the expenditures side of the budget. Government expenditures are constantly changing, both in amount and composition, and every change alters the state of equity. If the Carter Commission had really been concerned about equity, they might have recommended greater emphasis on expenditures (even though their terms of reference may have precluded a detailed analysis of expenditures). Government expenditures have the flexibility to carry out the redistributive role more precisely and with fewer adverse effects upon the economic system than taxation. As far as equity is concerned, therefore, it may be best to ignore what the Carter Report says, and concentrate attention on its discussion of the relation between taxation and the achievement of the other objectives of public policy.

9   Why Growth Should Not be a Policy Objective *

E. J. Mishan

What conceivable alternative could there be to economic growth? Explicit references to it are hardly necessary. When the Prime Minister talks with exaltation of a 'sense of national purpose' it goes without saying that he is inspired by a vision, a cornucopia of burgeoning indices.

---

*Reprinted by permission of author and publisher from E. J. Mishan, *The Costs of Economic Growth*, The Staples Press, London, 1967.

But to be tediously logical about it, there is an alternative to the postwar growth-rush as an overriding objective of economic policy: the simple alternative, that is, of not rushing for growth. The alternative is intended to be taken seriously. One may concede the importance of economic growth in an indigent society, in a country with an outsize population wherein the mass of people struggle for bare subsistence. But despite ministerial twaddle about the efforts we must take to 'survive in a competitive world,' Britain [and Canada are] . . . just not that sort of country. Irrespective of its 'disappointing' rate of growth, or the present position of the gold reserves, it may be reasonably regarded, in view of its productive capacity and skills, as one of the more affluent societies of the West, a country with a wide margin of choice in its policy objectives. And it is palpably absurd to continue talking, and acting, as if our survival — or our 'economic health' — depended upon that extra one or two per cent growth. At the risk of offending financial journalists and other fastidious scrutinizers of economic statistics, whose spirits have been trained to soar or sink on detecting a half per cent swing in any index, I must voice the view that the near-executive concern with industrial growth is . . . unimaginative and unworthy.

The reader, however, may be more inclined to concede this point and to ponder on a more discriminating criterion of economic policy if he is reminnded of some of the less laudable consequences of economic growth over the last twenty years.

Undergraduate economists learn in their first year that the private enterprise system is a marvellous mechanism. By their third year, it is to be hoped, they have come to learn also that there is a great deal it cannot do, and much that it does very badly. For today's generation in particular, it is a fact of experience that within the span of a few years the unlimited marketing of new technological products can result in a cumulative reduction of the pleasure once freely enjoyed by the citizen. If there is one clear policy alternative to pressing on regardless, it is the policy of seeking immediate remedies against the rapid spread of dis-amenities that now beset the daily lives of ordinary people. More positively, there is the alternative policy of transferring resources from industrial production to the more urgent task of transforming the physical environment in which we live into something less fit for machines, perhaps, but more fit for human beings . . . .

It is impossible not to dwell for a moment on the most notorious by-product of industrialization the world has ever known: the appalling traffic congestion in our towns, cities and suburbs. It is at this phenomenon that our political leaders should look for a really outstanding example of post-war growth. One consequence is that the pleasures of strolling along the streets of a city are more of a memory than a current pastime. Trucks, motor-cycles and taxis belching fumes, filth and stench, snarling engines and unabating visual disturbance have compounded to make movement through the city an ordeal for the pedestrian at the same time as the mutual strangulation of the traffic makes it a purgatory for motorists. The formula of mend-and-make-do followed by successive transport ministers is culminating in a maze of one-way streets, peppered with parking meters, with massive signs, detours, and weirdly shaped junctions and traffic circles across which traffic pours from several directions, while penned-in pedestrians jostle each other along narrow pavements. The Towns and cities have been rapidly transmogrified into roaring workshops, the authorities watching anxiously as the traffic builds up with no policy other than that of spreading the rash of parking meters to discourage the traffic on the one hand, and, on the other, to accommodate it by road-widening, tunnelling, bridging and patching up here and there; perverting every principle of amenity a city can offer in the attempt to force through it the growing traffic. This 'policy' — apparently justified by reckoning as social benefits any increase in the volume of traffic and any increase in its average speed — would, if it were pursued more ruthlessly, result inevitably in a Los Angeles-type solution in which the greater part of the metropolis is converted to road space; in effect a city buried under roads and freeways....

Other disagreeable features may be mentioned in passing, many of them the result either of wide-eyed enterprise or of myopic municipalities, such as the post-war 'development' blight, the erosion of the countryside, the 'uglification' of coastal towns, the pollution of the air and of rivers with chemical wastes, the accumulation of thick oils on our coastal waters, the sewage poisoning our beaches, the destruction of wild life by indiscriminate use of pesticides, the change-over from animal farming to animal factories, and, visible to all who have eyes to see, a rich heritage of natural beauty being wantonly and systematically destroyed — a heritage that cannot be restored in our lifetime.

To preserve what little is left will require major legislation and strong powers of enforcement. But one cannot hope for these without a complete break with the parochial school of economics that has paralysed the mind of all governing authorities since the industrial revolution. It will require a new vision of the purposes of life to stand up to the inevitable protests of commerce, of industry, and of the financial journalists, protests that employment, expansion, exports — key words in the vocabulary of the parochial school — will be jeopardized if enterprise is not permitted to develop where profits are highest.

Our policital leaders, all of them, have visited the United States, and all of them seem to have learned the wrong things. They have been impressed by the efficient organization of industry, the high productivity, the extent of automation, and the new one-plane, two-yacht, three-car, four-television-set family. The spreading suburban wilderness, the near traffic paralysis, the mixture of pandemonium and desolation in the cities, a sense of spiritual despair scarcely concealed by the frantic pace of life — such phenomena, not being readily quantifiable, and having no discernible impact on the gold reserves, are obviously not regarded as agenda.

Indeed, the jockeying among party leaders for recognition as the agents of modernization, of the new, the bigger and better, is one of the sadder facts of the post-war world, in particular as their claim to the title rests almost wholly on a propensity to keep their eyes glued to the speedometer without regard to the direction taken. Our environment is sinking fast into a welter of disamenities, yet the most vocal part of the community cannot raise their eyes from the trade figures to remark the painful event. Too many of us try not to notice it, or if occasionally we feel sick or exasperated we tend to shrug in resignation. We hear a lot about the 'cost of progress', and since the productivity figures over the years tend to rise we assume that on balance, and in some sense, we must be better off.

In the endeavour to arrest this mass flight from reality into statistics, I hope to persuade the reader that the chief sources of social welfare are not to be found in economic growth per se, but in a far more selective form of development which must include a radical reshaping of our physical environment with the needs of pleasant living, and not the needs of traffic or industry, foremost in mind. Indeed, . . . I shall argue that the social process by which technological advance is accommodated is, in any case, almost certain to reduce our sources of gratification in life . . . .

(b) Conflicts Among Objectives and their Resolution

10   The Concept of a "Trade-Off" *

R. G. Bodkin, E. P. Bond, G. L. Reuber and T. R. Robinson

In everyday life, individuals frequently face the difficulty of choosing among several goals, all of which are highly desirable in themselves but each of which is inconsistent with some of the others to some degree, thus making it impossible fully to achieve all of them. Among the many examples which could be cited are the following: the desire for income (requiring effort) vs. the desire for leisure; the desire for speed in transportation vs. the desire for safety; the desire to consume current income vs. the desire to accumulate assets. Few, if any, individuals opt for all work or all leisure, maximum speed without any concessions to safety, or starvation in order to save all of their income. Most individuals elect a compromise between these extremes: some income and some leisure; a "safe" speed; some consumption and some saving. In this sense we can say that individuals are willing to "trade off" income against leisure, speed against safety, and consumption against saving.

Nations frequently face similar difficulties in choosing among the objectives of economic policy. In the modern world, policy-makers in most, if not all, countries aspire to a wide range of economic objectives: full employment, a stable price level, rapid and sustained economic growth, balance-of-payments equilibrium, wide regional dispersion of economic development, and greater equality (of income, wealth, and opportunity) is an illustrative list. If it were merely a matter of compiling a list of desirable goals, questions of economic policy would be comparatively simple. However, if the various goals considered important by society conflict with each other to some extent, the compilation of such a list

*Reprinted by permission from R. G. Bodkin, E. P. Bond, G. L. Reuber, T. R. Robinson, *Price Stability and High Employment: The Options for Canadian Economic Policy*, Special Study No. 5 for the Economic Council of Canada, Queen's Printer, Ottawa, 1967.

is merely the beginning, not the end, of the process of formulating satisfactory economic policies. If all goals cannot be attained simultaneously, a hard choice must then be made as to how far to pursue one objective at the expense of the others. Under these circumstances, most societies, analogously to most individuals, can be expected to elect a compromise, trading off some portion of one objective in order not to fall further short on some other. It is true that the decision may not be a conscious one: the policy-makers may not view the matter in these terms or even if they take such a view, the 'objective' trade-offs may differ from those considered most probable by the decision-makers. Consequently, past actions by the policy-makers may be an imperfect guide to their preferences, given the uncertainties pervading most "real world" policy actions. Nevertheless, if a conflict between goals is present, some form of compromise is usually reached in practice; in this sense at least, the policy-makers may be said to have traded off one goal against one or more other goals.

How much of one objective must be traded off in order to gain a particular amount of another depends, of course, on the degree to which the objectives are in conflict. Conceivably, objective A might not conflict at all with objective B: in this case, A can be fully attained without impairing in any way the country's ability to achieve B as well and hence no choice between A and B is required. At the other extreme, it is conceivable that A and B are mutually exclusive. Here the choice is between all of A and none of B, or none of A and all of B — one can choose either A or B, but no combination of the two. It is, however, the view of the writers of the present study that many objectives of public policy . . . are neither completely independent of other objectives nor mutually exclusive of these other objectives, but lie between these two limits. Under these circumstances, a decision must inevitably be made, implicitly or explicitly, as to how far to pursue each objective. (In this context, an objective may be defined as the ideal that would be sought in the absence of conflicts.) Hence, in order to evaluate public policies a key question to be considered is how much of one objective must be foregone in order to move a step closer towards some other objective. In other words, what are the quantitative terms of the "trade-off" between goals A and B?

11   The Trade-off between Inflation and Unemployment*

The Economic Council of Canada

The reconciliation of high employment and reasonable price stability . . . remains a real and distinct problem for Canadian policy. In [an analysis undertaken for the Council], a number of so-called "trade-off" curves were derived showing,

*Reprinted by permission from *Third Annual Review, Prices, Productivity and Employment*, Queen's Printer, Ottawa, 1966.

under varying assumptions and conditions, the rates of price increase which would tend to occur at different levels of unemployment rates. One of the most important factors having a bearing on the estimated relationships between price changes and unemployment was the degree of foreign inflationary influence on Canadian prices.

For all the intricacies in the technical derivation of such "trade-off" curves, this analysis conveys a simple message: price increases tend to be relatively high when unemployment is low and the economy is buoyant; and conversely, price increases tend to be much lower when unemployment is high and the economy is slack. But the complexity of the factors and forces affecting such a relationship between rates of price change and levels of unemployment are such, both in theory and in the real world, that no specific "trade-off" curve can depict this relationship in a way that fits all (or even most) circumstances. [The chart], however, indicates a "trade-off zone" which, apart from illustrating the nature of this relationship, would generally reflect and accommodate actual experience in Canada since 1953 — an experience which encompasses diverse economic circumstances as regards the nature of external price influences, the postures of economic policy, the changing structure of the economy, the patterns of economic instability, the variations in expectations, and so forth.

Even after full allowance for qualifications, the central analysis of this special study strongly confirms the existence of an inherent reconciliation or trade-off problem between the goals of high employment and reasonable price stability in Canada in the post-war period. Moreover, careful evaluations of the results, together with some probing of pre-war experience in Canada and post-war experience of other countries, reinforces the view that the reconciliation problem is a persistent and pervasive phenomenon and has nowhere lent itself to easy solution, even under widely differing economic conditions and developments. The result is that this problem poses hard tasks for economic policy.

An especially useful feature of the trade-off concept is that it affords an illuminating way of viewing the roles of different kinds of economic policy. Some kinds of policies, for example, may be viewed as primarily tending to have the effect of moving the economy along a trade-off curve within the zone depicted in [the chart] either by moving towards a reduction in unemployment at the risk of eventually encountering greater price increases, or by moving towards a damping down of price increases at the risk of eventually leading to increased unemployment. Broad fiscal and monetary policies, acting upon total final demand and employment, are of this type.

These policies have a very important role to play in the economy, and the trade-off concept helps to show the situations in which changes in the basic strategies of these policies can be appropriate. It should be the purpose of these policies to help to keep the economy away from both the upper and the lower ends of the trade-off zone in [the chart]. That is, when actual output in the economy is falling persistently and substantially below potential output, with accompanying heavy unemployment and generally stable prices, it is clear that expansionary fiscal and monetary policies would be appropriate — and that it should be feasible to achieve a significant degree of inflation. Conversely, when actual output is tending to press strongly and persistently against potential output

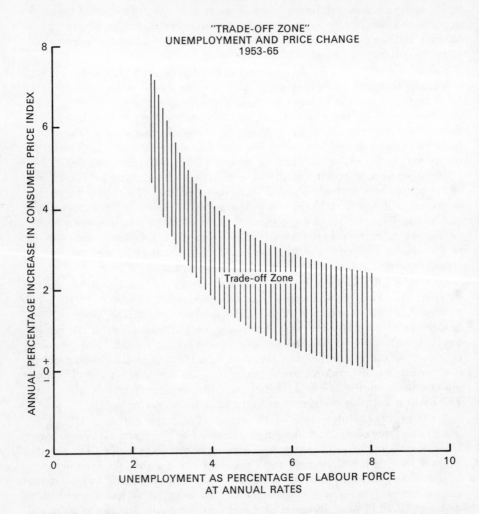

"TRADE-OFF ZONE"
UNEMPLOYMENT AND PRICE CHANGE
1953-65

(even though potential output is expanding), the general economic situation will almost invariably be one of very low unemployment and relatively strong general price advances. In these circumstances, it would be appropriate to deploy restraining fiscal and monetary policies — and it should be feasible to achieve a significant moderation of price and cost pressures without precipitating a substantial rise in unemployment. In short, the essential task of these so-called "big levers" of policy should be to try to keep the economy away from the upper and lower extremities of the trade-off zone.

There is, however, another very important range of policies whose task is a basically different one — that of trying to improve the trade-offs. In terms of the trade-off zone depicted in [the chart], the task of these policies is to try to shift the whole trade-off zone downward and to the left — that is, to seek ways of achieving less price increase for any given level of unemployment (and less unemployment for any given level of price increase). These are, in other words, policies whose basic task is more directly that of improving the reconciliation between the goals of high employment and the maintenance of reasonable price stability. Among the policies which would fall into this category are those designed to improve the mobility and adaptability of manpower, to strengthen productivity gains, to maintain effective competition, to facilitate adjustments to change, and to deal with pressure points and bottlenecks. These policies have been strongly emphasized in the Council's First and Second Annual Reviews as being essential to facilitate reconciliation between the goals of high employment and reasonable stability of prices set forth by the Council . . . .

In the light of post-war experience, the simultaneous achievement of these goals was clearly recognized by the Council to be extremely difficult, if not virtually impossible, without much more effective policies of these types . . . .

Nothing said here should be taken to imply that policies to improve the trade-offs are in any sense "better" than policies to prevent the economy from running into excessive price pressures or excessive unemployment. Both kinds of policies are needed. Both must play important roles.

12   The Conflict between Economic Growth and Equity*

The Royal Commission on Taxation

All taxes are likely to reduce economic growth; but many of the government expenditures financed by these taxes make an essential contribution to the growth of the economy. Other methods of financing government expenditures would probably have a more deleterious effect on economic growth.

The relevant question is not whether taxes reduce the rate of growth, but rather whether equitable taxes conflict with the growth objective more than inequitable taxes.

A tax system designed specifically to achieve the highest rate of growth would probably be considered highly inequitable. However, many inequitable provisions in the present tax system are also inimical to economic growth. These provisions can be eliminated and thereby both objectives can be achieved more completely.

If such costless increases in the rate of economic growth are achieved, it is then possible to adopt provisions to improve equity (even though such provisions

*Reprinted by permission from the Royal Commission on Taxation, *Report*, Vol. II, "The Use of the Tax System to Achieve Economic and Social Objectives", Queen's Printer, Ottawa, 1966.

would tend to reduce the rate of economic growth), without on balance suffering any reduction in the growth rate.

Specific provisions that would increase the equity of the tax system, but that would tend to reduce the rate of growth, often can be compensated for by adopting other provisions that would be favourable to growth without affecting the fundamental fairness of the system one way or the other.

It is essential, in evaluating the effects of our proposed tax reforms, that they be considered as a package rather than piecemeal. It is their overall impact on the rate of growth that is important.

Even if Canada has persistent but modest rates of unemployment and the rate of capital formation is correspondingly low, the rate of growth of potential GNP will be higher in the future than in the past if major wars and depressions do not occur. This suggests that Canadians could "afford" a more equitable tax system even if this were to reduce the rate of growth of output, for people could be treated more fairly and the increases in the nation's standard of living could still be maintained. We are confident, however, that if our reforms were adopted, they would improve the equity of the system without any reduction in the growth rate. Indeed, we are convinced our proposed reforms would make a positive contribution to growth.

13   Equity and Growth*

James Cutt

Critics of the Carter Commission Report have generally taken strong issue with the priority position accorded equity by the Commission. Explicitly it is argued that a priority position for economic growth would be more rational and in the long run more beneficial to lower income groups. Implicit in this argument is the view that redistribution as an objective is passé, that growth as a panacea would provide overall absolute improvements in wellbeing which would in turn minimize the need for concern over relative shares in an expanding cake.

The Concepts of Equity and Growth

Equity in taxation, according to the Commission, means taxation in accordance with "ability to pay"; the "benefit" principle of taxation is summarily rejected. The chosen index of ability to pay represents one of the most radical innovations suggested in the Report. The existing concept of income defined to include certain forms of accretion to economic wellbeing and to exclude others, and

---

*From *Canada's Tax Structure and Economic Goals*, York University, Toronto, 1967.

the possible alternatives of a wealth base or a consumption base, are rejected in favour of economic power, defined effectively as net accretion (consumption + gifts + increase in net worth) to economic wellbeing over the relevant period. Into this new comprehensive index would fall a wide variety of accretions presently excluded: capital gains, gambling winnings, gifts and bequests, etc. The index is further broken down into that part of economic power available for the "discretionary" use of the tax unit and the remaining part which is required for the maintenance of the tax unit. The fraction of income represented by discretionary economic power is considered to increase as income increases up to a maximum of $100,000 after which all further increments are considered to represent discretionary, and therefore taxable, economic power. Tax liability should then, the Commission contends, be proportionate to discretionary economic power.

Horizontal equity therefore requires that tax units with the same discretionary economic power, hereinafter "income", should pay the same proportion of that economic power in tax. The comprehensive definition of income is in itself a great contribution to horizontal equity, since differences in tax liability simply on the basis of different forms of accretion are eliminated. To further the pursuit of horizontal equity, however, the Commission recommends the adoption of the family as the basic unit of taxation; the recognition that organizations and institutions pay tax only as the representative of individuals and, accordingly, that the corporate and personal income taxes be completely integrated, the income tax liability of an individual tax unit being credited for tax paid in its behalf on both distributed and undistributed profits by the corporation; that a system of averaging be introduced to reduce discrimination under a progressive rate system against tax units with fluctuating incomes; and finally, that tax concessions to particular industries or to types of income be eliminated, such concessions being considered inequitable, frequently inefficient, and tending to distort the allocation of resources and erode the tax base. The last factor, the Commission's embrace of the principle of neutrality, has provoked much criticism of the Report by those groups whose special privileges would be curtailed.

Since discretionary income is taken to increase as a proportion of income as income increases, proportionate taxation of discretionary income implies an overall progressive rate structure. *Vertical equity* is thus given the conventional definition that those with greater ability to pay should pay higher taxes. The use of the tax system to redistribute income is thus explicitly stated by the Commission. The notion of discretionary income and its assumed rate of increase relative to total income lead the Commission to a precise scale of progressive tax rates. This particular scientific or pseudo-scientific justification of progression and a particular progressive scale of rates is really no better, and no worse, than the variety of sacrifice, faculty and other theories used to justify progression in the past. It is perhaps a pity that the Commission used the discretionary income theory as a cover for the clearly subjective notion of the appropriate degree of vertical equity which ultimately reflects, in Henry Simon's words, society's "ethical or aesthetic judgment that the prevailing distribution of . . . income is distinctly evil or unlovely". The Commission claims a consensus on its view of redistribution, and in this is probably generally justified — though again it might have been more frank to acknowledge that a consensus on a detailed scale of rates is clearly unattainable and that the rate scale reflects simply the judgment of a particular group of experts at a particular point in time.

Having stated that progression is desirable in the overall tax structure, the Commission examines in detail the inadequate progressivity of the present allegedly sharp scale of progressive rates which are avoided by high bracket capital income and apply in varying degrees to different types of earned income, and goes on to recommend reforms which would increase the overall progressivity of the tax structure. The greatly widened income base is again the major factor here, enabling the Commission to increase effective overall progressivity while reducing the highest marginal rate from 80 per cent to 50 per cent. As part of the move to greater overall progressivity the Commission also recommends increased reliance on the new comprehensive income tax and diminished reliance on sales taxation which tends to be regressive.

The *growth* objective of the tax system is initially stated as being ". . . to maximize the current and future output of goods and services desired by Canadians". A distinction is drawn between actual and potential growth of output, the latter being that rate of growth which would obtain if full employment prevailed. Further, since the Commission was concerned with taxation of income accruing to Canadian residents, potential GNP rather than potential gross domestic product is chosen as the appropriate index of growth.

The attitude to growth adopted by the Commission has two major aspects. First, in a positive sense, the proper rate of growth is taken to be that which would be attained by the allocation of resources according to market forces. Two policy conclusions follow: (a) departures from full employment cause growth of actual output to fall below growth of potential output, and the maintenance of full employment emerges as a major policy goal for fiscal policy; and (b), the Commission proposes to unharness the "invisible hand" by establishing a neutral tax system in which almost all concessions would be eliminated.

Second, in a negative sense, the Commission examines in detail the effect of its proposals on what it feels to be the three decisive determinants of growth: labour supply, technical change, and savings and investment.

The distinction thus emerges between "costless" growth, which results from the maintenance of full employment and the removal of misallocations of resources through market imperfections, tax concessions, and so on, and growth as a deliberate, specified policy goal. Though the Commission embraces only the first of these, it does provide, as mentioned above, some suggestions for growth by policy choice and an analysis of the costs of such a policy.

The Relationship Between Equity and Growth — Complementarity and Conflict

(i) Horizontal Equity: The Commission points out that the Canadian tax system has features which are both inequitable and growth inhibiting; the elimination of those features would thus further the attainment of both objectives:

> . . . fortunately, a tax structure designed to achieve horizontal equity also achieves neutrality with respect to industries and activities.[1]

The argument is that a more efficient allocation of capital can be obtained in a neutral tax system. The policy conclusions follow: first, the personal and corporate income taxes should be integrated and share gains fully taxed, eliminating the concern of corporations and investors for the form in which income generated from investment accrues; second, capital gains on other assets should also be fully taxed as income, correcting over-investment in such assets presently favoured by the zero rate of tax on capital gains; third, again to correct over-investment, the present favourable treatment of the mining and petroleum industries should be eliminated; and, finally, the dual rate of corporation income tax should be abolished. How large the alleged efficiency gains would be is difficult to estimate. The determination of the effect on resource use depends on estimating the inter-industry shift of real resources which is associated with a shift in financial investment away from previously favored areas. In the U.S.A. the efficiency loss due to over-investment in the non-corporate and under-investment in the corporate section has been estimated at about $2 billion, and R. A. Musgrave has offered a "guesstimate" that $200 million might be the order of gains in Canada. These gains represent simply an increase in the level of national income, and do not necessarily imply a long run higher growth rate.

The Commission further recognizes that the market itself discriminates against "the new, the unknown and the small" and is prepared to use the tax system to correct for these distortions. Immediate 100 per cent write-off of capital costs for certain small businesses and for the mining and petroleum industries is recommended. The accelerated depreciation implicit in the present system of capital write-offs also receives the blessing of the Commission. To encourage research and development, the exploration and development expenses of mining and petroleum firms, and the research and development funds of all firms presently receive immediate write-off; the Commission recommends the continuation of this provision. Finally, the discrimination of the market against risk investment should be compensated, the Commission allows, by much more generous loss offset and averaging provisions.

If one accepts the promise of the Commission that the optimum allocation of resources is achieved by the operation of market forces, it is difficult to dispute the policy inferences drawn. Paradoxically, it is against these very proposals which seek to free market forces to operate at maximum efficiency that the private sector briefs attacking the Report have railed! It seems clear, of course, that what is being attacked is simply the removal of special privileges and that the private sector is not advocating a more comprehensive overall role for tax policy in shaping the pattern and rate of economic growth.

---

[1] The Royal Commission on Taxation, *Report*, Vol. VI, Queen's Printer, Ottawa, 1967, p. 90.

The Report may be criticized for its failure to analyze in any detail the possibilities of a broad policy of "fiscal dirigism", defined as a fiscal policy aimed at the achievement of goals of public policy through the governmental insertion of incentives and disincentives into a basically market economy. The Commission might have been expected to explore the extent to which such a policy has been employed in Western countries since 1945; the success of many such policies suggests that the Commission's virtual identification of growth with neutrality may be overly facile. The only recognition of such policies given by the Commission is a hint that it might approve regional development policies.

(ii) Vertical Equity: It is a matter of simple arithmetic that if redistribution towards any group causes a fall in the rate of growth of national income, no matter how slight, there will be some date beyond which the *absolute* income of the initially favoured group will be less than it would have been if the redistribution had not taken place. The Commission is well aware of this dilemma:

> Equity, after all, has to be defined in terms of income received currently. There is little to be gained if, in the name of equity, the reformed tax system were to erode the sources of future income in order to redistribute current income.[2]

Having elected to redistribute income through the tax system largely by defining the new comprehensive income base, the Commission, in an attempt to offset adverse effects on work effort, suggests a drastic reduction in the marginal tax rates on upper income groups. As a result the tax liability of taxpayers *whose tax base is not widened as a result of the new definition of income* would fall sharply; the reductions at $10,000, $25,000, $40,000 and $70,000 are 11 per cent, 17 per cent, 27 per cent and 21 per cent respectively. In general, for recipients of work income, marginal rates are cut more sharply than average rates. That is, progression is reduced and, insofar as work effort is related to marginal tax rates, the general conclusion of the Commission that work effort will not be reduced, and may well be increased, by the tax proposals seems justified. It is perhaps fair to wonder, in the light of a substantial body of evidence in the literature that work effort is unrelated to tax liability, why the Commission found it necessary to recommend such drastic rate reductions. The Commission's argument that high marginal rates do affect work incentives is certainly not impressive:

> ... although we have no evidence to support our contention, we are convinced that high marginal personal rates of tax do have a negative effect on labour, managerial and professional effort.[3]

This conclusion is inconsistent with the findings of the special study done for the Commission on the subject.

With regard to saving, the Commission estimates that the reform proposals

---

[2]*Ibid.*, p. 73.
[3]*Ibid.*, Vol. II, p. 128.

would leave the level of private saving virtually unchanged. The Commission estimates that, had the proposed system been in operation in 1964, personal savings would have been lower by about $135 million or 4.5 per cent; business and foreign saving would have been the same; and government *revenue* would have increased by about $200 million. If the entire increase in government revenue is seen as government savings, there would therefore have been a small net increase in savings of $65 million. It might be noted here that many developing countries employ the device of forced savings via taxation and have found that unless revenue is earmarked for saving and investment or, at least, for consumption expenditure of a developmental or growth-oriented nature, much of the increase in government revenue finds its way into government expenditure of a purely current nature. In this way private saving is replaced not by government saving but by government consumption.

Although the Commission does not anticipate a significant change in the *level* of private savings, it does expect a significant change in their allocation. With regard to investment, the Commission estimates that the rise in share yields, following the integration of the corporate and personal income taxes relative to bond yields and non-corporate forms of equity investment, will significantly increase the flow of funds into corporate equity investment. Further, the taxation of capital gains is seen as possibly exercising a dampening effect on risk investment, and the Commission proposes to counter this reduction of incentive by greatly widened loss offset provisions, including unlimited carry-forward and deductability from all forms of income, and generous averaging of income for tax purposes. R. A. Musgrave has shown that by unlimited loss offset and averaging, it is possible to almost completely eliminate the discrimination against risk inherent in capital gains taxation. He also shows that in general, the diminished marginal rates and loss offset and averaging provisions operate to minimize the likelihood of significant substitution effects against labour effort, savings and equity investment. He suggests that significant adverse incentive effects and consequent negative growth implications are very unlikely indeed.

However, the Commission gives only passing consideration to what might be a decisive issue in resolving possible conflict between growth and vertical equity. In examining policies for the deliberate promotion of growth, the Commission briefly dwells on the possibility of permitting the deduction of specific forms of saving from gross income in determining taxable income, thus converting the income tax system into a partial expenditure tax system. Such a policy amounts, in fact, to compromising the equity objective only to the point of tolerating *functional inequalities* — defined as inequalities which can be shown to have positive growth implications. A comprehensive scheme of complete or partial exemption from tax of income *saved and invested in certain specified directions* would provide a delicate tool of dirigistic policy to influence the rate and pattern of growth, and would at the same time permit higher tax rates on that portion of income consumed. In effect, attention is switched from inequalities of income to inequalities of consumption which are the most disagreeable social manifestation of inequalities of income.

14   The "Faddiness" of Economic Objectives *

H. G. Johnson

The three goals of low unemployment, reasonable price stability and adequate rate of growth are all derived from recent brief historical experiences: low unemployment as a goal derives from the 1930's, price stability and growth from the late 1950's. Of the two recently added goals, it seems fair to observe that price stability is a goal generated by public opinion, to which economists have responded by producing ceremonially adequate theories of chronic inflation; whereas adequate growth is much more a creation of the [economics] profession itself, a reflection of the extent to which growth has become the test of efficient economic performance under the combined influence of the cold war and concern with the underdeveloped countries. Growth, as such, is not self-evidently an object of policy in a free enterprise economy; and the recent emphasis on the desirability of a high rate of growth seems to me to involve grafting on to a free enterprise system standards appropriate to a planned economy with military and political ambitions. I am not arguing that U.S. foreign policy may not require the support of a high domestic rate of growth, but simply that to pretend that it is a strictly economic goal can only confuse the issue. (In this respect the report is less honest than the staff papers, in failing to mention the political motivation for growth). Nor would I dispute the quite different proposition that there are many high-yielding investments in such things as education and basic research that private enterprise will not undertake, and whose undertaking by the state will result in faster growth.

The 'faddy' aspects of the goals of price stability and growth are well illustrated by some features of the report's discussion of them. With respect to price stability, the report begins by conjuring up the horrors of hyperinflation; though it admits that hyperinflation is not a real threat in the United States, and that arbitrary redistribution of income and wealth is far less drastic in a mild inflation, it nevertheless sets the avoidance of even mild sustained increases in the price level as a major goal. In so doing it ignores the now large body of empirical evidence to the effect that the arbitrary redistributions it abhors are difficult to detect in mild inflations, and the theoretical analysis indicating that economic behavior will adjust to inflation. It ignores also the fact that it mentions later that the upward bias in existing price indexes makes it very difficult to be sure that the upward movement of the indexes since 1953 represents genuine inflation. It is difficult to avoid the conclusion that the Commission has been guided by the *a priori* conviction that inflation is a terrible evil. With respect to growth, 'faddiness' is evidenced in the Commission's

---

*Reprinted by permission of author and publisher from "Objectives, Monetary Standards and Potentialities", *Review of Economics and Statistics*, Vol. XLV No. 1, Part 2, February 1963, pp. 139 — 142. The author was reviewing the report of the U.S. Commission on Money and Credit, *Money and Credit: Their Influence on Jobs, Prices and Growth*, Prentice-Hall, Englewood Cliffs, N.J., 1961.

expressed belief that the rate of growth has been inadequate, coupled with its inability to explain why it thinks so and its unwillingness to state a target rate of growth. (The report's only positive statement on this subject — "A growth rate below that which is obtainable in an economy operating at a high level of employment of our human and physical resources and at reasonably stable price levels is clearly not adequate" — is a masterpiece of high-sounding emptiness, quite apart from the ambiguity of the word "obtainable"; it amounts to saying that growth is not positively undesirable.)

The goals themselves are not ultimate objectives clearly related to a consistent concept of national economic welfare but, instead, are proximate objectives defined in terms of the operating characteristics of the economy, whose relation to economic welfare is not necessarily very close or direct. Each goal is defined by a modifying adjective — "reasonable", "low", "adequate" — indicating approval of the relevant characteristics of the economy's performance, evidently by public opinion or some sector of it. Just what satisfactory performance amounts to precisely is discussed only in connection with low unemployment. Despite the noncomparability and imprecision of the goals, the report asserts that they are equally important. Just how importance is assessed is nowhere explained. The Commission clearly does not have any operational definition in mind; presumably it believes that all goals are equal, but these are more equal than others.

Definition of the goals of public policy in terms of popularly approved characteristics of economic performance is perhaps the only legitimate approach in a democratic society, especially for a body like the Commission not entrusted with actual policy making. But to be useful as a guide to intelligent policy making or policy evaluation, a statement of goals in these terms should be accompanied not merely by recognition of the possibility of conflict between objectives, but also by consideration of factors relevant to making the optimal compromise in cases of conflict. The report stops far short of being useful in this respect. First, while it recognizes the possibility of conflict, its main argument is devoted to proving the compatibility of objectives. The one conflict it recognizes as likely — between low unemployment and price stability — it evades by appealing to other policies, confidence in whose likely effectiveness is not justified by experience here and in other countries. (Incidentally, the report seems to me to gloss over another conflict in its discussion of growth and inflation. The statistical evidence it quotes — to the effect that there is no association between the growth rate and the rate of price change for rates of price increase between zero and 6 per cent, but that countries with prices changes outside these limits experience lower growth rate — implies that normally growth and moderate inflation go together, not that "there is no basis for believing that inflation is needed to stimulate growth". Second, by confining the argument to the goals as defined by public opinion, the Commission deliberately evades confronting the problem of resolving conflict intelligently, and offers public opinion no guidance. The Commission regards the problem as one of "trading-off" one goal against the other; since the rate of price increase, the percentage of unemployment, and the growth rate are incommensurable, casting the problem in these terms fails even to call attention to the need for commensuration to resolve conflicts.

There are two possible approaches to efficient resolution of a conflict of objectives, both of which involve going behind the stated objectives to their economic content. I take the conflict between price stability and low unemployment as an example. One approach is to attempt to attach economic costs of a comparable kind to the nonfulfillment of objectives — say, the loss of income to the unemployed as against the loss of real income and property to the victims of inflation. The other is to investigate whether the social losses from nonfulfillment of an objective can be eliminated or mitigated by institutional changes — in the case of inflation, by indexing and other measures surveyed in Holzman's paper, in the case of unemployment, by more generous unemployment benefits as Galbraith suggested in *The Affluent Society*. Either, or both in combination, would be likely to lead to a more socially efficient resolution of conflict than reliance on an undefined social welfare function containing the rate of price increase, the level of unemployment, and the rate of growth as arguments would be.

I have used the example of conflict between price stability and low unemployment for a particular reason: in spite of the Commission, the staff papers, and a widespread agreement among the profession, it does not seem to me that the rate of growth belongs in the group of objectives with the other two. Both the rate of price change and the amount of unemployment can, for purposes of broad analysis, be taken to depend on the level of aggregate demand, and so to be amenable to "monetary, credit and fiscal policies"; the fact that they vary in opposite directions with demand poses the crucial conflict of objectives. But the rate of growth is a question of the allocation of resources between current uses and output-increasing activity. The choice between fiscal and monetary policy may influence this allocation; but there is no *a priori* reason why, other things equal, the rate of growth should vary with the average level of unemployment. In particular, contrary to the belief of the Commission and many economists, there is no *a priori* reason for expecting a higher normal level of employment, accompanied presumably by a higher rate of price increase, to produce a higher rate of growth.

In analyzing this problem it is necessary to recall that the rate of growth measures the proportionate and not the absolute annual increment of output, and that one should exclude the transitory effects of changes in the percentage of unemployment. Put very crudely in terms of the Harrod-Domar equation, the problem is whether a higher level of employment and income will raise the average proportion of income saved, lower the marginal capital-output ratio, or (more realistically) raise the savings ratio sufficiently to offset a raised marginal capital-output ratio. Both theory and empirical knowledge about these relationships give little grounds for the confident affirmative answer that many economists are inclined to give, and that is echoed in the report.

The report's conclusion that "measures to stimulate aggregate demand to attain low levels of unemployment are basic to an adequate rate of economic growth" is derived by extremely questionable arguments. The report credits low unemployment with both the immediate increase in output consequent on reduced unemployment, and the longer-term (but still once-over) effect of lower unemployment on the size of the effective labor force. The only possible permanent effect on the rate of growth of output it mentions is a decrease in the rate of reduction of hours of work, and this begs the question of the difference between real output and real income. The report recognizes that no firm conclusion can be reached concerning the effect of low unemployment or of the more appropriate measure of growth, the rate of growth of real GNP per man hour, but argues that special policies for increasing productivity can be introduced more easily when unemployment is low. This may be so: but the report loads the dice by assuming that demand is fixed and not increasing with productivity, so that increased productivity necessarily releases labor, and by arguing in terms of absolute rather than proportional increases in the productivity of the economy.

Similar objections can be raised against the Scitovskys' arguments for high employment as a growth stimulator, which also rely on counting transitional effects. Using an average multiplier, the Scitovskys calculate the reduction in investment necessary to increase unemployment by 1 per cent, find that it amounts to 10 per cent of net domestic capital formation, and argue that this will reduce the rate of growth by 10 per cent. Apart from its gross overexaggeration of the contribution of net capital formation to growth, this argument overlooks the effect of the reduction in demand on the denominator of the rate-of-growth equation.

In the same way, Klein's initial argument that, on the surface, growth and full employment are complements confuses the maximization of potential output at a point of time with increasing the growth rate. Klein goes on to a more sophisticated argument; on Harrod-Domar lines, to the effect that full employment has reduced the U.S. growth rate by encouraging high consumption; but his attribution of the fall in the aggregate savings ratio to full employment is not convincing. Only Chandler recognizes clearly that the rate of growth is a question of the composition of output, and that theory indicates no clear relation between it and the level of activity.

I conclude that it has yet to be demonstrated that lower unemployment as a normal situation (in contrast to a movement from higher to lower unemployment) is good for growth. Nor do the report and staff papers suggest any close relation between inflation and growth. It therefore seems that the report's treatment of price stability, low unemployment, and adequate growth as comparable policy objectives is a misclassification; that the objectives especially relevant to aggregative economic policy are price stability and employment, only; and that growth should be relegated to a position among the other objectives — economic freedom, defense, equitable distribution — that the Commission regards as desirable.

Though growth should not be ranked with price stability and low unemployment as an objective relevant to aggregative policy, growth policy might still be relevant to the attainment of these other objectives. The Commission, as already mentioned, looks to policies increasing competition and to economic statesmanship to resolve the apparent conflict between price stability and employment. An alternative policy (presumably what Klein recommends, though he does not spell out the logic adequately) would rely on the conscious promotion of increasing productivity to reconcile the rate of wage increase at low unemployment with price stability. The practicability of either solution seems doubtful: enforced competition and voluntary "economic statesmanship" are unlikely to be capable of overcoming a rate of price increase estimated to be of the order of 4 per cent at 4 per cent unemployment; and it is equally unlikely, even if the (Phillips) type of relation between unemployment and wage-rate change is reliable and independent of the rate of productivity increase, that the latter can be raised sufficiently by growth policy to achieve price stability. Thus the conflict between price stability and low unemployment is likely to persist. The economist is most likely to continue fruitfully to its resolution by further study of how far the conflict is created by our methods of measurement of prices and unemployment, what the costs of alternative compromises are, and how far the social costs of nonfulfillment of objectives can be mitigated.

Chapter Two
Government Expenditures

The previous chapter discussed the presumed basis of community policy objectives. This raises two further questions: what is the vehicle by which the community determines its objectives; and what arrangements exist to ensure that the objectives are implemented in accordance with the community's wishes. We know that governments do make decisions, but what we are concerned about is whether they are the right ones.

There are two main approaches to this problem. The first is to set up a theoretical construct of how the government *ought* to make economic decisions and to see how closely the institutions of government conform to our theoretical model. For example, we might ascertain the community's preference function by the use of public opinion polls, royal commissions, analyses of newspaper content and other devices, which we could present in a set of equations. We could then compare the solutions to our model with the actual solutions of government, as revealed in economic statistics and other empirical measurements. Any discrepancy between theoretical and observed results would measure the extent to which government is not fulfilling the community's objectives. This approach is undoubtedly of considerable value in a partial equilibrium analysis of government policy such as discussion of the balance of payments, full employment or price stability; however, the extent of value judgements involved and the dubious validity of short-run behavioural equations that emerge from this kind of procedure make it unsuitable in a general equilibrium setting.

The second approach is to analyze the actual decision-making process in government, explaining it in terms of a rational model. This approach also has its problems, notably the assumption that the political process that produced the government decisions that we are observing and analyzing has in fact revealed the community's preferences for public goods and services.

Our approach combines the two. While a purely theoretical solution to the community's objectives is not practicable, we cannot accept that the present system cannot be improved. By and large the democratic process does work, but it does not always work ideally in the economic sphere, either in maximizing efficiency or in maximizing welfare. Thus there is considerable scope for analyzing the effectiveness of present decision-making techniques and recommending improvements. This chapter contains three sections. The first explains the present method of decision-making in government. The second describes some of the techniques used in modern analysis of economic policy. Finally, the third section examines actual expenditures that have been undertaken by Canadian governments.

15   An Economic Theory of Democracy*

Anthony Downs

It does not unduly distort reality to state that most welfare economists and many public finance theorists implicity assume that the "proper" function of government is to maximize social welfare. Insofar as they face the problem of government decision-making at all, they nearly all subscribe to some approximation of this normative rule.

The use of this rule has led to two major difficulties. First, it is not clear what is meant by "social welfare", nor is there any agreement about how to "maximize" it. In fact, a long controversy about the nature of social welfare in the "new welfare economics" led to Kenneth Arrow's conclusion that no rational method of maximizing social welfare can possibly be found unless strong restrictions are placed on preference orderings of the individuals in society.[1]

The complexities of this problem have diverted attention from the second difficulty raised by the view that government's function is to maximize social welfare. Even if social welfare could be defined, and methods of maximizing it could be agreed upon, what reason is there to believe that the men who run the government would be motivated to maximize it? To state that they "should" do so does not mean that they will. As Schumpeter, one of the few economists who have faced this problem, has pointed out:

> It does not follow that the social meaning of a type of activity will necessarily provide the motive power, hence the explanation of the latter. If it does not, a theory that contents itself with an analysis of the social end or need to be served cannot be accepted as an adequate account of the activities that serve it.[2]

Schumpeter here illuminates a crucial objection to most attempts to deal with government in economic theory: they do not really treat the government as part of the division of labor. Every agent in the division of labor has both a private motive and a social function. For example, the social function of a coal-miner is removing coal from the ground, since this activity provides utility for

*Reprinted by permission of author and publisher from "An Economic Theory of Political Action in a Democracy", *The Journal of Political Economy*, Vol. LXV, No. 2, April 1957, pp. 135-150.

[1]Kenneth Arrow, *Social Choice and Individual Values*, Wiley, New York, 1951.

[2]Joseph A. Schumpeter, *Capitalism, Socialism and Democracy*, Harper & Bros., New York, 1950, p. 282.

others. But he is motivated to carry out this function by his desire to earn income, not by any desire to benefit others. Similarly, every other agent in the division of labor carries out his social function primarily as a means of attaining his own private ends: the enjoyment of income, prestige, or power. Much of economic theory consists in essence of proving that men thus pursuing their own ends may nevertheless carry out their social functions with great efficiency, at least under certain conditions.

In light of this reasoning, any attempt to construct a theory of government action without discussing the motives of those who run the government must be regarded as inconsistent with the main body of economic analysis. Every such attempt fails to face the fact that governments are concrete institutions run by men, because it deals with them on a purely normative level. As a result, these attempts can never lead to an integration of government with other decision-makers in a general equilibrium theory. Such integration demands a positive approach that explains how the governors are led to act by their own selfish motives. In the following sections, I present a model of government decision-making based on this approach.

An Economic Theory of Political Action in a Democracy

Democracy is a political system that exhibits the following characteristics:

(a) Two or more parties compete in periodic elections for control of the governing apparatus.

(b) The party (or coalition of parties) winning a majority of votes gains control of the governing apparatus until the next election.

(c) Losing parties never attempt to prevent the winners from taking office, nor do winners use the powers of office to vitiate the ability of losers to compete in the next election.

(d) All sane, law-abiding adults who are governed are citizens, and every citizen has one and only one vote in each election.

Though these definitions are both somewhat ambiguous, they will suffice for present purposes.

Next I set forth the following axioms:

1. Each political party is a team of men who seek office solely in order to enjoy the income, prestige, and power that go with running the governing apparatus.[3]

2. The winning party (or coalition) has complete control over the government's actions until the next election. There are no votes of confidence between elections either by a legislature or by the

---

[3] A "team" is a coalition whose members have practical goals. A "coalition" is a group of men who cooperate to achieve some common end. These definitions are taken from Jacob Marschak, "Towards an Economic Theory of Organizations and Information", in *Decision Processes*, R. M. Thrall, C. H. Coombs and R. L. Davis (eds.), Wiley, New York, 1954, pp. 188-189. I use "team" instead of "coalition" in my definition to eliminate intraparty power struggles from consideration, though in Marschak's terms parties are really coalitions, not teams.

electorate, so the governing party cannot be ousted before the next election. Nor are any of its orders resisted or sabotaged by an intransigent bureaucracy.

3. Government's economic powers are unlimited. It can nationalize everything, hand everything over to private interests, or strike any balance between these extremes.

4. The only limit on government's powers is that the incumbent party cannot in any way restrict the political freedom of opposition parties or of individual citizens, unless they seek to overthrow it by force.

5. Every agent in the model — whether an individual, a party or a private coalition — behaves rationally at all times; that is, it proceeds toward its goals with a minimal use of scarce resources and undertakes only those actions for which marginal return exceeds marginal cost.[4]

My central hypothesis [is that] political parties in a democracy formulate policy strictly as a means of gaining votes. They do not seek to gain office in order to carry out certain preconceived policies or to serve any particular interest groups; rather they formulate policies and serve interest groups in order to gain office. Thus their social function — which is to formulate and carry out policies when in power as the government — is accomplished as a by-product of their private motive — which is to attain the income, power, and prestige of being in office.

This hypothesis implies that, in a democracy, the government always acts so as to maximize the number of votes it will receive. In effect, it is an entrepreneur selling policies for votes instead of products for money. Furthermore, it must compete for votes with other parties, just as two or more oligopolists compete for sales in a market. Whether or not such a government maximizes social welfare (assuming this process can be defined) depends upon how the competitive struggle for power influences its behavior. We cannot assume *a priori* that this behavior is socially optimal any more than we can assume *a priori* that a given firm produces the socially optimal output.

Economic theory has suffered because it has not taken into account the political realities of government decision-making. Economists have been content to discuss government action as though governments were run by perfect altruists whose only motive was to maximize social welfare. As a result, economists have been unable to incorporate government into the rest of economic theory, which is based on the premise that all men act primarily out of self-interest. Furthermore, they have falsely concluded that government decision-making in all societies should follow identical principles, because its goal is always the maximization of social welfare. If my hypothesis is true, the goal of government is attaining the income, power, and prestige that go with office. Since methods

---

[4]The term "rational" in this article is synonymous with "efficient". This economic definition must not be confused with the logical definition (i.e., pertaining to logical propositions) or the psychological definition (i.e., calculating or unemotional).

of reaching this goal are vastly different in democratic, totalitarian, and aristocratic states, no single theory can be advanced to explain government decision-making in all societies. Nor can any theory of government decision-making be divorced from politics. The way every government actually makes decisions depends upon the nature of the fundamental power relation between the governors and the governed in its society; that is, upon the society's political constitution. Therefore, a different theory of political action must be formulated for each different type of constitution.

16 Governments Maximize Their Own Interest*

Albert Breton

In their efforts to analyse the behaviour of households and firms, economists have traditionally assumed that each of these units maximizes an index, such as a utility function, a profit function, or a present value function, which is taken to characterize its own interest. However, in analysing government policies these same economists have generally shied away from the maximization-of-own-interest assumption and have instead assumed that governments maximize a social welfare function or the common good; or they have proceeded by developing *ad hoc* hypotheses for each different problem. This is regretable, for the returns to the maximization-of-own-interest assumption in the analysis of household and firm behaviour have been impressive, even when due consideration is given to the simplification of reality that is involved. One cannot help suspecting that they might also be high in the analysis of government behaviour.

In consequence, in the present paper, following the lead of Schumpeter and Downs,[1] I suppose that governments are not primarily interested in maximizing a social welfare function, or the common good, or the public interest — whatever these may be — but that instead they seek to maximize their own interest. Specifically, following Downs and Wilson,[2] I assume that governments maximize the probability of their re-election, a probability which is dependent on the policies that are implemented as well as on the degree to which they are implemented. This relationship rests on the view that governments and their

*Reprinted by permission of author and publisher from "A Theory of Demand for Public Goods", *Canadian Journal of Economics and Political Science*, Vol. XXXII, No. 4, November 1966, pp. 455-467.

[1]J. A. Schumpeter, *Capitalism, Socialism and Democracy*, Harper, New York, 1950, p. 282. A. Downs, *An Economic Theory of Democracy*, Harper and Row, New York, 1957.

[2]J. Q. Wilson, "The Economy of Patronage", *Journal of Political Economy*, August 1961, pp. 369-380.

electorates are engaged in a sort of exchange in which policies are traded for votes; to maximize the probability of their re-election, governments endeavour to "produce" those policies which can be exchanged for the largest possible *quid pro quo*, that is, for the largest number of votes. Thus an analysis of government behaviour following a change in the preferences of consumer-voters, for example, would be to a large extent an analysis of changes in government policies. The potential number and variety of these policies, however, is so large that at first glance it seems impossible to proceed with a systematic analysis.

The strategy adopted here is to assume that government policies can be grouped into meaningful classes and to examine the factors underlying the implementation of policies for each of these classes. . . .

In a universe of certainty the only instrument of political action in the hands of consumer-voters is their power to vote,[3] but in a world of uncertainty they can join interest groups, participate in lobbies, make representations, generate unrest, organize manifestations, pressure their congressmen or representatives, stimulate organized protest, influence others by word-of-mouth, deliver speeches, give financial and other support to political action groups, and use the many other means that have been invented to influence politicians.[4] Individuals will be able to profit from these activities because in a world of uncertainty and competition, politicians do not know what the preferences of the electorate are, but they know that to maximize the probability of their reelection they have to obtain some knowledge of these preferences. Furthermore, given that individuals find it in their own interest under a system of benefit taxation not to reveal their true preferences for public goods, governments have to adopt a system of non-benefit taxation which, as we have seen, places all individuals in a situation of disequilibrium. If we now formulate the hypothesis that the propensity to join the political activities listed above depends *ceteris paribus* (to be specified below) on the difference between one's desired and one's actual position with respect to the supply of public goods, then, given any system of non-benefit taxation, it follows that an individual's participation in political activity, including voting, will reveal his true preferences for public goods. Indeed, it is at the level of political activity and not at that of market activity that the preferences for public goods are made known. The contrary contention, that individuals do not reveal their preferences for public goods, rests on the assumptions that individuals are not coerced to pay for public goods through a non-benefit system of taxation, and that the only relevant behaviour in the analysis of public goods is market behaviour.

Before proceeding with the argument, I should mention that individuals will not join the activities listed above randomly or haphazardly, nor will they join all of them. Let us adhere to the hypothesis that the propensity to join

---

[3]For an empirical study supporting the hypothesis that voting reflects the preference of voters, see V. O. Key, *The Responsible Electorate*, Harvard University Press, Cambridge, Mass., 1966.

[4]See E. C. Banfield, *Political Influence*, Macmillan, New York, 1961.

political activities is proportional to the difference between one's desired and one's actual position with respect to the availability of public goods. This propensity, however, will also be governed by the relative monetary and non-monetary costs of joining political activities and by the expected returns from joining which are a function of one's estimate of one's chances of influencing politicians. As Downs has shown, in a world of uncertainty some individuals will be able to influence politicians more than others, because some individuals can "deliver" more votes than others. One may suppose that politicians attribute to each individual, to each political group, to each block of interests, and in fact to each political activity in which people engage, a power coefficient which determines the "influence" that these individuals, groups, and blocks have on them. To each politician, the distribution of these power coefficients is his image of the power structure in society. We can derive three propositions from the above discussion. First, the larger the dispersion of tastes in a given jurisdiction, the larger the number of individuals who will join political activities. This follows from the fact that if the preferences of everyone in the jurisdiction are the same, no one will join in political activities, since a vote maximizing government will supply the amount of public goods which is desired for everyone. Secondly, holding returns and costs constant, if the propensity to join political activities is greater the larger the difference between the actual and the desired position of individuals, we should not expect all individuals to participate in political activities with the same degree of intensity; in fact, some individuals will not participate at all, while others will only participate symbolically. If instead of holding costs and returns constant, we hold the difference between the actual and the desired situation constant, those individuals who cannot expect to influence politicians will not join even if the cost is low; on the other hand if the costs are high, but the chances of influencing politicians higher, then the individual will join. Thirdly, since people's tastes vary between products, we should expect to find individuals joining more than one interest group, supporting the government on some policies and opposing it on others; individuals may also join political activities in relation to the supply of one public good and abstain the case of another.

Returning to our main argument, we can now say that the supply of public goods will be determined — under the assumptions made above — by the preferences of individuals for public goods relative to the amount available, by the "prices" that they have to pay for these goods, by the relative costs of joining political activities, and by the political power structure in society as seen by politicians. The presumption is that the supply of public goods and the system of taxation will tend to reflect the preferences of the more powerful group. This follows from the fact that these groups can "deliver" the largest number of votes and that politicians will cater to these groups to get the votes they "control". For this reason, the system of taxation will tend to be one where the "prices" paid by the more powerful groups will be below what they would be willing to pay for the amount made available, given what the less powerful groups are willing to pay; on the other hand the prices paid by these latter groups will of necessity be higher than the marginal utility of the public goods to them. In other words, the final grand equilibrium will reflect the preferences of individuals for private and public goods — and by implication for a given system of tax rates; it will also reflect the costs of producing these goods and what we can call, for short, the workings of the political process. It should be observed that even though individuals are in disequilibrium with respect to the supply of public and private goods considered in isolation of the political process, they are in full equilibrium once we take account of their political power which, of course, is always given in terms of the political power of others in society.

An important point that must be kept in mind, however, is that the power structure, like any other political, social, or economic phenomenon, can be thrown out of equilibrium by disturbances. It is not my intention to examine this problem in the present paper; however, I would like to indicate briefly that in a democratic society, the distribution of power or the power structure will not long endure if it is too skewed. To see why this is so, one need only reflect on the demand for public goods and the system of taxation implied by a very skewed power structure. The size of the disequilibrium of those not sharing in the power will lead them to try to break that structure, by creating new groups and new blocks.

Let me illustrate this argument by one of its implications. In "The Economics of Nationalism"[5] I have argued that nationalistic policies tend to redistribute income in favour of the middle class against the working class. This argument can be logically derived from the above theory on only two assumptions: that nationalism is a public good; and that the middle class considered as a group has more power than the working class. This power structure could not long endure if a nationalistic government single-mindedly pursued nationalistic policies because then the working class would "revolt" and engage in political activity to overthrow the party in power. To preserve equilibrium in the power structure — a structure which got it elected in the first place — the government will supply public goods designed to satisfy the working class. It is for this reason, I suggest, that political nationalism[6] and the welfare state tend to develop concomitantly, and that the most nationalistic states also tend to have the largest welfare programs. The above applies to democracies, but since dictatorships are subjected to the same basic forces, in the sense that a dictator cannot long stay in office if he throws the power structure too drastically out of equilibrium, it is not surprising that new and developing states which pursue nationalistic policies also have well-developed welfare programs.

One question still remains unanswered, namely the question of whether individuals, who by joining political activities reveal their preferences for public goods, will be able to hide their true political power. People's efforts obviously will tend to be directed at convincing politicians that their power coefficient is large while that of those who are not their "allies" is small. Can they be

---

[5]A. Breton, "The Economics of Nationalism", *Journal of Political Economy*, Vol. LXXII, No. 4, August 1964.

[6]For a distinction between political and cultural nationalism, see *ibid.*, p. 376.

successful in such an endeavour? The answer is that they will generally not be successful because it is not possible to convince a politician one day that so-and-so wields a lot of power and on the next day that he does not, and since this is true for all individuals and groups, politicians will know the distribution of political power.

Conclusion

In this paper, I have tried to bring together the theory of public goods and the economic theory of democracy. For that purpose, I have shown that because of certain characteristics of public goods, individuals would at one time or another be in such a situation that the amount of public goods they desired would be different from the amount available and that as a consequence of this disequilibrium they would endeavour to influence politicians so as to alter the amount of public goods forthcoming. This activity would generate a demand for public goods, but it would also in turn influence the structure of power in the society. In developing this analysis I have replaced the social welfare function by a political mechanism, so that the final grand equilibrium does not reflect the ethical values of society directly, but only to the extent that these are filtered through the political process. In fact, it is probably better to say that the final grand equilibrium does not reflect the ethical values of society as much as its "power structure".

17   Decision-making by Official Commission*

W. Irwin Gillespie

There is some reason to suspect that the political process and the corresponding voting mechanism is somewhat less than perfect in translating individual preference rankings into actual policies. There may be technical difficulties with multiple peaked preferences that result in arbitrary outcomes.[1] In a world of less than perfect information about budgetary issues where rational political parties seek to maximize votes, there is a tendency for upper income individuals to have a relatively greater influence on policy than lower income individuals, and there is a greater rate of abstention at the polls among lower income than

*Reprinted by permission from "Income Redistribution and Ability to Pay", *Report of Proceedings of the Twentieth Tax Conference,* convened by the Canadian Tax Foundation, Montreal, November 27-29, 1967, Canadian Tax Foundation, Toronto, 1968, pp. 245-246.
    [1]K. Arrow, *Social Choice and Individual Values,* Wiley, New York, 1951.

upper income individuals.[2] In other words, those preferences that do not become transmitted to the government are the very ones that we would expect, *a priori* to have an interest in the policy objective at hand, income redistribution. If budget policies reflect accurately the disproportionate influence of the upper income individuals, we would expect such policies to reflect the preferences of that group from which, in most cases, income is redistributed. Whatever the "true" preference ranking of all individuals concerning income redistribution alone, we would hardly expect the political process to perfectly capture it. The policymaker has direction from the voters, but it need not, nor rarely will, be direction towards an optional redistribution of income.

What reliance can the policymaker put in those principles or canons of taxation which from time to time have been put forward as guides to the selection of an optimal tax mix and policy objective mix? While such principles may provide some direction in connection with the optimal tax mix to achieve the desired policy objective mix, they are less than adequate in translating any information on individual preferences to the policymaker. Vertical equity, as one dimension of equity, comes closest to the issue of income redistribution by suggesting that persons in different positions should be treated in a different manner by the tax system. The implicitly understood next statement is that lower income individuals should pay lower tax rates than higher income individuals. If the principle had sprung from the people, then one might argue that it reflects a consensus of individual preferences for income redistribution. Let us grant the point; but are we any better off? The policymaker knows that the rich should pay more taxes than the poor, but this hardly permits him to frame legislation to that effect. The specification of the degree of vertical equity is crucial and it is absent.

Ability to pay as a principle of taxation has long been associated with the policy objective of redistribution of income through its link to the major vehicle of such redistribution, the progressive individual income tax. With the available evidence, we now know that the ability to pay principle defined as equal sacrifice does not lead to a clearly defined rate schedule for taxation and may not always imply a progressive rate schedule.[3] It does not provide the policymaker with enough information to effect whatever "desired" degree of progression is called for. Moreover, the use of the principle must follow from a postulated judgment about social values concerning the marginal utility of income; it does not itself describe those social values. Ability to pay as originally formulated does not provide the mechanism whereby rankings of preferences are translated from the individual to the policymaker.

With the political process and principles of taxation being less than satis-

[2]A. Downs, "An Economic Theory of Political Action in a Democracy", *Journal of Political Economy*, Vol. LXV, April 1957, pp. 135-150; A. Downs, *An Economic Theory of Democracy*, Harper and Row, New York, 1957; and E. S. Phelps (ed.), "Why the Government Budget is Too Small", *Private Wants and Public Needs*, rev. ed., Norton, New York, 1965, pp. 76-95.

[3]R. A. Musgrave, *The Theory of Public Finance*, McGraw-Hill, New York, 1959, pp. 90-115; and Walter J. Blum and Harry Kalven Jr., *The Uneasy Case for Progressive Taxation*, University of Chicago Press, Chicago, Ill., 1953.

factory as guides to translating individual preferences into policy objectives (and ultimately policy objective trade-offs) the potential of independent investigatory bodies, such as Royal Commissions or Task Forces for supplementing the information upon which policy decisions must be taken· becomes clear. Commissioners, not being in the business of maximizing votes, can afford to take a broad overview of the question at hand. A Commission potentially is a more perfect mechanism for extracting, distilling, and analyzing from the members of the collectivity a global social welfare function, or preference ranking of social values.[4]

The imperfections of the political process that lead ` to under-and over-emphasis on the preference rankings of the lower- and upper-income individuals respectively can be reduced, if not eliminated, by the researches of a Commission. The techniques of extracting such information may still require additional work and sophistication (ranging through briefs, public hearings, surveys of opinion, etc.), but the information once extracted need not be subject to a preferential ranking by the mechanism itself. This inherent value of a Commission permits it to match the true ranking of social values against the policy objectives possibility curve to determine simultaneously the optimal mix of policy objectives and budgetary policies to achieve that mix. In this way, the "desired" degree of income redistribution along with the optimal mix of quantities of other policy objectives can be determined. It would be unusual if such an optimal degree of income redistribution were identical with the "desired" degree of income redistribution arrived at by the political process, and it would consequently be unusual to find a successful Royal Commission *not* recommending major changes in the optimal budgetary mix following out of their derivation of the "desired" degree of income redistribution. Critics of the Royal Commission on Taxation are correct in pointing their remarks at the "underlying philosophy of taxation" as being the crux of most of their recommendations. Indeed, if this were not so and if the critics were silent on this point, we would strongly suspect that the Commission had not done a good job.[5]

To summarize thus far, there are a number of difficulties in determining the "desired" distribution of income. The first is the necessity to obtain a general equilibrium solution in which the optimal amount of income redistribution as a policy objective is determined simultaneously along with the optimal quanti-

---

[4]This view of Royal Commissions sees them as a periodic insertion of a Council of Social Values into an economy. This suggestion was put forward by Alvin H. Hansen, *Economic Issues of the 1960's*, Prentice Hall, New York, 1960, p. 91; and followed up in the *Final Report of the Special Committee of the Senate on Aging*, Debates of the Senate, Queen's Printer, Ottawa, February 2, 1966, Appendix, pp. 79-80.

[5]It may strike you as paradoxical to measure the "success" of a commission by the extent of the criticism of its recommendations and analysis, but to the extent that the existing budgetary (tax, transfer and expenditure) structure reflects the preference rankings of upper income and professional groups more accurately than lower income groups, then a change is going to give less weight to their social values: in such a world it is fair game to scrutinize carefully the underlying philosophy of the commission. This same point was put more succinctly by my bus driver who recently commented that, "The Carter *Report* must be what the common man wants; the establishment and all of organized society are against it!"

ties of the other policy objectives; the optimal mix of budgetary policies is, of course, determined as part of this solution. The second is to have at hand a mechanism that permits a translation of all individuals' preference rankings of the policy objectives into a set of social values that the policymaker can utilize in effecting the optimal mix of budgetary policies. The Royal Commission on Taxation is one such mechanism. Since the Commission was also in a position to analyze and examine the effects of various tax policies, it could extract some of the information that would form the basis of a policy objectives possibility curve. With information on possibilities and preferences, the Commission could derive and present one optimal mix of policy objectives and budgetary policies.

18   The Orthodox Model of Majority Rule*

James M. Buchanan and Gordon Tullock

We have made no attempt to relate our analysis directly to the history and development of political theory. . . . The "economic" approach to both the problem of constitutional choice and the analysis of decision-making rules is perhaps sufficiently differentiated from what has been the main stream of political scholarship to warrant independent treatment before the doctrinal setting has been completed. Moreover, in this respect the preliminary and exploratory nature of our whole analytical inquiry must be doubly emphasized.

Nevertheless, it will be useful at this stage to try to compare and contrast our models with the orthodox models of modern political theory, *as we conceive the latter*. We take this step, not for the purpose of comparison per se, but because in this way the content of our own analysis may be more clearly demonstrated, especially to noneconomist readers. We stand, of course, in danger of having our descriptions of the orthodox models labeled as straw men. Whether the constructions are straw or stone (and we are willing to leave this decision to others), we observe merely that, methodologically, straw men may also be useful . . . .

Our approach to collective action is avowedly individualist, rationalist, and secular. At the ultimate stage of constitutional choice, when decisions must be made among alternative means of organizing human activity and among rules for collective decision-making, full consensus of unanimity among all members of the social group seems to us to be the only conceivable test of the "rightness" of the choices made. This postulated unanimity rule for ultimate constitutional

*Reprinted by permission of authors and publisher from James M. Buchanan and Gordon Tullock, *The Calculus of Consent*, The University of Michigan Press, Ann Arbor, Mich., 1962, Chapter 17.

decisions allows us to divorce much of our analysis from the long and continuing debate concerning the validity of majority-rule as an absolute doctrine of popular sovereignty.

Unanimity and "Political Exchange"

In our view, both at the level of ultimate constitutional choice and at the level of analyzing the operation of particular rules, the issues have often been posed in terms of false alternatives. The alternatives are not those of majority rule *or* minority rule. One of the great advantages of an essentially economic approach to collective action lies in the implicit recognition that "political exchange", at all levels, is basically equivalent to economic exchange. By this we mean simply that *mutually* advantageous results can be expected from individual participation in community effort. Much of the debate surrounding the majority-rule doctrine seems to deny this possibility implicitly, even if such a denial is not explicitly stated. In this sense the discussion seems closely akin to the medieval arguments about the "just price". If, in market or exchange transactions, the loss to one trader must be offset by gains to the other, some rational basis for philosophical argumentation about the "justice" of prices would be present. However, the simple fact is, of course, that in normal trade *all* parties gain; there exist *mutual gains from trade*. The great contribution of Adam Smith lay in his popularization of this simple point, but full import of this conception for democratic political theory does not seem to have yet been appreciated.

Insofar as participation in the organization of a community, a State, is mutually advantageous of *all* parties, the formation of a "social contract" on the basis of unanimous agreement becomes possible. Moreover, the only test of the mutuality of advantage is the measure of agreement reached. Modern political theorists have perhaps shrugged off the unanimity requirement too early in their thinking. By noting that the attainment of unanimity is infeasible or impossible, they have tended to pose the false dilemma mentioned above. The early theorists (Hobbes, Althusius, Locke and Rousseau) did assume consensus in the formation of the original contract. They did so because the essence of any contractual arrangement is *voluntary* participation, and no rational being will voluntarily agree to something which yields him, in net terms, expected damage or harm. The categorical opposition of interests that many theorists assume to arise to prevent unanimity is much more likely to characterize the operational as opposed to the constitutional level of decision, and it is essential that these two levels of decision be sharply distinguished. It is at the operational level, where solidified economic interests of individuals and groups are directly subjected to modification and change by State action, that violent conflicts of interest can, and do, arise. At the "higher" constitutional level the problem confronted by the individuals of the group is that of choosing among alternative *rules* for organizing operational choices, and the discussion at this level will be concerned with the predicted operation of these rules. By a careful separation of these two levels of decision, much of the confusion inherent in modern interpretations of the contract theory of the State can be removed. Conceptually, men can reach agreement on rules, even when each party recognizes in advance that he will be "coerced" by the operation of agreed-on rules in certain circumstances. A potential thief, recognizing the need for protecting his own person and property, will support laws against theft, even though he will anticipate the probability that he will himself be subjected to punishment under these laws. Individuals at the level of operational decisions may accept results that run contrary to their own interest, not because they accept the will of the decision-making group as their own in some undefined, metaphysical manner, but simply because they know that the acceptance of adverse decisions (in our terminology, the bearing of external costs) is inherent occasionally in the "bargain" or "exchange" which is in the long run, beneficial to them. The expected external costs caused by adverse decisions may fall short of the added costs that would be involved in the participation in the more complex political bargaining process that might be required to protect individual interests more fully. In our construction, therefore, there is no necessary inconsistency implied in the adoption of, say, simple majority rule for the making of certain everyday decisions for the group with respect to those activities that have been explicitly collectivized, and the insistence on unanimity of consensus on changes in the fundamental organizational rules. The organizing principle or theme of our whole construction is the concentration on the individual calculus, and it is easy to see that both the unanimity rule at the constitutional level and other less-than-unanimity rules at the operational level of decisions may be based directly on this calculus.

While it is clear that something akin to the doctrine of inalienable rights — institutionally embodied in constitutional provisions limiting the authority of legislative majorities — can easily be reconciled with our construction, we should emphasize that this doctrine is not central to our construction. The fact that much of our construction can be reconciled with a strain of orthodox democratic theory, and vice versa, should not obscure the profound differences between our approach and the one which has been implicit in much political theory and philosophy, both ancient and modern. The most basic difference lies in the incorporation into our models of the economic meaning of the unanimity rule. . . .

Much political discussion seems to have proceeded as follows: "If the interests of two or more individuals conflict, unanimity is impossible. Some interests must prevail over others if action is not to be wholly stifled." This line of reasoning seems quite plausible until one confronts ordinary economic exchange. Note that in such an exchange the interests of the two contracting parties clearly conflict. Yet unanimity is reached. Contracts are made; bargains are struck without the introduction of explicit or implicit coercion. In this case, no interest prevails over the other; both interests are furthered. Our continued repetition of this simple analogy stems from our conviction that, at base, it is the failure to grasp fully the significance of this point that has retarded progress in political theory.

The "social contract" is, of course, vastly more complex than market exchange, involving as it does many individuals simultaneously. Nevertheless, the central notion of mutuality of gain may be carried over to the political relationship. When it is translated into individual behavior, mutuality of gain becomes equivalent to unanimous agreement among the contracting parties. The only test for the presence of mutual gain is agreement. If agreement cannot be reached, given adequate time for discussion and compromise, this fact in itself suggests the absence of any mutuality of gain. Moreover, where mutuality of gain is not possible, no criteria consistent with the individualistic philosophical conception of society can be introduced which will appropriately weight gains and losses among the separate parties to the institution taking the place of a contract (clearly, a relationship that does not embody unanimous consent is not a contract).

There may, of course, exist situations in which the formation of a "social contract" is not possible. When the negotiating parties are divided into groups that are classified on bases which seem reasonably certain to remain as permanent, independently of the decision-making rules that might be adopted, a "constitution" (in the sense that we have used this term throughout) may not be possible. The individual may never get the opportunity to participate (at the level of the Nation-State) in the choice process that we have been discussing. Under such conditions societies will tend to be controlled by some groups which will tyrannize over other groups. Such a situation must continue to exist, so long as genuinely mutual arrangements cannot be made.

Mutually Exclusive Alternatives

Situations such as these are not, however, what the orthodox theorist seems to have in mind when he makes statements like the one which we have attributed to him above. Implicitly, the orthodox theorist conceives all relevant political choice to take the form of selection between two mutually exclusive alternatives. An appropriate analogue is the choice confronted by the traveler at a fork in the road. He must either take one road or the other; the only other alternative is to stop. If, indeed, political decisions should assume this form, the statement imputed to the orthodox theorist above would be somewhat meaningful; but are the decisions that are confronted in the political process properly conceived as choices among mutually exclusive alternatives? Once more, let us turn to the analogy with market exchange. Such exchange could be converted into choices among mutually exclusive alternatives only if one partner to the bargain or contract should be required to secure gains *at the direct expense* of the other party. If such a rule were laid down in advance, any "solution" would require that the interests of one or the other of the parties prevail and the interest of the "loser" be subjected to "defeat". In game-theoretic terms, the assumption of mutually exclusive alternatives is equivalent to assuming that the game is zero-sum. The winnings must match the losings. If, in fact, this is the appropriate conception of the political "game", it is relatively easy to see that, once several persons (several players) are introduced, and if symmetry in preferences among individuals is postulated, the interests of the larger number (the majority) "should" or "ought" to prevail over the interests of the lesser number.

Clearly this would represent a wholly incorrect and misleading way of analyzing economic or market transactions. The implication of the approach would be that no exchange should take place at all because gainers balance losers in two-person trades and symmetry in preference is to be assumed present. In this approach, by contrast, the appropriate means of analyzing political transactions? By now it is perhaps obvious that we do not think that political choices should, at base, be conceived in terms of selection among mutually exclusive alternatives. The essence of the contractual conception of the collectivity, quite independently of the empirical validity of this construction, involves the mutuality of gain among all members of the group. However, *all* participants in a zero-sum game cannot win simultaneously. Games of zero-sum are played, and political choices on many occasions do reduce to mutually exclusive alternatives; but why do we observe zero-sum games being played in the real world? The answer is that such games are played because each and every participant has, implicitly, accepted the "contract" embodied in the rules of the game when he chooses to play. The zero-sum characteristic applies to the "solution" of the game; it does not apply to the "contract" through which all participants agree on the rules. At this second level there must be mutual gains, and the rule of unanimity must apply. At this level there is no way in which a zero-sum solution could apply; the game simply would not be played unless all participants expected some individual benefit at the time of entry.

This reference to game theory may be helpful, but we have not yet clearly shown the statement of the hypothetical orthodox theorist to be demonstrably false. Let us turn to a simple model of a three-man society, engaged in the formation of a "social contract". Let us call the three men A, B, and C. Suppose that the discussion is proceeding on the fundamental organizational rules that entering into a community or group life might involve. Let us assume that A is very interested in insuring that fishing is collectively organized, because he likes fish and because he also realizes that joint effort is much more productive than individual effort. If we limit our attention to this decision, we may reduce it to a yes-or-no question. Either the catching of fish will be collectively organized or will not. These appear to be mutually exclusive alternatives, and it seems impossible that agreement could be reached unanimously if, say C, who does not like fish anyway, does not agree to collective organization of this activity. This is the point at which our hypothetical orthodox theorist of the constitutional process seems to have stopped, but this represents the central error of his interpretation. Let us say now that C, in turn, is interested in insuring that the group allow the gathering of coconuts to be privately organized because he thinks he is a much better climber of trees than A or B. On the other hand, A and B both want to collectivize this activity as well as fishing. Suppose that B, in contrast to A and C, is really more interested in securing some defense against external attack than he is in either fish or coconuts. He wants, first of all, to organize some standing patrol or watch. Under these circumstances it becomes conceivable that the group can reach unanimous agreement of a "constitution" or contract. They can do so by making the appropriate compromises or "trades" among themselves. The only test for determining whether or not the organization of the community is or is not mutually desirable to all parties lies in the possibility that such an agreement can be reached. Our hypothetical orthodox theorist, therefore, errs in not following through beyond the confines of a single issue. Once several issues are introduced, and the variance of interests among individuals and over separate issues is allowed for, trades become possible. Moreover, when trade can take place, the analogy with economic or market exchange is appropriate. No longer must the group reach yes-or-no decisions at the constitutional level; no longer must alternatives be mutually exclusive. The existence of conflicts of interest does not preclude the attainment of unanimity; this merely makes it necessary that discussion proceed until the appropriate compromises are found.

If direct side payments among individuals are allowed for, even this modification is not needed. Return to our illustrative model. Suppose that the only decision confronted is that concerning the organization of fishing. A and B desire collectivization because of the greater efficiency, but C, not liking fish, is opposed. If side payments are allowed, the support of C for the collectivization of fishing for the group may be secured by the transfer of some item possessing real value to C by A and B (e.g., a few cigarettes) ; and only if C can be so convinced to support the collectivization of fishing will the entering into the agreement with A and B be worth while to him.

The Meaning of "Majority Rule"

We have shown that the attainment of unanimity is always possible if there exist mutual gains from entering into the "social contract", and that the orthodox theorist has tended to dismiss unanimity as a possible alternative to majority or minority rule too hurriedly because of a concentration on mutually exclusive alternatives. Our earlier models have shown, however, that the group may rationally choose less-than-unanimous decision-making rules for the carrying out of operational decisions for the collectivity. We now want to isolate a second major fallacy in the orthodox position. Even in these cases when unanimity is either not possible or not chosen as the rule by the group, we shall try to demonstrate that the dilemma posed by a majority rule-minority rule dichotomy remains a false one.

Recall that the unique feature of our models for constitutional choice was the demonstration that, unless equal intensity of preferences is postulated, there are no particular characteristics attributable to the 51 per cent rule for choice. This is only one out of many possible decision-making rules. The peculiar position that this proportion has assumed in orthodox thinking seems to be due to the idea that if less than 50 per cent are allowed to make a decision, the more than 50 per cent will be "concluded" or "coerced" into acceptance. Thus, the requirement of a qualified majority really amounts to allowing a minority to rule. If we may again put the words into the mouth of our hypothetical orthodox theorist, he might say: "If more than 51 per cent are required for political decision, this will really allow the minority to rule since the wishes of the 51 per cent, a majority, can be thwarted." In this construction there is no difference between the qualified majority of, say, 75 per cent and the simple minority rule of 26 per cent. Whereas in our constitutional models there may be a great difference in the external costs expected to be incurred under the 26 per cent minority rule and the 75 per cent majority rule, the orthodox theorist would deny this difference. Moreover, he would claim that the existing provision for amending the United States Constitution embody the rule of the minority.

Does the requirement of a qualified majority amount to the rule of the minority? Here, as before, the error of the orthodox theorist seems to reflect his emphasis on reducing all decisions to the yes-no, mutually exclusive type, and the implied failure to put quantitative significance on alternatives confronted. If we come to an issue analogous to the fork in the road mentioned above, and if this is the only issue, and if no side payments are allowed, the orthodox theorist would seem to be on reasonably safe ground in saying that the requirement of 75 per cent agreement would allow the 26 per cent to be really controlling for decisions.

However, if the requirement of a qualified majority of, say, 75 per cent is really equivalent to the minority "rule" of 26 per cent, what sort of decisions must be involved? Not only must the alternatives of choice be conceived as being mutually exclusive, but the alternative of inaction must be counted as equivalent to action. The fork-in-the road analogy mentioned above becomes too general because the alternative represented by stopping the journey is precluded. One way or the other must presumably be chosen. Suppose that there are 100 persons on a hayride and such a fork in the road looms ahead. Suppose that 74 of these persons choose to take the right-hand fork; 26 of them want to go to the left. With the 75 per cent rule in effect, neither road could be taken until and unless some compromises were made. With a 27 per cent rule in effect, the right-hand road would be taken without question in these circumstances. Surely these two rules produce different results. Failure to secure the required 75 per cent is not equivalent to granting "rule" to 27 per cent. If the third alternative of stopping the journey is allowed for, the 75 per cent rule will not allow action to be taken. The orthodox theorist would argue that such inaction, in this case, amounts to "victory" for the "recalcitrant" 26 persons making up the minority. Taken individually, however, these persons are thwarted in their desires in precisely the same way that the individual members of the larger group are thwarted. These individuals must also bear the costs of inaction. The argument may be advanced that, in such hypothetical situations as this, the interests of the greater number should be counted more heavily; but this, presumably, is a question that is appropriately answered only at the time when the decision-making rules are chosen. In our construction it seems wholly inappropriate to introduce this essentially irrelevant ethical issue at the stage of operational decision-making. When it is recognized at the ultimate constitutional stage that the larger the majority required for decision, the lower are the expected external costs that the individual expects to incur as a result of collective decisions being made adversely to his own interest, we may discuss the operation of the various rules quite independently of all attempts to measure utilities and to compare these interpersonally.

The orthodox theorist will not, however, accept this line of reasoning. He will say that the question to be decided in our illustration should be put as follows: Shall the group take the right-hand road or not? — Vote yes or vote no. In this way the qualified majority rule is made to appear equivalent to "minority rule". A minority of 26 per cent is empowered to block action desired by 74 per cent.

This argument is more sophisticated than the one considered previously, and it is more difficult to refute convincingly. To do so, we must, first of all, clarify the meaning of the terms "majority rule" and "minority rule". We have used these terms throughout our analysis to describe decision-making processes. Such general usage is no longer sufficient. We must sharply differentiate between two kinds of decisions: (1) the positive decision that authorizes action for the social group, and (2) the negative decision that effectively blocks action proposed by another group. If the group is empowered to make decisions resulting in positive action by/for the whole group, we shall say that this group effectively "rules" for the decisions in question. It does not seem meaningful to say that the power to block action constitutes effective "rule".

This relevant distinction between the power of determining action and the power of blocking action has not been sufficiently emphasized in the literature of political science. The reason for this neglect seems to be an overconcentration on the operation of simple majority rule. If a simple majority is empowered to determine positive action, there can be no other simple majority empowered to block the action proposed. Two simple majorities cannot simultaneously exist. The distinction becomes clear only when we consider "minority rule". If we adopt the meaning of this term suggested above, a group smaller than one of simple majority must be empowered to make positive decisions for the collectivity. For example, suppose we choose to consider a 40 per cent decision-making rule. This rule, under our definition, would be operative when 40 per cent of the voters, *any* 40 per cent are empowered to take action positively for the whole group. It is clear that the *same* rule could not also be applied to *blocking* action. If 40 per cent were also required to block action, then 40 per cent could not be defined as the "rule of the minority" at all. The rule for blocking action must always be $[(N + 1) — X]$ per cent, X being the percentage of the total group empowered to institute or to conclude positive action. Effective minority rule, therefore must require a *majority* to block legislation proposed by the minority. Effective "rule" by the 40 per cent minority must involve the requirement that 61 per cent of the voters are required to veto action proposed by a minority.

When the orthodox theorist suggests that qualified majority voting amounts to "rule" by the minority, he is referring to the rule for blocking action. If this line of reasoning is carried to its logical conclusion, we get this paradoxical result *that the rule of unanimity is the same as the minority rule of one.* Thus the rule of requiring unanimity among members of a jury to acquit or to convict becomes equivalent to the rule that would permit any individual juror to convict or to acquit. Instead of being at the opposing ends of the decision-making spectrum, as our whole construction suggests, the unanimity rule and the rule of one become identical. This paradoxical result suggests clearly that the power of blocking action is not what we normally mean, or should mean, when we speak of "majority rule" or "minority rule".

The distinction between the power of taking action and of blocking action proposed by others is an essential one; it represents the difference between the power *to impose external costs on others* and the power *to prevent external costs from being imposed*.

We may illustrate with reference to our familiar road-repair example. Let us assume that the constitution of our model township dictates that all road-repair decisions are to be made by a two-thirds majority. Under these conditions the power to institute action, lodged in any effective coalition of two-thirds of the voters, involves the power to impose external costs on the other one-third, either through the levy of taxes or the failure to repair certain roads to standard. One-third of all voters plus one have the power to veto or block any proposed repair project, but this power is effective only in the sense that a group of this size can prevent the additional taxes being levied. In no way can this minority group impose additional external costs on the other members of the group.

The Problem of Biased Rules

We have not yet satisfied the hypothetical orthodox theorist. He may conceivably accept all of our previous arguments but still try to stop us short by saying: What about the situation in which the issue confronted it whether or not a change in the rules should be made? Here the alternatives are mutually exclusive: change or no change. Moreover, should the established order (the *status quo*) operate in such a way as to benefit special minority interests, then surely the qualified majority rule for changing the "constitution" will allow the blocking power of the minority to be controlling. In effect, the maintenance of things as they are amounts to genuine "minority rule".

This argument gets us to the heart of the whole discussion of majority rule as a doctrine of popular sovereignty, to which we referred earlier in this chapter to some extent. We have discussed the applicability of the unanimity rule at the stage of making original constitutional decisions. At any point in time subsequent to the formation of the original "contract", the social organization must be presumed to be operating within the framework of certain established rules. These organizational rules define the way in which certain collective decisions will be made, including decisions to change the "contract". If these basic rules suggest that, for some decisions, more than a 51 per cent majority is required for positive action, it is surely the established order of affairs that may be said to be "ruling", and not the particular minority that may or may not be securing "benefits" through the continuance of this established order.

This is not to suggest that the established order must prevail for all time once it is accepted nor that either at its beginning or at any particular moment in time, this order is necessarily "optimal". The "social contract" is best conceived as subject to continual revision and change, and the consent that is given must be thought of as being continuous. However, the relevant point is that change in this "contract", if it is desirable at all, can always find unanimous support, given the appropriate time for compromise.

Again we revert to the game analogy. We may, if we like, think of players as being continually engaged in two kinds of mental activity. First, they are trying to figure out moves or strategies with which their own interests can be advanced within the context of a well-defined game. Secondly, and simultaneously with this activity, they can be conceived as trying to figure out a possible change in the rules that would make for a better game. In this second activity they will realize that they must choose rule changes on which all players can agree if the game is to continue. A proposed change in the rules (or in the definition of the game) designed especially to further individual or group interests, majority or minority, would be recognized to be possible. The other players could simply withdraw from the game.

Our conception of the constitutional-choice process is a dynamic one quite analogous to the game mentioned above. We do not conceive the "constitution" as having been established once and for all. We conceive the contractual aspects to be continuous, and the existence of a set of organizational rules is assumed to embody consensus. We think of the individual as engaging continuously both in everyday operational decisions within the confines of established organizational rules and in choices concerned with changes in the rules themselves, that is, constitutional choices. The implicit rule for securing the adoption of changes in the organizational rules (changes in the structure of the social contract) must be that of unanimity. This is because only through the securing of unanimity can any change be judged desirable on the acceptance of the individualistic ethic.

This does not imply, as is so often suggested, that the requirement of unanimity on changes in the rules (in the constitution) embodies an undue or unwarranted elevation of the *status quo* to a sacrosanct position. In the first place, the idea of *status quo* in terms of established organizational rules is hazy at best. The stability of the established rules for organizing public and private decisions does not, even remotely, tend to stabilize the results of these decisions measured in terms of the more standard variables such as income, wealth, employment, etc. The municipal-zoning ordinance may be accepted by all parties until someone has the opportunity to sell his own property to a developer at a huge capital gain. At this point in the sequence, the individual standing to gain would certainly desire a change in the rules to allow him to exploit this unforeseen opportunity, but it is precisely because this sort of thing is unforeseen that the zoning ordinance can be adopted in the first place. *Ex poste*, the individual faced with the opportunity to gain is likely to object strenuously to the *status quo* (that is, to the zoning ordinance), but securing a variance for one individual alone is equivalent to changing the rules of the ordinary game to the strategic advantage of one player. In the continued playing of the "social game", individuals will each confront situations in which they desire, strategically, to change the rules; but it is because these situations are distributed stochastically that agreement becomes possible. If a change in the rules (a change in the *status quo*) is mutually beneficial, it will, of course, be adopted. Empirical evidence from the operation of voluntary organizations suggests that rules are often changed.

An individual need not, of course, accept the "contract" that exists. He may rationally consider the rules to be undesirable. Faced with this conclusion, two choices remain open to him. He may seek to convert others to his point of view, and, if arrangements can be worked out through which all others come to agree, the "constitution" can be changed. Secondly, the individual may choose to reject the "contract" entirely; he may revert to a "state of nature" — in this case a revolt against established social order. On ethical grounds the individual must always be granted the "right" to make such a choice, but, once he has done so, the remaining members of the group have no contractual obligation to consider the revolutionary to be subject to the protections of the "contract". This "right of revolution" is not modified as it extends beyond the single individual to a minority or even to a majority of the population. In this, as in other aspects of our construction of the constitutional implications of a consistent individualistic philosophy, the shifts in the fraction of the population approving or disapproving certain changes are not of central importance.

Techniques for Economic Decision-Making

It is one thing to get agreement upon the objectives that policy-makers are aiming at, but it is quite another thing to translate the objectives into operational decisions. People may agree upon high-level general objectives but disagree violently over various subsidiary objectives subsumed under the general objectives. It is therefore not enough to agree upon the general areas in which governments ought to spend money, but we also need to determine how much money should be spent on individual projects. This is not difficult in principle: "Push expenditures for each public purpose to that point where the benefit of the last dollar spent is greater than or at least equal to the dollar of cost . . . . Equating marginal benefits and costs, if it could be done, would solve two problems of resource allocation. It would assure that every expenditure yields a benefit at least equal to the value of goods foregone in the private sector. Second, it would assure that an expenditure does not prevent a more valuable public expenditure in some other field. Thus, the principle assures that benefits of marginal expenditures exceed opportunity costs both in the private and public sectors."[1]

However it is difficult in practice. It is true that some benefits can be measured in dollars and cents in markets in which benefits can unequivocally be measured by market prices. But in many markets, prices are not a complete measure of benefits because of externalities, the benefits spilling over to persons who do not pay the

---

[1]Otto Eckstein, *Public Finance*, Prentice-Hall, Englewood Cliffs, N.J., 1964, pp. 23-24.

price.[2] The benefits of government expenditures on universities, for example, are not limited to the students who "buy" university education but are enjoyed by the whole community in the form of higher productivity, more rapid technological progress and a more rational discussion of public issues, among other things. A more important consideration is that for many government goods and services markets do not exist; yet —

> . . . clearly government programs can produce many items of value — such as defence capabilities, the saving of lives, improvements in race relations, better maintenance of law and order, a greater degree of equity, noise-abatement, and court decisions — for which there are no markets. These items are of value, for many people are willing to pay for increments in output. . . . Moreover, government programmes can produce many items of negative value — such as loss of life, impairments of race relations, deterioration of law and order, inequities, noise, and bad court procedures and decisions — for which there are no markets. Throughout the process of producing these positive and negative values, substitution possibilities are pervasive. Since there are no markets, what about shadow prices?[3]

Shadow prices may be inferred from econometric or programming models (in which case they will depend on the conditions of the model), they may be price relationships taken over from markets for similar items or from markets for the same items in other countries, or they may be derived by calculating the prices implied by governmental choices in other fields than the one in question.[4] As McKean points out, however, these implied price ratios are not necessarily the appropriate ones for the maximization of a particular preference function. The value of a human life is a case in point — the market value of an individual to society may be adequately represented by the discounted value of his lifetime earnings in working out the optimum level of government expenditures on road safety or public health, but it is unlikely that payment of such a sum to his relatives would be adequate compensation for the loss of his life. No price would satisfy both parties, and if a situation arose in which a decision between the two had to be made, it could be made only at the political level.[5]

---

[2]Formally, externalities arise when (a) interdependence exists among production or utility functions, and (b) the nature of the interdependence is such that payment cannot be extracted from the parties that benefit (nor compensation where a party suffers a loss). *Cf.* William J. Baumol, *Welfare Economics and the Theory of the State*, second ed., Harvard University Press, Cambridge, Mass., 1965, pp. 24-25.

[3]Roland N. McKean, "The Use of Shadow Prices", in Samuel B. Chase, Jr. (ed.), *Problems in Public Expenditure Analysis*, The Brookings Institution, Washington, 1968, p. 46.

[4]*Ibid.*, pp. 49-51.

[5]"There is a distinction between individual life and a statistical life. Let a 6-year-old girl with brown hair need thousands of dollars for an operation that will prolong her life until Xmas, and the post office will be swamped with nickels and dimes to save her. But let it be reported that without a sales tax the hospital facilities of Massachusetts will deteriorate and cause a barely perceptible increase in preventable deaths — not many will drop a tear or reach for their checkbooks." T. C. Schelling, "The Life You Save May be Your Own," in Chase, *op. cit.*, p. 129.

A similar type of question is the value to be attached to government expenditures that redistribute income in a manner that would be desirable on the grounds of equity, but which may contribute less to national product than alternative government expenditures. Such benefits are termed incommensurables, which though very real "cannot be measured in money by any objective and generally acceptable method".[6] Incommensurables will include the social and cultural benefits of government expenditures mentioned earlier. The lack of measurability does not mean that incommensurable benefits are intrinsically different from other kinds of benefits: "they may or may not be measurable in their own appropriate quantitative terms, in a manner helpful to the decision-maker (if not they are 'intangible' as well as incommensurable). Moreover, an *individual* can compare them subjectively with the other effects. Indeed, implicitly the decision-maker does translate these incommensurables into the common denominator when he makes a choice. But they cannot be expressed in terms of the principal or common unit in any *generally acceptable* manner."[7]

It may seem naïve, overly materialistic or perhaps barbaric to attempt to put dollar values on what may in the last resort be ethical or cultural things, but if government expenditures are positive it is unavoidable. If the benefits of government expenditures are not valued explicitly in a rational manner, they will be valued implicitly by the expenditure decisions themselves, perhaps at levels considerably different from what the policy-makers would have chosen deliberately.

On the other side of the ledger of public benefits will be the costs of government programs. These will include the direct costs of projects — wages and salaries of workers engaged on the projects, the fees of designers, architects, town planners and various other specialists involved in the preparation of projects, the materials used, the energy consumed, the transport charges, and so on. They will include external costs (negative external benefits) which are paid by people outside the project — smoke, noise and other nuisances created by the public project, reductions in the property values caused by location of highways, industrial projects and so on, in residential areas. The most important costs of a public expenditure program, however, will be opportunity costs, the value of alternative sets of public or private benefits that could have been provided with the same resources:

> The social opportunity cost of a public investment project is the value to society of the next best alternative use to which the resources employed in the project could have been put. If the funds of the public agency are limited, i.e. if the investment decision is made subject to capital rationing, the opportunity cost of any project is the social benefit of the best alternative project that the agency could undertake. . . . The appropriate measure of the social opportunity cost of a public project is the discounted value of the consumption stream that would have occurred had the project not been undertaken. . . . In short, a project's social opportunity cost is the present value of what society gives up in order to obtain the benefits of the particular project.[8]

[6]C. J. Hitch and R. N. McKean, *The Economics of Defense in the Nuclear Age*, Harvard University Press, Cambridge, Mass., 1965, p. 182.

[7]*Ibid.*, p. 182.

[8]Martin S. Feldstein, "Opportunity Cost Calculations in Cost-Benefit Analysis", *Public Finance*, Vol. XIX, No. 2, 1964, pp. 117-119.

These are some of the practical problems that must be solved in implementing a rational program of public expenditures to achieve given objectives. The following selections will give some indication of the kind of "techniques" that modern governments have been adopting to enable economic analysis to be brought to bear on the efficiency of public expenditures.

(a) Program Budgeting

The budget in a majority of countries is a financial document, and its form is dominated by financial accountability of the executive to the legislature. Appropriations are set out by spending departments and agencies rather than by purpose, and are limited to one year. The main difficulty with this approach is that the problems of modern government cannot be confined within the historically and politically determined administrative boundaries of the civil service. The major problems such as unemployment, poverty, air and water polution, educational needs and foreign investment come within the legal spheres of many departments. For example, federal expenditure with respect to manufacturing industry involves the Department of Trade and Commerce, the Department of Industry, the Department of Defence Production and the Department of National Revenue; federal expenditures on education are handled through the Departments of Agriculture, Finance, Fisheries, Indian Affairs and Northern Development, Labour, Manpower and Immigration, Public Works, National Research Council and the Secretary of State, to which should be added federal grants to the provinces for provincial educational institutions.

The objectives of modern government, which have been discussed in Chapter One, are not formulated with respect to departments of government. What matters is the degree to which the objectives are achieved. The way in which expenditures are distributed among departments in order to achieve these objectives is not really of major importance. Program budgeting is designed to force decision-makers in government to relate expenditures to community objectives rather than to administrative divisions of the civil service, and to provide techniques for the objective measurement of progress towards these objectives. Program budgeting has been most rigorously applied at the Federal level in the United States, following recommendations of the first Hoover Commission in 1949. The best-known application of the technique has been in the U.S. Department of Defense, where since 1961 decisions have been made on the basis of five-year programs relating to the national defence objectives as a whole, regardless of service distinctions. The following extract came from a Manual prepared by the Secretariat of the United Nations, which grew out of discussions of budgetary systems in various Budget Workshops held by the United Nations since the 1950's.

19   The Programme and Performance Budget *

The UN Department of Economic and Social Affairs

Development of the Management Approach in Budgeting

In the majority of countries, budgeting is conceived largely in financial terms. The financial accountability to the legislature is usually the overriding consideration and this permeates the entire budgetary process. Emphasis is placed mainly on the observance of appropriation limits. Moreover, the object-cum-organizational classification of expenditures in the budget does not enable identification of programmes or projects and, furthermore, is not related to the cost of major inputs or the work performed. In other words, the system of budgeting does not provide information on what a government is actually doing and what it gets for the money spent. Of course, it may be possible to compile such information from departmental reports or other supplementary documents, but in many cases this information cannot be linked directly with financial data as they appear in a budget or in the accounts because it does not constitute a basis for budget management. The absence of pertinent information of this type reduces the usefulness of this budgetary approach even for purposes of legislative review and appropriation. The sanctions resulting from this process then tend to be accorded to policy objectives that are not explicit in the budget.

The use of programme and performance budgeting developed essentially in response to the need for correcting this situation. It is intended to highlight management considerations in budgeting and in so doing to bring out the most significant economic, financial, and physical aspects of the budgetary activity. So far, this system has been given its most rigorous application at the Federal level in the United States.[1] In 1949, the first Hoover Commission recommended that "the whole budgetary concept of the Federal Government should be refashioned by the adoption of a budget based on functions, activities and projects"[2] and this was designated by the Commission as a "performance budget". It was pointed out that "such a budget would not detract from congressional responsibility and should greatly improve and expedite committee consideration". Following the recommendation, the Federal Government refashioned its budget in 1951 "to show programmes and activities under each appropriation request, and to introduce workload and other performance information in narrative form".[3] Initially, the appropriation structure was simplified, and pro-

---

*Reprinted by permission of the United Nations Department of Economic and Social Affairs from *A Manual for Programme and Performance Budgeting*, United Nations, New York, 1965, (UN Sales No. 66 XVI-1), pp. 1-3.

[1]This system of budgeting was introduced in the Philippines in 1954.

[2]Commission on the Organization of the Executive Branch of the Government, *Budgeting and Accounting*, Washington, 1949, p. 8.

[3]Joint Financial Management Improvement Programme, *Improvement of Financial Management in the United States Government: Progress, 1948-1963*, United States Government Printing Office, Washington, 1964, p. 8.

grammes were established within broad functional categories. Thus, in its early stages of development, improvement of Congressional review provided the stimulus and the emphasis was placed mainly on a budget classification. In its subsequent evolution, the form and content of performance budgeting have undergone many substantial changes. Among the important adjustments that have taken place, accounting support was provided ·for the programme classifications, accounting and budgeting have been integrated, and emphasis has been given to developing techniques of budgeting in terms of the cost of performance. In 1964, more than 80 per cent of the agencies provided costs information in their appropriation requests. These developments have strengthened the usefulness of the budget as a tool of management, and have provided effective means of both fund and programme control. The programme and performance budget provides unit cost data where such an approach is appropriate, and, as a supplement to this, current efforts are being directed towards developing productivity measures for different kinds of operations. In the initial attempt, productivity measures were evolved for selected organizations on an experimental basis,[4] and steps are being taken now to do the same thing in other agencies. Similar measures can be evolved in developing countries with respect to scarce resources.

Features of the Programme and Performance Budget

The programme and performance approach to budgeting is based principally on the use, in budget management, of three sets of interrelated considerations. In the first place, under this approach, meaningful programmes and activities[5]

---

[4]Bureau of the Budget, *Measuring Productivity of Federal Government Organizations*, Washington, 1964.

[5][A Programme is an instrument for performing functions by which goals can be set and undertaken, in principle, by high-level administrative units. An activity is a subdivision of a programme, preferably capable of some form of statistical measurement — in such terms of work-load, employee utilization, unit costs, etc. The UN Central American Workshop recommended the following functional classification of government transactions to be used for aggregating programmes and activities:

General services:
      General administration
      Justice and police
      General research and scientific services
Defence
Social and community services:
      Education
      Health
      Social security and special welfare services
      Community services
Economic services:
      Agriculture and non-mineral resources
      Fuel and power
      Other mineral resources, manufacturing and construction
      Transport, storage and communications
      Other economic services
      Multi-purpose projects
Unallocable expenditure]

are established for each function entrusted to an organization or an agency in order to show precisely the work objectives of various agencies. Secondly, the system of accounts and financial management are brought into line with this classification. Thirdly, under each programme and for its operational sub-divisions, action is taken to establish programme and work measures that are useful for evaluation of performance. Thus, "a performance budget is one which presents the purposes and objectives for which funds are requested, the costs of the programmes proposed for achieving these objectives and quantitative data measuring the accomplishments and work performed under each programme".[6]

In modern Governments, organizational responsibilities often cut across various functions. A most conspicuous example in many developing countries is presented by a ministry of public works. Such a ministry usually undertakes a variety of functional tasks, such as construction of school buildings, hospitals, roads and highways, irrigation projects, and housing. It would be much less meaningful if the activities of such an agency, fo rexample, were expressed solely in money terms and, furthermore, if the financial outlay were classified only into terms of object categories. On the other hand, much more could be gained for management purposes if the several functions of such an agency were clearly segregated and individual programmes and projects were identified under each function. A classification such as this would also contribute effectively to the over-all purposes of budgeting by improving executive and legislative review and decision-making and, further, by facilitating effective internal financial administration.

When the system of accounting and financial management is geared closely to the scheme of classification suggested above, a direct relationship can be established between programmes and their cost. The *purpose* of doing something and the *cost* of doing it are the twin considerations which are indivisible and indispensable to the most effective system of management. The calculation of cost in such a system, however, must be conceived in terms of actual receipt and use of resources required for the completion of a given project. In many countries, government accounts are kept either on a cash or obligation basis. Such accounts, although they are very useful for purposes of accountability and appropriation control, indicate only the payments made or obligations incurred and do not measure the true cost of providing various public services. However, if they are properly related to programmes, such accounts can initially be used in this budgetary approach, pending refinement of the accounting system.

Once the programmes and accounting data are inter-related, the development of physical measurement data and of the performance indicators for each programme and its sub-divisions provide a total perspective for effective budget management. In the process of budget execution, control of expenditure acquires a purpose and the accountability for operational activities becomes much more meaningful. An integrated view of these three factors helps to shift the emphasis from macro-considerations to micro-considerations in the appraisal

[6]Jesse Burkhead, *Government Budgeting*, Wiley, New York, 1956, p. 152.

and control of expenditures. The development of unit cost data and of productivity measures should enable, over a period of time, the establishment of norms and standards for comparison purposes. The use of such norms or standards in budget management in turn can bring about economy and efficiency in public expenditures. When finance is one of the limiting factors in the growth of developing countries, the need to economize this scarce resource and to get most out of public expenditures becomes overwhelmingly self-evident and impelling.

Between a plan and a programme and performance budget, there are certain structural similarities of form and common elements in the accounting for resource use. The basic features of a plan are its use, within a sector, of programmes or projects as operational units, the emphasis on their physical inputs and results or benefits and on their cost in relation to benefits. These are also the attributes of a programme and performance budget, in which objectives are first formulated at the functional level and then broken down, for operational purposes, into terms of specific programmes, projects or activities. Similarly, just as outlays in a plan represent the *cost* of providing goods and services and not merely expected disbursements or obligations to be incurred, a programme and performance budget can also lend significance, with proper accounting support, to workload data by developing their cost. Thus, in both cases, the intent and direction of resource use, the expected workload and its cost are related closely to each other. These similarities in form and operational orientation make programme and performance budgeting particularly suited for plan implementation and evaluation of plan progress in developing countries. The data obtained from budget execution, both of a physical and financial nature, can, moreover, be helpful in the subsequent revisions of a plan or formulation of new plans.

(b) Benefit-Cost Analysis

20   The Benefit-Cost Analysis Approach to Project Evaluation*

W. R. D. Sewell, J. Davis, A. D. Scott and D. W. Ross

Benefit-cost analysis may be used for three broad purposes:

(1) To assess the economic characteristics of a particular project:

(2) To determine which of a number of projects designed to serve

---

*Reprinted by permission of the publisher from W. R. D. Sewell, J. Davis, A. D. Scott and D. W Ross, *Guide to Benefit-Cost Analysis,* Queen's Printer, Ottawa, 1962.

a given purpose results in the largest ratio of benefits to costs; and

(3) To determine which of a number of projects designed to serve different purposes confers the largest net benefit on the economy as a whole.

So far benefit-cost analyses have been undertaken mainly for the first purpose and only to a limited extent for the selection of the most economically desirable project among alternatives. If for technical reasons, only one project can be undertaken to achieve a given objective, the study must necessarily be limited to a test of economic feasibility (i.e. to decide whether the benefit-cost ratio is greater than 1). But in other instances, where more than one project or program may be undertaken to serve a given purpose benefit-cost analysis must be extended to a comparison of the benefit-cost ratios of each of the projects in turn.

It is also possible to compare the benefit-cost ratios of projects or programs with quite different objectives, the purpose being to decide which confers the largest net benefit on the economy as a whole. These undertakings might be for different purposes such as the development of irrigation or the preservation of wildlife. Or, they might be located in widely different parts of the country. In any case it is necessary, as far as possible, to reduce the estimates of results and expenditures to monetary terms. Despite difficulties of measurement and the existence of widely different economic circumstances, this type of analysis organizes information in such a way that the final decision can be made in the context of prevailing social and political circumstances.

Essentially, benefit-cost analysis attempts to do, more methodically, what people are doing every day when they make decisions about the future. A businessman, for example, is always searching for the most profitable alternative. A similar challenge, leading to the maximization of benefits presents itself to government officials and agencies. The objective should always be to select the most economic alternative.

When assessing the merits of alternative proposals, the decision-maker must ask himself a number of questions:

(a) Which projects are feasible from a technical point of view?
(b) Which projects can also be defended on economic grounds? (i.e. Will the benefits which they produce exceed the costs involved?)
(c) Which, among these alternatives, is the most economical project, taking into account different basic assumptions as to market growth, interest rates, wage levels, and so on? (Which has the highest benefit-cost ratio?)

Another question which the analyst may have to bear in mind relates to financial feasibility. For a project to be financially feasible, the revenues must exceed the expenditures involved. Some proposals, though technically feasible and economically desirable, may be unable for some reason to attract funds necessary for their completion. In such instances they must be dropped from consideration for the time being.

In order to answer these various questions a great deal of information is required. Data describing the components of each alternative project and various project sequences must be examined in order to give a clear idea of which over-all plan or program will be most economic. The amount of effort involved in the analysis itself can, on the other hand, be tailored to suit the manpower, time and budgets available for this type of research. In the interest of efficiency those responsible for this work should consider limitations of a technical nature first. Economic and financial considerations may then be introduced.

Before a benefit-cost analysis can get underway, the various alternative technical possibilities must be identified. In any situation there are controlling factors which limit the range of choice. These factors may be physical, legal, or economic. For example in the case of a hydro power project, the topography often limits the range of choice. In some cases, legal rights may prohibit some developments. Having identified the various technical possibilities in this way, a number of questions relating to their benefits and costs may be asked. Clearly, unless the project or program can be shown to be technically possible, there is no point in launching an extensive economic analysis.

The next step is to determine the economic characteristics of the alternative projects or programs. It must be borne in mind that economic analysis, even at this stage, should go beyond a mere examination of project revenues and expenditures. Feasibility, in the economic sense, calls for a weighing of the relevant benefits and costs. Various side effects may have to be included — effects which are neither technical nor strictly financial in character. Measures which would help to stabilize prices, attract new industries, and generate more purchasing power, or employ idle workers, are all cases in point. By recognizing their existence, benefit-cost analysis helps us to gain a clearer understanding of the relative importance of various factors, some of which are bound to influence the decision-making process in any case.

If it can be shown that the total benefits of a given project or program exceed its total costs, it may be said to have passed the minimum test of economic feasibility. If this is the only possible way in which the designated need can be served, then this particular project or program will also be the most economic solution in sight. However, alternatives are often available to provide given benefits and must be assessed accordingly. Only that project or program with the highest benefit-cost ratio among these various alternatives is the most economically desirable. Benefit-cost analysis provides a mechanism for ranking these several projects or programs in their true order of economic merit.

The real test of optimum use is found in the answer to the question — "Could these resources be used more efficiently elsewhere by another firm or public agency, and in the satisfaction of an alternative need?" Society, in other words, is searching for a course of action which maximizes benefits relative to costs. A variety of needs may, of course, be met by projects or programs of widely different dimensions. The mere fact that one alternative offers more net benefits than another is insufficient proof of its economic desirability. It is possible to increase the amount of net benefits by spending more money on a given project. However, there may be more profitable ways of spending that money. The proper criterion, therefore, must be expressed in relative terms. The benefit-cost ratios which can be used to describe different alternatives, therefore, provide us with a much better test of which is the most economic thing to do.

It is true that the most economically desirable project or program may not always be financially self-sufficient, and, therefore, not of interest to private firms or to some local government agencies. Larger provincial or national organizations could undertake them and cover the costs because of their greater powers of taxation. Flood control projects and improvements in navigation facilities have sometimes been provided on this basis. Care must be taken, however, to make sure that estimates of non-reimbursable values are not exaggerated and that planning is not unduly biased in this way.

Enthusiasm for a particular project may sometimes obscure the fact that other alternatives exist. Such enthusiasm may lead to the claim that a given proposal is desirable simply because its benefits exceed its costs. Sometimes the mere size of the net benefits is also taken as a valid measure of economic desirability. Yet it should be apparent from what has already been said that the mere existence of net benefits is not enough. Even a large excess of benefits over costs falls short of being a final proof. Each alternative which is open to selection will have differing degrees of feasibility. To qualify they must be, first of all, technically feasible. The funds must also be available for construction and operation. But no one of the projects could be undertaken with confidence until it has been ranked against its competitors and its benefit-cost ratio has been shown to be greater than that of relevant alternatives.

Principles of Benefit-Cost Analysis

Benefit-cost analysis is based on the following principles:

(a) The goods or services produced by a project or a program have value only to the extent that there is, or will be, a demand for them;

(b) A project or program, in order to qualify as the best alternative for development, must be the most economic means, whether public or private, for supplying the goods or services for which it is designed. The cost of proceeding with the next best alternative, meanwhile, establishes an upper limit to the value of the labor, materials and other resources which may be employed in its construction and operation;

(c) The first-added, or most economic, alternative should be that project or program which exhibits the highest benefit-cost ratio. It should be remembered, however, that the selection of a given project or program for development usually changes the economic circumstances against which the remaining projects must be evaluated. It is, therefore, necessary to undertake further analyses after the decision to adopt a given project in a program has been made; and

(d) In order to determine the scale on which the first-added project should be built, it is still necessary to maximize its economic effectiveness. The point at which its benefit-cost ratio is a maximum is rarely the point at which the project can make its greatest economic contribution. This can only be determined by reference to its next best alternative. In order to optimize the first-added project, its scale must be increased to the point where its benefit-cost ratio is above, but only just above, that of its next best alternative. For instance, a benefit-cost analysis may show that projects A, B and C have ratios of 6:1, 5:1 and 4:1, respectively. The scale of Project A may be increased so long as its benefit-cost ratio does not fall below that of Project B.

Terms of Measurement

The products of any activity which can satisfy human wants are referred to in the *Guide* as "goods and services". To the greatest extent possible, the value of goods and services should be expressed in monetary terms, determined through the medium of the market place. Some goods and services demanded by the public, however, are not bought and sold in the market place. These items are sometimes referred to as "intangibles". In many cases it is possible to attach a monetary value to them . . . .

Evaluation of Benefits and Costs

When goods and services are allocated to a given purpose, the effect is obviously to preclude their use for any other purpose. This is the same thing as saying that the economic cost of utilizing a given supply of goods and services for a particular purpose is equivalent to the benefits foregone, i.e. the value which would have been realized had they been employed in their best alternative use. In circumstances where the resources of labor and materials are fully employed, it may be assumed that the value of the goods and services in question is reflected in the volumes consumed and the market prices paid for them. Alternative applications would presumably have used these amounts and paid the same prices for them. Hence, these are the values which represent the true economic cost of goods and services diverted from other uses and employed in a given project or program.

Viewpoint for Economic Analysis

The viewpoint from which project and program effects are evaluated is of fundamental importance to the economic analysis. The viewpoint of an individual assessing the positive and negative effects of a given course of action upon his own immediate interests may well be different from that of the community as a whole. Similarly, the outlook of a small group of individuals organized either as a private firm or as a municipal undertaking could differ from that of a provincial authority or of a federal agency. Projects which are national in scope necessarily involve a more comprehensive approach to the evaluation of benefits and costs, since at this level a greater number of alternatives frequently present themselves.

Guide to Benefit-Cost Analysis

Appropriate allowances must, of course, be made for all transfers, cancellations and offsetting influences. This warning becomes progressively more important as the viewpoint of those responsible for the analysis is expanded to cover neighboring areas and related sectors of the economy. It also turns out that, as the viewpoint adopted in the analysis broadens, some of the secondary effects tend to cancel each other out. In other words, secondary considerations tend to be of lesser importance and the results of the analysis rests more directly on an assessment of primary benefits and costs as the scope of the exercise is increased.

Provincial authorities may, however, include in their analyses effects, some of which can be properly ignored by the federal authorities. Because of these legitimate differences, it is important that the secondary benefits and costs be clearly identified so that negotiations in respect of these differences can proceed in an intelligent manner.

It is apparent, from what has already been said, that the results of benefit-cost analysis may differ according to the viewpoint adopted by the corporation, agency or department carrying out these studies. Whether the viewpoint is local, provincial, regional or national, public or private, however, it should be clearly stated in the analysis. In this way comparisons can be made and negotiations conducted in objective terms.

Project and Program Formulation

The following principles and procedures, while they are frequently described in terms of single projects, are also applicable to identifiable segments of projects and to entire programs which consist of a number of projects.

The analysis from beginning to end, is essentially a matter of weighing alternatives. Each transportation route, each power site, and each recreational area is considered for possible development. The most promising site or location is then selected by a process of elimination, the one exhibiting the highest ratio of benefits to costs coming out on top. This site or location must then be examined by itself with a view to optimizing its scale.

The first step in a detailed benefit-cost analysis is the estimation of demand for goods and services which can be met by developing the project or program in question. This initial estimate may have to be revised at a subsequent stage:

(1) If substantial reductions in cost are in prospect; or

(2) If higher costs are indicated, thus altering the prices (and so the volumes) of the goods and services demanded. Revisions of this kind may have to be made several times depending upon the number of stages through which the analysis is carried.

Usually the analyst is presented, at the outset, with a specific proposal. A project may have been selected, on the basis of preliminary investigations. Certain technical and financial data are available and, from this, benefits and costs can be calculated in a preliminary way. Conclusions can also be drawn as to:

(a) The extent to which these benefits and costs vary with the size or scale of the project;

(b) The benefits and costs involved in including or leaving out selected projects from a given program;

(c) The benefits and costs involved in including or excluding certain purposes from a multi-purpose project or program.

The optimum scale for a given development occurs at the point where its net benefits are at a maximum. This is the point at which the benefits added by the last increment of scale have fallen to the point where they are just equal to the costs involved in adding this same increment. These increments cannot, of course, be less than the smallest physical additions of plant and equipment that are practical. The same considerations apply when selecting a sequence of projects to form a program.

21   Problems of Differential Measurability in Benefit-Cost Analysis*

Anthony Downs

The final problem that concerns me is the use of variables that are simply not measurable and their incorporation into the analysis. This does not apply to Rothenberg's paper alone; many of the studies presented at this conference fall into a category of analysis which I call a horse-and-rabbit approach. There is an old joke which says that a fifty-fifty proposition offered by a shyster resembles a horse and rabbit stew: each partner puts in one unit — you contribute the horse and he contributes the rabbit. In the analyses we have been hearing about here, this joke takes on a new slant. The tiny rabbit is minutely examined and exhaustively analyzed with sophisticated techniques before it is placed in the stew — but then we go out and get any old selected-at-random horse and throw him in. Thus it often seems that we are doing an exhaustive analysis of certain variables which are capable of being analyzed, then making wild guesses about relatively incommensurable variables which are in fact much more important in determining the outcome. We are making a stew with a scientifically-prepared rabbit and a random-chosen horse. The quality of such a stew is bound to be rather indeterminant.

Consequently, it seems to me that this type of analysis cannot be directly applied to decision-making. In many benefit-cost analyses containing relatively

*Reprinted by permission of the publisher from Robert Dorfman (ed.), *Measuring Benefits of Government Investments*, The Brookings Institution, Washington, 1965, Anthony Downs, "Comments on 'Urban Renewal Programs' ", by Jerome Rothenberg, pp. 350-351.

immeasurable variables, the size of probable errors in estimating the variables is larger than the variation necessary to change our policy from one alternative to another. Hence we are not in a good position to make decisions on this type of analysis alone. About all we can do is to (1) specify all the particular effects the decision-maker should look at, (2) indicate which effects are measurable and which are not, and (3) try to measure the effects which are measurable. This will at least tell the decision-maker what things he ought to consider and give him a rough measurement of those which can be measured. Since the decision-maker is generally a politician, it will then be up to him to make up his mind. He will have to estimate the immeasurables and balance the gains of some groups against the losses of others. I think that benefit-cost analysis, if approached from this point of view, can perform an extremely useful service indeed.

Chapter Three
Federal-Provincial Relations

In the previous chapters, the problems of taxation and public expenditures have been discussed as though only one level of government was involved. From the economic point of view, the basic questions of growth, stability and equity are the same whatever the institutions of government decision-making. It is obvious that the implementation of any economic policy must be dispersed both vertically and horizontally: a government that required all decisions including the trivial ones to be made at Cabinet level and that ignored unique local conditions would soon strangle itself in red tape. In fact, from the point of view of efficiency, the appropriate size of a unit will vary according to the nature of the public function: the larger the externalities, the larger the appropriate size. Thus the appropriate size for defence is the nation, the appropriate size for highways may be the province, and the appropriate size for garbage collection services would be the municipality. There may be a different optimum size for each government function.

On the other hand, the cost to the community of decision-making rises steeply as the number of decision-making units increases, and at some point, the benefit from making policy decisions at the most efficient scale of organization will be exceeded by the cost of maintaining one more time-consuming committee.[1] The most efficient number of units may be a second best solution, the number that will keep to a minimum the deviations of size of decision-making units from their optima. This condition will be easier to state in general terms than to define for a particular country, and it will obviously vary from place to place and from time to time. Since the optimum governmental structure will vary over time, governmental structures that are defined rigidly at one point in time may be placed under considerable strain when there are changes in the social and economic conditions to which they were originally made to conform. This is a situation which has become familiar in Canada, as well as in other federal systems.

The problem of assigning decision-making responsibility to the most efficient level of government is not an insuperable one in a unitary state, such as Great Britain, because although authority may be delegated from the central government to the lower levels, the central government retains the ultimate authority. The analogue

---

[1]James M. Buchanan, *The Public Finances*, Irwin, Homewood, Ill., 1965, pp. 503-509.

in the private sector is the head office delegating day-to-day decision-making to the branch office, but if anything goes wrong at the branch office, the head office can take over. Under a federal system, however, there are two levels of government which are legally independent of one another: the central government, having no authority in matters that are constitutionally within the responsibility of the provincial or state governments; and the state or provincial governments having no authority over matters which the written constitution assigns to the central government, although they do have ultimate authority over local governments.

Among economists there are two main attitudes towards federal government, and these are to a large extent reflected in their policy recommendations. There are those who regard a federal form of government as intermediate between several independent states with interests in common, on the one hand, and a unitary state, on the other; for them the aim of policy in a federation should be to facilitate the transition to a single, central government. "One group of writers has in mind the confederating or amalgamation of disparate peoples, to obtain certain 'economies of scale' in national and international affairs while retaining a maximum of regional self-determination. They may anticipate that this action will lead to mobility and centralization eventually, but in their present observation, the federation is somewhat like a military or economic alliance of nation-states."[2]

The other point of view is represented by the federalists, who believe that a decentralized form of government is inherently preferable to a centralized one. "Federalism is here praised as an ideal for *any* society, however culturally unified. Its attractiveness lies in its ability to preserve and encourage individualism, by allowing like people to migrate freely, and congregate into local, provincial or other types of political jurisdiction. Here the rule of majorities will tend toward unanimity, for minorities can always emigrate to political units of similarly-inclined people."[3]

The approach of Canadian writers tends to be pragmatic, and therefore avoids the extreme views. Canadians have to live with a federal state. As W. A. Mackintosh put it, "those who live in federal states know that their scheme of government, in so far as it is federal, was devised and adapted to cope with particular stubborn difficulties and that it has little relation to any abstract ideal. Most federations have been born in travail when dissolution, defeat or deadlock impended."[4] As far as Canada is concerned, "the deep line between the French-speaking Catholics and English speaking Protestants [was an instance] of particularism which made federalism the only road to national unity. The only piece of rhetoric in Canadian constitutional history is Lord Durham's statement: 'I expected to find a contest between a government and a people; I found two nations warring in the bosom of a single state. I found a struggle not of principles but of races'."[5]

The second reason for preferring a federal state to a unitary one in Canada was the great distances, in which the costs and delays of a centralized administration would have been intolerable, especially in the middle of the nineteenth century.

---

[2]A. D. Scott, "The Economic Goals of Federal Finance", *Public Finance,* Vol. XIX, No. 3, 1964, p. 245.

[3]*Ibid.,* p. 245.

[4]W. A. Mackintosh, "Federal Finance", in *Federalism: An Australian Jubilee Study,* F. W. Cheshire, Melbourne, 1952, p. 80.

[5]*Ibid.,* p. 81.

Both of these sorts of difficulties establish a need for decentralization. Usually this is thought of as a need for decentralization in administration but that is something which is possible with a unitary government. It has not essentially anything to do with federalism. What federalism really does is to provide for decentralization of legislation. In the smaller compartments of the . . . provinces, it is possible to achieve a greater homogeneity of legislators and executives than is possible in the larger national union. It is this provision for diversity without disunion which is the essence of federalism and which creates its own peculiar problems. It was to this that Justice Holmes of the U.S. Supreme Court referred when he deprecated anything which would "prevent the making of social experiments that an important part of the community desires, in the insulated chambers afforded by the several states, even though the experiments may seem futile or even noxious to me and to those whose judgment I most respect".[6]

The Canadian federal system is not, of course, the only one to face the problem of adapting the constitutional structure to economic change. Similar strains have appeared in all the older federal systems.[7] Yet the federal form of government is still being adopted by some of the newer nations of the world, and the economics of federalism seem more likely to flourish than to wither away. As Musgrave notes, "recent years have shown a trend away from the unitary bias, and for good reasons . . . . Across the Atlantic, fiscal thinking in multi-unit terms has been stimulated by the movement for European economic integration. There the problem is one of rearranging and synchronizing the tax structures of associated countries, so that economic frontiers can be eliminated and efficiency gains from tariff reduction can be realized without being offset by distorting tax differentials. This problem raises the issue of tax shifting in the open economy, and thus the tools of fiscal and trade analysis are brought together. Similarly there arise the questions of how stabilization policy may be made to work in the open economy, and how the interests of domestic and balance of payments stability may be reconciled."[8]

The main issues in federal economics are represented in the following extracts. The first two define the federal problem. Sir Kenneth Wheare's book is the definitive work on federal government, and he clearly sets out the Canadian case in legal and political terms. Dr. Ratchford, a noted authority on the financing of federations, analyzes the Canadian constitution from the economist's point of view.

The second section presents some of the many proposals made for greater economic efficiency in the Canadian federation. The official reports include a summary of the famous Rowell-Sirois Report (The Royal Commission on Dominion-Provincial Relations, 1940), The Carter Commission (the Royal Commission on Taxation, 1967), and statements made by the Federal Government and two of the Provincial Governments. The other extracts represent three types of federalist solution to the problem of Canadian federation, and an outline of a formula solution proposed for the United States but not yet considered for Canada.

---

[6]*Ibid.*, p. 81.

[7]G. Findlay Shirras, *Federal Finance in Peace and War*, Macmillan, London, 1944, *passim.*

[8]R. A. Musgrave (ed.), *Essays in Fiscal Federalism*, The Brookings Institution, Washington, 1965, p. 4.

22 Federal Government Defined*

Kenneth C. Wheare

By the federal principle I mean the method of dividing powers so that the general and regional governments are each, within a sphere, co-ordinate and independent. . . . In the case of a federation, the fundamental principle is that general and regional governments are co-ordinate. The fact that both operate directly upon the people is an illustration of this principle, but it is not enough in itself to ensure that they are co-ordinate, as the example of South Africa shows. What is necessary for the federal principle is not merely that the general government, like the regional governments, should operate directly upon the people, but, further, that each government should be limited to its own sphere and, within that sphere, should be independent of the other. . . .

The Canadian Constitution — the British North America Act, 1867, and certain subsequent amending acts — divides the powers between provincial and Dominion legislatures in such a way that the provinces have exclusive legislative control over a list of enumerated subjects, and the Dominion has exclusive legislative control over the rest, which, 'for greater clarity', were enumerated also, though not exhaustively. The legislatures of Dominion and provinces are distinct in personnel from each other; neither has power to alter the Constitution so far as the distribution of powers is concerned. That power belongs to the United Kingdom parliament alone. The Courts may be invited to declare Dominion or provincial laws void on the ground that they transgress the field allotted to the respective legislatures by the Constitution. So far the federal principle is rigidly applied. But there are certain important exceptions. The executive of the Dominion has power to disallow any Act passed by a provincial legislature, whether or not the act deals with subjects falling within the legislative field exclusively assigned to the provinces. Further the Dominion executive appoints the Lieutenant-Governor of a province, that is, the formal head of the provincial government. It can instruct the Lieutenant-Governor to withhold his assent from provincial bills and to reserve them for consideration by the Dominion executive, and it may refuse assent to such reserved bills if it thinks fit. Finally, appointments to all the important judicial posts in the provinces are in the hands of the Dominion executive. These are all unitary elements in an otherwise strictly federal form of constitution. They are matters in which the regional governments are subordinate to the general government, and not co-ordinate with it.

These are substantial modifications of the federal principle. Consider the powers of disallowance and of veto alone. They mean that, as a matter of law, the Dominion executive could prevent a provincial legislature from making

---

*Reprinted by permission of publisher from K. C. Wheare, *Federal Government*, fourth ed., Oxford University Press, for the Royal Institute of International Affairs, London, 1963.

laws upon its own allotted subjects, if the Dominion executive happened to disapprove the policy involved in the laws. The powers of disallowance and veto are quite unrestricted in law.[1] They extend to financial legislation as much as to any other. The Dominion executive could prevent a province from raising revenue or spending money if it disapproved of its financial legislation. Could there be a more powerful weapon for centralizing and unifying the government than this? It is true that the Dominion parliament cannot itself legislate upon provincial subjects; it can only prevent the provincial legislature from doing so. In this respect the Canadian Constitution differs from that, for example, of South Africa, where not only may the executive of the Republic veto provincial ordinances but the parliament of the Republic can itself also legislate upon provincial matters. The federal principle is not completely ousted, therefore, from the Canadian Constitution. It does find a place there and an important place. Yet if we confine ourselves to the strict law of the constitution, it is hard to know whether we should call it a federal constitution with considerable federal modifications. It would be straining the federal principle too far, I think, to describe it as a federal constitution, without adding any qualifying phrase. For this reason I prefer to say that Canada has a quasi-federal constitution.

But the matter cannot be left at that. The law of the constitution is one thing; the practice is another. What do these unitary elements amount to in practice? The power of disallowance has not been a dead letter, but at the same time it has been used sparingly.[2] Sometimes the Dominion executive has taken the view that disallowance should not be used unless a provincial act is obviously *ultra vires*. So exercised it could become part of the machinery to ensure observance of the federal principle in the Constitution. However, as this function can be performed by the Courts in Canada, and as they are less likely to be interested parties than the Dominion executive, it would be better to leave questions of *ultra vires* to them. But the use of the power of disallowance has not been confined to cases where a provincial act was thought to be *ultra vires*. It had been used also to nullify legislation of which the Dominion executive did not approve. The power of veto has been similarly used to destroy provincial bills. As late as 1937 both disallowance and veto were used by the Dominion to destroy legislation by the province of Alberta where a 'social credit' government of unorthodox economic views was in power.

The powers of disallowance and veto, therefore, are not dead. But it is clear that the Dominion executive is careful not to use them frequently. Such use would be most unpopular among the people of Canada who desire to be left alone in the exercise of their own provincial powers. So far these legal powers

---

[1]This had been disputed but was settled by the Supreme Court of Canada in 1938 by their decision in *In re Disallowance and Reservation* (1938), S.C.R. 71.

[2]For an account of the way in which the powers have been exercised see W. P. M. Kennedy, *The Constitution of Canada*, Chapter XXIII; E. Forsey, *Canadian Journal of Economics and Political Science*, Vol. IV, 1938, pp. 47ff.; Harlow J. Heneman, *American Political Science Review*, No. 1, 1937; *Report of the Royal Commission on Dominion-Provincial Relations* (referred to hereafter as the *Rowell-Sirois Report*), Queen's Printer, Ottawa, 1940, Book I, pp. 49, 253-254.

which might turn Canada into a unitary state have been subordinated to the federal principle in practice.

Constitutional custom goes further. It is true that the law of the Constitution empowers the Dominion executive to appoint the Lieutenant-Governor of a province and that by law the Lieutenant-Governor appoints the ministers of the province. But by convention the system of cabinet government prevails in the Dominion and provinces of Canada. The Lieutenant-Governor is bound by the convention that he must appoint as his ministers only such persons as can command a majority in the provincial legislature.[3] It is the provincial legislature and electorate which decide who shall form the effective executive government of the province; and the Dominion executive must accept their choice. Similarly, although the Dominion executive appoints the principal provincial judges, it has exercised these powers with discretion and has not attempted to pack the courts with partisans opposed to provincial powers. The fact is that Canada is politically federal and that no Dominion government which attempted to stress the unitary elements in the Canadian Constitution at the expense of the federal elements would survive.

From what has been said, it seems justifiable to conclude that although the Canadian Constitution is quasi-federal in law, it is predominantly federal in practice. Or, to put it another way, although Canada has not a federal constitution, it has a federal government.

23   The Constitutional Basis of Public Expenditure in Canada*

B. U. Ratchford

The preamble to the British North America Act states that the uniting colonies wished to have a federal state "with a Constitution similar in Principal to that of the United Kingdom".[1] Had it not been for the complications presented by a federal state, it might have been possible to have stopped with that one statement and thus to have adopted for Canada the British Constitution by reference. But the problem of federal finance was a major obstacle; which level of government should make what expenditures and how should the funds be raised?

---

[3]On this topic see John T. Saywell, *The Office of Lieutenant-Governor,* University of Toronto Press, Toronto, 1957.

*Reprinted by permission of author and publisher from "The Constitutional Basis of Public Expenditure in Canada", *Canadian Tax Journal,* Vol. VIII, September-October and November-December 1960.

[1]*British Statutes,* 30 Victoria, Ch. 3.

As has been true with other federal states, this question threatened to prevent the original federal agreement, and it has persisted over the years.[2]

It is the purpose of this paper to examine the constitutional bases of the powers of federal and provincial legislative bodies in Canada to authorize public expenditures.

General Nature of the Constitution

The written part of the Canadian Constitution is found in the British North America Act (BNA Act), 1867, and its several amendments. Technically, that Act is an ordinary statute of the British Imperial Parliament and can be amended by, and only by, that Parliament.[3]

Prominent features of the written Constitution are: (a) the power of the British government to disallow Dominion acts within two years of their receipt in London; and (b) the power of the Governor General to refuse to assent to Dominion bills or to reserve them for the signification of the Queen's pleasure. These powers have not been exercised for a very long time and are now constitutionally obsolete.

Since the Canadian Constitution is in the British tradition, it is different in several basic respects from the constitution of a republic which is starting afresh with no usages or precedents to follow.[4] By indicating their preference for a constitution of the British type, the colonies incorporated, by reference, a large but indefinite number of customs, traditions, and conventions into their Constitution.

Dawson points out that the BNA Act

> . . . does not pretend to be a comprehensive document, such as, for example, the Constitution of the United States; and there is thus little of well-rounded, balanced description and enumeration of authorities and functions which so frequently characterize those written constitutions which aim to cover all the essentials of government within a limited number of carefully articulated sections. There are many — very many — vital things about the government of Canada (to say nothing of the provincial governments) which are not stated or even hinted in the British North America Act . . . .
>
> . . . the unwritten constitution is every whit as important as the British North America Act, and, indeed . . . much of the latter is transformed and made almost unrecognizable by the operation of the former . . . .[5]

---

[2]The overriding importance of federal-provincial relations in the constitutional area is illustrated by a very minor and routine catalogue procedure used in Canada's Library of Parliament. Under the heading "Canada — Constitutional Law", there is only one cross-reference; "See also: Federal and Provincial Relations (Canada)".

[3]The lack of any prescribed or generally agreed method of amending the Constitution is one of the major constitutional problems of Canada. See my "Introductory Statement" in A. R. M. Lower, F. R. Scott, et al. (eds.), Evolving Canadian Federalism, Duke University Press, Durham, N.C., 1958, p. 13.

[4]See my Public Expenditures in Australia, Duke University Press, Durham, N.C., 1959, pp. 56-57.

[5]Robert MacGregor Dawson, The Government of Canada, third ed. rev., University of Toronto Press, Toronto, 1957, pp. 67, 70.

Examples of important features of the unwritten constitution are: the greatly changed position of the Governor-General; the great importance of the Prime Minister and the Cabinet, which are not even mentioned in the BNA Act; and the fact that the Prime Minister and the Cabinet must have seats in Parliament and must always command the support of the House of Commons. Dawson concludes that "almost all the above are reproduced in miniature in the provincial governments".[6]

In hammering out their Constitution, the Canadians were greatly influenced by the experience of the United States and in the 1860's they "were contemplating the awful spectacle of its disruption".[7] Perhaps the most important conclusion they drew from that conflict was that the American states had retained too much power. They resolved not to make the same mistake and set about to create a stronger central government. In this they were aided by the strong preference of John A. Macdonald for a unitary state. "Evidences of the unitary principle run all through the B.N.A. Act".[8]

First, the residue of powers — those not specifically allotted either to the Dominion or the provinces — rests with the Central government (sec. 91), while the provinces were restricted to 15 enumerated matters and "Generally all Matters of a merely local or private Nature in the Province". (Sec. 92 (6).) Second, in taxation the provinces were restricted to direct taxes, (sec. 92 (2) and "in 1867 the privilege of direct taxation was rather empty one; the people had had no experience with direct taxes and provincial treasuries dependent on them would have remained empty".[9] Third, the Parliament of Canada could "declare" any local work, "although wholly situate within the Province . . . to be for the general Advantage of Canada" and thus bring it under exclusive federal control (sec. 92 (10) (c)). Fourth, the federal government appoints the Senators from each province (sec. 24), appoints, pays, and can remove (for cause) the Lieutenant Governors of provinces (sec. 58, 59, 60), and appoints and pays the judges of all superior provincial courts (secs. 96, 100). Finally, "to cap the structure of federal dominance, Ottawa was given the power to disallow any new provincial statute within one year of its adoption".[10] (Sec. 90.) Taken together, these provisions certainly went a long way toward the creation of a strong central government.

In one respect the Canadian Constitution is similar to that of Australia but different from that of the United States; it contains nothing resembling a Bill of Rights. In the present context this means that there is no "due process" clause in it and hence no procedural restriction on action by the central government.

---

[6]*Ibid.*, p. 69.

[7]A. R. M. Lower, "Theories of Canadian Federalism — Yesterday and Today", in *Evolving Canadian Federalism, op. cit.*, p. 12. John A. Macdonald, The Father of Confederation, "was an assiduous reader of Hamilton's doctrines in *The Federalist*. He possessed a copy of this work which he annotated freely in the margins". *Ibid.*, p. 13.

[8]F. R. Scott, "French-Canada and Canadian Fedralism", in *Evolving Canadian Federalism, op. cit.*, p. 62. The section numbers which follow refer to the BNA Act.

[9]Lower, *op. cit.*, p. 46.

[10]Scott, *op. cit.*, p. 63. Since Confederation there have been 112 disallowances, the last in Alberta in 1943.

Provincial Constitutions

The various provinces have constitutions which, in general form, are similar to that of the federal government. Section 90 of the BNA Act extends to the provinces, with minor adjustments, the provisions of the federal constitution dealing with appropriation and tax bills, the recommendation of money votes, the assent to bills, the disallowance of acts, and the signification of pleasure by the representative of the Crown on bills reserved. The Lieutenant Governors can refuse assent to bills (which they have done 28 times since Confederation), or reserve bills for signification of the Governor General's pleasure, in which case they do not become effective unless the Dominion Government explicitly assents within one year. A total of 69 bills have been reserved, the last three in Alberta in 1937; only 13 later received Dominion assent.

In addition to these general provisions, some provinces are affected and bound by provisions in the statutes of the Canadian Parliament which admitted them to the union. With these exceptions, the provinces have flexible constitutions with respect to purely local matter; that is, "A provincial legislature has constituent powers and the entire framework of government in the province (except for the office of Lieutenant-Governor) can be altered by the passage of any ordinary statute."[11] Using this power, four of the provinces have abolished one house of their legislatures and all of them have extended their original four-year term to five.

The Distribution of Powers

The most important and the most difficult task accomplished by the Constitution was the distribution of legislative powers between the federal government and the provinces. This was done primarily in sections 91 to 95 of the BNA Act.

Federal Powers

In order to make sure that the federal government remained dominant and retained the residual powers, the Constitution made a double statement of its powers. First, there was the broad, sweeping statement at the beginning of section 91 that the federal Parliament has the power to legislate ". . . for the Peace, Order and good Government of Canada, in relation to all matters not coming within the Classes of Subjects by this Act assigned exclusively to the Legislatures of the Provinces;". Then, ". . . for greater Certainty, but not so as to restrict the Generality of the foregoing Terms of the Section", the Act enumerated 29 (now 31) specific matters falling within the federal sphere. The most important of those for our purpose were: the public debt and the borrowing of money; the regulation of trade and commerce; taxation; the postal service; the defence power; navigation and shipping; banking, currency, coinage, bills of exchange, and legal tender; interest; weights and measures; bankruptcy and insolvency; patents and copyrights; and certain works exempted from provincial control. These last included steamship lines, railways, canals, telegraph and other works serving two or more provinces or foreign countries and any other work declared by the federal parliament to be for the general

---

[11]Dawson, op. cit., p. 92.

advantage of Canada or of two or more provinces. In addition, section 132 gave the federal Parliament ". . . all powers necessary or proper for performing the Obligations of Canada or of any Province thereof, as Part of the British Empire, towards Foreign Countries, arising under Treaties between the Empire and Such Foreign Countries". Later amendments added to the list of matters on which the federal Parliament could legislate; they include unemployment insurance, old age pensions, and the right to make limited amendments to the Constitution on purely federal matters.

Provincial Powers

The provinces received no broad or general grant of powers; rather, they were given the power to legislate with respect to 16 enumerated matters. These included: the amendment of provincial constitutions, except for the office of Lieutenant-Governor; direct taxation; borrowing; municipal institutions; and, most important of all, "Property and Civil Rights in the Province". In a separate section (93) education was carefully and firmly placed under the exclusive control of the provinces, with specific provisions to protect the Roman Catholic and Protestant minorities. Finally, section 92 (16) gave the provinces jurisdiction over "Generally all matters of a merely local or private Nature in the Provinces".

The last provision and the one dealing with property and civil rights have proven, in application, to be very broad and indefinite and have given rise to most of the constitutional controversies which have raged in the past 75 years.

Concurrent Powers

Section 95 gave concurrent powers to the Dominion and the provinces over two matters — agriculture and immigration. In case of a conflict of legislation, federal law takes precedence. An amendment to the BNA Act in 1951 added section 94A, which gives concurrent jurisdiction over old age pensions, but here the precedence is reversed because it is specified that no law of the federal Parliament ". . . shall affect the operation of any law present or future of a Provincial Legislature in relation to old age pensions".

Financial Arrangements and Grants

The financial arrangements which were an essential part of Confederation were the most difficult and complicated of all the problems which had to be faced. After long and heated negotiations the following major settlements were agreed and included in the BNA Act: (1) all duties and revenues of the provinces, except those specifically reserved to them, were taken over by the Dominion to form "one Consolidated Revenue Fund, to be appropriated for the Public Service of Canada . . ." (sec. 102); (2) all stocks, securities and cash of the provinces were taken over by the Dominion as a reduction in the debts to be assumed (sec. 107); (3) all public lands were to belong to the provinces (sec. 109); (4) the debts of the provinces, with certain exceptions, were assumed by the Dominion (sec. 111).

The above arrangements, plus the denial of indirect taxes to the provinces, left the provinces wholly unable to meet their financial requirements; some system of federal grants was essential. After much hard bargaining the system finally agreed upon provided (sec. 118) for specific annual grants to each of the provinces which amounted to a total of $260,000 plus an annual grant of 80 cents per head of population.[12] In an apparent attempt to prevent a reopening of the question, the Act then provided that "Such Grants shall be in full Settlement of all future Demands on Canada. . . ." Seldom has a full settlement fallen so far below the payments actually made.

The BNA Act contains no provision giving the federal government general power to make grants either to the original provinces or to any which might be admitted later. Yet this has in no way prevented the development of a system of grants which has steadily grown in variety and size; apparently no constitutional question has ever been raised about it. A narrow and literal interpretation would be that, since the BNA Act provided a system of grants in full settlement of all future demands, the Dominion would be precluded from making any further payments. But a broader interpretation, and the one followed in practice, is that the general spending power of the federal government is broad enough to enable it to make any grants it wishes to the provinces, so long as such action does not encroach upon powers specifically reserved to the provinces. As Dawson expresses it, "the financial adjustments have taken place largely on an extra-constitutional basis".[13]

Delegation of Powers

The distribution of powers outlined above is such that at times certain elements of a problem will fall within the jurisdiction of the provinces while other elements are within federal jurisdiction. Perhaps the most familiar one is that dealing with the grading and marketing of agricultural products which later enter inter-provincial or foreign trade. The logical arrangements would be for one party to delegate its powers to the other so that an agency might be set up to deal with the whole problem. Yet it seems that ". . . in all likelihood neither Dominion nor province can delegate its powers to the other. Such a change, if permitted, would in effect be an amendment to the British North America Act."[14] Several attempts by provinces to make such delegations have been held *ultra vires* by the courts.

Constitutional Development Through Amendments

Of all the changes which have been made in the Canadian Constitution, only a very few have come through formal amendment of the BNA Act. Of those, only two are of importance for our purpose here; the others have dealt with such matters as the admission of provinces and representation in the federal Parliament. The paucity of formal amendments has been the result, at least

---

[12]There was an additional annual grant to New Brunswick for a period of ten years (sec. 119).

[13]Dawson, *op. cit.*, p. 97.

[14]Dawson, *op. cit.*, p. 92.

in part, of the lack of any agreed method of amending the BNA Act and of the ability of any one province to block action on important matters.

In 1940, Mr. Mackenzie King, "taking advantage of the fact that his Liberal Party controlled all the provincial governments except Alberta", put through an amendment giving the federal government jurisdiction over unemployment insurance. "This was the first time since 1867 that a formal transfer of legislative power had been made."[19] Earlier, in 1935, the government of Prime Minister Bennett, had enacted a law setting up a system of unemployment insurance as a part of the "Bennett New Deal" but the courts held it *ultra vires*, as noted below.

The second major change was an amendment in 1951 giving the federal government concurrent jurisdiction over old age pensions. Under the generally agreed interpretation of the federal spending power at that time, this move was hardly necessary and it "merely regularized the fact that the federal Parliament was already legislating in this field".[20]

Constitutional Development Through Interpretation and Practice

Most of the changes in the Canadian Constitution have come about through court interpretations and through changing practices and usages. It is not feasible here to give more than the briefest summary of these complex developments. The ruling cases were decided by the Judicial Committee of the Privy Council in London until appeals were abolished in 1949.

General Trend

During the first 20 years or so after Confederation, the courts followed the evident intention of the framers of the Constitution to give the federal government the dominant power. But, as Dawson states,

> The Judicial Committee later divided the Dominion grant of powers into two separate parts, general and enumerated; it followed this bisection with the astounding discovery that the general Dominion grant was not the governing one but was *"in supplement of* its enumerated powers", and it then proceeded to relegate this general and now degraded power to a position of inferior strength and authority. The enumerated Dominion powers, which had begun as illustrations of Dominion authority, thus became of greater consequence than the general power which they were supposed to illustrate.[21]

The Courts held that the Dominion could use its general grant of power only in emergencies and it defined emergencies very narrowly and illogically.[22]

---

[19]Scott, *op. cit.*, p. 76.

[20]*Ibid.*, p. 77.

[21]Dawson, *op. cit.*, p. 108.

[22]Thus drunkenness constituted an emergency permitting the Dominion to enact a prohibition law, but "an economic cataclysm, such as the world depression of the thirties, was apparently not considered grave enough to warrant the invocation of this emergency". *Ibid.*, p. 110. When however, the emergency power was successfully invoked, as during a war, it was "held to override any or all of the provincial powers which stand in the way of the National interest", *Ibid.*, p. 109.

Once this has been done, the interpretation of the legislative powers of the Dominion and the provinces "settled down to a competition between the specific enumerated heads of sections 91 and 92". In this race the provinces had the advantage because in section 92 they had two headings capable of broad interpretation — the civil rights provision and the general provision — while the Dominion had, in section 91, only one such heading — the one dealing with the regulation of trade and commerce — "and it received a restricted interpretation".[23]

Effects of Court Decisions

The net effect of the court decisions was that, until after World War I, the Dominion suffered a constant erosion of its areas of legislative competence while the provinces had gained additional powers to legislate on such things as intra-provincial regulation of production, trade, and marketing; wages; hours of labour; unemployment insurance; workmen's compensation; industrial disputes; trade unions; health; and insurance. As industrialization progressed these areas expanded steadily and required more government activity and regulation; this imposed added financial requirements upon the provinces, and they were unprepared to meet them. At the same time the problems which were emerging in these areas soon expanded beyond provincial boundaries and became national problems. But the federal government was unable to cope with them; as Corry has said:

> The Dominion could not have carried out during the depression of the nineteen-thirties measures comparable to the New Deal in the United States because the British North America Act, as interpreted by the Privy Council, reserved most of such measures to the provinces.[24]

Dawson expresses much the same thought in these words:

> Residual power had thus slipped away from the Dominion and had re-appeared in a somewhat altered guise in Section 92; property and civil rights had become, indeed, the true residual clause.[25]

The additional opportunities and responsibilities for government action thus gained by the provinces were not matched by added sources of revenues. The provinces, and especially the poorer ones, were squeezed more and more; their usual reaction was a demand for larger federal grants.[26] This was the cause of much of the trouble in the financial relationships between the Dominion and the provinces.

---

[23]*Ibid.*, p. 108. See also J. A. Corry, *Democratic Government and Politics*, University of Toronto Press, Toronto, 1946, pp. 362-363.

[24]Corry, *op. cit.*, p. 362.

[25]Dawson, *op. cit.*, p. 109.

[26]See J. R. Mallory, *Social Credit and the Federal Power in Canada*, University of Toronto Press, Toronto, 1954.

The Social Security and Labour Conventions Cases

The administration of Prime Minister Bennett came to power shortly after the onset of the depression. In an effort to cope with the problems of that economic disaster he secured the enactment of a series of measures which came to be known as the "Bennett New Deal". They dealt with unemployment insurance, hours, minimum wages, agriculture and other matters. In a series of decisions the courts held most of the acts *ultra vires* of the federal Parliament. These cases perhaps marked the climax and turning point of the old, narrow trend of constitutional interpretation.

First, however, it is necessary to note two cases which perhaps gave Mr. Bennett some basis for hoping that the courts would uphold his measures. In 1932 the Judicial Committee had rendered two decisions which upheld the power of the federal Parliament to regulate aeronautics[27] and radio communications.[28] The legislation in the first case was passed to implement the provisions of an Empire treaty; in the second, to implement the provisions of a Canadian treaty. The legislation was upheld on the ground that the federal Parliament had the power to implement treaty provisions.

If these two cases were upheld on the basis of treaty powers, why not find a treaty base for other desirable legislation? In the Versailles Treaty the contracting parties had agreed to undertake legislation to promote the welfare of workers. So most of the "New Deal" acts alleged, *inter alia*, the necessity of implementing the Versailles Treaty.

The Labour Conventions case[29] involved three acts dealing with a weekly day of rest, maximum hours, and minimum wages. The Supreme Court of Canada divided 3-3 on the case, but the Judicial Committee held all the acts *ultra vires* on the ground that they dealt with matters within the exclusive jurisdiction of the provinces, and the treaty power did not give the federal government jurisdiction because "the Dominion cannot, merely by making promises to foreign countries, clothe itself with legislative authority inconsistent with the constitution which gave it birth".

The Social Security, or Unemployment Insurance, case dealt more directly with the spending power of Parliament. The Act in question had set up a contributory system of unemployment insurance. The preamble to the Act alleged the necessity of implementing the Versailles Treaty but the Attorney-General, in his argument before the courts, did not attempt to use that as a justification. The Supreme Court of Canada held the act *ultra vires* by a vote of 4-2. Before the Judicial Committee, counsel for the Dominion argued that: (1) unemployment was a threat to the body politic of Canada and the purpose of this Act was to abate that evil; (2) in appropriating funds the Parliament of Canada was not limited to the items enumerated in the BNA Act; (3) since unemployment was a problem which did not exist when the Act was framed, it was not specifically provided for in that Act and hence it was "a matter with respect to which legislative jurisdiction must be found in one or other of the

---

[27]*In re The Regulation and Control of Aeronautics*, [1932] A.C. 54.

[28]*In re Regulation and Control of Radio Communications*, [1932] A.C. 304.

[29]*Attorney-General for Canada v. Attorney-General for Ontario*, [1937] A.C. 326.

residuary classes of ss. 91 and 92."[30] The Judicial Committee held that this was not emergency legislation and that it could not be sustained under the treaty power; therefore it would have to be judged on the basis of the taxing and spending power of the Dominion. There was consideration of the question whether the compulsory premium payments were a tax. Their Lordships held it was not necessary to decide that question finally, although "It might seem difficult to discern how it differs from a form of compulsory insurance. . . . But assuming that the Dominion has collected by means of taxation a fund, it by no means follows that any legislation which disposes of it is necessarily within Dominion competence."[31]

The Committee continued and concluded:

> If . . . in pith and substance the legislation invades civil rights within the Province, or in respect of other classes of subjects otherwise encroaches upon the provincial field, the legislation will be invalid. To hold otherwise would afford the Dominion an easy passage into the Provincial domain . . . in pith and substance this Act is an insurance Act affecting the civil rights of employers and employed in each Province, and as such is invalid.[32]

Thus, in effect, the Act was held invalid not because the subject of the expenditure was improper but because the Act contained substantive legislation which affected civil rights. In this respect the case was remarkably similar to the *Pharmaceutical Benefits* case in Australia[33] and to the *Butler* case in the United States.[34]

Later Developments

Since 1937 many things have happened to give the federal government a wider scope of action and more freedom in spending.

First, two specific amendments to the BNA Act have given the Dominion power to legislate with respect to unemployment insurance and old age pensions.

Second, the Dominion was able to use its defence power during two long intervals — World War II and the Korean War. The defence power has never been defined accurately, and apparently the courts have never been asked to pass on the question; but, as noted above, in such emergencies the federal government has great freedom of action. Further, the question as to how long such an emergency lasts "is essentially a political one and the courts are therefore very loath to question the decision of the Dominion Parliament on the length of the emergency period".[35]

Third, the Judicial Committee, in one of the last cases it decided before

---

[30]*Attorney-General for Canada v. Attorney-General for Ontario*, [1937] A.C. 355 at pp. 358-363.

[31]*Ibid.*, at p. 366.

[32]*Ibid.*, at p. 367.

[33]*The Attorney-General for Victoria v. The Commonwealth*, 71 C.L.R. 254 (1945).

[34]*U.S. v. Butler*, 297 U.S. 1 (1936).

[35]Dawson, *op. cit.*, p. 109.

the abolition of appeals, stated that the true test of the Dominion's power to legislate

> . . . must be found in the real subject matter of the legislation; if it is such that it goes beyond local or provincial concern or interests and must from its inherent nature be the concern of the Dominion as a whole (as, for example, in the *Aeronautics* case and the *Radio* case) then it will fall within the competence of the Dominion Parliament as a matter affecting the peace, order and good government of Canada, though it may in another aspect touch on matters specifically reserved to the Provincial legislatures.[36]

Fourth, in 1947 the Judicial Committee recognized the right of Canada to abolish appeals to that Committee.[37] There is as yet no adequate basis for judging the performance of the Supreme Court of Canada as the court of last resort, especially since it has not considered any major case involving the issues under study here. But perhaps it may be hoped that the court will be responsive to the extensive and critical literature of the past two decades and will follow a broader and more realistic line of interpretation. Perhaps one small indication of that is given by a case decided in a lower court (the Ontario High Court) in 1956.[38] The point at issue was the power of the federal government to control atomic energy works. Defence of the legislation was based on three provisions of the BNA Act: (1) the general grant of federal powers; (2) the defence power; and (3) the power to declare a work of general advantage to Canada. The court held that the control of atomic energy was clearly a matter beyond local or provincial control and was "a matter which from its inherent nature is of concern to the nation as a whole". Therefore federal acts and regulations concerning it were "within the powers of Parliament to make laws for the peace, order and good government of Canada".[39] While the Act might conceivably have been upheld under either of the two specific grants of power, the court chose to sustain it under the general grant of federal powers. Having done that, the court ruled that it was unnecessary to pass on the arguments concerning the specific powers.

Finally, the federal government has been able to expand its scope of activities without running into constitutional limitations by a more extensive use of grants. For several years the Dominion has been making substantial and increasingly larger grants for two functions which definitely are reserved for the exclusive control of the provinces — health and education. The grants to the universities are unconditional but the health grants are based upon a complex system of conditions. While there has been some discussion of the constitutionality of these grants, apparently no serious challenge has been raised.

---

[36]*Attorney-General for Ontario v. Canadian Temperance Federation*, [1946] A.C. 193 at p. 205.

[37]*Attorney-General for Ontario v. Attorney-General for Canada*, [1947] A.C. 127.

[38]*Pronto Uranium Mines v. Ontario Labour Relations Board, et al.*, 5 D.L.R. (2d), 1946, 342.

[39]*Ibid.*, p. 348.

General Nature of the Spending Power

By way of summary, what can be said as to the general nature of, and the constitutional limitations on, public expenditures in Canada? Recently one writer stated:

> Almost any activity of government is now *prima facie* legitimate and the task of the elector and of the judge has become merely one of deciding whether it is an activity appropriate to the Dominion or to the provinces.[40]

Since expenditures are closely tied to activities, this statement may be taken as applying to expenditures also. The provinces present few constitutional problems; they seem to have ample power under the Constitution to engage in any activity they desire and can finance. There are few serious problems in the federal domain because the restrictions on federal activities and expenditures have been relaxed as described above.

Two recent statements about the federal spending power may be regarded as reflecting the generally accepted view on this point. Professor Frank R. Scott expresses it this way:

> What Ottawa collects as taxes, it can distribute as gifts or subsidies. It can select the recipient at its choice, be he an individual or body politic. Like the Prince of old, The Queen of Canada can scatter her largesse. She may go further, and attach conditions to the gift. All conditional grants are made on this basis. Making a gift not being the same as legislating in the field which is the object of the gift, since there is no change in the law and no compulsion to accept, a policy of offering to subsidize what it cannot directly compel by legislation opens to the federal government a wide road into positive social planning based on induced provincial consent.[41]

In January 1957, Prime Minister St. Laurent, speaking in the House of Commons, stated the view that federal grants to universities and for other similar purposes were constitutional. He pointed out that this doctrine was not new; the federal government, since 1917, has distributed many millions of dollars as research grants, family allowances, pensions, old age assistance, and for many other similar purposes. All of these payments, he said, had three features in common: (1) they are financed through the Consolidated Revenue Fund; (2) they do not involve any element of compulsion; and (3) "they apply to classes of responsibilities which relate to matters within the legislative jurisdiction of the provinces but they do not amount to legislation controlling the administration or the operation of these functions". He said, further, that

> From the origin of confederation provincial governments have accepted most of these programs and have participated in the financing of some of them without questioning their constitutional validity. They themselves have used the royal prerogative to apply public funds to matters that would be

---

[40]Mallory, *op. cit.*, p. 197. Since the provinces control the municipalities, what is said about the former may be taken as applying to the latter as well.
[41]Scott, *op. cit.*, pp. 77-78.

of value to the national development or to the welfare of the nation as a whole.[42]

As an example of the latter he mentioned grants made by the province of Quebec to the University of Ottawa, which is outside the boundaries of the province.

Both of these statements stress the fact that there is no compulsion attached to the grants. Technically and legally that is correct. But practically and financially there may be considerable compulsion. Indeed, the grants are often deliberately designed to induce (or coerce) the provinces to do certain things which might be beyond the constitutional powers of the federal government to do directly.

Finally, it may be appropriate to consider briefly the sanctions for any constitutional limitations on the spending power which may exist. Apparently there is not in Canada, as there is in the United States, any court rule which prevents a citizen from bringing action to restrain any public expenditures unless he, as a taxpayer, can show a significant and demonstrable financial interest in the question.[43] Yet apparently there has been no such suit. Professor Corry has given some of the reasons:

> At first glance it seems extraordinary that no one has challenged the constitutionality of the assumed spending power before the Supreme Court . . . . Yet a little reflection will show that proof of the unconstitutionality of federal spending for objects outside federal legislative power would prove far too much for almost anybody's comfort. A great many of the substantial interests of the country now derive advantages from it, and the rest of them have not given up hope of doing so. The provincial governments . . . do not want to challenge it. Federal spending now supports so much of the established political, social, and economic structure of the country that prudent men hesitate to take steps that might wipe it out.[44]

Conclusion

There are many technical and complex questions of constitutional law involved here but the one major problem which emerges is the one which besets all federal states — the correct division of power and functions (and therefore of expenditures) between the federal government and the provinces. Since the provinces in Canada do not have sufficient funds to finance all their own functions they are not attempting to expand their functions, so the problem boils down to the extent to which the federal government can and should expand its expenditures.

At one stage — in the 1930's — the federal government was seriously hampered by constitutional limitations and was rendered helpless to embark on

---

[42]*Hansard*, January 29, 1957, p. 754.

[43]See my paper "Some Constitutional Aspects of Federal Expenditures", *The Journal of Finance*, Vol. X, 1955, pp. 459-482.

[44]J. A. Corry, "Constitutional Trends and Federalism", in A. R. M. Lower, F. R. Scott, *et al.* (eds.) *op. cit.*, p. 119.

programs which the nation needed very much. Within the past twenty years or so, however, it has managed to remove or evade most of those limitations. This has been accomplished by two formal amendments to the BNA Act, the expanded use of grants, and to some extent by a changed attitude on the part of the courts. At present the federal government is not significantly handicapped by any constitutional restraint on spending, although in a few instances it must do indirectly what it might otherwise do directly.

24   The Rowell-Sirois Views on Canadian Tax Policy *

J. Sirois, J. W. Dafoe, R. A. Mackay and H. F. Angus

The Report which the Commission has prepared is the outcome of two and a half years of carefully planned study. In the present summary the aim is to set out the principal recommendations embodied in the Report and to indicate briefly the reasons for them. At the heart of the problem lie the needs of Canadian citizens. The basic problem before the Commission lies, therefore, in finding a way in which the financial position of the Provinces could be improved and assured, without disastrous financial consequences to the Federal Government on whose efficient functioning all Provinces are dependent. National unity must be based on Provincial autonomy, and Provincial autonomy cannot be assured unless a strong feeling of national unity exists throughout Canada.

The Commission did find one onerous function of government which cannot, under modern conditions, be equitably or efficiently performed on a regional or Provincial basis. This function is the maintenance of those unemployed who are employable and of their dependents. In reaching this conclusion (which is amply supported by the Evidence and the research studies) the Commission merely confirmed conclusions which had been reached by earlier Commissions. So firmly is the Commission convinced of the validity of this conclusion that even when it comes to consider the situation which will arise if its main recommendations are not implemented, it proceeds on the assumption that the relief of the unemployed who are able and willing to work will become a Federal function.

Another function closely analogous to that of relief for employables is that of assistance to a primary industry (e.g. agriculture) in the form of operating cost advances. When relief is on a small scale the responsibility can be borne without difficulty by the Province. But in the event of widespread disaster with

*Reprinted by permission from the Royal Commission on Dominion-Provincial Relations, *Report*, Queen's Printer, Ottawa, 1940, Book II, Section G.

which a Province is unable to cope without assistance from the Dominion, or in the event that the Dominion by such means as an exclusive marketing organisation has already established effective control of the industry concerned, the Commission recommends that the Dominion should assume direct administrative and financial responsibility rather than render indirect assistance by way of advances to the Provinces affected.

The Commission's treatment of these expensive functions of government may be contrasted with its treatment of another expensive function, namely the payment of non-contributory old-age pensions. As the Federal Government is already paying as high a proportion of their cost as it can reasonably pay without assuming control of the administration of the pensions, and as the Commission was convinced that it is more satisfactory that the Provinces should continue to administer non-contributory old-age pensions, it could not recommend any further financial help to the Provinces in this connexion. But the Commission is of the opinion that if non-contributory old-age pensions were to be superseded or supplemented by a contributory system the latter should, for various reasons, be under the control of the Dominion.

There is, however, an important financial burden of which Provincial Governments can be relieved without any sacrifice of autonomy. This is the deadweight cost of their debt service. The burden taken up by the Dominion, if it were to assume this deadweight cost, would be less than the burden of which the Provinces were relieved because, as maturities occurred, the debts could be refunded more advantageously by the Dominion than by the Provinces. To this extent a saving would accrue to Canadian taxpayers. The Commission has, therefore, recommended that the Dominion should assume all Provincial debts (both direct debts and debts guaranteed by the Provinces) and that each Province should pay over to the Dominion an annual sum equal to the interest which it now receives from its investments. The reason for this proviso is that it would not be expedient that the Dominion should take over liability for a debt which represented a self-liquidating investment retained by a Province. . . . If the Provinces are relieved, in accordance with this recommendation, of the deadweight burden of their debt, it is not unreasonable that they should surrender to the Dominion the subsidies, whatever their character, which they now receive. . . .

The Commission had also to consider how to provide the Dominion with sources of revenue which would enable it to carry its new burdens. This enquiry (as will be seen) was combined with the consideration of efficiency and equity in taxation specifically entrusted to the Commission. There could be no question of increasing the legal taxing powers of the Dominion since these are already unlimited. But the Provinces, in return for the benefits which they would receive, and for further payments which the Commission finds it necessary to recommend, should be prepared to renounce some of the taxes which they employ (or are entitled to employ) at present. The Dominion, for its part, should be able and willing to refrain from competing with the Provinces in respect of sources of revenue left to them and should leave the Provinces free to collect these revenues in whatever way appears to them most efficient even if the method of indirect taxation should be involved.

Just as the assumption of Provincial debts by the Dominion will lead to savings in interest from which taxpayers will benefit, so there are several taxes from which, if they are under unified control, as great a revenue can be obtained as at present with less hardship to the taxpayer. What is more important, a reorganisation of these taxes, of a character which is possible only if they are under unified control, can remove many hindrances which in the recent past have been detrimental to the expansion of the national income (i.e. to the sum-total of the incomes of all citizens of Canada). As this income expands, as the result of what may be fairly termed greater efficiency in taxation, the same revenue as at present can be obtained by taxes imposed at lower rates than those of today.

The first of the taxes which the Commission recommends that the Provinces should renounce is the tax on personal incomes. Not all Provinces impose this tax. Those which get most revenue from it are often taxing incomes which other Provinces think that they should have a share in taxing, because they are in part at least earned in them although they are received in those Provinces in which investors live, or in which large corporations have their head offices. Nor is this all. The general equity of the whole Canadian tax system — and the Commission has been instructed to concern itself with equity as well as with efficiency in taxation — requires that the tax on personal incomes, which is one of the very few taxes capable of any desired graduation, should be used to supplement other taxes and should be uniform throughout Canada.

The Second . . . includes those taxes imposed on corporations which individuals or partnerships, carrying on the same business as the corporation, would not be required to pay, and taxes on those businesses which only corporations engage in. They include, therefore, the tax on the net income of corporations and a multitude of taxes devised to raise revenue from particular classes of corporations which a Province cannot conveniently subject to a tax on net income. They do not include *bona fide* licence fees, the power to impose which would remain with the Province. These Provincial corporation taxes are peculiarly vexatious to those who pay them and particularly detrimental to the expansion of the national income. The cost of tax compliance is high. The tax is often payable by a corporation which has no net income. The tax is very likely to be a tax on costs rather than on profits. These taxes are also a frequent source of interprovincial jealousy. Great benefits may be expected if they are swept away and the equivalent revenue raised by Federal taxes chiefly on corporate net income.

To ask the Provinces to give up the entire revenue which they now derive from taxing corporations would, however, intensify a grievance of which the Commission received complaint in more than one Province; for the Dominion would receive a tax on income which was in part derived from the depletion of irreplaceable natural wealth. It is clearly desirable that revenue of this character should be used for developmental work which will compensate for the damage which has been done to the resources of a Province. The Commission has, therefore, recommended that the Dominion should pay over to the Province concerned 10 per cent of the corporate income derived from the exploitation of the mineral wealth of the Province. When what is required is the conservation of natural resources by maintaining their productivity, rather than compensation for depletion by new investment, the Provinces are in a position to use their own taxing power.

The third tax which the Commission recommends that the Provinces should forgo consists of various forms of succession duty. . . . The use made of them by the Provinces has given rise to bitter complaint because the Provinces have not made equitable arrangements with one another so as to tax each item in an estate in one Province only. The differences in rates between Provinces, and the dangers of double taxation, seriously distort investment in Canada.

At this point there must be a refinement in the calculations. What is significant for the purposes of the Commission is the size of the surplus or deficit which would exist in a Province if it were to provide the normal Canadian standard of services and impose taxation of normal severity. It is not the services which each Province is at present providing, but the average Canadian standard of services, that a Province must be put in a position to finance. It is not the revenue which its taxes yield at their present level which matters, but the revenue which it would derive from them if its people were as heavily taxed as Canadians in general. Just as in the case of debt it is necessary to take account of the fact that some Provinces are more accustomed than others to provide services for their people through municipalities or other agencies instead of directly. The Commission has, therefore attempted to compute, Province by Province, what the cost would be if the Province and its municipalities taken together were to provide services on the Canadian standard. Adjustments have been made for the cost of the developmental services appropriate to the Province, and for the weight of taxation in the Province. The result has been that the Commission has been able to make a recommendation as to the amount, if any, which each individual Province should receive from the Dominion annually to enable it to provide normal Canadian services with no more than normal Canadian taxation. The Commission recommends that each Province found to be in need of such a payment should receive it by way of an annual National Adjustment Grant from the Dominion. This grant as originally fixed would be irreducible. The Commission recommends, however, that National Adjustment Grants should be re-appraised every five years. For special emergencies, which might arise in respect of any Province (and which exist in one Province to-day), special provision should be made, as it would be undesirable either to fix an annual grant in perpetuity on the basis of conditions that are transitory, or to fail to provide for serious emergencies. . . .

The recommendations which have been described would, if implemented, safeguard the autonomy of every Province by ensuring to it the revenue necessary to provide services in accordance with the Canadian standard. Every Provincial Government (including those whose position will be so good as to make adjustment grants unnecessary) would be placed in a better financial position than it is in to-day. And the financial position of every Province would be immeasurably more secure than it is to-day. The Commission looks on this as its primary achievement. It is convinced that this fundamental problem must be faced and it has not been able to discover any alternative way in which it could be solved.

The recommendations which the Commission has made must be judged as a whole. They cannot with fairness either to the Provinces or to the Dominion be considered in isolation for any one of them taken alone might produce grotesque results.

At what cost, it may be asked, will the Provinces have secured these advantages? There will be a certain cost to the Dominion and, therefore, to the Dominion's taxpayers. The taxes forgone by the Provinces, if replaced by Dominion taxes of equal yield, would not provide all the money which the Dominion will probably be called on to pay under the Plan. It is necessary to say "probably" because the Dominion, unlike the Provinces, will be left with highly variable expenditures (e.g. those on unemployment relief) and variable revenues. The long-run effects of the proposed arrangements should, as has been explained, be to increase employment and to increase the national income and, therefore, the national revenue. But the expectation of the Commission is that the Dominion, in the first instance, will have to increase taxes somewhat. Even without increasing tax rates it will obviously increase the taxes payable by citizens of those Provinces which have no personal income tax to-day. It is hardly necessary to add that, in view of the end to be attained, the price seems low.

25   The Carter Views on Canadian Tax Policy*

K. L. Carter, A. E. Beauvais, S. M. Milne, J. H. Perry, D. G. Grant and C. E. S. Walls

In trying to devise a federal tax system we are forced to consider a very large part of the tax structures of the provinces because much of each province's tax structure is the same as or similar to the federal tax structure. Any change in the federal tax structure, therefore, has significant implications for provincial taxation. For example, the federal personal income tax base and the provincial income tax bases are either identical or very similar. To recommend a change in the federal income tax base is tantamount, therefore, to recommending a change in provincial income tax bases. In our view it would be a tremendous loss to all Canadians if this common income tax base was not maintained. To

*Reprinted by permission from the Royal Commission on Taxation, *Report*, Queen's Printer, Ottawa, 1967, Vol. VI, Ch. 38.

recommend that the federal government move from a manufacturer's sales tax to a retail sales tax obviously is of great significance to the provinces because most of them now impose a form of retail sales tax. We are persuaded that great advantages would be gained if the provinces and the federal government were to adopt a common retail sales tax base.

Even greater uniformity of tax bases than now prevails among governments would be highly desirable, as would uniformity of rates. Indeed, our proposed federal tax system would fall far short of the objectives we have sought if the provinces and the federal government were unable to harmonize rates of tax on a common income tax base. In particular, our recommendations with respect to the integration of corporation and personal income taxes would lose some of their effectiveness unless co-ordinated rates were applied at both levels of government. Likewise, some of the advantages of including gifts in the personal income tax base would be lost if the provinces continued to impose death taxes.

Canada should avoid, if possible, the duplication of administrative and compliance costs that may result when the federal and provincial governments levy essentially the same kind of tax on the same taxpayers. It is most desirable that agreements be reached between the federal and provincial governments for the collection and administration of each type of tax by one or the other in a way that protects the interests of both.

We are under no illusions that it would be an easy matter to achieve common tax bases, harmonized tax rates and joint tax collection arrangements. The drive for greater provincial autonomy is extraordinarily strong. The desire to have complete fiscal independence for each province as a matter of right, and as a tool for achieving provincial objectives, would make it difficult to persuade some of the provinces to work more closely with the federal government and other provincial governments in the tax field. The potential gains from success are so great, and the potential losses from failure so heavy, that we have no hesitation in urging the federal government to strive to attain these goals despite the serious obstacles that may be encountered.

In arriving at the conclusions and recommendations given in this chapter, we have been guided by the following considerations:

1. The federal government must continue to have the major voice in the determination of personal and corporation income tax bases. While consultation with the provinces is essential, particularly now that the provinces obtain such a large share of personal income tax revenues, the federal government must be more than a benevolent chairman of a committee of the provinces. This is also true, but to a lesser extent, with respect to sales taxes.

2. The federal government must ensure that the tax system does not become either a weapon with which the strong provinces tyrannize the weak provinces or a means of erecting barriers between provinces.

3. Although it has no constitutional obligation to do so, the federal government has taken primary responsibility in the past for the redistribution of personal income. It has determined the progressiveness of the personal rate structure, and federal transfer payments have been largely responsible for

offsetting regressive property taxes. At least until the provinces take a greater interest in the redistributive effects of the tax system, the federal government should continue to assume this responsibility.

4. . . . the federal government should resist further increases in personal income tax abatements in order to keep the personal income tax as an effective tool of discretionary fiscal policy. Only when a joint stabilization strategy is developed, and the provinces can play an effective stabilization role in co-operation with the federal government, should this restriction be relaxed.

5. The relative importance of sales and property taxes in the overall Canadian tax mix should gradually be reduced. This would not hurt Canada's international competitive position or the rate of economic growth, but would improve the equity of the Canadian tax system. If, over time, the proposed tax system did not yield adequate government revenues, personal income taxes should be raised. If tax cuts were required to offset the revenue drag, sales and property taxes should be reduced. Because of the greater long-run elasticity of income taxes, persistent adherence to the foregoing rules would, in our opinion, substantially improve the tax mix.

26   The Objectives of Canadian Federation: A Federal View *

Mitchell Sharp

It is evident to us that the federalism of the future must recognize even more than the federalism of the past that intergovernmental arrangements must serve the two purposes which concerned the Fathers of Confederation. One was to establish a federal system which would define the roles of the federal and the provincial governments in the management of the public affairs of Canada. The other purpose was to provide the means for promoting the social and cultural development of our two societies, a goal which has come to include the culti-vation of the enriching heritages that have come to us from other lands. In this twofold purpose lies the uniqueness both of the spirit of Canadian federalism and of the intergovernmental arrangements which our system calls for.

It will be equally self-evident, I think, that the economic and social develop-ments of our first century have changed substantially the roles both of the

*Reprinted by permission from *Federal-Provincial Tax Structure Committee*, September 14th and 15th, Queen's Printer, Ottawa, 1966. The Tax Structure Committee was estab-lished by the Federal-Provincial Conference of Prime Ministers and Premiers in 1964, and was given the task of conducting "a joint review of the nature and extent of federal and provincial taxes in relation to the financial responsibilities which nowadays have to be carried by federal and provincial governments".

federal and the provincial governments, and the inter-relationship between these roles. The Depression, the war and then the years of reconstruction taught governments everywhere that they must assume the new and difficult task of managing their economies, in the interest both of full employment and balanced economic growth, and the Federal Government assumed the primary responsibility for this role in Canada. These years taught us, too, that Canadians everywhere want and expect certain basic government services wherever they live, and that they expect their federal and provincial governments to find the methods by which this can be achieved.

It was during these years too that the role of the provinces was similarly enlarged, by the expectations imposed upon them by the people of the provinces, by the technological changes and urban developments which created new needs, and by the renewed realization of provincial potential by provincial politicians. So the responsibilities of provincial governments grew both in scale and in scope, involving programmes in the fields of health and welfare, education, urban development, transportation, and resource and economic development.

Out of these developments emerged still another and a different role for the Federal Government, and new interpretations of the role of the provinces. The Federal Government assumed the responsibility for ensuring that the poorer provinces should, through a system of equalization payments, be put in a position to finance their new and heavier responsibilities. The provincial governments in turn, exercised both their taxing and spending powers in such a way and on such a scale as to increase, in practical terms, both their fiscal powers and their influence over the nation's economy. In the process of these changes, many of the programmes of the federal and the provincial governments, each of them acting within its own constitutional domain, have come to overlap, with the consequent need for harmonization of government plans and programmes.

These are the forces the federalism of the future must accommodate. We must somehow fashion machinery which will permit a strong Federal Government to accomplish the economic and social responsibilities which properly belong to it, but without impairing the fiscal freedom and responsibility of the provinces. We must on the other hand fashion machinery which will strengthen the ability of the provinces to provide the greatly expanded and improved public services which are expected of them, but without at the same time hobbling the Federal Government or forcing it to have different laws for different parts of Canada — differences which might have the effect of obscuring or weakening its proper role as a government which governs all Canadians and protects equally the interests of all of them.

We in Canada, in other words, cannot solve the problems of twentieth century federalism by subordinating one level of government to another. Nor can we do so by adopting a kind of compartmental federalism, under which the federal and provincial governments would attempt to function in isolation. We must find another way.

Any general appreciation of the objectives of federalism in Canada, such as this, must lead to a statement of the guiding principles which flow from it, if it is to be useful in discussions such as those we are about to begin. The following, then, are the principles by which we believe we should be guided in trying to develop a system of federal-provincial fiscal arrangements which will be consistent with the federalism of the future.

(1) The fiscal arrangements should give both the federal and provincial governments access to fiscal resources sufficient to discharge their responsibilities under the constitution.

(2) They should provide that each government should be accountable to its own electors for its taxing and spending decisions and should make these decisions with due regard for their effect on other governments.

(3) The fiscal arrangements should, through a system of equalization grants, enable each province to provide an adequate level of public services without resort to rates of taxation substantially higher than those of other provinces.

(4) They should give to the Federal Government sufficient fiscal power to discharge its economic and monetary responsibilities, as well as to pay its bills. In particular they should retain for Federal Government a sufficient part of the income tax field in all provinces — both personal and corporate — to enable it to use variations in the weight and form of that tax for economic purposes and to achieve a reasonable degree of equity in the incidence of taxation across Canada.

(5) They should lead to uniform intergovernmental arrangements and the uniform application of federal laws in all provinces.

(6) The fiscal arrangements should seek to provide machinery for harmonizing the policies and the priorities of the federal and provincial governments.

27   A Provincial View of Federation*

John P. Robarts

Each premier has an obvious duty and obligation to advance the interests of the citizens of his own province; at the same time, in developing policies and guiding the decisions of his government, he must consider what is best for Canadian federalism and all the citizens of this nation. Before spelling out explicitly the position of the Ontario Government, I should like to set forth

*Reprinted by permission from *Federal-Provincial Tax Structure Committee*, September 14th and 15th, Queen's Printer, Ottawa, 1966.

some of the principles which underlie Ontario's position and our central object-ive to achieve a system of public finance in Canada which allows all govern-ments to meet their expenditure responsibilities without detracting from the growth potential in the private sector of the economy.

The first principle is that the revenue requirements and priorities of the federal and provincial governments must be reconciled and coordinated in a manner which recognizes the need for balanced growth of the public and private sectors of the economy. This in turn means that total governmental expenditures must be contained within the limits of a tolerable level of taxation and debt and that the tax structure must distribute that burden among different types of economic activity according to sound economic principles. It also means that a mechanism must be sought through which all governments can reach a consensus on economic and social goals and priorities. What does this nation, including its federal and provincial governments, wish to accomplish in terms of economic and social progress and in what order and at what rate? We have had, for the past two years, a firm indication from the Economic Council of Canada of the type of economic opportunities which lie ahead and of the obstacles to the achievement of these goals. The matter of priorities is closely related to the question of sharing from a given tax package because only by assessing our priorities can we assess our relative financial and tax requirements. The Ontario Government believes that the Economic Council of Canada can make a valuable contribution to the setting of national goals. We also believe that the Tax Structure Committee should be maintained as a means of provid-ing for inter-governmental cooperation in the area of taxation policy.

The second principle is that a viable system of federal-provincial finance should be based on the allocation of limited tax resources in a manner which closely matches the expenditure responsibilities of the two levels of government. This involves more than a division of existing revenues to match existing expenditures. Rather, it means that tax resources must be allocated so that, over time, total federal and provincial revenues increase proportionately to the anticipated growth of expenditures at each level. It also means that existing tax resources must be allocated in a way which equalizes relative federal and provincial burdens of subsequently raising additional tax revenues or borrowing.

The third principle is that the reorganization of federal-provincial arrange-ments must be based on a comprehensive treatment of all the main areas or forms of inter-governmental finance — tax sharing, cost sharing and equali-zation. Although each of these areas has its unique features and separate ob-jectives, it is apparent that changes in one area cannot be finally evaluated until the accompanying changes in the other areas are fully known.

The final principle is that the objectives, principles, mechanisms and range of federal-provincial financial arrangements should be simplified and rational-ized. The tendency in the past to treat and patch arrangements in a piecemeal and uncoordinated fashion is one of the main factors contributing to the com-plexity and profusion of inter-governmental programmes, payments and trans-fers. However, apart from the need to improve the administrative flexibility and efficiency of the system, this principle also involves the encouragement of a greater degree of public awareness and discussion of the financial structure of Confederation and its evolution in response to changing conditions and requirements.

Given the overall objectives and guiding principles of the reorganization of federal-provincial financial arrangements, I should like to stress the order in which we believe the arrangements should be discussed and dealt with. We believe that attention should be given first to the question of tax sharing, followed by cost sharing, including higher education and medicare, and equalization. This ordering is based on the belief that tax sharing is of vital and central importance in that it determines the provinces' independent access to tax resources. The other types of arrangements may be viewed as of secondary importance in that they provide federal funds which augment the provinces' basic financial capacity. Tax sharing is of central importance, also, because it has important implications for the other areas. For example, the greater the province revenue resources *vis-a-vis* their expenditures, the less will they need supplementary federal aid through cost sharing. Similarly, in the sphere of equalization payments, the greater the fiscal capacity of the wealthier provinces, the larger is the basis upon which transfers to the less-developed provinces are determined.

28   The Inseparability of Cultural and Financial Autonomy in a Federation *

Daniel Johnson

We would like, at the outset, to dwell as briefly and clearly as possible on certain ideas which we feel duty-bound to outline because we consider them fundamental. For, in order to get a clear understanding of Quebec's positions at this conference, it is necessary to have full knowledge of the outlook of the citizens represented here by our delegation. This outlook is not new; several generations of our forebearers held similar views.

We believe that there is in Canada, in a sociological sense, a nation of French speech, whose home is in Québec. This nation has every intention of continuing its self-assertion by obtaining, with due respect for order and justice, all the instruments required for its development.

Specifically, what does Québec want? As the mainstay of a nation, it wants free rein to make its own decisions affecting the growth of its citizens as human beings (i.e., education, social security and health in all respects), the economic

*Reprinted by permission from *Federal-Provincial Tax Structure Committee*, September 14th and 15th, Queen's Printer, Ottawa, 1966.

development, (i.e., the forging of any economic and financial tool deemed necessary), their cultural fulfilment (which takes in not only arts and literature, but the French language as well), and the presence abroad of the Québec community (i.e., relations with certain countries and international organizations).

To this end, the new Québec Government is committed to the fundamental task of obtaining legal and political recognition of the French-Canadian nation: among other things, this will require a new constitution to guarantee equal collective rights in our country to English-speaking and French-speaking Canadians, as well as to give Québec all the powers needed to safeguard its own identity. Obviously, this is not a matter for decision by the Tax Structure Committee; still, the questions within the Committee's terms of reference have such broad implications that we felt it advisable to draw everyone's attention to the over-all problem which confronts us and which we firmly intend to solve. In fact, while revenue sharing between governments is to some extent separate from the socio-cultural problem arising out of the French-Canadian nation's presence and determination to assert itself, the two cannot be kept in different compartments.

Joint Programmes

In our view, this brief statement of Québec's aims puts the problem of joint programmes in its true perspective. In the long run, despite the immediate financial benefits which some may offer initially, these programmes impede the free growth of our people by imposing on them priorities likely to upset those they would otherwise adopt, in addition to reducing their effective budget autonomy. For a province, shared-cost programmes can be regarded as financial aid with more or less annoying conditions attached. For a nation like ours, their effect is to freeze its sources of taxation and take away full control over areas of activity which are rightfully its own. Joint programmes therefore are generally incompatible with the basic aims pursued by the French-Canadian nation.

For that reason, when the current transition period ends, Québec does not plan to renew joint programmes from which it has opted out. On the contrary, its contracting-out will be made final after agreement has been reached on a fiscal compensation based on a fair estimate of present and future costs. Québec, however, is still ready to take part in any federal-provincial conferences called to discuss matters pertaining to these programmes after the transition period has ended.

Furthermore, Québec will not enter any new shared-cost plans in fields of exclusive provincial jurisdiction. Instead, it will insist on receiving unconditional compensation with which to provide Québec's population with services fitted to their own needs, the terms of such compensation being worked out according to the nature and duration of programmes involved.

Our position on joint programmes in which Québec still participates will be determined in the light of the principles set forth here.

Let this point be understood once and for all: for social and cultural reasons, Québec absolutely insists on full respect for its fields of jurisdiction under the constitution; federal interference in these fields, direct or indirect, will not be tolerated.

We would like here to caution the federal government against one seeming solution: it may be tempted, because of Québec's objections to joint programmes generally, to abandon with compensation shared-cost programmes from which Québec has already opted out, but which have been continued in the other provinces. Such a course would force those provinces, reluctant though they might be for reasons which we understand and accept, to adopt a system which, in the final analysis, was designed to solve a problem unique to Québec.

This roundabout way of coping with a situation caused by attitudes peculiar to Québec and based on grounds not necessarily found in the other provinces would, we are convinced, lead inevitably to widespread misunderstanding. At best, it would give the federal government a fleeting impression of leadership, while running the risk of pleasing neither Québec nor the other provinces. It would surely bring about new difficulties later, as a result of failure to understand that Canada is not made up of ten identical territories known as provinces, but of ten separate entities, none really like any other, including one — Québec — which is the heartland of a nation. To us, these are basic truths. Acceptance of them, far from implying automatic disintegration of the country, would prove to Québeckers that they can be part of Canada without being forced into a common mould, thereby risking loss of the cultural distinctions which make their lives meaningful.

Re-Arrangement of Revenues and Functions

The Québec Government firmly believes that Canada's stability depends on Québec's being able to attain its basic aims. From the outset therefore, it is imperative that every field of jurisdiction given to the provinces by the present constitution be fully respected. For that reason and in provision for the new constitution, it is also vital to proceed without delay with a re-arrangement of revenues and functions between the Governments of Canada and of Québec. By this process, the Québec Government would gradually become solely responsible within its territory for all public expenditures on every form of education, old age security, family allowances, health, employment and training of the labour force, regional development and, in particular, municipal aid programmes, research, fine arts, culture, as well as any other social or cultural service within our jurisdiction under the present constitution. Existing federal programmes in these fields would be taken over by Québec, which would maintain their portability where applicable.

All this leads logically to a new division of revenues. In our view, the new sharing formula should have two features: first, as a corrective to the present situation, it should provide for a net transfer to Québec and the other provinces of revenues now held by the federal government, in order to bridge the gap — brought to light by the work of the Continuing Committee on Economic and Fiscal Matters — between the provinces' current revenues and the cost of their present responsibilities; second, it should provide adequate compensation to Québec for the new obligations which it is to assume.

The best possible way of redistributing revenues between Québec and the federal government would be, in our opinion, to set aside for Québec's use 100% of the tax sources to which it is entitled under the constitution: personal and corporate income tax, as well as succession duties. According to our calculations, the revenue which the federal treasury would collect from these sources in Québec for 1971-72 comes close to the amount which Québec should receive for that year from the net transfer of revenue required to close the gap between its present responsibilities and current income sources, fiscal compensation for new obligations assumed, and equalization measures.

29   Conditional and Unconditional Grants in Theory*

Anthony D. Scott

While production has an objective, or at least a money counterpart, the measurement of satisfaction comes up against many obstacles, not the least of which, in the case of federal finance, is the absence of any indication as to whose satisfaction should be maximised. We can, for a while, avoid this issue while analysing possible situations, but must return to it at a later stage. As in the 1950 "Note", we shall use the words 'province', 'state' and 'local' interchangeably; and we shall designate the main body as the 'general', 'federal' or 'central' government. Both levels of government provide 'services' and 'amenities', which mean the same thing.

If the grant is 'conditional', the implication is that it is to be used only for the purpose specified, and the details of the service are to conform to certain universal standards for the provinces set by the central parliament. Furthermore, it is almost always specified that the grant is made on condition that the province shall 'match' it, or a certain fraction of it, from its own revenue resources. To give a complicated example, in the United States' social security old-age assistance scheme, three-quarters of the first twenty dollars of pension has been provided by the federal government, and beyond twenty dollars the federal government matches the state's contribution to a maximum pension of fifty dollars. If the pension is greater than fifty dollars the entire difference must be made up by the state.[1]

*Reprinted by permission of author and publisher from A. D. Scott, "The Evaluation of Federal Grants", *Economica* N.S., Vol. XVIV, November 1952.

[1]*Cf. Social Security Bulletin*, September 1946, pp. 2-8 and 25-30; *Social Security Yearbook*, 1947, p. 63; and W. J. Cohen and J. L. Calhoun, "Social Security Legislation", *Social Security Bulletin*, July 1948, pp. 3-14.

The particular virtue claimed for conditional grants is that the taxing authority — the central government — is keeping the responsibility for the spending of
the taxes: ". . . the old theoretical ideal that each unit of government must raise
the revenues necessary for all the functions which it administers. . . ."[2] If we
imagine the central government to be a maximising body, then the power to
stipulate the use of grants made to the provinces will enable it to maximise the
satisfactions obtained from spending the revenues it has collected. Handing the
grants to the provinces *unconditionally*, on the other hand, removes from the
control of the central parliament, which is responsible to all the taxpayers, the
method of spending the amounts collected.

Unconditional grants, on the other hand, have claimed for them different
virtues. Although constitutional and efficiency criteria suggest governmental
income transfers from the centre to the state, there remains the argument that
conditional grants "interfere with the right of the State to decide by itself what
service it shall perform . . . (they may) stimulate a service which would not
otherwise have been performed and for which money would not otherwise have
been raised by the States",[3] and the cautious Rowell-Sirois Commission in
Canada commented, in 1940: "The Dominion in respect to conditional subsidies
had to impose either such rigid and detailed conditions (often unsuitable to
local conditions), involving such minute inspection and regula⁺ion as to be a
major infringement on provincial autonomy and practical only in a unitary
state, or general conditions which were only nominally observed and no real
check on any irresponsible expenditure."[4]

Professor Simons, in his summary of the United States income tax policy has
said: "First of all, the federal government must eschew arrangements which
would enable it, through the distribution, to influence state and local policies
(except perhaps in matters of income and inheritance taxation). Conditional
grants-in-aid are unobjectionable so long as they involve only modest contributions to worthy causes. Such devices are totally undesirable, however, in connection with distribution of the magnitude here in question".[5]

Unconditional grants, on the other hand, put income into the hands of the
provinces so that they can reduce taxes and provide the present standard of
services, provide further amenities without increasing taxes, or increase both
taxes and amenities.

In most countries both types of grants are now used. Constitutional provisions
in the United States, by preventing the federal government from promoting

---

[2]A. N. Hansen and H. S. Perloff, *State and Local Finance in the National Economy*,
W. W. Norton, New York, 1944, p. 123.

[3]H. M. Somers, *Public Finance and National Income*, Blakiston, Philadelphia, 1949,
p. 461.

[4]Royal Commission on Dominion-Provincial Relations, *Report*, Queen's Printer, Ottawa,
1940, Book II, p. 127.

[5]H. C. Simons, *Personal Income Taxation*, University of Chicago Press, Chicago, Ill.,
1938, p. 216. The Rowell-Sirois Commission, *loc. cit.* and Dr. M. Newcomer in *Taxation
and Fiscal Policy*, Columbia University Press, New York, 1940, p. 53-54 show, however,
that even conditional grants may lead to local spending programmes totally at odds with
the intentions of the central legislature.

certain services directly, have forced it to use conditional grants widely, and for reasons connected with the transformation of the Poor Law administration into the present social services, the largest part of English local government grants are for specific expenditures.[6] In Australia and Canada constitutional commitments have dictated the use of an array of unconditional grants and subventions (which we shall also call 'lump sum' grants or 'block' grants).[7]

We hope in this part to make explicit the matters involved in discovering whether a conditional grant is likely to over-ride the preference of a province in spending a given expenditure. Specifically, the method is an adaptation of the indifference curve analysis of Messrs. Peacock and Berry of the relative advantages of specific subsidies and income subsidies.[8] For a federal grant is analogous to a subsidy; it can be used to augment individual incomes (budgets) or to cheapen certain products (services). The redistribution which can be brought about is of three kinds: (a) from rich to poor throughout the federation, regardless of province, through the action of the federal income tax; (b) from rich to poor within the province, through the combined effect of the reduction of dependence on provincial regressive taxes and the larger grants for social services; and (c) from the wealthier provinces to the poorer provinces. Here we are speaking of the third type of redistribution. . . .[9]

It should . . . be emphasised that while the diagrams will only show indifference between two alternatives, there are here choices among at least three alternatives of importance: between personal income (or its loss by taxation) and the quantity of government services in general, and between government services in general and the quantity of services of the amenity favoured by the federal grants. If we use taxation and federally-sponsored services on the axes, then the enjoyment of other provincial government services is implicit in the indifference curves. A slightly easier way to look at the matter is to put on one axis the quantity of service A, on the other the quantity of service B, and put into the indifference curves not only the utility of having these amenities, but also the dissatisfaction of the taxes necessary to pay for them. In the following diagrams we will use this second arrangment. . . . The curves thus show the attitude to dividing a given budget between two types of service.

In Diagram I the curves are drawn showing the collective attitude of the province to the provision of varying quantities of A and B. A, shall we say, includes sanitation, public works, police and justice, and housing expenditure. The number of units of all of them can only be measured in terms of money.

---

[6]Cf. Little et al., "The Effects of the Local Government Act, 1948, and other recent legislation on the finances of local authorities", Accounting Research, Vol. II, July 3, 1951.

[7]It is interesting to note that in Jugoslavia the taxing and spending power is greatest at the provincial ("republic") level. "Grants" are made, in this country, from the republics to the central government, cf, [London] Times, January 24, 1951 p. 7.

[8]A. T. Peacock and D. Berry, "A Note on the Theory of Income Redistribution", Economica, N.S., 1951, pp. 83-90.

[9]The analysis of (a) and (b) is the analysis of income redistribution in the usual, unitary state, sense.

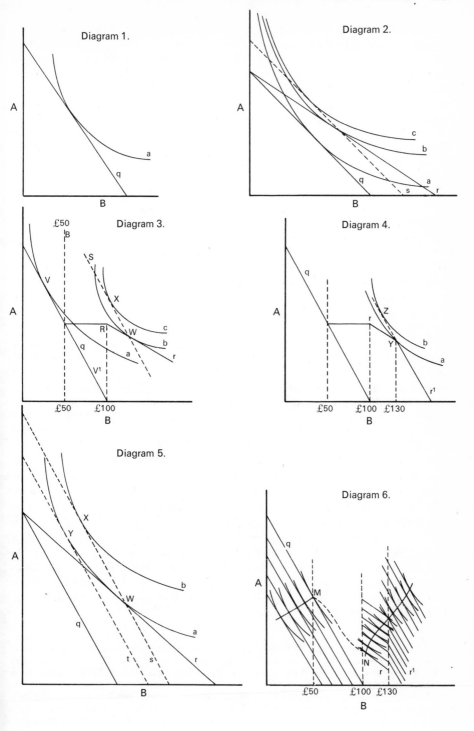

The distribution of expenditure among them is assumed to be optimal.[10] B, on the other hand, represents expenditure on a service not willingly undertaken by the province, say, unemployment expenditure. As in such diagrams, the sloping line represents by its position the tax income of the provincial treasury — its budget — and by its slope the relative costs of providing the two types of services. The point of tangency shows the distribution of expenditure between A and B in order to achieve the greatest community satisfaction.

The first conditional grant to be considered is the simple 'matching' case (Diagram 2). It is directly analogous to the subsidy on a commodity. Where before 100 persons could receive relief, now 110 can, and with the same *provincial* outlay. With the tastes depicted in the curves, the result has been that the province has received more of both services, and has moved to curve *b*. But by the usual reasoning it could be shown that the same total expenditure by the province aided by central government *un*conditional grants could be more efficiently spent, so as to touch curve *c*, with less of service B, however. In fact, while it is not certain that after the subsidy more will be spent on B (owing to the action of income and substitution effects), it is true that a conditional grant will lead to more being spent on B, and less on A than would be the case if the province had been given a block grant. In both cases, the province will be on higher indifference curves but the highest will be reached with the grant in unconditional form.

The next case (Diagram 3), however, is more complex. Here we portray a conditional grant of the following type. The federal contributes nothing till the provincial government has contributed £50. After that, the federal government will match the £50 and each additional contribution from the province. This *type* of conditional grant is found in the dominion-province old age pension system in Canada and in the United States scheme outlined above. The cost-line *q* touches the highest indifference curve *a* at V. It should be noted that V may well be below the point where *q* cuts the £50 line, at V^1 on diagrams 3 and 10.

However, the same total expenditure, if devoted more to B and less to A, would enable the province to cross the £50 threshold and move immediately out to curve *r* which has twice the slope of *q* (to signify that the federal government is matching local expenditure) and also has its origin at B = 100. The indifference curve to which *r* is tangent may or may not be in the segment from B = 100 to the B axis. If it is, then the expenditure on A and B will be set at those coordinates. If not, the point R is the most advantageous position. Let us call this point W, on *b*. As in the previous analysis, there will be some more advantageous point than W involving the same total expenditure which could be reached if the grant were unconditional rather than conditional.[11] *s* shows the original cost relationship, and the new tangency point is at X, on *c*.

---

[10]We could equalise the marginal rates of substitution between all types of government expenditure, taken two at a time, and between them and tax-free income. The assumption that A represents an optimal distribution implies that these choices have already been made.

[11]There is an exception to this. In Diagram 10 we draw two indifference curves *a* and *b* touching *r* and *q* respectively. (If the slope of *r*, say, is greater than twice that of *q*, *a* can touch *r* at W, say. If it is less than twice the slope of *q*, *a* will touch the extreme R.)

Diagram 4 shows the same type of conditional grant, with the condition that after its contribution has reached a certain figure, say £65, the federal government will contribute no more, i.e. when the total expenditure reaches £130, the original cost relationship again holds, if the province continues on its own to spend on B. This introduces a kink into the line r, so that r and r^1 may easily not be tangent to any indifference curve but cut them only at their intersection, say Y. Then Z, on b, would be a more desirable position.

If it were true that most provinces were led by this system to extend themselves to make full use of the federal grant, then their indifference curves would probably be steeply sloped and touch r^1 beyond Y. If the point of tangency is beyond Y, along r^1, the result is the same as with a block grant, for r^1 is parallel to q. In fact, U.S. experience with the old-age pension scheme has shown the states spread all the way along r, with the average state at a position to the left of Y.[12] Thus it cannot be said that the federal government is urging and helping the States to do things which they would be only too glad to do for themselves.

In all the above cases there is an alternative method of statement. It may be our desire, not to maximise satisfaction with a given expenditure, but to minimise outlays while achieving certain standards of satisfaction. The indifference curve approach to this is to be seen in Diagram 5, where we see, analogously with the tax-and-subsidy demonstrations, that the satisfaction to the provincial residents shown by a could be achieved with a smaller total expenditure by giving an unconditional grant t, than with the conditional expenditure r which is equal to s and greater than t. Hence the least expensive way of reaching a given standard of satisfaction is through an unconditional grant.

Note on the Indifference Curves

As mentioned in our discussion of the "community indifference curves" used here, there are good reasons for rejecting the assumption that the changes contemplated do not involve deliberate redistributions of income. This at once places our problem outside the purview of that portion of welfare economics which as developed the Kaldor compensation principle, the de Scitovsky double criterion, and further arguments leading to an unambiguous definition of economic welfare. (See Kaldor, E. J., 1940; de Scitovsky, *Review of Economic Studies*, 1941; Robertson, *Manchester School*, 1951). That approach to welfare involves the *possibility* of an income redistribution after an economic change so that the sufferers would be as well off afterwards as before while the winners, after recompensing the sufferers, still enjoy improved welfare. Now our problem can be treated in this way as long as it involves only the choice between accepting or rejecting a federal grant, which then is similar to an increase in real income.

Then the province would prefer to be at V *without* the grant than at R or W with it. The province might accept a matching grant because it was free, maximise its satisfaction at R, or W, then find it would have been better off with the old distribution of expenditure *without* the grant. This situation could not arise if V were below S at V¹; or if the grant were unconditional in which case the federal grant will inevitably increase satisfaction.

[12]*Cf.* J. A. Maxwell, *The Fiscal Impact of Federalism in the United States*, Harvard University Press, Cambridge, Mass., 1946, p. 128.

But since the problem also involves the ways of spending the grant, which clearly leads to a redistribution of income, the community indifference curves may cross and give us no indication as to desirability of contemplated changes. (See Baumol, *Review of Economic Studies*, **XIV** (1) and **XVII** (3), and Stolper, *Schweizererische Zeitschrift für Volkswirtschaft und Statistik* for discussions of these curves and their construction.)

It therefore appears that in discussions of Public Finance, it is not possible to avoid interpersonal comparisons of utility, as was indeed ceded by Mr. Kaldor to Professor Robbins in his paper mentioned above. Mr. Little has recently gone to some trouble to point out that value judgments about the distribution of income are always necessary, even in the first class of cases, and there has recently been a discussion between Mr. Henderson, Mr. Little and Mr. Buttrick (*Review of Economic Studies*, **XVI** (1), **XVII** (1) and **XVIII** (3)) which, while recognising that ends *could* be selected by anyone, or in any way, has, at least in the papers of Mr. Henderson and Mr. Buttrick, investigated the rights of the Cabinet to do so. Earlier, Bergson's "Reformulation of certain aspects of welfare economics" (Q.J.E., 1938) had stressed the importance of value judgments about the sharing of national income in constructing an economic welfare function. In other words, where it is intended to redistribute income, it is essential that interpersonal comparisons be made.

In the curves used in this paper this unpalatable task has been assigned to its customary performer, the state and provincial legislature. The choices are those of the members, acting together, not of the whole economy. Moving to a higher indifference curve means greater satisfaction to this body, not to the community at large. To the extent that the legislature is out of sympathy with all or part of the community, choices made on the basis of majorities, large or small, will be different from those which would lead to greater economic welfare. This is a regrettable defect of the analysis, but after all little more regrettable than that legislatures do exist which do not reflect the popular will or act in its interest. It should be emphasised, however, that even if the legislature is in close contact with the electorate, the duty of making interpersonal comparisons will still remain, and hence moving on to a preferred indifference curve in the above analysis may well make some persons worse off, without possibility of redress.

30   The Principles of Federal Finance and the Canadian Case*

R. Dehem and J. N. Wolfe

The essence of federalism is the division of sovereignty between two levels of government. In any system of government, there are sovereign and delegated authorities. In a unitary government all sovereign powers are concentrated in the central government, although decentralization for the purpose of administrative efficiency may result in the delegation of certain powers from the central and supreme government to the regional and local subordinate authorities. In a federal state, on the other hand, regional governments, as well as the central authority, are invested with sovereign powers.[1] In no actual case, however, do both levels of government enjoy sovereignty in all domains, since complete concurrence of jurisdictions would lead to incessant conflicts of coordinate authorities. For this reason, federal constitutions indicate, in a more or less precise way, the special fields of absolute competence of the central and the regional authorities. Partial concurrence of jurisdictions may not be excluded, in which case the problem of bringing about agreements between the sovereign powers arises.

Administrative efficiency in a federal state requires both centralization and decentralization of executive functions, in much the same way as in a unitary state. If subordinate functions are delegated to the regional governments, these governments become subordinate to the central authority in these fields. On the other hand, administrative efficiency may require the centralized administration of certain matters in the realm of provincial supremacy, for example, the collection of provincial taxes. In this case, the central governments would act as an agent of the provincial governments, and be subordinate to them. The two types of powers — sovereign and delegated — must be clearly distinguished in order to prevent unnecessary conflicts of authority.[2]

The financial organization that is adequate in a particular federal state depends upon the objectives that are pursued by the federation and upon the material conditions which form the framework of its operations. These material conditions include: the distribution of populations and resources among the provinces; the type of industrial organization; the regional concentration of industries; the interregional distribution of per capita income; and the vulnerability of the

---

*Reprinted by permission of authors and publisher from "The Principles of Federal Finance and the Canadian Case", *Canadian Journal of Economics and Political Science*, Vol. XXI, February 1955, pp. 64-72.
[1]K. C. Wheare, *Federal Government*, third ed., Oxford University Press, London, 1953, p. 11.
[2]The scope of this paper is restricted to federal finance. For a discussion of the functions of government and their distribution in a federal state, see R. Dehem, "Du Bien public et de sa réalisation dans un Etat fédéral", *Actualité économique*, Vol. XXX, pp. 5-21.

whole economy and of its regional sectors to external cyclical disturbances.

As the mutual independence of central and regional governments in their respective jurisdictions is essential to a federal state, it is usually argued that the financial organization should, wherever possible, provide independent sources of revenue to the separate governments. Otherwise, it is feared, financial dependence may make federation illusory. Financial independence involves financial responsibility, each government having to levy on its own constituents the revenue it needs. The decentralization of fiscal responsibilities is, however, quite compatible with centralized devices for administrative efficiency, namely the collection of certain provincial taxes by the federal government.

The distinction made in this paper between the terms financial independence, financial responsibility, and financial autonomy is of some importance. Financial independence is said to exist if a province receives no income from other governments. Financial responsibility is said to exist when any increase in expenditure by a province must be met entirely by an increase in the taxes levied by that province. Financial autonomy exists when there is no pressure on a province, either directly or through conditional grants, to make expenditure or perform actions it would not otherwise wish to do. It will be assumed in this paper that a fixed statutory unconditional grant made in perpetuity does not seriously affect a province's independence, responsibility, or autonomy.

The working of the principles of independence and responsibility may, however, give rise to three types of objections: (1) interregional differences of tax rates will induce shifts and misallocation of resources, which will be detrimental to the country as a whole; (2) regional counter-cyclical fiscal policies are likely to be ineffective if not co-ordinated, and regional financial independence is likely to stand in the way of effective federal action; (3) interregional inequalities of per capita income remain unaltered, and these inequalities may become intolerable in cyclically depressed areas. These objections appear to provide arguments for the centralization of economic power in the hands of the federal government.

To meet the first objection would require uniformity of tax rates wherever undesirable migration of labour, capital, and entrepreneurship is feared. Differences in the taxation of personal income and business profits will have to be avoided, unless they are obviously compensated by differential provision of public services. In so far as public spending is redistributive, the migration effects will be stronger the greater the differences in the rates of progressivity in income taxes. In order to avoid the emigration of their wealthiest citizens, provincial governments may be tempted to minimize progressivity of taxation, in which case they would not fulfil the general wish for less inequality.[3] Uniformity in tax rates can be brought about by the centralization of the relevant taxing powers in the hands of the federal government. But it can also be the result of interprovincial agreement.

---

[3]See J. A. Maxwell, *The fiscal Impact of Federalism in the United States*, Harvard University Press, Cambridge, Mass., 1946, p. 262; and A. H. Hansen and H. S. Perloff, *State and Local Finance in the National Economy*, W. W. Norton, New York, 1944, p. 251.

The fear of deep depressions has led some economists[4] to believe that it would be safer to entrust the most extensive taxing and spending powers to the central government, which has sole responsibility for stabilizing aggregate economic activity. This thesis, based on a pessimistic outlook, underestimates the efficacy of alternative instruments of policy, namely, monetary controls and exchange-rate management. It also exaggerates the extent to which the spending and taxing powers need to be centralized to be effective in coping with the cycle. Yet the dampening of economic fluctuations will be considered here as one among the several objectives of a rational fiscal organization.

Interprovincial income redistribution is another aim that is generally assigned to a federal fiscal system. The mechanism of redistribution would work permanently, but most intensively in periods when the different provinces are unequally affected by the economic fluctuations, owing to the specialization of their resources.

Some arrangements for accomplishing these aims are, however, strongly objectionable as they undermine the independence of regional governments. If grants are given for specific purposes and closely supervised by the central authority, the federal principle is obviously disregarded. If, on the other hand, the federal government gives unconditional grants but bargains separately with each individual provincial government, its monopolistic position may bring about unfair terms to certain provinces, especially to those which are ready to pay a price for regional autonomy.

How then are the basic principles of federal finance to be reconciled? The following principles are here considered as ideal: (a) financial independence and responsibility co-related to functional autonomy; (b) adequacy of means relative to needs;[5] (c) lessening of interregional inequalities of per capita income; (d) interregional uniformity of tax rates in so far as such is necessary to prevent misallocation of resources; (e) counter-cyclical flexibility of tax rates and expenditures; (f) administrative efficiency.[6]

If, in a country with rather uniform interregional distribution of per capita income, revenue adequate to finance strictly provincial activities could be derived from provincial public assets (royalties and profits from public enterprises) and from taxes with negligible interprovincial incidence, no problem would arise. This could be called the *ideal case*. The federal government would have the responsibility for dampening the business cycle through the manipulation of its own expenditures and revenues. The federal government's credit and exchange-rate policy could be used to complement fiscal policy.

The problem of devising compromises between the several objectives arises when the functions of the provincial governments are so extensive that their

---

[4]See M. Lamontagne, *Le Fédéralisme canadien, évolution et problèmes*, Presses universitaires Laval, Québec, 1954.

[5]More explicitly: each provincial community, and the nation as a whole, should be able to bring about its preferred allocation of income between public and private goods and services.

[6]Compare B. P. Adarkar, *The Principles and Problems of Federal Finance*, P. S. King, London, 1933, pp. 218-224, where principles (c), (d), and (e) are not mentioned.

financing requires taxation with interprovincial incidence, such as taxes on personal and business income, and also when the need is felt for redistributing income between the provinces. Any compromise involves the sacrifice, to a certain degree, of one or more ideals. However, one should aim at *optimum* policies, that is, compromises which involve no unnecessary sacrifice.

Solving the problem of an optimum financial organization in a federal state by sacrificing the federal principle is deceptively easy; it amounts to negating the problem altogether.[7] In this paper, any solution which would involve an encroachment by the federal government upon the restricted realm of provincial autonomy is excluded *a priori*.

The data of the problem differ from one federal state to another. The solutions appropriate to each individual case will depend upon the geographic, economic, and cultural characteristics of the country, and also upon the constitutional division of sovereign powers. In general, one may say that the fewer the sovereign powers allocated to the regional governments, the easier it will be to devise adequate financial arrangements, as the ideal case will thus be approximated. If, for instance, responsibility is so divided that the provincial budgets become cyclically vulnerable, as they were in most federal states during the 1930's, inevitable emergency measures on the part of the federal government may infringe violently upon the federal principle. This may have lasting consequences. Thus, one may suggest that, in order to safeguard provincial autonomy at all in a rational economic organization, the field of autonomy should be restricted to the essentials of regional particularism, for instance, cultural matters in a multicultural state. Any unnecessary extension of the domain of sovereign competence of the provincial governments may endanger autonomy altogether, as the problems of co-ordination with the central and with the other regional governments become insuperable and tend to have centralizing solutions.

It is the purpose of this section to consider briefly the extent to which Canadian practice has managed to achieve the ideals we have mentioned. No attempt will be made to describe the actual working of the various systems, since such material is already easily available.

In the 1920's many provinces levied their own personal income and corporate income or corporation taxes, and many cities and towns imposed such taxes as well. The provinces depended on their own taxation for revenue, except that there were certain fixed statutory subsidies from the federal government, of considerable importance in many provinces. The system provided more or less complete financial autonomy, and involved no serious breach with either responsibility or independence.[8] This result was achieved, however, only at the cost of much double taxation, and a high cost of tax compliance, together with considerable misallocation of resources. There was little provincial redistribution, nor did the federal government take very vigorous steps towards inter-class redistribution. .

In the depression of the thirties this system broke down to a greater or less

---

[7]Compare Lamontagne, *op. cit.*, especially pp. 245-249.

[8]Financial independence can only be said to have been assured because the various federal subsidies were arranged on a statutory basis.

degree. While differential tax rates persisted, many provinces became quite incapable of carrying on without federal help. Conditional grants by the federal government, which had existed in certain forms for some years, were much increased. There were direct federal subsidies and loans, especially to the Prairie Provinces. There could hardly have been said to be a federal policy on inter-class redistribution, though conscious interprovincial redistribution now became a reality. In general, we may say that the cyclical instability of demands upon the provinces, implied by their responsibility for relief payments, had brought a virtual disruption of the old Canadian federation. Provinces in many cases were no longer autonomous, responsible, or really independent.

The *Royal Commission on Dominion-Provincial Relations,* reporting in 1940, proposed that the most cyclically volatile provincial functions (relief to employables) and revenue (personal and corporate income taxes and the more stable corporation taxes) should be given up by the provinces, together with succession duties. The federal government alone should levy these taxes, assuring a uniform rate. The provincial governments would be compensated by a *National Adjustment Grant,* whose size would be great enough to ensure each province an average Canadian standard of governmental services. *A Finance Commission,* which would be appointed by the federal government, would make recommendations to the federal government about the size of these grants. The suggestions of the Royal Commission, if they had been adopted, would have given the federal government almost complete control over the progressivity of taxation. They would, too, have rendered the revenues of the provinces more stable cyclically. On the other hand, they would have almost completely destroyed provincial financial independence and responsibility, even if autonomy were maintained. The plan would have resulted in considerable loss in good times, moreover, to Ontario, Quebec, and British Columbia. Although the plan provided for increased revenue to a province which lagged behind while others were gaining, it did not provide very well for the increase of the general level of provincial expenditure when income grew or prices rose.

The adoption of the wartime tax agreements after the failure of the *Dominion-Provincial Conference of 1941* need not concern us here. The expedients then agreed upon in a wartime atmosphere are hardly likely to be repeated. After the war the federal government decided that central control of the income and corporate tax fields was essential. The provinces were offered, very roughly, certain per capita[9] sums for the surrender of their tax rights in these fields for a five-year period. These grants were to be unconditional and the payments were to be adjusted for growth of population and of national income. The agreements made in *1952* did not much change the general form of the earlier ones, although they raised the minimum level of payments, and provided an optional basis of payment designed to persuade Ontario to sign the agreement.[10]

The scheme now in operation assures equal tax rates if all provinces agree

---

[9]There were in fact three options in the original scheme and four in the 1952 agreements.

[10]The reader is warned that this is all very much simplified. For an account of the details of the agreements, see *Canada Year Book,* 1952, pp. 1055-1058.

to it. It provides, too, for cyclical stability of provincial revenues, as well as for changes with growth of population, real income, and prices. It provides for re-distribution of income between provinces and allows the federal government more or less complete control over progressivity of income taxation, with the assistance, such as it may be, that this confers on the government's anti-cyclical policy. On the other hand, when taken together with the federal government's various conditional grants, it seems to remove to a large extent the autonomy and financial independence of all the provinces.[11] Since, at the time of writing, Quebec has not agreed to it, the advantages of equal tax rates and total federal control over progressivity are lost to a certain extent.

The Canadian federation has certain characteristic features.[12] In the first place the number of regional governments is relatively small. Secondly, there is a considerable disparity in per capita income between the provinces. Thirdly, at least one of the provinces, Quebec, is culturally very different from the other provinces, extremely conscious of its individuality, and anxious to preserve it. Fourthly, judicial interpretation of the constitution of the federation has given extensive power to the provinces in the fields of business, labour, and social services, as well as over roads, conservation, and development. Fifthly, financial and business institutions are concentrated in two provinces, but there is con-siderable interprovincial mobility of both capital and entrepreneurship. Finally, the federal government has complete power over the banking system. In gen-eral, the strength of a few provinces and the cultural individuality of one of them make any simple centralizing solutions unrealistic.

In order to attain the advantages of both financial independence and finan-cial responsibility, it would be necessary to grant to the provinces power suffi-cient for the raising of all needed taxes. In practice this must mean access to income taxes, personal or corporate, or both. At the same time, if the desire for governmental services were more uniform than the level of per capita income, unequal tax rates in the different provinces might induce some uneconomic shifts of men and resources.

Two alternative solutions to the problem of devising a financial organization that would respect the federal principle are here suggested. They are not based solely on the abstract ideal principles. They are meant to be possible solutions

---

[11]For a statistical account of the financial dependence of the provincial governments upon the federal authority, see A. M. Moore and J. H. Perry, *Financing Canadian Fed-eration*, Canadian Tax Foundation, Toronto, 1953, pp. 78-89.

[12]On Canadian federalism, see especially the following: Moore and Perry, *ibid.*; Royal Commission on Dominion-Provincial Relations, *Report*, Queen's Printer, Ottawa, 1940; V. W. Bladen, "The Economics of Federalism", *Canadian Journal of Economics and Political Science*, Vol. I, 1935, pp. 348-351; W. A. Carrothers, "Problems of the Cana-dian Federation", *ibid.*, Vol. I, 1935, pp. 26-40; J. A. Corry, "The Federal Dilemma", *ibid.*, Vol. VII, 1941, pp. 215-228; H. A. Innis, "The Rowell-Sirois Report", *ibid.*, Vol. VI, 1940, pp. 562-571; W. J. Waines, "Dominion-Provincial Financial Arrangements", *ibid.*, Vol. XIX, 1953, pp. 304-315; W. A. Mackintosh, "Federal Finance" in G. Sawer (ed.), *Federalism: An Australian Jubilee Study*, F. W. Cheshire, Melbourne, 1952, pp. 80-109.

to the specific Canadian problems, account being taken of the basic political data.

Proposal I

The provinces would retain the right to raise income taxes on the condition that they would agree on a definition of taxable income and on a common exemption and tax schedule. The federal government would be free to levy its own taxes in order to finance federal services, to counteract the business cycle, and to transfer income to the poorest provinces in the form of unconditional grants. These grants could be used by the regional governments in the ways that would best suit provincial needs, be it economic development, education, housing, family allowances, or what not.[13]

These direct federal subsidies undoubtedly threaten the financial independence of the provinces receiving them. To minimize the dangers involved, it is important that they be drawn up on the basis of some rational formula, that the formula be fixed for long periods at a time, and that the payments be self-adjusting with respect to changes in provincial population and national income. Even so, it would be essential that the formula be arranged so that the wealthy provinces, and especially Quebec, receive no federal subsidy.

In order to prevent harmful short-term variations in provincial revenues, this scheme could be provided with a built-in stabilizer: the federal government would guarantee each province's revenues from income taxes up to, say, 80 per cent of the proceeds in the preceding period. The transfer of the volatile business income tax to the federal government, if it could be arranged, would be favourable to stability in provincial finances. This would also avoid the administrative problem of imputing corporate income to the provinces where it originated. Moreover, such an arrangement would induce the provinces to levy adequate royalties for the use of their natural resources.

Proposal II

The provinces could gain more autonomy *vis-à-vis* the federal government by assuming themselves the main part of interprovincial income redistribution. They would have to agree upon the coefficient c_1, c_2, c_3 of the following formula determining each province's share in the aggregate proceeds of provincial income taxes:

$$r_i = c_1 + c_2 p_i + c_3 y_i$$

---

[13]In this case, grants should be unconditional, because they are purely redistributive. Their use is, in principle, indifferent to the federal government. Mr. A. D. Scott has clearly demonstrated the wastefulness of conditional grants as compared with unconditional ones, under the present assumption. See "The Evaluation of Federal Grants", *Economica*, Vol. XIX, 1952, pp. 377-394. [See selection 29 in this volume.] There are, in fact, certain exceptions which ought to be made to this general rule, dealing principally with the possibility that one province may attempt, directly or indirectly, to exploit the social services of another. They need not, however, concern us here.

where r_i, p_i and y_i stand for respectively the ith province's share of revenue, population, and aggregate income; c_1 is a constant designating the cost of administration in the least populated provinces, determined at a reasonable level by agreement; c_2 is a sum per head of population; whereas c_3 is a fraction of provincial aggregate income. The third term of the second member of the equation would prevent too drastic redistribution, to which the wealthier provinces might object. It provides correlation between tax revenues and per capita income.

Once agreement is reached on the values of c_1, c_2, c_3, the federal government could add to the sum of the r_i's its own fiscal needs, in conformity with the general economic conditions, and would establish a single income tax schedule. It would be sovereign in the determination of the tax schedule, which gives it complete fiscal control of the business cycle. Provincial autonomy would be preserved, subject to the inter-provincial agreement.

If, owing to the bargaining power of the richer provinces, inter-provincial redistribution were deemed insufficient by the federal authority, it would still be feasible for the central government to adjust the rate of progressivity of its own tax schedule in such a way as to increase the relative fiscal burden of the richer provinces.

The agreement would cover a period of several years. It would thus provide steadily growing revenues to the provinces. The federal share of revenues would bear the brunt of the cyclical variations.

The solutions presented here depend essentially upon the argument that each province is in the best position to know its own needs, so that federal supervision of expenditure is, with a few exceptions, best avoided wherever possible. Such an assumption, however, is to some extent dependent upon the administration of the provinces being as capable, as honest, and as well meaning as that of the federal government. Whether or not all the provincial governments fulfil these conditions is a question which must be left to the reader. Certainly there is considerable room for improvement in the civil services of some provinces. If the federal government were to give serious consideration to the implementation of these proposals, then it should certainly exhort all provinces to set up judicial committees empowered to make recommendations looking towards an improvement of the calibre of the provincial bureaucracies. Again, there is some reason to believe that the present power of the federal government goes some way to protect minorities in certain provinces. Another point for which the federal government should press is, therefore, the provision of a bill of rights in all provinces, or at any rate a gentleman's agreement that minority rights will be respected.

The solutions we have sketched are by no means ideal in every respect. They both involve some compromise of the principle of financial independence. But they assure the complete financial independence of the wealthier provinces, including Quebec. And they allow complete financial autonomy and responsibility to all the provinces. They both ensure, moreover, that there will be no unintended interference with the most efficient allocation of resources, and at the same time they provide for inter-provincial redistribution. Proposal II calls, however, for a very great measure of co-operation among the provinces. Proposal I requires agreement only upon allocation of income, definition, and rates. But what if even this measure of agreement is not forthcoming? If this were to happen there would be no means of implementing the proposals we have suggested. The best arrangement that could be hoped for would be necessarily much inferior. Possibly the most satisfactory under the given circumstances would be the following: the provincial governments would give up their corporation income taxes and corporate taxes altogether, but would be free to set any personal income tax rate they desired. This would lead to some misallocation of resources, but probably not very much, since the shifting caused by variations in personal income taxes is not likely to be very great.[14] The federal government would provide unconditional subsidies for the poorer provinces. Such an arrangement would safeguard the financial autonomy of all provinces, as well as the independence and responsibility of the richer ones. The federal government should guarantee the revenues of all provinces up to a certain percentage of a moving average figure in order to ensure cyclical stability. The federal government should, moreover, reduce its own personal income tax somewhat in order to allow the provincial governments to enter the field more easily. A great drawback to this arrangement is that under it the federal government would not have sole control of inter-class income redistribution.

We have suggested two ways in which the problems of federal finance in Canada could be met. Each of them is a compromise between desirable goals. A third suggestion has been mentioned above which provides a possible approach in case interprovincial negotiation breaks down. One provision is respected by all these suggestions: the wealthy provinces, and most particularly Quebec, must somehow be assured of complete financial separation from the federal government. No solution which does not free this province from any dependence whatsoever upon arbitrary federal grants can hope to stand for long, and it might damage the unity of the nation while it lasts.

---

[14]The provinces might alternatively receive a certain share of a uniform corporation tax, as was the case under the Tax Rental Agreements from 1947 to 1952.

31   The Fiscal Equity Principle*

John F. Graham

A. The Principle of Fiscal Equity as a Criterion for Fiscal Adjustment

The principle of fiscal equity, developed by Buchanan as a criterion for fiscal adjustment, is an extension of the widely accepted and fundamental doctrine of equal treatment of equals, or "horizontal equity" as it is sometimes called. Horizontal equity is only one of the two aspects of the doctrine of equity, the other being "vertical equity", which is concerned with the far more difficult problem of the equitable treatment of unequals: Both are intrinsic parts of the other.[1] Horizontal equity is of primary interest here, since it is particularly relevant to the equalization aspects of fiscal adjustment: but sufficient attention must also be given to vertical equity, which is the relevant aspect in considering the distributive effects of a fiscal system, to indicate how it should be taken into account.[2]

The doctrine of equal treatment of equals is frequently used in evaluating the equity of tax systems; but Professor Buchanan insists, quite correctly, *that benefits from public services as well as burdens of* taxation should be taken into account in determining whether similarly situated individuals receive the same fiscal treatment. The principle of fiscal equity as the term is used here, simply means that similarly situated individuals[3] in different provinces and localities should receive equal fiscal treatment, taking both benefits from public services and burdens of taxation into account.

---

*Reprinted by permission of author and publisher from John F. Graham, "Fiscal Adjustment in a Federal Country", in R. Robertson (ed.), *Inter-Government Fiscal Relationships*, Canadian Tax Foundation, Toronto, 1964.

[1]Compare Richard A. Musgrave, *Theory of Public Finance*, McGraw-Hill, New York, 1959, pp. 160-161.

[2]For a brief explanation of how vertical equity must also be taken into account, see John F. Graham, *Fiscal Adjustments and Economic Development: A Case Study of Nova Scotia*, University of Toronto Press, Toronto, 1963, pp. 183-187. In short, assuming it is desirable that the fiscal system be egalitarian in its redistributive effects, it is necessary to add the egalitarian postulate that the *fiscal residuum of benefits minus burdens must decrease as income rises.* This requirement could be met even with a regressive tax system, providing the regressive tax burden increased more rapidly than benefit as income increased. Of course, the more progressive the tax system and the greater the extent to which public services particularly benefit lower income groups, the more egalitarian the fiscal system will be. At the same time, care must be taken that the fiscal system leaves more productive labour and capital with larger rewards than less productive labour and capital. Otherwise the system would not only be unjust, it would be uneconomic, for it would tend to drive labour and capital into less productive uses. The important problem remains, of course, of determining how egalitarian the fiscal system should be.

[3]The term "similarly situated individuals" pertains to individuals in the same economic circumstances according to such indices as income (from salaries and wages,

Even with perfect allocation of resources in accordance with the principle of marginal productivity, average income and other indexes of fiscal capacity would vary from province to province and from locality to locality because of lack of uniformity in the distribution of natural resources, and consequently, in occupational distribution. Equalizing transfers would therefore still be necessary to implement the principle of fiscal equity and to prevent distortion from the optimum allocation of resources. If fiscal treatment of otherwise similarly situated individuals in different provinces or localities is not equal, taking both benefits and burdens into account, there will be pressure on the less favourably treated ones in the poorer provinces or localities to move themselves or their capital, or both, to richer provinces or localities where the treatment is more favourable, even though they may be more productive in the poorer provinces or localities. Equalizing transfers to the poorer provinces and localities are necessary to eliminate differential fiscal pressures and their consequent distortion of allocation of resources from the optimum. The implementation of the principle of fiscal equity is desirable, then, both on the ethical ground that it permits equal treatment of equals and on the economic ground that it is conducive to optimum allocation of resources.[4]

A prime virtue of the principle of fiscal equity is that it puts the emphasis on the effect of the fiscal system on the individual, rather than on political units. It makes sense to speak of equalization, where questions of economic welfare and justice are at issue, only with regard to individuals and not, in any ultimate sense, with regard to provinces or localities.

Fiscal Residuum

Buchanan also developed the concept of the "fiscal residuum", already referred to, defined as being equal to an individual's tax burden minus his benefits from public services, as a means of measuring the fiscal pressure on similarly situated individuals in different provinces or localities. (It is more convenient to define

---

interest, dividends, rent, annuities, social security payments, etc.), value of property, age, and size of family. In considering questions of equity (fairness), it is necessary to think in terms of similarly situated individuals in different provinces and localities. In considering questions of fiscal effects on allocation of resources, it is preferable to think in terms of the fiscal pressure on the same individual in different provinces or localities, although for convenience the term "similarly situated individuals" is used here even in the latter context.

[4]In fact, resource allocation is far from perfect, that is resources are not perfectly mobile: but this does not invalidate the applicability of the principle of fiscal equity on efficiency grounds, as is demonstrated in Section III.

Mention might be also made at this point of the fact that variations in costs of providing a public good of given quality will affect the amount of transfers required to enable any given province or locality to provide a service at a prescribed standard with uniform tax rates. For example, if there are economies of scale in the production of public goods, the amount of transfers required will be affected by the size of the recipient province or locality. And if public goods were "Giffen-goods", that is, if the demand for them varied inversely with income, the burden of providing them in the low-income provinces, and therefore the amount of transfers required to equalize fiscal pressure, would be all the greater.

the fiscal residuum the other way round, as being equal to benefits minus burdens, so that it will have a positive value when benefits exceed burdens. This
change does not affect its use.) Buchanan argued that if such individuals'
residua are equal their fiscal treatment is equal.[5] If this proposition were correct, satisfaction of the fiscal equity criterion would require only that the residua
of similarly situated people in different provinces and localities were equal,
rather than the more restrictive condition that such people receive the same
levels of services and incur the same burdens of taxation.

Unfortunately, equalizing of residua of similarly situated individuals will not
necessarily equalize their fiscal treatment, for their welfare is partly determined
by the *level* of public services they receive. Since legislators or councillors have
to determine the level of public services (as well as of taxes) for *all* of the residents of a province or locality, some residents will feel that their welfare would
be enhanced by more public services and less private goods, and some the reverse.
An individual will not feel equally well off in two places if there are substantial
differences in the levels of services even if his fiscal residuum would be the
same in both.[6] He would do so only if public and private services were perfect
substitutes, which they are not. The more imperfect their substitutability, the
greater the resulting differences in his welfare in the two places.[7] Using the
fiscal residuum in making comparisons of similarly situated individuals in
different provinces and localities where there are wide variations in services
and tax rates is still superior to making such comparisons in terms of tax rates
or service alone, for it does take some account of differences in benefits and
in burdens; but the complete application of the fiscal equity principle would
require that individuals in different provinces or localities with the same income, expenditure, and value of property should incur the same tax burdens
and receive the same levels of services, wherever they live in the country.
An approximation to this result or, for that matter, to the equalizing of residua
of equals can be attained only if there are sufficient equalization transfers to
the poorer provinces and localities.

---

[5]J. M. Buchanan, "Federalism and Fiscal Equity", *American Economic Review*, Vol.
XL, No. 4, September 1950, p. 591.

[6]For example, a resident in a locality where there are low taxes but is inferior education for his children may feel much worse off than he would in another locality where
there are high taxes but is superior education, even if his fiscal residuum would be
identical in either place.

[7]Compare Richard A. Musgrave, "Approaches to a Fiscal Theory of Political Federalism", *Public Finances: Needs, Sources, and Utilization*, National Bureau of Economic
Research, Special Conference Series, Princeton University Press, Princeton, N.J., 1961.
"If state taxes, imposed to finance public services, are allocated on a benefit basis, all
citizens of the federation will be taxed on a benefit basis by their respective states. In
this case, no central equalization is needed since the requirement of horizontal equity
is met by the very condition of universal taxation according to benefits received.", p. 119.
State and provincial taxes, as Professor Musgrave is of course aware, are not all allocated
on a benefit basis, but, even if they were, the requirement of horizontal equity would
not be met unless benefits and taxes were uniform, for, as has just been explained, a
zero residuum, or any other particular value, does not assure equality of fiscal treatment,
unless public and private goods are perfectly substitutable.

Equity v. Need

It might well be asked whether there is any substantial difference between making transfers according to the principle of fiscal equity and making them according to the more familiar concept of fiscal need, about which much of the discussion of federal equalization payments to the provinces has centred in recent years. While fiscal need can perhaps be construed to mean about the same thing as fiscal equity, it need not be and generally is not. Fiscal need is a vaguer concept and it fails to provide the clear rationale for fiscal adjustment implied in the concept of fiscal equity. Sometimes fiscal need is used with respect to any transfers which have some equalizing effect. Sometimes, as in the case of the proposal of the Royal Commission on Dominion-Provincial Relations for national adjustment grants to the provinces,[8] it is used more specifically to pertain to transfers designed to enable all provinces to provide levels of certain services equal to the national average with average rates of taxation.

A further and more fundamental objection to the concept of fiscal need used even in its more specific sense — one which would remain even if the above objection were somehow met — is that it is usually used with reference to political units as such and so implies an organic concept of the state, (in fact, the very term "fiscal need" seems to have come to imply this), while the principle of fiscal equity more clearly implies a concept of a state as a collection of individuals, which it has already been argued is the only appropriate concept, certainly the most useful one, where questions of equity and optimum resource use are being discussed.[9] At the same time, the principle of fiscal equity provides a clear rationale for fiscal relations between governments, a test any principle of fiscal adjustment must meet if it is to be practicable. To sum up: the advantage of the principle of fiscal equity over fiscal need, as the latter is usually construed, is that by focusing on individuals rather than on political units as such, the goals of fiscal adjustment and the means of implementation can be more clearly defined and determined with respect to both equity and efficiency.

The Political Unit

The fiscal equity principle could be applied solely by each province with respect to its localities, leaving disparities in the fiscal treatment of similarly situated people as between provinces. But Buchanan gives two cogent arguments to support his contention that the appropriate political unit for the application of the principle is the whole country, in spite of the economic and social heterogeneity of the provinces or states which is inherent in a federation. One argument is economic, the other ethical.

First, since the economy is national in scope, the diversified political framework notwithstanding, the fiscal system should be designed to *interfere as little*

---

[8]"National Adjustment Grants", Royal Commission on Dominion-Provincial Relations, *Report*, King's Printer, Ottawa, 1940, Vol. II, Ch. 5, pp. 125-130.

[9]Compare J. M. Buchanan, *op. cit.*, p. 586. Fiscal transfers and alterations in the distribution of functions and revenue sources must, of course, be made between political units, and the decisions to make them must be taken by governments, but the intent and the effects can be meaningfully considered only with respect to individuals.

as possible with the optimum allocation of resources on a national scale. Because the provinces vary in their fiscal capacity, as measured by indexes appropriate to the particular tax bases used, fiscal transfers are necessary to make possible equal fiscal treatment of similarly situated persons in different provinces.[10] Otherwise, people in poor provinces, poor in terms of fiscal capacity, will be subjected to greater fiscal pressure than they would be in rich provinces, and will have an incentive to move themselves or their capital, or both, to the richer provinces. In other words, a poor province will likely have much labour and capital which are more productive in it than they would be elsewhere. In the absence of equalizing transfers, the heavier fiscal pressure that will be exerted on individuals of any given economic circumstances in a poor province will induce some uneconomic movements of labour and capital from poor to rich provinces and impede some economic movements of labour and capital from rich to poor provinces.[11] As Buchanan puts it:

> Requiring state areas to remain integrated in the national economy is inconsistent with the forcing of the governmental units of these areas to act as if the economies were fiscally separate and independent. This inconsistency can only be removed by centralization of fiscal authority or by the provision of some intergovernmental fiscal adjustment.[12]

Second, income distribution is arrived at through market forces operating over the whole nation. If one of the functions of a fiscal system is to alter this distribution according to some concept of social justice, then the "fiscal system ... should operate in a general manner over the whole area of the economy determining the original distribution". Otherwise, "the system necessarily operates in a geographically discriminatory fashion".[13]

An important consequence of the acceptance of the fiscal equity principle, as Buchanan points out, is that "the principle establishes a firm basis for the claim that the citizens of the low-income states within a national economy possess the 'right' that their states receive sums sufficient to enable these citizens to be placed in positions of fiscal equality with their equals in other states".[14]

---

[10]Probably the best single index of fiscal capacity is income *per capita*; but it may not be an adequate measure of fiscal capacity, for yields from particular important sources, such as natural resource income and corporate and progressive personal income taxation, may not be closely correlated with average income. It is possible, for example, that a province with a lower personal income *per capita* than another province might obtain a higher yield *per capita* from the same set of rates of progressive personal income tax because of a more uneven distribution of income. On this subject see [United States] Advisory Commission on Intergovernmental Relations, *Measures of State and Local Fiscal Capacity and Tax Effort*, Superintendent of Public Documents, Washington, D.C., October 1962.

[11]As pointed out above, even with optimum allocation of resources throughout the nation, there will be inter-provincial disparities in *per capita* income and other indices of fiscal capacity because of inter-provincial differences in endowment of natural resources and consequent differences in resource mix. Some provinces are bound to have larger proportions of people in low-income occupations than others.

[12]Buchanan, *op. cit.*, p. 590.

[13]*Ibid.*, p. 590.

[14]*Ibid.*, p. 596.

Although "right" may be too strong a term to use, even in quotation marks, the strong economic and ethical arguments for equalizing transfers do remove from them the stigma of being regarded as subsidies that smack of being hand-outs, as they have often been regarded in the past. Strong though these arguments are, for this rationale for fiscal adjustment to be acceptable in the context of a federal state, the provinces must accept the idea of redistribution from rich to poor people as a national principle, regardless of whether their own citizens will gain or lose.

Acceptance of the principle of fiscal equity by both federal and provincial governments as the basis for fiscal adjustment would have not only the strong economic and ethical virtues just described, but would also have a unifying effect on the country — since the object would be to dispense the same measure of fiscal justice to all individuals throughout the country — as opposed to the divisive effect of the periodic wrangling over equalization that takes place at present between the federal and provincial governments, and the provincial and local governments, on the spurious basis of fiscal adjustment between these political units as such.

It is essential that the equalization should not stop at the federal-provincial stage. For the principle of fiscal equity to be applied in a federal country it must be followed through at the provincial-municipal stage. The federal government makes grants to provincial governments, not to individuals. Whether the fiscal equity principle is implemented or not depends upon the effects on individuals of the provinces' uses of the grants. Moreover, a provincial government has considerably more freedom to effect adjustment between itself and its municipalities, since they are its own creatures, than has the federal government to effect adjustment between itself and the provinces, which possess large spheres of sovereignty in their own right. Adjustment among localities is easier than adjustment among provinces. A province, holding the power that it has over the localities is free, to a degree the federal government in dealing with the provinces is not, to use conditional or unconditional grants or to alter the powers of the localities, without being concerned about poaching on the powers of another jurisdiction. If, for example, a province considers it desirable on the one hand that the localities have responsibility for education and on the other that specified minimum standards be maintained throughout the province, it is free to charge the localities with this responsibility, even to specify the way their share of the necessary revenue is to be raised, to define the minimum standards in as much detail as it chooses, and make grants, if it deems them necessary, to enable these standards to be maintained. Not only are there no constitutional barriers to provincial municipal fiscal adjustment,[15] but the greater uniformity of the local than of the provincial tax structure makes the application of the fiscal equity principle a simpler, though still by no means an easy, task.

It is important to be clear that applying the fiscal equity principle with respect to provinces or municipalities *does not mean equalizing their fiscal capacity*. To

---

[15]There may, of course, be barriers imposed by considerations of practical politics.

achieve such an end would require that all tax bases, such as income, expenditure and wealth *per capita*, and the distribution of income, be made equal for all the political units at each tier, a requirement quite inconsistent with optimum resource allocation. What it does mean is compensating them for their differences in fiscal capacity *in the provision of public services*.

Fiscal Flexibility

An important modification of the argument is necessary to allow for fiscal flexibility in determining revenues and expenditures. Fiscal flexibility at each level of jurisdiction is generally regarded as a desirable feature of any fiscal system. It is essential in a federal system, because of the social and economic heterogeneity of the provinces and their possession of sovereignty in some spheres. Without this flexibility, provincial and local autonomy would have little significance. No scheme of adjustment that puts governments at any level in a fiscal strait-jacket would or should have much chance of being implemented. Provinces and localities should always be *free at least to determine the levels of services* which are primarily of provincial and local concern and to raise the levels of services of general national or provincial interest above nationally or provincially established minimum levels. Such flexibility is, however, inconsistent with complete equalization according to the fiscal equity principle, for when it is present, wealthier provinces and municipalities will always be able to supplement general services or provide higher than average provincial and local services with less additional tax burden than poorer provinces and municipalities.[16] It is not claimed, therefore, that it is possible or desirable to achieve complete implementation of the fiscal equity principle; but rather that the principle can and should be implemented with respect to minimum levels of services.[17] With this

---

[16]In considering burdens of taxation, it is important to be clear that a tax levied at a given rate is no more burdensome in a low income province or locality than in a high-income province or locality. A 15 cent per gallon gasoline tax would affect a given tax-payer in the same way regardless of whether he lived in a high or low-income province. Both provinces have their low-income groups; their unemployed, penniless widows, indigent aged; and both have their wealthy, and the others in between. A given type of tax imposes a heavier burden in one place than in another only if the rate is higher, assuming, in the case of taxation of expenditure, that costs are similar.

[17]As Professor Tiebout has pointed out, variations among localities in types and levels of public services combined with the opportunity of people for interspatial movement would help to accommodate the varying tastes of individuals if their incomes (and therefore fiscal capacities of localities) were equal. Under such conditions there would be a tendency for people with similar fiscal tastes to move together. Where incomes of individuals (and therefore fiscal capacities of localities) vary, differences in costs (taxes) also influence location and an individual will be able to obtain a given level of services at lower cost to him in a wealthy locality because of the high contributions being made by others. See Charles M. Tiebout, "An Economic Theory of Fiscal Decentralization", *Public Finances: Needs, Sources, and Utilization*, National Bureau of Economic Research, Special Conference Series, Princeton University Press, Princeton, N.J., 1961, pp. 92-94; and the same author's "A Pure Theory of Local Expenditures", *Journal of Political Economy*, October 1956, pp. 416-424. The latter proposition is much the same thing as saying that under such conditions ensuing differences in fiscal capacity exert differential fiscal pressure on otherwise similarly situated individuals. The application of the principle

modification, transfers made according to the fiscal equity principle, far from impairing provincial and local autonomy, give positive content to it. Autonomy means very little to the poorer provinces and localities unless they have sufficient financial resources to perform their functions at levels comparable to those in other provinces and localities.[18]

B. The Geographical Neutrality, Implied in the Fiscal Equity Principle, and Optimum Resource Allocation

A policy of fiscal adjustment based upon the fiscal equity principle can be called "neutral" in that it neither reinforces nor impedes geographical movements called for by the marginal productivity principle. If an individual, regardless of where he lived in the country, received the same level of public services and incurred the same tax burdens with respect to his given income, wealth, expenditure, and whatever other tax bases were used, there would be no differential fiscal pressure on him to move himself or his capital if both were employed where their marginal productivities were highest.[19] If his marginal productivity, or that of his capital, or both, were higher elsewhere, the inducements for him to move himself or his capital would remain.

It might be argued against a geographically neutral scheme of fiscal adjustment that there is a tendency towards optimum resource allocation only under conditions of perfect competition, whereas imperfect competition is the typical condition in the real world. While it is true that the geographically neutral system of fiscal adjustment resulting from the application of the fiscal equity principle would not eliminate departures from the optimum allocation of resources in an imperfectly competitive world, it may still be the best system if more specific information is lacking as to the kinds of fiscal adjustments which are required to compensate for imperfections. It also has the virtue of not impeding the implementation of other types of policy aimed at correcting the departures. It appears that a geographically neutral system of fiscal adjustment is also consistent with a "second best" solution for resource allocation, since the burdens of taxation and the benefits from public services would be uniformly applied with respect to all similar factors of production.

---

of fiscal equity to the degree proposed here would retain the same variety in the patterns of public goods that would exist if fiscal capacities were equal and at the same time eliminate most of the distortion in resource allocation stemming from differences in fiscal capacity.

[18]It is not argued that all localities should provide the same levels of all services — that a resident of a settlement in the Northwest Territories should receive the same services he would in Toronto. Some services appropriate for urban localities are not appropriate for rural areas — street lighting, public water supply and sewage disposal, for example — and some services appropriate for a large city are not appropriate for a small town — a symphony orchestra, for example. What is argued is that localities of each type in a province should be enabled to provide similar services with similar tax burdens.

[19]This proposition is strictly valid only if services and benefits are measured in real terms or if the inter-provincial and inter-local variations in the value of money are not substantial.

Effect on Mobility

Related to the above discussion is the argument that has been advanced that fiscal transfers to poor provinces have a distortive effect on the allocation of resources — that permitting, as they do, higher levels of services and higher real incomes there, they impede the desirable outward movement of labour and capital according to the marginal productivity rule.[20] This argument does not hold up if transfers are made in accordance with the principle of fiscal equity, for a number of reasons.

If there were perfect mobility of resources, there would still be differences among provinces and localities in average income and in other indices of fiscal capacity, because of differences in occupational distribution and in wealth. Fiscal transfers would therefore be required to eliminate differential fiscal pressure, which would otherwise distort the allocation of resources from the optimum. Where there is not perfect mobility, and perhaps is even persistent and deeply rooted immobility, it is unlikely that all labour and capital should move out; what is more likely is that some amounts of some kinds of capital and labour should move out and some amounts of some kinds should move in. To oppose fiscal transfers on the ground that they impede mobility is to ignore this possibility. Without transfers, differential fiscal treatment will exert pressure indiscriminately on factors to move from a poor province or locality, even factors that are well located there, and will inhibit the inward movement of factors from richer provinces and localities, even ones that would be better located in the poor province or locality. As has already been pointed out, the implementation of the principle of fiscal equity, in eliminating differential fiscal pressure on similarly situated individuals, would be geographically neutral in that the inducement of higher rewards elsewhere would still operate with respect to poorly located factors at the same time that differential fiscal pressure was eliminated with respect to well-located factors.

The Atlantic Provinces provide a useful illustration. Differences in marginal productivity probably call for a continued net emigration of some labour and capital. But the withholding of federal transfers from the Atlantic Provinces in order to accelerate the movement of labour and capital from that region would not be economically sound, for it would encourage not only the desirable movement of factors whose productivity is relatively low there, but also the undesirable movement of factors whose productivity compares favourably with what it would be in other parts of the country. It would also discourage the desirable inward movement from other parts of the country of factors whose productivity would be greater in the Atlantic Provinces.

There is another compelling reason for rejecting the argument that fiscal transfers distort resource allocation by impeding mobility, to the extent that this

---

[20]For a discussion of this and related questions, see: A. D. Scott, "A Note on Grants in Federal Countries", *Economica*, Vol. XVII, November 1950; J. M. Buchanan, "Federal Grants and Resource Allocation", *Journal of Political Economy*, Vol. LX, June 1952; A. D. Scott, "Federal Grants and Resource Allocation", *Journal of Political Economy*, Vol. LX, December 1952; and J. M. Buchanan, "A Reply", *Journal of Political Economy*, Vol. LX, December 1952.

argument relies on the push of poverty and adversity as a corrective.[21] This argument assumes that the push of adversity exceeds the stimulus to mobility of self confidence and resourcefulness that stem from a people being well-educated and healthy, which in turn depends upon there being good standards of public services, particularly in the fields of education, health, and welfare. To be effective, adversity must be severe and, even then, move only people with certain qualifications; a policy of letting it provide the spur may do little to eliminate costly, deeply rooted, self-perpetuating poverty which, though commonest in Canada in the Atlantic Provinces, is to be found in sections of practically all provinces. If, on the other hand, through the pursuit of a contrary policy, people are well-educated and healthy, they will both be potentially more productive and more likely to see and seize upon opportunities for betterment in their present locations or elsewhere, and there are more likely to be alternatives open to them. There is likely to be a far greater responsiveness to differential rewards reflecting differences in productivity. If this were the case, intra-regional, as well as inter-regional, mobility would be facilitated. This is important. Mobility within a region such as the Atlantic Provinces will, for some factors of production, be a more appropriate corrective than movement out of the region.

Viewed in this way, fiscal transfers made according to the principle of fiscal equity, while geographically neutral with respect to the treatment of similarly situated individuals, may, by permitting higher standards of public services, exert a powerful and dynamic influence both in increasing the inherent productivity of labour and in making it more mobile and otherwise more adaptable. Moreover, to the extent that public policy, by fiscal adjustment and other means, facilitates external and internal economic adjustment, inter-area differences in fiscal capacity, and therefore the amounts of fiscal transfers required to implement fiscal equity, will probably be reduced, though they will never be eliminated.

Resource Allocation

Also relevant to this discussion is the danger of confusing the effect of an egalitarian fiscal system on resource allocation with the effect of fiscal adjustment on resource allocation. In an egalitarian fiscal system public services may form a large part of the real income of low-income groups and therefore make private rewards relatively less important for people in the groups when they compare their positions with the possibly better positions they can obtain elsewhere in other provinces or in other localities. But this situation is a result of the decision of society that the provision of public services on such a scale by means of an egalitarian fiscal system is desirable.[22] It is no argument for providing inferior services or imposing heavier tax burdens in poor provinces and localities. People, especially poor people, in rich localities as well as in poor ones, have their incentives to move blunted because the public services make

---

[21] I am indebted to Milton Moore for suggesting the argument in this paragraph.

[22] A similar point is made in J. E. Meade, *The Theory of International Economic Policy*, Vol. II, *Trade and Welfare*, Oxford University Press, London, 1955, p. 419.

them better off than they would otherwise be and so diminish the pull of the higher private incomes they could attain by moving. Even so, if their marginal utility of income is higher than for rich people, their incentives to move in response to any given income differential will be still greater. The blunting effect, which depends upon their being some substitutability between private and public goods, is not the result of equalizing transfers. On the contrary, such transfers, as has been shown, are necessary to equalize the fiscal pressure on similarly situated individuals in rich and poor provinces and localities and so to encourage optimum use of resources.

It appears that the argument that fiscal transfers induce, accentuate, or perpetuate misallocation of resources, although initially plausible, and possibly valid in some instances, is too tenuous theoretically and too remote empirically to be taken seriously as a general proposition, if the transfers accord with the principle of fiscal equity. This conclusion holds whether or not there is initial misallocation and, if there is, whether or not it is transitional or deeply rooted.[23] At the same time, it must be recognized that some systems of transfers could be conducive to misallocation of resources, for example, those in excess of the amounts required to implement the principle of fiscal equity.

The pattern of intergovernmental fiscal relations is not the most direct, and may not be the most potent, means in the realm of public policy for influencing the allocation of resources in the private sector of the economy. Anti-combines legislation, tariffs, subsidies, tax concessions, construction of public works, and transportation policy are some of the other means. Nevertheless, the total effect of fiscal relations is likely to be considerable and it is therefore important that it be conducive to, or at least compatible with, optimum resource allocation.

In so far as the marginal productivity principle, or some modification of it, is valid as a guide to optimum resource allocation its operation will be undermined to the extent that governments sustain uneconomic industries by such means as tariffs and subsidies which permit the payment of wages and salaries, interest, and profits, comparable to those paid in other industries. But this result is presumably the policy objective of the government. Whether it is wise or foolish from economic and other points of view, it is the result the government aims to attain. Given this end, it follows that those factors connected with such industries should receive the same fiscal treatment as similar ones elsewhere.

---

[23]For a more detailed discussion of these points, relating particularly to Nova Scotia, see John F. Graham, *op. cit.*, pp. 153-170, 180-182, 187-189.

32 The Economics Component of Canadian Federalism *

David M. Nowlan

Puzzles have solutions, problems don't; problems have responses, and one man's response will inevitably give rise to another man's objection. No anodyne logic from an economist's armoury of professional devices will obliterate the fact that we in Canada are faced with a problem in our desire to secure some appropriate distribution of fiscal responsibilities among our various levels of government. As political, social and economic pressures build, a piecemeal alteration in the distribution of these responsibilities takes place; this has happened in the past and will continue to happen in the future. While no disgrace should be attached to such piece-by-piece economic evolution (I confess that I distrust visionary reconstruction), we have now got what one large newspaper has called a "confused web of federal-provincial relations in the fiscal field". If we wish to avoid compounding this confusion, we should be talking, thinking and arguing about the respective fiscal responsibilities that should fall on the federal, provincial and municipal governments in Canada. The current confrontation between Quebec and Ottawa has tended to obscure the fact that this problem is confederation-wide. I have no illusions that economic theory can provide an ultimate rationale for any particular distribution of power but it can be of some help in setting goals against which our piecemeal manoeuvring may be assessed. Theory is as theory does; and theory does deal with abstractions and ideal forms. The trick is to see if these abstractions can be put to work for us.

It will quickly become evident, however, that I do not stick to my last and confine my remarks to accepted theoretical considerations in the economics of federalism. My view is that the economic responsibilities of the provinces, in both fiscal and monetary matters, should be greatly increased, and I am writing as much about this view as I am about economics. One desirable consequence of such a shift in responsibilities would be the diminished role Ontario would have in influencing the economic policies of the country. The massive economy of this province has tended to dominate federal economic policy, a current example being the move afoot to slow down the inflow of foreign capital. This of course would have little impact on an established industrialized area with easy access to Canadian savings, but it could severely harm the economies of the less developed hinterland provinces.

It is generally agreed that over the last ten years or more the economic role of the provinces has been increasing. Statistics on expenditure by various levels of government confirm this general agreement, but the extent of the shift is

*This article is slightly abridged from a paper entitled "Centrifugally Speaking: Some Economics of Canadian Federalism" written for and to be published in T. Lloyd and J. McLeod (eds.), *Agenda 1970: Proposals for a Creative Politics*, University of Toronto Press for the University League for Social Reform, Toronto, forthcoming, November 1968.

sometimes exaggerated. Of the total expenditure on goods and services by all levels of government, the federal government accounted for roughly 53 per cent in 1955 and only 35 per cent in 1964. Provincial-government expenditure rose from 18 per cent of the total to 23 per cent over the same period. However, if defence spending is excluded from this total, the federal share fell from 25 per cent to 21 per cent between 1955 and 1964, and the provincial share also fell, from 28 per cent to 27 per cent; the share spent by municipalities increased. Of course it is completely open for discussion what is the best way to measure relative federal-provincial economic power or influence. If transfer payments, in which educational expenditures play a large role, were included, the increasing role of the provinces would again be shown.

In what follows, I have divided my comments into three parts. The first deals with the theory of public spending and its bearing on the division of spending responsibilities among the various levels of government. The second part deals with interprovincial income transfers and their impact on resource allocation and economic growth. The third section is a comment on the potential role of the provinces in income stabilization policy. My discussion is focussed on the economics of federalism, a focus that takes as given the various political or fiscal units in Canada. This avoids the rather barren land of the pure theory of fiscal decentralization.[1]

Federalism and the Theory of Public Spending

Goods and services the use or consumption of which by one individual does not diminish the amount available to others are defined as public goods; a public park is a simple example. It is with these kinds of goods that the theory of public spending deals. The basic theorem, which was established by Professor Samuelson,[2] is that a decentralized market mechanism, a competitive market for example, is not capable of providing the best or efficient levels of public goods. This means that whenever such public goods exist a competitive market will not allocate resources in the best way.[3] If an efficient allocation of resources is our overriding goal, we are left with the prescription that public goods ought to be provided free of charge, presumably by the government for reasons mentioned below. The government should provide for general use parks, roads, emergency hospital care, national defence, museums, welfare services and so on, taking care not to exclude the agencies now in the United Appeal (except that the provision of Y.M.C.A. services to businessmen might be left in private hands).

---

[1]The homogeneity assumptions needed do not make very good fertilizer, as may be seen in an essay such as that of Charles M. Tiebout, "An Economic Theory of Fiscal Decentralization", *Public Finance: Needs, Sources and Utilization*, National Bureau of Economic Research, Princeton University Press, Princeton, N.J., 1961.

[2]"The Pure Theory of Public Expenditures", *Review of Economics and Statistics*, Vol. XXXLV, November 1954.

[3]Formally, a best or optimal allocation of resources exists when no one person in the economy can be made better off without some other person being made worse off. To be quite strict, the theorem does not apply to public goods that have a zero cost to the society. These, a competitive market would allocate efficiently; they would be free.

The private market, which requires payment for goods and services, could not efficiently provide these goods; nor could they be provided by voluntary subscription, even if the benefits were then made freely available to society, because each individual would be inclined to under-contribute and society as a whole would have less than optimal amounts.

The actual level at which public goods and services should be provided is in general indeterminate without specifying some desired distribution of income.[4] This is where the government enters. By deciding the extent to which public goods will be provided to the public, governments at all levels must take an implicit or explicit stance on the appropriate distribution of income; there is, I assume, no other body to which we would be willing to delegate this responsibility.

To carry this line of thought one step further, I assume, or perhaps it is a definition, that the government distributes income in a socially desired fashion. If this is accepted (the only way to dispute it would be to provide a more generally accepted definition of a socially desired income distribution), it follows that if resources are allocated efficiently or optimally between the private and public sectors, there is no meaning in asking whether the appropriate (i.e. the socially desired) amounts of public goods are being provided. It is only when the allocation is inefficient that it can definitely be said that public goods are available in inappropriate amounts. Inefficiency of this sort will exist any time public goods are provided by the free market or by subscription, even if they are also provided by government. Thus, the basic public-spending theorem may be used to criticize the government for not providing certain services that are being provided by the private sector but it cannot be used to press for an increase in or establishment of services that are not provided privately. Of course it is open to any individual or group to lobby for additional amounts of government-provided goods or services whether the initial public-private distribution is efficient or inefficient.

The theorem is occasionally wrongly used in its reverse form. Nothing that has been said should be taken to imply that it is inefficient for the government to provide non-public goods.

It is possible to make this comment on public goods with some confidence only because the related policy goal, an efficient resource allocation, is likely to be widely accepted. But now, even with agreement that government ought to provide public goods, the problem of dividing public-spending and revenue-raising responsibilities among the various levels of government in a federal country is much less tractable partly because the range of defensible goals is broad, and partly because more than one government becomes responsible for income redistribution. Arguments favouring any given division of responsibilities may be based on considerations of national unity, constitutional absolutism, administrative efficiency or efficiency in resource allocation; or they may rest on straight paternalistic grounds. Intermingled with these more substantive

---

[4]In other words, there are any number of different ways in which the available resources may be allocated efficiently, each one corresponding to a different distribution of income among members of the society.

principles are emotional or philosophical biases, which appear primarily as either a desire to have more centralization or a desire to have more decentralization of government functions; a centripetal bias versus a centrifugal bias. In using these labels I shortchange a considerable body of writing that attempts to rationalize one or other of these positions.

A centripetal bias is manifest in the general belief that public-spending responsibilities should rest primarily with the federal government, and should be delegated to lower levels only if warranted on the ground of some substantive argument. The centrifugalist, on the other hand, argues that such responsibilities should automatically fall on the lowest level of government, unless an acceptable case can be made for moving a responsibility up one level. These biases are important primarily when the application of some substantive principle to a particular case produces a less than completely decisive outcome.

In a search for some substantive ground on which to base the allocation of public-spending rights and responsibilities among the federal, the provincial and the municipal governments in Canada, it is natural for the economist to turn first to the already-introduced notion of efficiency and to ask what might constitute an efficient allocation of these spending responsibilities. Approaching the problem this way, we may make at least an initial advance; the argument, it turns out, is in part analogous to the logic leading to the recommendation that public goods (as defined) should be provided by the government. Now, instead of having a government and a private market, we have three levels of government.

Consider this example. Part of Ontario's highway network benefits residents of other provinces. The highways provide both access routes to Ontario centres and through routes for western residents travelling to eastern Canada and for eastern residents travelling to western Canada. If Ontario decided to charge tolls to non-residents (something in addition to gasoline taxes which introduce a general element of inefficiency affecting both resident and non-resident) for the use of through highway routes, then some non-residents would decide not to use this Ontario service, a service which could in fact have been provided to any individual non-resident completely free of any cost to Ontario. Resources would not be allocated efficiently and this would provide an argument for having a higher-level government (the federal government) responsible for providing a highway route through the province free of charge to all Canadians.

To generalize would be to argue this way: any time a non-resident could or does benefit from, but must pay for, a provincial service that costs nothing extra to provide, resources are allocated inefficiently and this inefficiency provides an opportunity for arguing that the federal government should take over responsibility for the service. Similarly, if a municipality charged non-residents of that municipality for the use of a service that costs nothing extra to provide, one could argue that the province should take responsibility for the service and provide it free of charge to all provincial residents. The logic of this argument is the same as the logic behind the prescription that the government (a government, we would now say) should expand its provision of any public good that is being sold in the private market.

This particular form of the efficiency criterion for the distribution of spending responsibilities has, however, limited application. In the first place, there are few services provided, or likely to be provided, by lower-level governments (a province or a municipality) for which non-residents are charged more than residents; and secondly, an alternative to moving the responsibility for the service up one level of government is simply to abolish the discriminatory pricing against non-residents. If this latter alternative were followed, we would have public goods provided (hopefully free, but at least at an equal cost to all Canadians) by a government and, as I have previously argued, there appears to be no question whether appropriate amounts of these goods or services are being provided; we take for granted that the government is providing the right amount.

But, now that we are dealing with three levels of government, can we take for granted that any one government will provide the appropriate amount of a public good or service? Consider first the efficiency aspect of this spending. With only one government to contend with, we could reasonably assume that if a group of citizens were willing to pay for the extra cost of providing additional levels of a public good but the government did not respond to this willingness, then the private market would provide the good or service. This would indicate an inefficient allocation of resources and policy could be guided accordingly. If the government were the only agent who could legally provide this service, then pressure by the citizens could be brought to bear on the government. But, to revert to the highway example, if Manitobans wanted a better through highway in Ontario, and were willing to pay the extra construction and maintenance costs, they would have no way of pressuring Ontario into providing this better service. The Manitobans are economically disenfranchised, at least with respect to the provision of highway services in Ontario. This leads to inadequate amounts of Ontario-provided through highways. Resource allocation is inefficient. Inefficiencies of this sort could exist any time the services provided by a lower-level government benefit without cost residents of another jurisdiction. Thus we do end up with a widely applicable efficiency criterion for the distribution of spending responsibilities.

The efficiency criterion of the previous paragraph can be strengthened by considering the income-distribution aspect of spending by lower-level governments. To take the highway example once again, if expenditures on through highways in Ontario benefit other Canadians, why should other Canadians not bear part of the tax burden needed to finance these highways? The distribution of spending responsibilities will be inequitable (which is not the same as being inefficient) if a lower-level government is charged with providing a service that benefits residents of other jurisdictions as well as its own. Thus we can add an equity criterion to the efficiency criterion in setting up a substantive principle to guide the distribution of spending responsibilities.

In summary, if the spending of any one provincial government benefits without cost the members of another province, the spending has external or spillover effects, and to get an efficient and equitable allocation of spending the federal government ought to take over responsibility for that particular good or service. In an economy with a hierarchy of governments we might usefully subdivide the general category of public goods into "federal-public" goods, "provincial-public" goods and a residual category of "municipal-public" goods. Provincial-public goods cannot efficiently and equitably be provided by municipalities acting in their own interests and federal-public goods cannot efficiently and equitably be provided by provinces acting in *their* own interests.

On this basis, therefore, the federal government should clearly be responsible for such federal-public goods as national defence spending, harbour construction and maintenance, the publication of statistical material and the administration of at least some aspects of external affairs, to mention only a few broadly dispersed functions. For reasons of administrative efficiency as well as spillover effects, the federal government might well carry out desired public research in various scientific and technical fields. However, the spillover argument is scarcely capable of providing justification for federal spending, including grants-in-aid (conditional grants) to lower levels of government, on, for example, parkland, local construction projects (or even national-linkage construction projects beyond a certain point), ARDA and other regional planning projects, hospitals and technical or educational facilities. The external effects of provincial or municipal expenditures on such items are probably not absolutely nil, but I would judge that they are sufficiently small, and the goods or services sufficiently basic, that each lower level government would be as likely as the federal government to provide optimal levels of output. Such a conclusion betrays my centrifugal bias; a centripetalist might rule in favour of federal control whenever the least amount of spillover was suspected.

A serious practical obstacle may arise in the attempt to persuade all governments concerned to accept federal responsibility even for goods or services that are clearly federal-public. The obstacle is that inter-provincial income redistribution (or inter-municipal redistribution, if provincial-public goods are being considered) operates through, in part, the spending pattern of the federal government. This does not invalidate the notion that, to bring about efficiency in allocation, all responsibility for federal-public goods should fall on the federal government; but it does mean that a particular province may not favour the federal takeover of a federal-public service, because inter-provincial income distribution may be altered to its detriment. In fairness to the centripetalists, I should also emphasize what is frequently neglected; that the spillover argument in no way stands against a higher-level responsibility for what is clearly a lower-level public good.

Shared-cost arrangements between Ottawa and the provinces for joint provision of public goods may easily lead to inefficient overall amounts of such goods. Each level of government tends to regard the cost of shared-cost program in terms of its own outlay; no decision-making body oversees the total expenditure. This will generally lead to the over-provision of a shared cost good or service, the distorting effects of which may partly be the underprovision of other provincial-public or federal-public goods. If there were only one body responsible for and paying for the regional provision of highways or medicare, it is possible that, with unchanged government expenditure in total, outlays on these items would decrease and more resources would be devoted to the public support of, for example, education, research activities or housing. With the partial vision of shared-cost programmes eliminated, this allocation of resources would necessarily be more desirable.

The argument that shared-cost programs are desirable because they help establish various services at levels considered appropriate by the federal government is really an argument for the outright federal provision of the service. Such shared-cost programmes influence the marginal or last dollar spent by the provinces, and not only, if at all, the initial dollars spent. It follows that the federal government is encouraging spending right up to the total level of service ultimately provided. If this is desirable, it clearly is even more desirable that the provinces leave the field to the federal government alone. The establishment of regulations imposing on the provinces a minimum level of service is a slightly different matter and may be defended on paternalistic grounds, about which I comment below.

An independent argument may be made for the federal provision of public insurance schemes such as unemployment insurance, old-age pensions, workmen's compensation, medicare provisions (if this is treated as an insurance scheme) and so on. If payments and benefits are uniform throughout the country, people can move more easily from province to province, and such freedom of movement is a desirable component of nationhood.

Aside from the economic aspects of the issue, there are other substantive points to be considered in a discussion of the distribution of spending responsibilities. These I raise and comment on very briefly just to show my own biases and not because I feel that they can be dealt with adequately in a few paragraphs.

In considering federal versus provincial responsibilities I generally disagree with centralizing arguments based on grounds of paternalism ("Ottawa knows best") or administrative efficiency. There seems little reason to suppose that the federal government can judge better than the provinces the nature and level of provincial-public services that provincial residents want. In considering the possibility that some governments might be more astute or effective in providing public services, Professor J. S. Dupré has suggested, as an example, that provincial discrepancies in the level of youth-allowance payments and loans to university students "are not likely to be tolerated" by provincial residents.[5] Not only are safeguards of this sort likely to exist if a maximum degree of decentralization occurred but also a wider range of public services would probably be introduced, perhaps in single provinces at first and then more widely if they appeared to be successful and desirable. I find it hard to believe that the central government would have more imagination and initiative than the ten provincial governments combined. If cross-Canada homogeneity in public services is what is desired, Professor D. V. Smiley offers reassurances here. With the decentralization of responsibilities, he argues that "as elites concerned with particular public amenities become more influential, the expectations throughout that society

[5]*Report of the 1964 Conference*, Canadian Tax Foundation, Toronto 1965, p. 214.

about the appropriate levels of particular public services will become more homogeneous".[6]

When it comes right down to the question whether or not the provincial civil servants or politicians are sufficiently competent to handle increased fiscal responsibilities, it seems to me that one cannot settle the question by pointing to past inefficiencies or incompetences. In any case the past record, especially in recent years in fields such as economic planning, is not by any means biased in favour of the federal government. The presumption for the future surely must be that the brilliant civil servant and the enlightened politician will go where the power lies.

Bases of administrative efficiency or paternalism as support for provincial control of municipal-public goods, such as welfare services and educational facilities, are, I think, much stronger. In a small municipality particularly, there may well be major gaps in representation on governing bodies; and this gap may be sufficient to require some paternalistic overseeing. I see no harm in being arbitrary in this matter,[7] in pushing, within limits, for decentralization down to the provincial level and centralization up from the municipal level.

Arguments for federal control in certain fields based on the ground of national unity leave me unconvinced, mainly because I fail to understand the meaning of the ground. Such arguments frequently seem to be no more than definitional declarations: "if Quebec takes sole responsibility for these spending fields, national unity as we know it, will not survive". This is not a direct quotation from any person, but I think it captures the essence of a lot of talk; and it clearly does not provide us with any insights into the problem.

Unwavering devotion to the letter of the constitution does not really form a rallying point for discussions of spending responsibilities. On these responsibilities, the constitution provides for divisions on such general grounds, and leaves so much open for negotiation, that there is little support on which to hang an argument. But when notions of provincial financial independence and financial responsibility[8] are combined with fixed concepts, derived only partly from the constitution, about the division of revenue-raising rights between federal and provincial governments, they lead automatically to a stance on the division of spending responsibilities; there are simply no residual degrees of freedom. It is clear that independent positions cannot be taken on both spending responsibilities and taxing rights within a framework of fiscal responsibility. If taxing rights are believed to be fixed, this determines within limits the revenue-raising powers of the various levels of government and this in turn leads to the view that the provinces, to take the current example, cannot undertake more spending, except through federal grants, because they do not have the revenue-raising capacity.

Some form of fiscal responsibility certainly should be imposed on the provinces. Although the desire for provincial income redistribution and for full-

---

[6]*Ibid.*, p. 221.

[7]Aside from the merits of this case, being arbitrary is a convenient way to delay the day when one is computer-programmed out of a job.

[8]These terms are used by R. Dehem and J. N. Wolfe in "The Principles of Federal Finance and the Canadian Case", *Canadian Journal of Economics and Political Science*, Vol. XXI, February 1955. The limits within which financial or fiscal responsibility might operate are commented on in the next paragraph.

employment policies provides reasons why a provincial dollar spent need not be matched by a provincial dollar raised, each province should be faced with the full opportunity cost of providing additional public goods or services; i.e. the resources used for providing them should be provincial except when the province raises outside loans or receives grants from the federal government that are intended to redistribute provincial income. But to achieve an efficient allocation of resources, it is vital, I believe, not to assign taxing rights until after spending responsibilities have been decided upon, and even then the taxing arrangements should be flexible enough to leave the provincial and federal governments freedom to decide the levels at which they should exercise their respective spending responsibilities. Tax rental agreements result in unnecessary revenue rigidity; the 1962-67 federal-provincial fiscal arrangements provide a desirable departure from previous postwar agreements. The present tendency in Ottawa to try to come to some agreed division of the income-tax revenue between the federal and provincial governments is similarly undesirable. Ottawa's view that this division is related to the amount of control it can exercise over aggregate demand seems to me unfounded, since this control operates through absolute changes in revenue and spending and it makes no difference whether a given absolute change in spending or in taxes is eight per cent, say, rather than five per cent of the total federal-government revenue.

Income Transfers, Resource Allocation and Economic Growth

Income redistribution between governments must be set by a higher-level government. It follows from the arguments of the previous section that if an efficient use of resources is to be made, transfers of money among the provinces should be in the form of unconditional grants; but of course this is not the only form of provincial income redistribution. Much federal-government spending has a differential regional impact and to this extent is also a redistributive device. Such redistributive spending is not inefficient, but I have argued that it should not be undertaken except on federal-public goods or services.

Under most circumstances it is generally agreed that lump-sum income transfers among individuals do not result in an inefficient resource allocation. But where the transfers are among regional governments, the possible inter-regional migration of factors of production such as capital or labour may lead to overall national inefficiency in the allocation of these factors. The question then arises, do attempts on the part of the federal government to equalize provincial incomes necessarily result in such inefficiency?

Professor Anthony Scott, in what turned into a debate with Professor James M. Buchanan,[9] argued that income transfers from the rich to the poor provinces

---

[9]See A. D. Scott's articles "A Note on Grants in Federal Countries", *Economica*, Vol. XVII, November 1950; "The Evaluation of Federal Grants", *Economica*, Vol. XIX, November 1952; and "Federal Grants and Resource Allocation", *Journal of Political Economy*, Vol. LX, December 1952; and J. M. Buchanan's "Federalism and Fiscal Equity", *American Economic Review*, Vol. XL, September 1950; and "Federal Grants and Resource Allocation", *Journal of Political Economy*, Vol. LX, June 1952. John F. Graham in his book *Fiscal Adjustment and Economic Development*, University of Toronto Press, Toronto, 1963, deals with this controversy at some length.

in Canada impeded the movement of factors from areas of low marginal productivity, such as the Maritimes, to areas of high marginal productivity, such as Ontario. Buchanan argued that efficiency in resource allocation was best achieved by providing in all areas the same "fiscal residual" which he defined as benefits received as a result of public spending less tax costs incurred. The fiscal residual is clearly a rather hazy concept, but in broad outline I agree with Buchanan's position, even though dissenters have recently forced him to backtrack somewhat.[10]

The argument against Scott is this. Factors of production, men and capital, move from region to region in response to the prospect of greater total benefits or income. This income consists of two parts: money returns to the factor, which are assumed to bear some relation to marginal productivity, and services or goods provided by the public sector. To the extent that a rich region can provide higher levels of public goods relative to tax costs, resources are drawn to the region independently of marginal productivity criteria. Since efficiency in the allocation of resources requires factors to be used where their marginal productivity is highest, different provincial levels of the fiscal residual may encourage inefficient inter-provincial allocation. Therefore our desire for an efficient allocation of resources would lend support to transfers designed to equalize provincial revenues, quite aside from the fact that some degree of equalization is likely to be a federal goal in any case. The same argument may be used to support inter-municipal income transfers by the provincial governments. The tendency of industry to locate in rich urban areas, where the level of public services relative to tax costs is high, may result in inefficiencies (heightened by the many external dis-economies to an overcrowded community of having industry locate in it) that could be overcome by subsidies to poorer or smaller municipalities, with such subsidies being used either to increase the level of public services or to reduce the local tax rate.

Scott's argument has considerable currency, however, and for this reason it should be looked at more carefully. He begins with the implicit assumption that we know beforehand the desirable direction for factors to move, i.e., the direction that will lead to a more efficient allocation. Implicit in the argument of Buchanan is that we do not know this. At first glance, this latter position might seem untenable; surely it is obvious that marginal products are higher in Ontario than in the Maritimes, and that, at the very least, Ontario and not the Maritimes should form the major Canadian growth area. Frequently such a view is based on one or both of two propositions: that the regions most rich in natural resources are those that can most efficiently employ additional factors of production (this roughly is Scott's contention) or that economies of scale in production exist, and resources should therefore be channeled to established and relatively large industrial areas. The validity of the first proposition depends, first, on the relationship between the natural-resource endowment and the current use of other productive factors (a natural-resource-poor area might have a relative capital shortage, for example) and, second, on the nature of the industry under consideration. That all growth is related to natural-resource endowment

---

[10]See his comments in *Public Finance: Needs, Sources and Utilization*, National Bureau of Economic Research, Princeton University Press, Princeton, N.J., 1961.

is a position of geographical determinism that, unfortunately, comes easily to Canadians bred on the staple theory of economic growth. In fact, the production of natural resources is a notoriously bad indicator of economic maturity; the *consumption* of natural resources is a good indicator, but an area can consume such resources without producing them. The second proposition, that relating to economies of scale, is, in its baldest form, generally founded on a misunderstanding. If such economies exist this does not constitute a basis for recommending the transfer of resources from small producing units to large. To say that economies of scale exist is only to say that *average* unit costs will fall with an increase in output. For any industry, even when different firms in different locations use the same technology, the smaller firm might have lower *marginal* costs and efficiency might therefore be enhanced by moving resources from larger to smaller units.

These points strengthen the case for, or at least weaken the arguments against, increasing inter-provincial equalization payments above current levels. Until the 1962-67 federal-provincial tax agreement, equalizing transfers were made on the basis of provincial per capita revenues that would result from the application of a standard tax rate on personal income, on corporation profits and on inheritances. Under the current arrangement there is a belated, halfhearted recognition that other sources of revenue should be taken into account: 50 per cent of the per capita three-year average of revenues from natural resources are now counted in deciding the level of equalization payments. A backward step was also taken, however, in that these payments are now made on the basis of the average per capita yield for all provinces rather than on the basis of the per capita yield of the richest two. The importance of natural-resource levies for some provinces is shown in data compiled by Marion Bryden in a recent Canadian Tax Foundation study: for the year 1963, 29.4 per cent of Alberta's revenues (excluding intergovernmental transfers) came from these levies, as did 10.1 per cent of Saskatchewan's revenues and 12.5 per cent of British Columbia's revenues. The Canadian average was 6.6 per cent. Small taxing bases force poorer provinces into higher levels of regressive consumption taxes. Across Canada, provinces in 1963 raised 28.7 per cent of their revenue from consumption taxes; in Newfoundland the percentage was 58.6; in Prince Edward Island, 47.8; in Nova Scotia, 41.1; and in New Brunswick, 39.2

As well, the poorer provinces should, I think, be concerned about the drain of savings to richer, more developed regions. It is difficult to pin down a case for concern about this movement and easy to say that it indicates a gratifying mobility of funds in search of higher returns. Studies of the availability of capital in the Atlantic Provinces have concluded that it is not, in general more difficult for any given class of borrower to obtain funds in that area than in other provinces, and these findings have tended to produce some complacency. But the wider issue is not whether current borrowers can obtain funds, but whether steps should be taken to encourage greater entrepreneurial initiative, and hence an even greater demand for capital, in some of these areas.

I have already indicated some reasons why an outward flow of capital is not necessarily an efficient response to marginal productivity differentials. Given the conservative nature of the institutions through which these funds are channeled, (and I am thinking now especially of life insurance companies and the chartered banks), one might present an even stronger case for suggesting that more risk capital should be directed to the less well developed provinces.

I would not, however, press these arguments to include income-equalization payments to all sub-provincial underdeveloped regions. The provinces provide a useful arbitrary geographic area within which attempts might be made (by the provinces) to reallocate resources in what was considered to be an efficient manner. Federal operations on resource allocation among sub-provincial units leave me most unimpressed. The subsidies provided to coal producers in Cape Breton and gold producers in Northern Ontario have been nothing short of ridiculous. It is not clear that expenditures on ARDA and other federal regional redevelopment schemes are in the overall interest of the provinces in which such expenditures are made. Recently, officials from 35 Western Ontario municipalities protested, with justification, that the federal-government designated-area scheme discriminated against their communities by not including them. In this federal scheme, 81 areas were designated on the bases of unemployment figures and average income levels as qualifying for grants and tax concessions. If the money for these projects was available to the provincial governments, those governments could spend it in accordance with some pre-planned design for provincial growth and we might see the end of indiscriminate support of areas with little long-run economic potential. My general position is that grants to bolster low-growth or low-income areas should be made on a provincial basis in the form of equalization or special non-tied transfers, and that incentive resource mobilization should be planned by the provinces on an intra-provincial basis.

Income Stabilization

In both the United States and Canada the bald, unadorned view that the federal government alone is responsible for counteracting cyclical income fluctuations seems to meet with little argument. As long as this is the general attitude, the provincial governments are unlikely to press for greater responsibilities in this matter because to assume them is rather invidious in an era when the desire to stamp out price increases weighs more heavily than the desire to eliminate unemployment, which means that tax increases will appear to play a larger role in government policy than tax cuts. Indeed, complete federal responsibility might be justified if unemployment and income levels across Canada moved together, if full employment in one area was matched by full employment in all other areas and if federal action had an equal impact in all areas.

It appears to be the case, however, that a regionally differentiated fiscal policy is frequently required. If industrial employment is taken as a current indicator of provincial business cycles (no better indicator is available at the provincial level), it may be seen that between provinces the provincial cycles are frequently out-of-phase. Moreover, it is well known that even where provincial cycles are in-phase, the unemployment level may vary greatly between the provinces. Because Ontario is so large and so rich, the situation prevailing there dominates the aggregate Canadian data on which federal economic decisions are based.

This is hardly a desirable situation for the Atlantic Provinces this year, Quebec that year or the Prairie Provinces some other year; it is a situation that strongly suggests that the provinces should take over from the federal government a large measure of the responsibility for contracyclical policies.

If provincial responsibility in this regard were strengthened, at least one desirable side benefit might accrue. Of the eleven governments acting to stabilize income and employment, at least one might recognize what Ottawa seems to neglect, that in the interest of efficiency in resource allocation it is primarily, if not entirely, taxation levels and not government-spending levels that should be altered. If a government takes a stand, in some period with full employment, on the appropriate levels at which government goods and services should be provided then it is inappropriate to alter these in order to fend off inflation or deflation.[11] Instead, taxation levels should be increased or decreased, the idea being that if the government is successful in its policy the desirable or previously determined distribution of output between the public and the private sectors will be achieved. If a decision is made to cut government expenditure when inflation is anticipated or add to government expenditure when a falling off of economic activity is expected, the result is too little or too much government participation in the economy. The argument also applies to situations where the economy is inflated or deflated, but then the overriding desire to get back to some appropriate level of aggregate demand may warrant a contracyclical alteration in government spending.

Although my remarks have related to fiscal policy, there is no reason why provincial governments should not be encouraged to pursue an active monetary policy as well. To this end the provinces should have access to the Bank of Canada. The flexibility of provincial-government economic policy would be enhanced if they were permitted to engage, where the central bank deemed is was warranted, in a bit of inflationary financing.

It should be made clear that while I am pushing for a far greater degree of autonomy for the provinces in the taxation field, I recognize that it is necessary for the rate of progressive taxation to be generally uniform throughout Canada. Progressive taxation is a device for the redistribution of personal income and if it initially differed significantly from province to province there would be a tendency for the tax structure of all provinces to be pulled down to the structure of the least progressive; otherwise the high income earners would tend to leave the provinces with the most progressive tax structures. A similarity in tax structure would not imply that tax rates for any given income level would be equal; these could still vary, but their variation would be related to the degrees of government spending.

---

[11] I suspect that an alteration in the level of government spending is popular partly because generations of policy advisors have been brought up and continue to be brought up on textbooks of elementary economics that lay great stress on the demonstration that the multiplier effect of a dollar of government spending is greater than the multiplier effect of a dollar change in tax revenues.

33 Revenue-Sharing Between Federal and Provincial Governments*

A. J. Robinson

One of the dilemmas in the federal system arises out of the disparity between the constitutional and political responsibilities of governments and their revenue-raising capacities. The federal government derives the bulk of its revenue from personal and corporate income taxes, and the progressive rate structure of these taxes ensures that so long as national income grows, revenues from these taxes will increase at a faster rate. The provinces and municipalities, however, which bear the burden of basic government services such as health, education, transportation and communications, and protection of persons and property, have less elastic revenue sources, the main ones being sales taxes, property taxes, licence fees and profits from liquor sales. Their revenue from autonomous sources increases more slowly than national income, and certainly much more slowly than the income-elastic demands for government services in modern society.

The consequence of this disparity in revenues and responsibilities has been that the provinces have had to seek funds from the federal government. On the one hand, this has been said to encourage fiscal irresponsibility among provincial politicians, since they are enabled to freely spend funds in the collection of which they have made no effort and have not incurred the odium which it is presumed attaches to political parties which increase taxes. On the other hand, the dependence of provincial treasuries upon federal handouts may undermine that sovereignty of the provinces which is vital to the federal system of government. It is certainly the case that conditional grants from the federal government to the provinces do inhibit provincial sovereignty to some extent, because each province has to distribute its funds according to federal rather than provincial priorities; for example, a province might have to devote resources to the construction of interprovincial highways because that is the sector for which funds are available, even though the provincial government might regard slums and water pollution in the cities as a more urgent social problem. "The essence of federalism", in the words of W. A. Mackintosh,[1] "is [its] provision for diversity without disunion . . . . In the smaller compartments of the state or provinces, it is possible to achieve a greater homogeneity of legislators and executives than is possible in the larger union." This "diversity in tastes among residents of different states and local communities and differences in resources undoubtedly leads to wide differences in priority orderings within the public sectors of these jurisdictions. Additional grants-in-aid tend, however, to require conformity to a uniform standard, a conformity that is inconsistent with meaningful consumer sovereignty as the determining force in decisions

---

*Not previously published.

[1]W. A. Mackintosh, "Federal Finance", in G. Sawer (ed.), *Federalism: An Australian Jubilee Study*, F. W. Cheshire, Melbourne, 1952.

about the allocation of resources in the public sector and between the private and public sectors of the economy."[2]

A recent proposal to increase the revenue of the states and provinces of a federation without undermining their autonomy in expenditure decisions is revenue-sharing, better known as the "Heller Plan" because its chief advocate has been Professor Walter W. Heller, Chairman of the Council of Economic Advisors under Presidents Kennedy and Johnson.

The essence of the plan is that it "would distribute a specified portion of the Federal individual income tax to the states each year on a per capita basis, with next to no strings attached. This distribution would be over and above existing and future conditional grants. The Federal government would each year set aside and distribute to the states 1 to 2 percent of the Federal individual income tax base (the amount reported as net taxable income by all individuals)."[3]

Heller links the states' share to the income tax *base* rather than to federal income tax revenues, firstly because taxable income is more stable than revenues, and, secondly, because it would be independent of the level and structure of federal income tax rates, and would not interfere with federal fiscal policy. The revenues collected would be placed in a trust fund, which would be shared periodically among the states on the basis of population.[4] The larger states would get more than the smaller states in total, but because the given per capita sum derived from the nation as a whole would be a larger proportion of per capita income in the poorer states than it would be in the richer, there would be a transfer of funds from high to low-income states.

The virtue of the plan, according to Heller, is its simplicity: "its provision of a large and automatically growing source of revenue to the states; the freedom of movement it offers the states; the consequent relief from gradual hardening of the categories under the conditional grants program; and its contribution to the vitality and self-determination that will make the states stronger partners in our federalism. Its supporters also cite the equalizing fiscal effects of the revenue-sharing plan and its effectiveness in maintaining a progressive distribution of Federal-State-local fiscal burdens."[5]

There have been major and minor criticisms of the plan. The minor criticisms relate to whether expenditure of funds should be wholly or mainly unconditional — Heller, for example, believes that civil rights conditions should be attached to the funds, and he apparently would not oppose restriction of the use of funds in a broad sense, say to education, health, welfare and community development programmes. Other minor points are whether it should be 1 or 2 or some larger percentage of the income tax base, and whether some incentive should be given to states to increase their own fiscal effort.

The major criticisms of the plan come from those who really are opposed

---

[2]Harvey E. Brazer, "The Federal Government and State-Local Finances", *National Tax Journal*, Vol. XX, No. 2, June 1967, p. 160.

[3]Walter W. Heller, *New Dimensions of Political Economy*, Norton, New York, 1967, p. 145.

[4]*Ibid.*, pp. 146-147.

[5]*Ibid.*, p. 148.

to the continuation of the federal system itself. As Pechman has noted, "reaction to such general purpose grants depends largely on attitudes toward the relations between the federal and state governments. They are opposed by those who wish to control the use of federal funds in great detail, who have little faith in the willingness or ability of state governments to use the funds wisely, and who believe that general purpose grants will weaken the role of conditional grants. They are supported by those who wish to strengthen the role of the state governments and to limit federal control over state-local spending, and who believe that conditional grants are already overworked in the federal system. Some oppose the expansion of federal assistance either in the form of conditional or general purpose grants, on the ground that separation of the expenditure and financing functions will lead to excessive and wasteful expenditures. However, in a tax system which restricts state and local governments to the lease desirable and responsive tax sources, a general purpose federal grant makes sense as a supplement to conditional grants."[6] Brazer also regards "the block grant, along lines suggested by the 'Heller Plan,' [as] a most promising device ... for improving the general fiscal capacity of the states, for equalizing that capacity, and for reducing the disparity among the states in the tax load imposed on similarly circumstanced residents per dollar of public expenditures."[7]

It has not been the purpose of this note to make any recommendations or even suggestions regarding the application of the Heller revenue-sharing formula to federal-provincial financial relations in Canada. However, it is interesting to observe that, on the basis of 1965 Canadian data, 1 per cent of the federal income tax base would be about $14 per capita, and redistribution of this amount would increase provincial revenues by about 6 per cent. Heller's proposal was to redistribute one or two per cent of the income tax base, and as Brazer pointed out, this figure could be raised to 3 per cent or 4 per cent or any other percentage, with corresponding increases in the importance of a redistribution in provincial budgets.

---

[6]Joseph A. Pechman, *Federal Tax Policy*, The Brookings Institution, Washington, D.C., 1966, pp. 229-230.

[7]Brazer, *op. cit.*, p. 164.

Chapter Four
Taxation in Canada

Taxation is the primary mode of financing government expenditures in Canada. This chapter examines the tax system at the federal and provincial levels of government; a subsequent chapter examines taxation at the municipal level.

The federal tax system in Canada has not evolved in a systematic or planned manner. Rather it has emerged in response to a series of historical crises of one sort or another, particularly the depression of the 1930's and the two World Wars. Almost all the existing federal taxes appeared first in the statute books during the turmoil of World War I, scarcely the optimal moment for rational appraisal of the structure of the various measures and their long-run implications.

Most of the basic conceptions were simply borrowed from other countries. The possibility of reform toward the end of the 1920's disappeared with the economic crisis of the early 1930's and the useful suggestions of the Rowell-Sirois Commission were lost in the chaos of World War II. Consideration of some of the basic issues in the tax system at the end of the 1940's was submerged in the exigencies of the Korean War. Since then, the increasing demands of the provinces, and the problem of financing rapidly increasing federal expenditures on social welfare, have subordinated examination of the structure of the tax system to the immediate priority of increasing revenue. Of the existing federal tax system, one of the members of the Royal Commission on Taxation had this to say:

> . . . our federal taxation hastily thrown together at its origin, was subject to its greatest changes during periods of national stress, . . . the alterations made in these conditions were on a purely pragmatic basis and tended to persist once the crisis had passed, and . . . never yet has there been a thorough examination of its underlying objectives and philosophy. For half a century we have gone along on a hand-to-mouth basis that has produced each year more problems than it has ever solved. . . . Only by establishing some basic underlying principles on which to build a solid structure is there any escape from ultimate complete frustration.[1]

Faced with relatively elastic expenditure commitments, particularly on education,

---

[1] J. Harvey Perry, "The Anatomy of a Tax System", *1967 November Conference of the Canadian Tax Foundation*, pp. 7-35.

and relatively inelastic revenue sources, the attention of the provinces in the post-World War II period has been primarily directed to increasing tax revenue rather than to reforming tax systems.

In the 1960's the long-postponed thorough appraisal of the federal and several of the provincial tax systems was carried out and published in a series of Royal Commission Reports. Of particular significance, of course, is the Carter Commission Report on the federal tax system. It remains to be seen whether the recommendations of the various Commissions will be implemented. The fact remains that a vast new fund of analysis of taxation in Canada is now available, and it seems appropriate to bring together a group of readings which reflect the old system, if system it may be called, and the new proposals.

The first selection in this chapter supplements the previous examination of policy objectives by setting out the associated principles of taxation, which must be taken into account in addition to the basic tax objectives in the formulation of an appropriate tax mix and the implementation of tax policy.

The second selection is the most recent examination of the incidence of taxation in Canada. Using data for 1961, the selection used is more contemporary, and also more comprehensive, than the earlier study by Irving Goffman.[2]

The first general part of the chapter is completed by two selections which set out the major taxes at the federal and provincial levels. Both selections are from the excellent annual summaries published by the Canadian Tax Foundation.

The remaining selections cover particular forms of taxation. The personal income tax is examined first, under the heads of the definition of income, the inclusion of capital gains, the unit of taxation, the rate structure, and income averaging. The corporation income tax is examined next, emphasis being directed to the question of its integration with the personal income tax. The neglected issue of taxes on testamentary and *inter vivos* transfers at the federal and provincial levels follows. Particularly interesting here are the different approaches taken by the federal and provincial tax Commissions. The section on taxes on commodities and services examines the present structure and proposals for reform of the Manufacturers' Sales Tax and the various provincial sales taxes. Finally, some relatively novel tax devices — the Turnover Tax, the Value-Added Tax, the Negative Income Tax, and Selective Employment Tax — are briefly examined.

The Principles of Taxation

It is more fashionable these days to discuss "objectives of taxation" than "principles of taxation". The Carter Commission accordingly framed its consideration of the federal tax system in terms of objectives. Although, on balance, such a "functional" approach to taxation is clearly superior, a group of eminently desirable tax principles tend to be disregarded in the process. It is one of the services of the Smith Committee on taxation in Ontario that it drew attention to these tax principles. After a detailed consideration of the paramount principle of equity, the Report proceeded to an examination of "Other Principles of Taxation".

---

[2]I. J. Goffman, "Incidence of Taxation in Canada", *Public Finance*, Vol. XIX, 1964, pp. 44-67.

34 Other Principles of Taxation *

The Ontario Committee on Taxation

Equity is the prime, but by no means the sole, characteristic of a good tax system. After due consideration, we have selected no fewer than nine principles which, together with equity, should form the basis of a sound revenue structure. Some of these are derived from considerations of equity, others are prompted by the need for efficiency. We enumerate them here for the sake of convenience and will proceed to discuss them in turn. They are:

1. adequacy
2. flexibility
3. elasticity
4. balance
5. neutrality
6. certainty
7. simplicity
8. convenience
9. economy of collection and compliance.

Adequacy

This principle requires virtually no explanation. It is a self-evident proposition that to be satisfactory, a tax system must be capable of providing the flow of funds that a government deems appropriate in any given period. We note, however, that the principle of adequacy can become highly relevant when the relative merits of grants and taxes are discussed in connection with provincial and municipal revenue systems.

Flexibility

By flexibility is meant that a tax system should be so constituted that government, by discretionary action, can readily increase or decrease the flow of tax funds in response to changing circumstances, which can stem either from considerations of expenditure requirements or of economic policy. Obviously, some taxes, such as those on property and on personal income, are more flexible than others, in that rate alterations can be graded so as to accommodate small as well as large changes in revenue requirements. The principle of flexibility can thus be deemed to be satisfied if a revenue system is comprised in part of flexible taxes.

Elasticity

The principle of elasticity is closely related to those of adequacy and flexibility. This principle requires that a revenue system be composed in part of

---

*Reprinted by permission from the Ontario Committee on Taxation, *Report*, Queen's Printer, Toronto, 1967.

161

taxes whose yields respond closely to changing economic circumstances without deliberate changes in rates. It is important that the principle be fulfilled for two reasons. First, elasticity enables governments to meet rising service demands occasioned by economic growth without the disturbance of frequent rate changes. Second, elastic tax yields are an important adjunct of fiscal policy in that they can serve as automatic stabilizers, leaving a greater proportion of income in the private sector in times of adversity and dampening inflationary pressures in times of prosperity.

Balance

This principle is to be found in certain textbooks under such names as "multiplicity" or "plurality", but we have chosen the term "balance" in order to emphasize the kind of plurality that a tax system should possess. The need for a balanced plurality of taxes is grounded partly in the requirements of flexibility and elasticity, partly in equity, and partly in administrative considerations. As to flexibility and elasticity, it is readily apparent that some taxes are more flexible, others more elastic. Thus the property tax is relatively unresponsive to economic change but highly flexible, whereas consumption taxes are rather more elastic but relatively inflexible. A tax system should therefore have a sufficient multiplicity of taxes to take account of these characteristics. In the domain of equity, if a tax system is to conform to the basic rule of equal treatment of equals, it must not only be able to take differing individual situations into account but also be virtually foolproof in terms of evasion.

Multiplicity, then, is an important key to elasticity, flexibility and equity. But it is not an end in itself. For one thing, the number of taxes that reflect elasticity, flexibility and equity is limited. Too great a multiplicity of taxes may dissipate altogether tax payer consciousness of the cost of government, consciousness that is certainly desirable in a constitutional democracy. Thus we subscribe only to that multiplicity of taxes consistent with flexibility, elasticity, equity and sound administration — in short, to a principle of balance.

Neutrality

The principle of neutrality is directly related to the objective of efficiency in the use of the human and material resources of society. We do not suggest that, in order to be neutral, a fiscal system must exert no influence on the economic behaviour of persons or businesses. When the fiscal operations of all levels of government in Canada involve, as they do, almost one-third of gross national product, it is clear that no such thing is possible. Our approach to neutrality is rather in terms of applying the rule of least price distortion in the choice of taxes. If one assumes that the pattern of relative prices determined by competitive market forces tends to encourage the most efficient allocation of the nation's resources, then to the extent that a tax system minimizes its distortion of relative prices, it minimizes its interference with productive efficiency. An important implication follows, namely that the more general a tax, the less it will normally interfere with individual choices on the part of producers, resource owners and consumers. From this point of view, such general taxes as those on income and retail sales are to be preferred to selective excise taxes applied to a narrow range of commodities.

Understood in terms of least price distortion, the principle of neutrality is violated if consumers are taxed on their expenditures for goods but not for services. The principle is likewise violated if governments provide tax concessions in order to induce particular firms or industries to locate in areas where, in terms of the most efficient use of resources, they would not otherwise go. In its broad context, however, the efficient use of resources involves not only the private costs incurred by a firm but also the social costs arising from its operation in a particular location. Again, neutrality will be violated where the revenue system imposes heavier taxes on some legal forms of business organization than on others. To be neutral, the tax system should provide similar treatment for individual proprietors, partnerships, co-operatives and all forms of corporate enterprise.

We do not wish to argue that neutrality is a principle of taxation that should be followed under any and all circumstances. It is appropriate only when economic efficiency is a prime criterion of policy. On frequent occasions, governments are legitimately more concerned with other goals and will consciously depart from neutrality in order to further these objectives. What should be recognized, however, is that where tax neutrality is abandoned, the efficient allocation of resources, in the short run at least, will be impeded.

Certainty

The principle of certainty as to the time, manner and amount of payment of tax has been advocated for centuries. Adam Smith regarded a small degree of uncertainty as a much greater evil than "a very considerable degree of inequality", in that it subjected the taxpayer to the arbitrary decisions of the authorities. A further argument for certainty is the desirability, in an era of high government expenditure, that the citizen be well informed of his tax burden so that he may relate it to the benefits he derives from public services. If the individual is not well informed, he may make decisions about government spending that might have been different had he been aware of the facts. A particular risk is that being only dimly aware of his total tax burden, he will underestimate the cost of the public services with which he is provided. This is particularly likely where many of his taxes are hidden in the prices of the goods and services he purchases, rather than imposed upon him directly.

If the principle of certainty is valid, and we believe that it is, then those direct taxes that cannot be shifted, or that can be shifted only to a limited degree, are superior to any taxes that can be hidden or easily shifted. On this basis, the personal income tax is superior to corporation income tax which sooner or later must be borne by individuals as consumers, shareholders or employees. Similarly, a visible retail sales tax is superior to a consumption tax levied at the manufacturer's level. Again, as it affects the relative merits of subsidies or tax concessions as forms of government financial assistance, the principle of certainty favours subsidies, for their costs are more readily ascertainable to government and public alike than are the costs of tax concessions or exemptions.

Finally, the principle of certainty should apply with force to the content of tax statutes. At the very least, no tax law should be written in such a way that it contains provisions that the government either cannot or will not enforce effectively.

Simplicity

We wish to comment only briefly on the relation between certainty and simplicity. The principle of simplicity will lend strong support to certainty provided it is applied with care. The point is, of course, that indiscriminate striving for simplicity will yield statutes that leave too much unsaid and hence that can only be applied with a wide scope for administrative discretion — discretion that will unduly impinge on certainty. Again, undue simplicity may make it impossible to recognize the varying circumstances of particular taxpayers. Hence the principle of simplicity must be considered as dictating the greatest charity within the limits set by certainty and equity.

Convenience

The principle of convenience is highly significant in relation to the time, place and manner in which a taxpayer is called upon to discharge his obligations. It is in accordance with this principle that municipalities have developed instalment systems for the payment of property taxes and have, in some instances, permitted payment through chartered banks and other specified places of business. The principle of convenience is not simply a matter of good public relations. Observance of this principle redounds to the direct advantage of government by simplifying compliance and by reducing costs. With regard to the latter, there can be no doubt that the deduction of income tax at the source, a practice introduced by the Dominion during World War II, has greatly simplified government fiscal operations by increasing the speed of cash flows and hence reducing the need for short-term borrowing.

Economy of Collection and Compliance

The principle of economy applies both to the costs incurred by government in collecting taxes and to those incurred by the taxpayer in complying with his tax obligations. The principle of economy, especially in relation to the costs incurred by government, dictates not the lowest possible cost but the lowest cost consistent with equity and effective enforcement. Thus it is blatantly false economy for governments to employ unqualified assessors at rock-bottom rates of remuneration. Such practices can result only in inefficiency, discrimination, and multiplying appeals and hence increasing the cost of taxpayer compliance. Properly understood, the principle of economy requires the employment of competent public servants in sufficient numbers.

Conflicts of Tax Principles

It is the better part of wisdom to recognize that among the many tax principles that we have outlined there exist numerous occasions for conflict. Decisions concerning the most appropriate mix of taxes will accordingly require some consensus as to which principles should be given priority, a consensus that even among responsible and reasonable people may be difficult to formulate. Thus thorny problems may arise because of differing interpretations of the principle of ability to pay, or because this principle conflicts with benefits received or with neutrality or with simplicity or with economy of collection and compliance. Then too, it may be that convenience or the reasonable opportunity to appeal — an essential aspect of equity — conflicts with economy. Whatever the nature of the conflict, we wish to stress that among all the principles that we have discussed, those relating to equity are of fundamental importance in the formulation of tax policy. This is by no means to deny that in specific circumstances equity may legitimately be subordinated to other principles, but where such is argued, we place the burden of proof squarely on the proponents of the case.

Tax Principles and Social Policy

We wish to close this [section] by noting that there will be instances where certain tax practices depart from principles not because of conflict between the principles but because certain generally accepted goals of social policy are held to override the principles. To cite but three well-known examples, let us briefly examine the tax treatment of alcohol and tobacco, the exemption of churches and charitable organizations from property tax, and tax discrimination based on location.

In all countries whose revenue systems we have studied, alcohol and tobacco are taxed more heavily than other foods and beverages. This is a violation of the principle of neutrality, sanctioned historically in part by the widespread belief that such commodities are luxuries whose consumption, within limits, should be discouraged. We are not convinced that many governments have seriously sought to attain sumptuary objectives of this kind by taxation, or that where they have, the pricing mechanism represents the most appropriate or effective means of achieving these objectives. Stronger justification for the relatively high taxation of these products undoubtedly rests on the fact that their heavy consumption by many individuals imposes substantial costs on society. But the very high taxation of alcohol and tobacco in many jurisdictions must ultimately rest on social policy and consensus.

The exemption of churches and charitable organizations from real property taxes — a common practice in Canada, the United States and other countries — violates the principles of benefits received, equal treatment of equals, and neutrality. The social policy underlying such exemptions and other preferential treatment may be defended in terms of the valuable contributions that these institutions make to their supporters and to society generally, and because of the difficulty of providing support for churches through direct subsidy.

Social policy frequently finds expression in tax discrimination on the basis of the location of the taxpayer. Such discrimination clearly violates the principles of equal treatment of equals. Among the areas of discrimination that have come to our attention are provincial and municipal tax concessions offered to induce firms to select a particular location.

That social policy may from time to time override the principles of taxation is a fact of life. And it can be argued that in a democratic setting, social policy based on a deep-seated popular consensus should have priority over principles in that it represents the will of the people. The danger of this argument, however, is that if pushed too far, it sanctions indiscriminate trampling on the principles of taxation and hence invites revenue-raising by caprice, which is hardly compatible with constitutional democracy.

The Incidence of Taxation

A meaningful concept of incidence must clearly refer to the incidence of budget policy as a whole — in other words, must examine the distribution of tax burden on the one hand, and the distribution of expenditure benefits on the other. The result may be referred to as "budget incidence", or "net fiscal incidence".

The incidence of government expenditures is examined elsewhere in this study. The following extract is from the most recent examination of the incidence of taxation in Canada. The income base chosen for the study is referred to as "broad income" and includes money income, such as wages, salaries, rent, and interest, certain forms of non-money income such as food and fuel grown and consumed, and the imputed interest of financial intermediaries, and certain other adjustments. These latter include the imputation to shareholders of both retained corporate earnings and the unshifted portion of the corporation income tax, and the addition to the income of wage earners of that portion of social security contributions which falls on wage earners. The base thus defined is taken to *exclude* the operations of the public sector, i.e., taxes are not deducted from income, and government expenditures on goods and services, and transfer payments, are not included. An alternative base which includes the operations of the public sector, referred to as "adjusted broad income", provided very similar results.

35　The Incidence of the Total Tax Structure*

W. I. Gillespie

The tax revenues that are examined in some detail are shown in Table 1. This table differs somwhat from the usual published statistics of D.B.S. The taxes are for net general revenue, and the provincial and municipal data are on a comparable basis for the fiscal year 1961. The tax rental payments to the provinces have been treated as provincial tax revenue for the year 1961. In addition, social security contributions have been included in the tax estimates.

TABLE 1
TOTAL TAX PAYMENTS, 1961 *

Revenue Source	Total Tax Payments		Total Tax Payments Exclusive of Taxes Exported to Foreigners	
	Millions (1)	% (2)	Millions (3)	% (4)
1. Individual income tax	$2,137	21.4	$2,137	22.9
2. Corporate profits tax	1,610	16.1	1,191	12.8
3. Succession duties	151	1.5	151	1.6
4. General sales taxes	1,400	14.0	1,400	15.0
5. Selective excises	1,482	14.8	1,440	15.4
6. Import duties	535	5.3	535	5.7
7. Property tax	1,399	14.0	1,300	13.9
8. Social Security	600	6.0	600	6.4
9. Other taxes	676	6.8	575	6.2
10. Total taxes	9,990	100.0	9,329	100.0

*For all levels of government: Inter-governmental transfers are deleted.
Source: D.B.S., *Financial Statistics of Federal, Provincial and Municipal Governments, 1961.*

Shifting Assumptions

The Individual Income Tax

The individual income tax is assumed to rest with the initial payee, i.e., the tax is not shifted. This tacitly assumes that total factor supplies, labour and capital, are fixed. While this is a limiting assumption, if secondary changes are more or less neutral in their distributional implications, it is not so restrictive as it first might seem.

---

*Reprinted by permission of author and publisher from W. I. Gillespie, "The Incidence of Taxes and Public Expenditures in the Canadian Economy", *Studies of the Royal Commission on Taxation*, Queen's Printer, Ottawa, 1966.

The Corporate Profits Tax

The corporate profits tax is assumed to fall partially (one half) on profits, while the remainder is shifted forward to consumers. That portion of the tax that falls on profits is allocated by a distribution of dividends received. The part of the tax shifted forward to consumers is allocated by a distribution of total consumption. This treatment of the corporate profit tax arises out of the lack of consensus concerning the incidence of the tax.

General Sales Tax on Consumer Goods

The general sales tax on consumer goods is assumed to be borne by the consumer. The tax is allocated by a distribution of total consumption expenditures. This treatment is based on the general consensus among economists that the sales tax on consumer goods is, in fact, borne in proportion to total outlays on consumption.

Two Canadian taxes fall within the scope of a general sales tax on consumer goods — the general manufacturers' sales tax, and the provincial retail sales tax.

Selective Excise Taxes

Selective excise taxes are assumed to fall on the consumers of the taxed products. The main excise taxes are on sales of liquor, tobacco, and motor fuel; there are many minor excise taxes which range from radios to playing cards and amount in total to no more than eleven per cent of all excises. Selective excise taxes are allocated by the distribution of consumption expenditures on the taxed articles, i.e., the excise tax on tobacco is allocated to smokers and it is distributed by a percentage distribution of consumption expenditures on tobacco, by income class.

The Property Tax

The property tax is of considerable importance, both because of its importance as a revenue source on the local level, and, due to this, its decisive weight in the allocation of the tax payments among the lower income groups. To the extent that the real property tax is applied to the *value of land* it cannot be shifted, and thus rests on the owner. That part of the property tax yield from business land is borne by business owners and is allocated by the distribution of dividends received. The portion of the property tax yield from farm land is borne by farm operators who own their own farms, and is allocated by the distribution of the estimated value of farm property (exclusive of the farm operator's house). That part of the property tax yield from residential-owner-occupied real estate is borne by the home owner and distributed by the estimated value of owner-occupied homes, while the tax yield from residential-renter-occupied real estate is borne by the landlord and is allocated by the distribution of net rental income. That part of the property tax yield from business and farm improvements is in the nature of an excise tax on the value of buildings and, as such, is capable of being shifted to consumers. Assuming these portions of the property tax are shifted, then the former is allocated by a distribution of total consumption while the latter is allocated by a distribution of expenditures on food products.

That part of the property tax on the assessed improvements of owner-occupied homes is again assumed to remain with the owner; and it is allocated by a distribution of the estimated value of owner-occupied homes. In the case of renter-occupied homes, though, the property tax on improvements is, in effect, an excise tax on the cost of providing rental units. Our assumption is to allocate the entire tax share falling on rental improvements to the tenant.

Selective Factor Taxes

It is assumed that a tax on the earnings of a certain factor (e.g., wages) remains with the recipient.

Succession and Estate Taxes

It is assumed that all succession and estate taxes can be allocated to income-recipients in the open-end upper income bracket.

Hospital Insurance Premiums

It is assumed that hospital insurance premiums or taxes remain with the payee; that is, such taxes are not shifted. This tax is allocated by a distribution of hospital insurance tax payments.

Customs Import Duties

It is assumed that customs duties are shifted to the consumers of the taxed commodities. In this manner import duties are similar to a general excise tax on consumption.

"Other" Taxes

The category "*other*" taxes includes: (i) motor vehicle licences, (ii) natural resource revenues, (iii) taxes on the premium income of life insurance companies, and (iv) municipal business taxes. Motor vehicle licences are allocated by a distribution of expenditures on automobiles. Taxes on life insurance premiums and municipal business taxes are allocated by distributions of the value of life insurance paid and total consumption, respectively.

Empirical Results: The Standard Pattern of Tax Incidence

With these qualifications in mind, taxes are allocated by the assumptions given above and the results are expressed as a per cent of income. The resulting pattern of total tax incidence for the year 1961 is set forth in Table 2 and illustrated in Chart 1. Table 2 contains the effective tax rates for each income class for all taxes. The total tax structure (line 18) is regressive over the first four income classes — up to an income level of $5,000 — and mildly progressive throughout the remainder of the income scale. When the "adjusted broad income" base is used, the regressivity over the lower income brackets extends up to an income level of $3,000 beyond which the total tax incidence is progressive. Due to the uncertain nature of the effective tax rate in the upper income bracket, it is not clear just how progressive the tax system is over the upper income brackets. In general, though, the incidence of the total tax structure is regressive *at least* up to an income level of $3,000 (using the "adjusted broad income" base) and *at most* up to an income level of $5,000 (using the "broad income" base).

The federal tax structure (line 1) is regressive over the first two brackets and progressive beyond. This pattern is the result of several contrasting forces: first, the individual income tax (line 2) is progressive throughout the entire income range. The corporate profits tax (line 3) is regressive up to an income level of $5,000, and progressive beyond; such regressivity over the lower income brackets is explained by the portion of the tax that is shifted forward, and which is distributed by total consumption expenditures. The general sales tax, selective excises and import duties, all exhibit regressivity up to an income level of $5,000, proportionality from $5,000 to $10,000, and regression beyond.

The provincial and municipal tax structure (line 9) is regressive over the first three income brackets, and almost proportional beyond. The proportional pattern beyond an income level of approximately $4,000 is a result of the element of regression being slightly more than offset by an element of progression. The progressivity is inserted by the individual income tax and the corporate profits tax, although these taxes bear nowhere near the weight in the provincial and municipal tax structures that they do in the federal tax structure. Besides the sales and excise taxes, the property tax also lends weight to the regressive nature of the total provincial and municipal tax structure over the lower income brackets. The property tax (line 15) is regressive over the entire income range. Hospital insurance taxes are regressive over the entire income range, but their weight is minor within the provincial and municipal tax structure.

To sum up, given certain assumptions as to the incidence of each tax, the evidence — with due allowance for some unquantifiable margin of error — suggests that the distribution of effective tax rates is regressive up to an income level of *at least* $3,000 and *at most* $5,000, and progressive beyond. It is this element of regressivity of the tax structure that is important when considerations of tax equity are involved. In total, one third of all families are affected by the regressiveness up to $3,000, while almost two thirds are affected by the regressiveness if it persists up to an income level of $5,000.

The Tax Structure in Canada

The following three extracts are taken from the annual summaries of fiscal statistics produced by the Canadian Tax Foundation. The first extract presents in brief summary form the complete tax revenue picture for the three levels of government, excluding intergovernmental transfers. The second sets out the tax structure and revenue at the federal level. The third presents in tabular form the complete tax structure and revenue therefrom in the provinces.

TABLE 2

EFFECTIVE TOTAL TAX INCIDENCE FOR THE TOTAL TAX STRUCTURE, 1961 *

Line	Tax Source	Family Money Income Class							
		Under $2,000	$2,000-2,999	$3,000-3,999	$4,000-4,999	$5,000-6,999	$7,000-9,999	$10,000-and Over	Total
		Percentages							
1.	FEDERAL TAXES, total	27.3	16.9	18.0	17.3	19.3	20.7	23.8	20.2
2.	Individual Income Tax	1.1	1.9	3.3	4.5	7.2	8.8	10.4	6.9
3.	Corporation Income Tax	6.5	3.4	2.8	2.3	2.4	2.7	6.1	3.4
4.	Sales Tax	8.0	4.2	4.2	3.7	4.0	4.1	2.7	3.9
5.	Selective Excises	4.3	2.6	2.6	2.3	2.5	2.4	1.5	2.3
6.	Import Duties	4.7	2.3	2.2	1.9	2.0	2.0	1.3	2.0
7.	Estate Duties							1.4	.3
8.	Social Security Contributions	2.7	2.5	2.9	2.6	1.2	.7	.5	1.5
9.	PROVINCIAL & LOCAL TAXES, total	32.7	16.0	14.2	13.1	13.5	13.5	14.6	14.5
10.	Individual Income Tax	.1	.3	.5	.7	1.1	1.4	1.6	1.1
11.	Corporation Income Tax	2.0	1.1	.9	.7	.7	.8	1.9	1.0
12.	Sales & Excises	8.2	4.5	4.6	4.3	4.7	4.5	3.0	4.4
13.	Succession Duties			.7	.5	.4	.3	1.5	.3
14.	Hospital Insurance Premiums	2.6	.9	.7	.5	.4	.3	.1	.5
15.	Property Tax	16.3	6.8	5.4	4.8	4.3	4.0	3.8	4.8
16.	Other Taxes	2.7	1.6	1.4	1.3	1.4	1.5	2.2	1.6
17.	Social Security Contributions	.8	.7	.8	.8	.9	.9	.5	.8
18.	TOTAL TAXES, ALL LEVELS	60.0	32.9	32.2	30.5	32.8	34.2	38.4	34.7

* Using the "broad income" base.

Note: Details may not add to totals due to rounding.

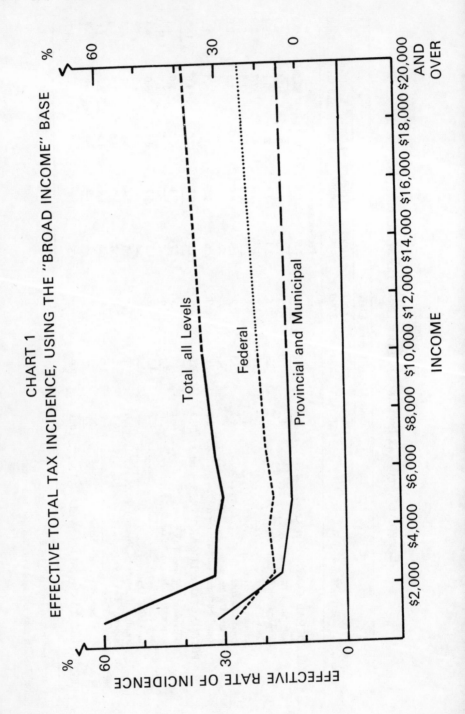

CHART 1

EFFECTIVE TOTAL TAX INCIDENCE, USING THE "BROAD INCOME" BASE

Total all Levels

Federal

Provincial and Municipal

EFFECTIVE RATE OF INCIDENCE

INCOME

$2,000 $4,000 $6,000 $8,000 $10,000 $12,000 $14,000 $16,000 $18,000 $20,000 AND OVER

36 An Overview of Tax Revenue in Canada*

The Canadian Tax Foundation

In Table 1, page 174, the consolidation shows that in 1963-64 the provinces had almost exclusive occupancy of the motor fuel tax field and about 49% of the death tax field, although only three provinces levied their own succession duties at that time — the federal government collecting for the others. The provinces obtained only 32% of sales tax revenue in that year with the municipalities collecting 3% and the balance of about 65% going to the federal government. The municipalities had over 99% occupancy of the property tax field. The federal government had sole use of customs and excise duties and the non-resident income tax.

With regard to non-tax revenue, the provinces collected almost 92% of privileges, licences and permits and received 58% of total revenue paid out by government enterprises and 45% of proceeds from sales and services. The municipalities got 12% of the earnings of government enterprises and the federal government received the balance of 30%.

---

*Reprinted by permission from *Provincial Finances, 1967*, The Canadian Tax Foundation, Toronto, 1968.

TABLE 1

NET TAX REVENUE OF ALL GOVERNMENTS
EXCLUDING INTERGOVERNMENTAL TRANSFERS
1963-64[a]
($ million)

Revenue Source	Total Amount Collected				% of Total Collected		
	Fed.	Prob.[b]	Mun.	Total	Fed.	Prov.	Mun.
TAXES							
Income							
Individuals	1,374.7	412.2	—	1,786.9	76.9	23.1	—
Corporations	2,167.7	389.3	—	2,257.0	84.8	15.2	—
Interest, dividends, etc. going abroad	124.5	—	—	124.5	100.0	—	—
General and other sales	1,277.8	632.1	61.6	1,971.5	64.8	32.1	3.1
Motor fuel and fuel oil sales	—	539.0	.9	540.0	—	99.8	.2
Customs and excise duties and excise taxes	1,247.2	—	—	1,247.2	100.00	—	—
Real and personal property and business	—	9.1	1,673.5	1,682.6	—	.5	99.5
Estate tax and succession duties	90.7	85.7	—	176.4	51.4	48.6	7.8
Other	.2	197.9[c]	16.7	214.8	.1	92.1	7.8
TOTAL TAXES	6,282.8	2,265.3	1,752.6	10,300.7	61.0	22.0	17.0

[a]Fiscal year 1963-64 for federal and provincial governments and calendar year 1963 for municipal governments. [b]Includes revenue of territories. [c]Includes hospital insurance premiums totalling $124.4 million.

Source: D.B.S. *Consolidated Public Finance—Federal, Provincial and Municipal Governments, 1963*, Queen's Printer, Ottawa, 1963.

37   The National Revenue Structure*

The Canadian Tax Foundation

1. Personal Income Tax

This tax is imposed under the provisions of the *income tax act*. Individuals resident in Canada are liable for the tax on income from all sources, domestic and foreign alike. Individuals who are not resident in Canada must account for the tax on income arising in Canada.

As indicated, Canadian residents are liable for tax on income from all sources. The scope of the tax is narrowed, however, by the exclusion of capital gains, gifts and inheritances, by the specific exemption of such items as family allowances receipts, unemployment insurance benefits and veterans' disability pensions — to mention only the most important. The tax base is further reduced by the personal exemptions and other deductions to which taxpayers are entitled.

The personal exemptions are as follows: for persons taxed as single — $1,000, and as married — $2,000 (reduced by the excess of the spouse's income over $250 and up to $1,250); for persons 70 years of age and over and those from 65 to 69 not receiving Old Age Security — an additional $500; for each child, niece or nephew wholly dependent on the taxpayer and qualified for family allowances, $300; for each other such dependant not so qualified and under the age of twenty-one years, $550; for each other such dependant over twenty years provided that he is either incapacitated or is a full-time student, $550. For a parent, grandparent, aunt or uncle who is incapacitated, and for a brother or sister who is either under 21, incapacitated or in full-time attendance at an educational institution, the tax-payer can deduct the amount spent in support of such dependant up to $300 if the dependant is qualified for family allowances, otherwise up to $550. Some of the exemptions for dependants are limited to dependants resident in Canada.

Other deductions which may be taken in computing the taxable amount include medical expenses in excess of 3% of income and charitable donations up to a maximum of 10% of income. Contributions to registered pension plans and to registered retirement savings plans are also deductible subject to maxima set out in the *income tax act*. Of less importance are the deductions for union dues, professional membership dues, fees for students and a restricted list of expenses incurred in connection with employment. An optional standard deduction of $100 may be claimed in lieu of the deduction for medical expenses and charitable donations.

The amount which remains after deducting the aggregate of personal exemptions and other allowances is known as "taxable income" and it is to this that the rates are applied.

---

*Reprinted by permission from The Canadian Tax Foundation, *National Finances 1967-1968*, Toronto, 1968.

TABLE 2
FEDERAL TAX REVENUE
Fiscal Years 1958 and 1965 to 1968
($ million)

	1958	1965	1966	1967	1968[a]
TAXES					
Taxes on income					
Personal income tax[b]	1,499.8	2,103.3	2,142.5	2,473.8	2,815.0
Corporation income tax[b]	1,234.8	1,523.8	1,606.6	1,593.2	1,570.0
Non-resident withholding tax	64.3	143.7	170.0	203.6	190.0
Total[d]	2,798.9	3,770.8	3,919.1	4,270.7	4,575.0
Estate tax (or succession duties)	71.6	88.6	108.4	101.1	110.0
Excise duties					
Spirits and beer	171.9	240.1	264.8	271.4	382.0
Cigarettes, tobacco and cigars	131.7	177.2	187.1	196.4	120.0
Less refunds	—3.5	—5.9	—6.1	—6.9	—7.0
Total[d]	300.1	411.4	445.8	461.0	495.0
Sales Tax[b]	703.2	1,204.6	1,395.1	1,513.6	1,655.0
Other excise taxes					
Automobiles	72.3	—[c]	—[c]	—[c]	—[c]
Cigarettes, tobacco and cigars	142.4	218.3	238.1	251.4	272.0
Television sets, radios and phonographs	16.9	23.5	27.0	31.2	33.0
Other	18.5	27.8	31.4	33.4	35.0
Less refunds	—.7	—.3	—.3	—.5	—
Total[d]	249.4	269.1	296.2	315.6	340.0
Customs import duties	498.1	622.1	685.5	777.6	815.0
Other taxes	1.5	.2	.2	.2	—
TOTAL TAXES	4,622.8	6,366.8	6,850.3	7,439.7	7,990.0
OLD AGE SECURITY TAX REVENUE					
Personal income tax	135.0	431.9	494.9	576.6	785.0
Corporation income tax	60.7	145.2	152.3	149.5	161.0
Sales tax	175.8	383.2	522.1	559.5	564.0
Total[d]	371.5	960.3	1,169.3	1,285.6	1,510.0
CANADA PENSION PLAN					
Personal income tax	—	—	94.9	587.5	—

[a]Budget forecast after tax changes (detailed breakdown is our estimate). [b]Excludes Old Age Security tax revenue, which is shown separately below. [c]Tax repealed June 20, 1961. [d]Does not necessarily add owing to rounding.
Sources: Budget Speech; Public Accounts; Canada Gazette, September 9, 1967.

The Rates

The basic rates of federal tax in effect since 1960 start at 11% on the first $1,000 of taxable income and increase on successive layers to 80% on taxable income in excess of $400,000. An amendment to the *income tax act* effective July 1, 1965 provided for a deduction of the lesser of $600 or 10% of the "basic tax" (that is, the federal tax before the 1965 reduction and before the provincial abatement). A further amendment, effective about June 1, 1966, rescinded the 1965 tax cut and replaced it with a deduction equal to the lesser of $20 or 20% of the "basic tax".

The federal rates also are reduced in respect of income earned by an individual in a province of Canada. The provincial abatements, expressed as a percentage of the federal "basic tax", are:

16% for the 1962 taxation year
17% for the 1963 taxation year
18% for the 1964 taxation year
21% for the 1965 taxation year
24% for the 1966 taxation year
28% for the 1967 taxation year

In respect of income earned in 1967 in the province of Quebec the abatement is further increased by 22% of the "basic tax" — 19% representing the compensation to Quebec for "opting out" of certain federal-provincial programs and assuming responsibility under the *established programs (interim arrangements) act* and the remaining 3% as compensation for Quebec's assumption of the costs of a program of schooling allowances similar to the federal program under the *youth allowances act*.

In addition to the tax calculated in accordance with the schedular rates, investment income from sources outside Canada in excess of the greater of (1) $2,400 or (2) the personal exemptions and certain deductions to which a taxpayer is entitled, is subject to a 4% surtax.

Individual taxpayers are also liable for the Old Age Security Tax on taxable income as calculated under the *income tax act*. For 1967 the rate of tax is 4% with a maximum tax of $240 (previously $120). The Old Age Security tax is not taken into account in calculating the provincial share of the income tax.

Provincial Situation

The current fiscal arrangements between federal and provincial governments require all provinces to enact their own personal and corporation tax in order to continue receiving revenue from these sources. By agreement, the federal government collects any taxes on income that the provinces impose, provided the bases remain identical with the federal definition. Eight provinces accepted the federal offer to collect both their personal and corporation income taxes. Ontario accepted the offer only for personal income tax and is continuing to collect its own tax on the income of corporations. Quebec continues to levy and collect its own personal and corporate income taxes and is not participating in the federal-provincial tax collection arrangements. It is, however, eligible for equalization payments under the new fiscal arrangements. The Yukon and Northwest Territories are not covered by the *federal-provincial fiscal arrangements act*. No income taxes are levied by the territories and the federal abatement is not extended to income earned in the territories.

2. Corporation Income Tax

This tax, like the personal income tax, is in the main also imposed under the *income tax act*. However, 3% of the "total rate" is imposed under the *old age security act*. The principles dealing with the scope of the tax and the distinction between resident and non-resident taxpayers parallel those applicable to

TABLE 3
PERSONAL INCOME TAX —1967[a]
Federal and Provincial Marginal Rates

Federal Marginal Rates after Provincial Abatement			Provincial Marginal Rates			Marginal Rates Federal and Provincial	
Taxable Income	Quebec[b]	Other Provinces[c]	Quebec[d]	Manitoba and Saskatchewan	Others	Manitoba and Saskatchewan	Others[d]
$	%	%	%	%	%	%	%
1	3.30	5.72	5.50	3.63	3.08	9.35	8.80
1,001	7.00	10.08	7.00	4.62	3.92	14.70	14.00
2,001	8.50	12.24	8.50	5.61	4.76	17.85	17.00
3,001	9.50	13.68	9.50	6.27	5.32	19.95	19.00
4,001	11.00	15.84	11.00	7.26	6.16	23.10	22.00
6,001	13.00	18.72	13.00	8.58	7.28	27.30	26.00
8,001	15.00	21.60	15.00	9.90	8.40	31.50	30.00
10,001	17.50	25.20	17.50	11.55	9.80	36.75	35.00
12,001	20.00	28.80	20.00	13.20	11.20	42.00	40.00
15,001	22.50	32.40	22.50	14.85	12.60	47.25	45.00
25,001	25.00	36.00	25.00	16.50	14.00	52.50	50.00
40,001	27.50	39.60	27.50	18.15	15.40	57.75	55.00
60,001	30.00	43.20	30.00	19.80	16.80	63.00	60.00
90,001	32.50	46.80	32.50	21.45	18.20	68.25	65.00
125,001	35.00	50.40	35.00	23.10	19.60	73.50	70.00
225,001	37.50	54.00	37.50	24.75	21.00	78.75	75.00
400,001	40.00	57.60	40.00	26.40	22.40	84.00	80.00

[a]Excluding Old Age Security tax of 4% with ceiling of $240: also excluding 4% surtax on investment income from non-Canadian sources. [b]Abatement is 50% of basic federal rates. [c]Abatement is 28% of basic federal rates. [d]Note that an amendment to the Quebec Act in 1967 exempts from tax single persons earning less than $2,000 and married persons earning less than $4,000.

individual income taxpayers. Broadly speaking the rules governing the determination of taxable income, i.e., the taxable amount and the rates of tax, are
the same for all corporations; thus the tax can be said to be of general application to corporations resident in Canada and to non-resident corporations carrying on business in Canada.

TABLE 4

CORPORATION INCOME TAX

COMBINED FEDERAL AND PROVINCIAL EFFECTIVE RATES[a]

as at April 1, 1967

(%)

Taxable Income $	Federal Tax only	Combined Federal and Provincial Tax		
		Quebec & Ontario	Newfoundland Saskatchewan & Manitoba	Other Provinces[b]
10,000	11.0	23.0	22.0	21.0
15,000	11.0	23.0	22.0	21.0
25,000	11.0	23.0	22.0	21.0
50,000	19.7	31.7	30.7	29.7
100,000	29.9	41.9	40.9	39.9
500,000	38.0	50.0	49.0	48.0

[a]Includes 3% Old Age Security tax. [b]This rate applies also to Yukon and Northwest
Territories and to taxable income earned outside Canada.

Rates of Tax

Under the federal *income tax act* the corporation income tax rates are 18%
on the first $35,000 of taxable income and 47% on that portion in excess of
$35,000. In addition, corporations are liable for Old Age Security tax at 3%
on total taxable income. When this is added, the rates are 21% on the first
$35,000 of taxable income and 50% on the remainder. These rates are before
the provincial abatement. As of 1962 all provinces had entered the corporate tax
field and, under fiscal arrangements between the federal and provincial governments, the federal government agreed to allow an abatement of a percentage
— 10% (increased from 9% in 1967) — of the corporation's taxable income
earned in a year in a province. By virtue of the abatement the federal rate
(including Old Age Security tax) on that portion of a corporation's taxable
income attributed (on a sales and wages basis) to the provinces is reduced to
11% on the first $35,000 of taxable income and 40% on the remainder. No
abatement is available in respect of the taxable income earned in the Northwest
Territories or the Yukon where the full federal rates apply.

Provincial Rates

The return of taxing powers to all provinces became effective for the 1962
and subsequent years. Five provinces levy a corporation income tax of 10%,

Manitoba, Saskatchewan and Newfoundland 11%, Ontario and Quebec 12%.

Combined Rates

For 1967 the combined federal and provincial rates including Old Age Security tax are as follows: Ontario and Quebec — 23% on the first $35,000 of taxable income and 52% on the remainder; Manitoba, Saskatchewan and Newfoundland — 22% and 51% respectively; and all other provinces and territories 21% and 50% respectively.

3. Estate Tax

The *estate tax act* came into force January 1, 1959, and applies to the estates of persons dying on or after that date. The *dominion succession duty act* applies to estates of persons who died on or before December 31, 1958.

The *estate tax act* distinguishes between estates of those who were domiciled in Canada at the time of death and estates of persons who were domiciled elsewhere.

For a deceased domiciled in Canada all property is subject to tax. If the estate has an aggregate net value of $50,000 or less it is exempt. From the aggregate net value, which broadly speaking is the value of the property minus debts, encumbrances and funeral expenses, there is a minimum deduction of $40,000. If the deceased left a wife the minimum deduction is $60,000 plus $10,000 for each dependent child. Other deductions are provided in respect of an incapacitated surviving husband and for orphans. The rate structure applicable to estates of domiciled Canadians is similar to the individual income tax rate structure in that successive layers of the taxable amount are taxed at progressively higher rates. The first $5,000 of the taxable amount is taxed at 10%, the next $5,000 at 12% and so on up to $2,000,000 beyond which point the remainder is taxed at 54%. The tax, as determined by the rate schedule, is subject to reduction in respect of provincial death taxes, foreign death taxes, and gift tax. The *federal-provincial fiscal arrangements act* provides for a provincial abatement or payment to the provinces of 75% of the federal estate tax collections in a province.

Where the deceased was domiciled outside Canada at the time of death any of his property that was situated in Canada is subject to a flat rate tax of 15%. The $50,000 exemption and the deductions for survivors do not apply, although the tax is waived if the estate is less than $5,000; and if the estate is more than $5,000 the tax must not reduce the value after tax to less than $5,000. The Canada-U.S. Estate Tax Convention raised this ceiling to $15,000 for domiciliaries and citizens of the United States.

4. Gift Tax

The gift tax is imposed under Part IV of the *income tax act* on individuals resident in Canada and applies to *inter vivos* gifts whether the property is situated inside or outside of Canada. The aggregate taxable value is computed after deducting an exemption of at least $4,000 and the tax is levied at rates ranging from 10% to 28% payable by the donor. It does not apply to gifts in the nature of bequests, those made to charitable organizations, or to gifts of less than $1,000. Gifts made to Canada, to any province or to a municipality are also exempt. There is, in addition, a special exemption available once in a lifetime of an amount up to $10,000 for a transfer to a spouse of a house to be occupied jointly by the spouse and the donor or for the transfer of a farm from a parent to a child.

. . . the purpose of the gift tax is to protect the revenue arising from the estate and personal income taxes rather than to raise substantial revenue itself.

5. Non-Resident Withholding Tax

Persons (including corporations) not resident in Canada are liable for federal income tax at the regular rates only on income from employment in Canada or from carrying on business here. Other forms of income such as dividends, interest, rents, management fees, alimony and royalties, when paid or credited to non-resident persons are subject to special taxes under Part III of the *income tax act*. These taxes, which must be withheld by the payer, are levied on the gross amount of the payments at a rate of 15% or less. The 15% rate of withholding on dividends, for example, is reduced to 10% where the corporation paying the dividend has the required "degree of Canadian ownership".

In addition to the tax under Part III, non-resident corporations carrying on business in Canada are subject under Part IIIA of the *income tax act* to an additional tax of 15% on after-tax earnings minus an allowance for increases in capital investment. The purpose of the tax is to equalize, at least roughly, the tax burden on Canadian branches and Canadian subsidiaries of foreign corporations.

6. Commodity Taxes

i. Excise Taxes

The *excise tax act* is the statutory basis of the excise tax structure, the main component of which is the general manufacturers' sales tax. The sales tax is a tax of general application in that it applies to all goods manufactured or produced in Canada or imported into Canada unless the goods are exempted by a provision of the Act. Included in the list of exemptions are: most foodstuffs, electricity and fuels, materials incorporated into manufactured goods, and many items of machinery for farming or mining.

The tax is applied, in the case of goods manufactured and produced in Canada, on the manufacturer's selling price exclusive of all other excise taxes but inclusive of excise duties. When the goods are imported, the tax is imposed on the duty-paid value. The rate of sales tax was raised from 11% to 12% (including the 3% Old Age Security tax) with effect from January 1, 1967. The remainder of the excise tax structure consists of *ad valorem* taxes on a prescribed list of goods and of certain specific taxes. These taxes are in addition to the general sales tax.

Ad valorem taxes at 15%, are levied on television sets, phonographs, and cigars, and at 10% on toilet articles, cosmetics, jewellery, watches, slot machines, matches, tobacco, pipes, etc. The *ad valorem* taxes are imposed on the same tax base as the sales tax. The most important specific excise taxes are on cigarettes at the rate of 2½ cents on each 5 cigarettes, and on manufactured tobacco at 80 cents per pound. The other specific excise taxes apply to playing cards and wines.

ii. Excise Duties

The excise duties, which are authorized by the *excise tax act*, apply only to specified products. Following are the most important dutiable items and the rates of duty:

(1) Liquor (other than brandy) ....$13.00 per proof gallon
(2) Brandy ....$11.00 per proof gallon
(3) Spirits used in medicines, extracts, etc. ......$ 1.50 per gallon
(4) Beer ....$ .38 per gallon
(5) Cigarettes weighing not more than
     3 pounds per thousand ....$ 4.00 per thousand
(6) Other cigarettes ....$ 5.00 per thousand
(7) Manufactured tobacco ....$ .35 per pound
(8) Cigars ....$ 2.00 per thousand

Unlike the excise taxes, which apply to domestic and imported goods alike, the excise duties are levied on domestic products only.

7. Customs Import Duties

Background

The basic form of the Canadian tariff has not been changed since the general revision of 1907. Until the United States–Canada trade agreement, effective January 1, 1936, the bulk of commodities entered under the General Tariff. Subsequent to that date imports from the United States were subject to duty under the Intermediate Tariff, and the General Tariff became relatively insignificant. Since that agreement, the major changes have been as follows: United Kingdom–Canada trade agreement of 1937; United States–Canada trade agreement of 1938; War Exchange Conservation Act and other temporary wartime changes in 1940-45; the General Agreement on Tariffs and Trade (GATT) 1948; the imposition of temporary surcharges in 1962-63; the Canada–U.S. Auto Agreement in 1965; and the Kennedy Round of GATT trade negotiations concluded on June 30, 1967.

Present Position

The tariff is composed of specific and *ad valorem* duties of three general levels on a wide range of imports into Canada. The three schedules of rates, which are progressively higher, are the British Preferential Tariff (limited to countries within the British-Commonwealth), the Most-Favoured-Nation Tariff (restricted to other countries with which Canada has trade agreements including the participating countries to GATT) and the General Tariff. The General Tariff is of negligible importance, since it applies to only a few countries with which Canada had little trade.

While primarily regarded today as an instrument of foreign commercial policy, the customs tariff is an important source of federal revenues. Surprisingly few groups of commodities account for the bulk of the revenues. For example, the iron and steel group in recent years has accounted for about one-third of the total. The second most important group is textiles. Almost no revenue is derived from basic raw materials such as iron ore, petroleum, coal, and unmanufactured cotton and wool, which are for the most part admitted free.

8. Old Age Security Taxes

The Old Age Security taxes on personal and corporate income and on sales are not included in budgetary revenue but are channelled into the Old Age Security Fund which is separated from the budgetary accounts.

At present the taxes are 3% on corporate income, 3% on sales, and 4% on personal income (up to a maximum of $240).

38   Provincial Tax Revenue*

The Canadian Tax Foundation

The provinces derive their revenue from three main sources: taxes, non-tax receipts and payments from the federal government. In 1966-67 taxes were expected to contribute 68% of total revenue, non-tax receipts, 22% and federal payments, 10%.

The *British North America Act* of 1867 empowers the Parliament of Canada to raise "money by any mode or system of taxation" and restricts each provincial legislature to direct taxation within the province in order to raise revenue for provincial purposes. Thus, while the federal government employs both direct and indirect taxation across all of Canada, the provincial governments are confined to levying direct taxes within their own boundaries.

---

*Reprinted by permission from The Canadian Tax Foundation, *Provincial Finances*, 1967, Toronto, 1967.

TABLE 5
NET TAX REVENUE
ALL PROVINCES
Fiscal Years 1957 and 1964 to 1967
($ million)

NET TAX REVENUE	1957	1964	1965	1966a	1967ab
			Current and capital combined		
Taxes					
Corporation (non-income)c	20.3	60.9	59.2	48.3	54.7
Income: Corporation	62.2	412.2	455.1	508.2	573.4
Individual	36.4	389.3	507.7	744.2	1,046.8
Property	7.9	8.8	9.9	10.1	11.9
Sales:d General	177.9	562.0	725.7	767.2	1,002.6
Amusements and admissions	20.3	27.0	31.8	33.5	39.2
Motor fuel and fuel oil	300.2	538.0	582.7	650.8	738.1
Tobaccoe	16.7	30.2	63.4	52.4	75.5
Other commodities and servicesf	7.5	12.8	14.9	26.3	30.0
Succession dutiesg	64.6	85.7	92.2	99.0	114.5
Otherh	18.4	137.0	155.6	173.7	281.7
Total tax revenuei	732.2	2,263.9	2,698.1	3,113.7	3,968.5

aEstimates. bFunctional breakdown of 1967 expenditures excludes British Columbia's expenditures as this information was not made available to D.B.S. cTax on premium income of insurance companies in all provinces. Ontario and Quebec also impose various other non-income taxes on corporations. dCommissions allowed to retailers and gasoline and other agents included in revenue and expenditure figures as follows: gasoline tax—1957, $3,488,000; 1964, $5,167,000; 1965, $5,784,000; 1966 and 1967, not available; general and other sales taxes—1957, nil; 1964, $14,985,000; 1965, $18,662,000; 1966 and 1967, not available. eCovers specific tobacco taxes in all provinces except Nova Scotia, British Columbia and Alberta. Tobacco is taxed under general sales tax in Nova Scotia and B.C., but not at all in Alberta. fMainly Quebec hospital tax on meals, Nova Scotia tax on long distance tolls, and tax on electricity and telephone services in Manitoba. gIn 1957 only Quebec and Ontario imposed succession duties. British Columbia has imposed succession duties as of 1963. hIncludes hospital and medical insurance premiums where applicable, security transfer and property transfer taxes in Ontario and Quebec and other minor taxes. iMay not add owing to rounding.

Source: D.B.S. *Provincial Government Finance, Revenue and Expenditure,* 1956 and 1963 to 1966.

A direct tax may be defined as one "demanded from the very person who it is intended or desired should pay it". Income and property taxes are good examples of direct taxation. By legislating provincial sales taxes in Canada as consumer purchase taxes and designating retailers as agents of the Crown for purposes of collection, they have been made to fall within the direct tax category.

In this chapter we describe the taxes imposed at the provincial level of government. There is some controversy as to what actually constitutes a tax. For example, annual registration fees for corporations are sometimes based on a flat rate or they may be dependent upon the capital of the company.

The following table gives the principal taxes levied in each province. Since natural resource revenues are considered by many as a form of tax applying to their business activities, we have listed them at the end of the table even though they are described in the non-taxation chapter.

The rates and details of taxes shown in Table 6 are those in effect on January 1, 1967.

Type & Basis of Tax	Newfoundland	Prince Edward Island
Amusement:		
Admission price of amusements	5¢ flat rate	31¢ to $1: 2¢ to 10¢ Over $1: 5¢ on every 50¢ or fraction of 50¢
Pari-mutuel betting	11%	10% (4½% net)[g]
Consumption:		
Retail Sales	6% on 17¢ and over	5% on 25¢ and over
Tobacco	12% average	10% average
Alcoholic beverages	Sales tax	10%
Meals	Sales tax	Sales tax over $1
Motor fuel per gal.	Gas and Diesel 19¢[e]	Gas and Diesel 18¢
Other	1¢ per gallon fuel oil —	Nil
Corporations:		
Profits[a]	11%	10%
Capital taxes	Nil	Nil
Place of business	Nil	Nil
Persons:		
Income[b]	3.08% to 22.4%	3.08% to 22.4%
Succession duties	Nil	Nil
Hospital and medical premiums	Nil	Nil
Public officers	Nil	Nil
Property taxes	Nil	⅖ of 1% of assessed value of lands not situate in an incorporated municipality
Insurance premiums:		
Fire marshals tax[c]	8%	Nil
All premiums	2%	2%
Miscellaneous taxes	Public utilities: See text	Crop insurance premiums
Natural resources:[d]		
Minerals		
(i) Net income or profits	Iron ore: 20%[f] on profits over $5,000. Others: 5% on profits over $5,000.	Nil
(ii) Royalties	Nil	Nil
(iii) Other bases	Up to 10 mills on assessed value of minerals on the Island of Newfoundland	Nil
Logging	Nil	Nil

	Nova Scotia	New Brunswick	Quebec

	¢ to 70¢: 5¢
	ver 70¢ to $1: 10¢
	ver $1: 10¢+5¢ on every
	50¢ or fraction of 50¢
		Theatres, average 11%.
		Others, up to $1: 2¢ to 10¢;
		  thence 5¢ for every 50¢ or
		  fraction of 50¢
			Nil[h]

	% (6½% to 8%)[g]	11% (3% to 4½% net)[g]	7% to 9%
	% on 16¢ and over % average les tax les tax over $1 as 19¢, Diesel 27¢ ng Distance calls, 5¢ on every 50¢ or fraction of 50¢. Tolls under 25¢ exempt	6% on 15¢ and over 10% average Sales tax Sales tax over $1 Gas 18¢, Diesel 23¢ Nil	8%[hh] on 11¢ and over 12% average 8%[hh] 8%[hh] over $1.24 Gas 16¢; Diesel 22¢ Hotel rooms: 8%[hh] Telecommunications: 8%[hh]
	% l l	10% Nil Nil	12% $\frac{1}{10}$ of 1%. See text $25 to $50
	8% to 22.4% l	3.08% to 22.4% Nil	5.5% to 40%[hh] See text

	l
	l
		Nil
		Nil
			Nil
			20% on fees over $3,000
			  earned by public officers
			  and registrars

	wners of 1,000 acres or more
	l % of assessed value; fire
	protection 75¢ per 100 acres
		School and business tax:
		  $1.50 per $100 of real
		  property assessment
			Nil

	of 1% maximum: present ates ½ of 1%	1% maximum	Nil

	⁊
	blic utilities: see text
		2%
		Public utilities: See text
		Licensed insurers: costs of
		  administering Insurance
		  Act
			2%
			Security transfer: See text.
			  Hydraulic power: 15¢ per
			  1,000 KWH.

	per ton	7% to 9% on profits over
		  $10,000
			9% to 15% on profits
			  over $50,000

	text for detail	Coal: 14¢ per ton Nil	Nil $1 acreage tax on unde- veloped mineral lands
		Nil	10%; no tax if income is not over $10,000. 15¢ per cord cut

Type & Basis of Tax	Ontario	Manitoba
Admission price of Amusement:	76¢ to 92¢; 6¢ to 8¢, thence 10%[i]	61¢ to 70¢—1¢ to 3¢ 71¢ to $1—5% Over $1—10%
Pari-mutuel betting	6%	10%
Consumption:		
Retail sales	5% on 21¢ and over	Nil[k]
Tobacco	5% average	20% average
Alcoholic beverages	Sales tax[i]	Nil[l]
Meals	Sales tax over $1.50	Nil[m]
Motor fuel per gal.	Gas 16¢, Aviation fuel 2¢, Diesel 22¢	Gas 17¢, Aircraft gas 2¢, Diesel 20¢
Other	Nil	5% purchase tax on electricity, natural and manufactured gas, coal, steam and hot water[n]
Corporations:		
Profits[a]	12%	11%
Capital taxes	$\frac{1}{20}$ of 1%[j]	Nil
Place of business	$20 to $50[j]	Nil
Persons:		
Income[b]	3.08% to 22.4%	3.63% to 26.4%
Succession duties	See text	Nil
Hospital and medical premiums	Hospital: $3.25 single, $6.50 family, per month Medical: $5 single, $10 per family of two, $12.50 per larger family per month	Hospital: $2 single, $4 family, per month
Property taxes	1½% of market value in unorganized territory	Nil
Insurance Premiums:		
Fire Marshals Tax[c]	1% maximum: present rate, 2/3 of 1%	1% maximum
All premiums	2%	2%
Miscellaneous taxes	Land Transfer: 1/5 of 1% up to $25,000, 2/5 of 1% on remainder Security Transfer: See text	Crop Insurance Premiums

PROVINCES—JANUARY 1, 1967
BASIC RATES OR RANGE OF RATES

Saskatchewan	Alberta	British Columbia
Nil	Nil	Nil
%	5%	12%
% on 15¢ and over	Nil	5% on 15¢ and over
0% average	Nil	Sales tax
Sales tax at 5% on 15¢ and over	Nil	Sales tax
Nil	Nil	Nil
Gas 15¢, Diesel 18¢	Gas 12¢, Diesel 14¢	Gas 13¢, Aircraft gas 1¢, Diesel 15¢
Nil	Nil	½¢ per gallon on fuel oil
1%	10%	10%
Nil	Nil	Nil
Nil	Nil	Nil
.63% to 26.4%	3.08% to 22.4%	3.08% to 22.4%
Nil	Nil	See text
Hospital: $2 single, $4 per family per month	Nil	Medical: Basic premium— $5 single, $10 per family of 2, $12.50 per larger family per month[q]
Medical: $1 single, $2 per family per month		
ates fixed annually for unorganized territories	Rates fixed annually for special areas and improvement districts	Unorganized territory: Agricultural land: ½ of 1%
	Grazing land: tax equal to amount payable under the lease	Improved, forest and tree farm land: 1%
		Timber land: 1½%
		Wild land: 3%
		Coal land: class A—7% class B—2%
		Mineral claims: 25¢ per acre
		Pipelines: 1%
%	⅓ of 1%	1% maximum
%°	2%	2%[r]
op Insurance Premiums	Crop Insurance Premiums	Crop Insurance Premiums

Type & Basis of Tax	Ontario	Manitoba
Natural Resources:[d]		
Minerals		
(i) Net income or profits	6% to 12% on income over $10,000	6% to 11% on income
(ii) Royalties	Nil	12½% on oil
(iii) Other bases	Natural gas: ½¢ on every 1,000 cu. ft. for home consumption, 2¢ per 1,000 cu. ft. for export Acreage tax: 10¢ per acre	8 mills on assessed value of crude oil mining claim tax $10
Logging	10% on profits over $10,000	Nil

[a]As of the 1967 taxation year these taxes may be deducted from federal corporation income tax up to 10% of taxable income in the provinces: for prior years the rates were 10% in Quebec and 9% in the other provinces. [b]All provincial taxpayers were entitled to an abatement of federal personal income tax of 21% of tax in 1965, 24% of tax in 1966 and 28% in 1967. (Provincial rates of personal income tax rose accordingly.) In addition to this basic abatement, Quebec and any other province that withdrew from federal-provincial shared-cost programs gained a further adjustment. In all provinces except Quebec, Manitoba and Saskatchewan the provincial rates were equal to the abatement in 1965, 1966 and 1967 (i.e. they were 21%, 24% and 28% of the federal rates). In Manitoba and Saskatchewan they were 26% and 27% respectively of the federal rates in 1965. In 1966 they were 29% of the federal rates in both provinces and in 1967 they were 33% of the federal rates. [c]Levied on fire insurance premiums in addition to the levy on all premiums of fire, life, accident, etc. [d]Natural resource charges are classified by D.B.S. as "non-taxation revenue—privileges, licences and permits". [e]Effective April 1, 1967, increased to 6%, the 1 percentage point increase earmarked for education; the budget address of March 15, 1967 announced an increase in gasoline taxes to 20¢ per gallon, effective April 1, 1967, and a corporate income tax rate of 11%. [f]Limited to equivalent of 10¢ per ton on first 1½ million tons and 8¢ per ton thereafter, or a flat

Saskatchewan	Alberta	British Columbia
ee text on Royalties	Nil	10% on income over $25,000
ee text	See text for detail	See text for detail
creage tax: 3¢ per acre on non-urban mineral rights[p] roducing tract tax: currently 8 mills on assessed value of coal, petroleum, natural gas and potash in producing area; maximum 10 mills	Acreage tax: maximum 5¢ per acre on owners of mineral tracts; for 1966 the rate is 3¢ per acre. Principal mineral tax: for 1966 the rate is 8 mills per $ on assessed value of principal minerals in a producing area. Oil and gas conservation tax: maximum 10 mills per $ on assessed value of oil and gas property; no tax if assessed value is less than $3,000.	Mineral property tax: maximum 10% of assessed value of minerals; present rate 8%
il	Nil	10%; no tax if income is not over $25,000.

2¢ per ton escalated with the price of iron ore. [g]If tax is remitted within 7 days, the ace Association may deduct from 5% prior to and 8% after October 1 in Nova Scotia, om 6½% to 8% in New Brunswick and 5½% in Prince Edward Island of the amounts agered as commission. [h]10% tax imposed by municipalities. [hh]The Quebec budget address announced that the tax on sales, hotel rooms, meals and telecommunications would e increased to 8%, effective March 16, 1967; rebates of personal income tax would be made to single persons earning $2,000 or less and to married persons earning $4,000 or ss, effective January 1, 1967. [i]For entertainments where liquor is served: 10% of arges, maximum $1. [j]These taxes are payable only to the extent that they exceed the % tax based on income. [k]A 5% sales tax is to go into effect June 1, 1967. [l]To be subject sales tax of 5%. [m]Meals $2 or over will be subject to sales tax. [n]Except on domestic eating fuels and electricity, when used for heating. [o]Tax on persons insuring with nlicensed insurers, 10% of premium. [p]The 3¢ per acre acreage tax does not apply to dividuals or to coal rights. [q]British Columbia pays from 50% to 90% of basic premium low income subscribers. [r]Tax on persons insuring with unlicensed insurers, 5% of emiums.

Sources: Correspondence and interviews with Provincial Treasurers; Provincial atutes; D.B.S. *Principal Taxes and Rates*; *CCH Tax Reporters*.

Taxes on Personal Income

The Definition of Income

Equity in taxation is generally taken to mean taxation according to "ability-to-pay" rather than according to "benefits received". The question then arises as to an appropriate index of "ability-to-pay". The tax base generally accepted in preference to "consumption" or "wealth" has been "income", variously defined. The concept of taxable income which has gained increasing acceptance among economists has been that of total accretion, whereby income is defined to equal consumption during a given period, plus increase in net worth. It is perhaps fair to contend that this broad definition of income has become the 'conventional wisdom', and that the onus of proof in debate on the subject now falls to the proponents of a narrower definition.

The following two extracts focus on the definition of income for tax purposes in Canada. The first is partly historical, partly conceptual and sets out the acceptance in Canada of a compromise definition of income, reflecting both the "English" and the "American" concepts. The second is the unequivocal embrace by the Carter Commission of the accretion concept. In later sections of the Commission Report (not included below) the accretion concept is tempered slightly by administrative feasibility — realization is to be preferred to accrual, and imputed rent must be excluded.

39   The Canadian Concept of Income*

J. Harvey Perry

The General Concept of Income

At the outset, since the subject is an "income" tax, it is not unnatural to inquire "What is income?" This question would, of course, seem highly irrelevant to salary or wage earners (the majority of the taxpayers) since there is seldom any cause for doubt as to whether or not their remuneration is to be classed as income. They would therefore be the more surprised to learn that "income" is one of the most disturbingly elusive concepts in the whole field of taxation. One would almost be safe in saying that "income" for tax purposes is not a concept at all; that there is no universal and unchanging principle by which an amount of money may be measured and tested to determine whether or not it is of the species.

In judging such matters one turns ordinarily to the terms of the statute, to see what meaning may have been given the subject of the tax by legislation. In the Canadian Income Tax Act, however, the legislators have not even pretended to define income, much less capital, a concept of equal significance.

---

*Reprinted by permission of author and publisher from J. Harvey Perry, *Taxation in Canada*, third ed., University of Toronto Press, Toronto, 1961.

In this respect our law differs little from that of any other country. The statute is normally of little help.

The English Concept of Income

Under the English Income Tax Act tax is charged not on income in total but on segments of income which, taken in the aggregate, amount to total income. Schedule D of the Act charges a tax on "the annual profit or gain arising or accruing . . . from any kind of property whatever . . . and from any trade, profession, employment or vocation. . . ." This is the schedule with which we are principally concerned.

It will be readily understood that the English courts, in interpreting this wording, have occupied themselves not with general consideration of the nature of "income" but with the question of the nature of annual profit or gain from a trade or employment. As a result they have apparently adopted a more restricted view of income than might have been the case under a more general wording. The over-all result of their decisions was summarized in the report of the 1920 Royal Commission on the Income Tax, as follows: "Casual, non-recurring or occasional profits arising from transactions that do not form part of the ordinary business of the person who makes them are accordingly held not to be within the scope of the Income Tax, and consequently escape taxation."

In the English approach, therefore, many forms of gain, particularly speculative and casual gains, are not subject to tax, since they are not part of the returns that are normally associated with a trade or employment. Such gains in common parlance are usually known as "capital" gains, to distinguish them from "income" gains. In truth, however, there is no such concept in English law as a "capital" gain and the only test that is material to the result is whether or not the gain is the return from a trade. It follows, therefore, that when the regular possibility of making a "capital" gain presents itself in carrying on such a trade as a stockbroker's business, for example, or where the making of capital gains is the main purpose of a venture, the gains may be taxed as income of a trade. What degree of regularity makes the difference between casual gains and income cannot be established in advance.

The American Concept of Income

In contrast to the English, the American approach to a concept of income is significantly broader. The taxation of "capital" gains, for example, has been apparent in American law from the beginning of its experience with an income tax. The Revenue Act of 1862, which imposed the first American income tax under a general definition of income, was interpreted to apply to profits made on the sale of real estate. The charging section was broadened by the 1864 act specifically to include "all income or gains derived from the purchase and sale of stocks or other property, real or personal." In the act of 1867 this wide definition was dropped but was replaced by a narrower specific charge on profits made from real estate transactions. The general charging section of the 1867 act imposed a tax on "the gains, profits and income of every person, . . . whether derived from any kind of property, rents, interest, dividends, or salaries, or from any profession, trade, employment or vocation, . . . or from any other source whatever" and, in addition, it specifically included as income "profits realized within the year from sales of real estate purchased within the year, or within two years previous to the year for which income is estimated. . . ."

While the original American law (which was first enacted in 1913 following the Sixteenth Amendment) made no specific mention of "capital" gains, there has been little doubt in the minds of the judges from the beginning that the statute was intended to include such gains within its ambit.

Judicial interpretation reflected the attitude of the average American citizen that "capital" gains were income and should be taxed as income, along with poker winnings, prizes from quiz shows, and lucky tickets on the Irish sweeps. In this view the courts seem to have simply taken cognizance of the dynamism of enterprise in a rapidly growing economy. None of the later American cases or amendments to the Internal Revenue Code have disturbed the basic proposition that capital gains are taxed as income in United States. For the most part the special provisions of the Internal Revenue Code relating to capital gains, such as the reduced rate of tax, are in recognition of the fact that the gains so taxed in one year may represent an increment that has accrued over several years and because of this "lumping-up" should be given some relief through a lower tax rate than ordinary income of the year. It is interesting to note in this connection that no distinction whatever was made between capital gains and other income in the tax rates until 1921, and even today such gains are treated as ordinary income if the asset has been held for less than six months.

The Canadian Position

Historically the Canadian position has been an intermediate one, a role in which we not infrequently find ourselves. For our income tax we borrowed our statute law substantially from the United States and our jurisprudence from England. The definition of income contained in the Income War Tax Act enacted in 1917 has an unmistakable resemblance to United States income tax statutes and bears no resemblance whatever to the English act. Yet the interpretation given it has followed with few exceptions the decisions of the English courts.

This is not to say, of course, that in recent times "capital" gains have not been taxed in Canada simply because of slavish adherence to the English cases. It is probably closer to the truth to say that as a matter of policy and custom such gains are not now taxed, a view confirmed by the statement of the Hon. D. C. Abbott in his 1950 Budget Speech. Undoubtedly the actual content of the exemption will alter from time to time, and in post-war years transactions formerly disregarded have been brought to tax, the most striking being frequent or substantial transactions in real estate. However, the general position is still that of the British.

40 A Comprehensive Definition of Income*

The Royal Commission on Taxation

Economic Power

In order to allocate taxes in accordance with the equity principles we espouse, we must specify a tax base that would estimate consistently the economic power of each individual and family relative to others. There is, of course, a variety of methods by which economic power, the ability to command goods and services for personal use, can be estimated. Some are conceptually pure but impossible to administer; others are readily administered but depart significantly from the spirit of the concept. The problem is to specify a tax base that maintains the integrity of the concept without creating insuperable administrative difficulties.

Changes in economic power are measured over a period of time rather than at a particular point in time. The choice of any time period is inherently arbitrary. The conventional choice is, of course, the calendar year. Using this unit of time, a tax unit's economic power can be measured as the sum of the following:

1. The market value of the goods and services used up by the tax unit during the year to satisfy its own wants (consumption).
2. The market value of the goods or services given to other tax units during the year (gifts).
3. The change over the year in the market value of the total *net* assets held by the tax unit (current saving = change in net worth = change in wealth). This may be either a positive or a negative figure in any time period.

The proposed tax base must of necessity take into account all of a person's net gains over the year. All gains, after meeting the expenses necessary to generate them, must be reflected in the base because all of them must be disposed of in one of the three ways we have specified in the tax base. The distinction between wages, interest, dividends, business income, gains on shares, bequests, sweepstake winnings, and so on, all would disappear. Because it encompasses more than the present tax base, we have called our new concept the "comprehensive tax base".

We believe that the comprehensive tax base would measure the relative economic power of individuals and families on a consistent basis. Its very consistency would in fact produce a radical change from the present income tax base. Whether one wishes to consider it as a great broadening of the concept of income or as a fundamentally different tax base is of little consequence. Certainly we do not think that anything is to be achieved in this context by a debate about the meaning of words. It ultimately does not matter whether

---

*Reprinted by permission from the Royal Commission on Taxation, *Report*, Queen's Printer, Ottawa, 1966, Vol. III.

capital gains, gifts and bequests are or are not called "income". What does matter is that these things increase the economic power of those who are fortunate enough to receive them, and therefore should be taxed like wages, salaries, rent, dividends, interest and so on. If economic power is increased it does not matter in principle whether it was earned or unearned, from domestic or foreign sources, in money or in kind, anticipated or unanticipated, intended or inadvertent, recurrent or non-recurrent, realized or unrealized. When we use the term "income" in the context of the tax system we are proposing, we mean the comprehensive tax base as we have just described it.

The Comprehensive Tax Base Reformulated

The comprehensive tax base has been defined as the sum of the market value of goods and services consumed or given away in the taxation year by the tax unit, plus the annual change in the market value of the assets held by the unit. It would be futile to write such a definition into a taxing statute because it does not provide sufficient delineation, either to taxpayers or tax administrators, to make compliance and enforcement possible. In particular, it would be impossible to measure directly the value of the goods and services consumed by each Canadian individual or family each year. Similarly, an annual valuation of all assets is impractical.

Fortunately, the comprehensive tax base can be restated in such a way that most of the compliance and enforcement problems can be substantially solved without a major departure from the basic concept. By taxing all the net gains, appropriately defined, of each tax unit on an annual basis, it is possible to achieve the same result as taxing each unit's "consumption plus gifts plus change in net worth", while avoiding the problem of measuring the value of the unit's annual consumption.

The definition of "net gains" is, of course, of crucial importance. The following reformulation of the comprehensive tax base in terms of net gains provides a useful starting point, although we discuss later how this formulation also requires extensive modification, essentially for administration reasons:

1. The tax base of each unit would include the annual net gains less net losses, from:

   (a) the provision of personal services;
   (b) the disposal of tangible or intangible property;
   (c) the receipt of gifts or legacies from other tax units;
   (d) the receipt of windfalls;
   (e) the ownership of tangible or intangible property;
   (f) any combination of these "sources".

2. Gains can take one or all of the following forms:

   (a) the receipt of cash;
   (b) the acquisition of rights to, or interests in, property;
   (c) the receipts of benefits in kind as a *quid pro quo*;

(d) a change in the value of a right to, or an interest in, property;
(e) the personal use and enjoyment of property that could have been rented to others — that is, gains forgone.

3. Cash, or rights to, or interests in, property disposed of by the unit in the expectation of generating or acquiring a net gain should be deducted from the gross gain to determine the net gain or loss.

4. Net gains and losses should be determined on the basis of fair market value.

5. Net gains that could be realized by the tax unit, but are not so realized because the property in question is transferred to another unit as a gift or for an inadequate consideration, should be included in the tax base of the donor, and the amount by which the consideration is inadequate should be included in the tax base of the donee.

Some of the salient features of the "net gains" formulation of the comprehensive tax base, as we have just defined it, should be emphasized:

1. The tax base would include gifts and bequests received from other tax units. This is appropriate because these amounts represent an acquisition of economic power. In view of this concept, the estate taxes and gift taxes would be withdrawn.

2. The tax base would include imputed income, that is, the gains realized when a person uses or consumes his own personal services or his own property. In most circumstances, however, the valuation and administrative problems involved in including such amounts in income are insuperable.

3. The money value of gains in kind would be included on the same basis as money gains. Here, too, there are valuation problems.

4. When the market value of rights to, or interests in, property changes, the tax unit has a net gain or loss, according to our formulation of the comprehensive tax base. This means, in effect, that gains and losses would be included in the base on an accrued rather than on a realized basis. Once again we are confronted with serious valuation problems.

5. *All* of the expenses reasonably incurred to earn gains, other than personal living expenses, would be allowed as deductions from such gains. Distinctions between the forms of taxable gains, or considerations of whether a gain was actually made, would not be relevant in determining whether the expenses were deductible. The major question would be when, not whether, the expenses incurred in the expectation of obtaining a net gain would be deducted.

6. No personal consumption expenditure would be deducted. This follows from the basic concept we have already enunciated, which involves taking all changes in economic power defined as "consumption plus gifts plus change in net worth". The need to prevent the deduction of personal consumption expenditure has some far-reaching consequences. Three of the more important can be briefly described:

(a) A tax unit which makes gains cannot be allowed to deduct from those gains general living expenses.
(b) The net losses incurred in operating a "business" where there is

no expectation of earning a net gain from the business, even in
the long run, should not be deductible from income derived from
other sources. The presumption must be that the owner is obtaining personal satisfaction from operating the business and that the
losses of the business are therefore disguised personal living expenses.

(c) Gifts are not expenses incurred in the expectation of generating
net gains and should not be deducted from gross gains or receipts.

The Taxation of Capital Gains

The inclusion of capital gains in income for tax purposes is one of the major questions
in the definition of income issue, examined previously. Capital gains could, of course,
be taxed quite separately from other income, or might be taxed at special, usually
concessionary, rates within the income tax structure. The general question of taxing
capital gains is examined in the first of three extracts below. The second extract sets
out the philosophy by the Carter Commission on the inclusion of capital gains in
income for tax purposes in Canada. A rigorous interpretation of the comprehensive
definition of income would require the taxation of accrued capital gains. Administrative considerations, however, lead the Commission to recommend the inclusion only of
realized capital gains. The third, very brief, extract is a purple passage by J. Harvey
Perry.

41   Capital Gains – To Tax or Not To Tax*

Ronald Robertson

The arguments criss-cross through considerations of economics, equity, administrative feasibility, law, accounting, business and revenue raising, creating a
rather muddled assembly.

The "Cons"

1. A capital gains tax would inhibit the flow of risk-taking capital investment
which is essential for the development of a young and growing country like
Canada.

---

*Reprinted by permission of author and publisher from Ronald Robertson, *Canadian
Tax Journal*, Vol. XIII, September-October 1965.

2. A closely related "Con" argument is that a tax on gains arising from the appreciation of corporate share values would probably have the effect of increasing shareholder pressures for the distribution of corporate earnings. This could result in less funds being available for reinvestment in business and the reduced corporate retentions would, in turn, have unfavourable effects on growth.

3. The revenue yields would be negligible and in fact might result in revenue loss. The reasoning here is that, assuming a capital gains tax were imposed at a flat rate, the odds are that many borderline cases now caught at full income rates in Canada would soon get capital gains treatment at the lower rate. Critics also suggest that U.S. figures on capital gains collections have little relevance in Canada for this reason.

Further, if capital losses were allowed, it can be argued that they would largely offset gains. A similar point is that Canada's attractiveness to risk capital from countries where there is a tax on capital gains would be diminished. This in turn would result in Canada losing the tax payable on regular income from such investment as is lost.

4. A capital gains tax would result in such complicated legislation that the present tax laws would look like child's play by comparison. The U.S. experience, and more recently, the experience in Great Britain, tends to underline this point.

5. The tax is costly to collect and, as a corollary to 4, a nightmare for taxpayers and revenue officials alike.

6. A capital gains tax would lead to more avoidance and evasion than we have now, and result in a lessened regard for our tax laws.

7. A capital gains tax gives no assurance of equity, but merely shifts the line. While in Great Britain, the stringent new tax provides for deemed realizations at death, in the case of gifts, and at 15 year intervals where settled property is involved, it is generally conceded that as a practical matter, with few exceptions, only realized gains can be taxed. This being so, the person who realizes his gains several times in a lifetime may suffer a relatively heavier burden than a person who can hold on to his property.

8. If a capital gains tax is exigible on death, and is followed by a death tax on the balance, a double tax bite is felt. As noted, this is the case with Great Britain's broadened capital gains tax. The Americans have discussed this point for years. A similar argument is that death taxes should be considered a once-in-a-lifetime capital gains tax and this should be sufficient for the purpose of equity.

9. The tax on long-term capital gains may be largely a tax on inflated values and not on real gains. Where a taxpayer has to replace an asset upon which a monetary gain has been realized he must buy at the inflated price. In effect, therefore, he suffers a capital rather than a capital gain tax. In some countries an allowance is made for inflation before tax is imposed. [note] that it is not only the prices of capital assets that become inflated over time. Inflation also hits wages and other forms of income which are subjected in most countries to graduated income tax rates.

10. Where time periods are introduced to distinguish between long-term and short-term capital gains, the market mechanism is impeded to the extent that people are "locked into" investments until a long-term gain taxable at lower rates may be realized. Conversely, where losses occur taxpayers may tend to sell investments prematurely in order to realize deductible short-term losses.

11. A capital gains tax at regular graduated rates is inequitable and virtually confiscatory where the gain has accrued over a period of years, but is taxed at a high marginal rate in one year.

12. Where capital gains are taxed at special rates, the need to distinguish between a capital gain and regular income still exists.

It will be noted that several of these points concern the form as much as the existence of a capital gains tax. However, it seems highly unlikely, short of some sort of general averaging provision, that a capital gains tax can be devised against a background of graduated rates and not contain a number of inequitable and distorting side effects.

The "Pros"

1. There is no doubt about the main argument put forward in favour of taxing capital gains. It is that such a levy makes the tax system more equitable. The reasoning here is simply that a capital gain is as much income, in the economic sense of providing command over goods and services, as any other kind of receipt and the ability to pay concept requires its inclusion in the tax base. The same can, of course, be said for family allowances, unemployment insurance benefits, gifts and a wide variety of fringe and other benefits whether received in cash or in kind.

One's passion for or against a tax on capital gains tends to vary with the facts and status of the person who received it. The farmer who makes a gain on the sale of his farm after a lifetime of toil seldom invokes the rancour which an economically similar gain will produce if it is realized by a city slicker in a year or two. However, capital gains come in all shades of equitable white, grey and black.

2. This leads to the second argument, namely, that those who make capital gains might be better off with a capital gains tax than they are at present in Canada, since the legal capital gains-income line would probably soften, and more gains which are now taxed at full rates would get capital gains treatment. This seems to be what has happened in the United States.

3. It is also suggested that a capital gains tax would provide for greater certainty in the taxation of capital receipts. This, it can be argued, would enhance risk-taking rather than work against it.

4. If capital losses were allowed to offset capital gains, or preferably ordinary income, more risk capital would be forthcoming. In connection with this argument, however, it should be noted that many capital gains tax enthusiasts shy away from allowing capital losses against ordinary income. But if the main test is equity, and if equity means ability to pay, it is hard to see why capital losses should not be permitted to be offset against any other kind of

income. In principle, at least, ability to pay should not be a one-way street.

5. The revenue from a capital gains tax is not as inconsiderable as suggested, (the contrary arguments might be recalled). Here the U.S. figures are usually cited. In the United States, tax revenues from the tax on capital gains amount to about 5% of individual tax revenues. In 1959, the late Dr. Kenneth Eaton estimated the potential Canadian yield at that time as about $100 million a year.

6. With respect to business capital gains, it is argued that business exists to make a profit, and a profit is a profit whether in the form of a capital gain or not. In fact, there seems to be one school of thought among accountants that, under "generally accepted accounting principles", capital gains and losses should be reflected in the statement of earnings.

7. Inclusion of capital gains would widen the tax base and the revenue from a tax on general gains should permit some lowering of the general tax rates — perhaps producing a trade-off between high personal income tax rates and a flat-rate on capital gains.

8. The taxing of capital gains would remove some of the impetus to strip corporate surplus. It is the magic of transforming undistributed income into tax-free receipts that provides the main "dividend stripping" incentive. When the difference in tax consequence can be between zero and 80%, or even between zero and 15%, the attraction is quite strong.

9. It is the lack of a capital gains tax that induces some Canadians to sell out to American buyers. It can be argued that Americans buy and hold business interests because so far in the U.S. there is no capital gains tax on transfers at death. In Canada, on the other hand, it is sometimes argued that the absence of a capital gains tax may act, surprisingly as an inducement for Canadians to sell out family companies and retire to a sunnier climate on the proceeds. That is, there is no benefit to be gained from holding on to assets until death in Canada while there is in the United States.

10. The administrative complexities are not so impossible as opponents suggest. The U.S. manages to impose a capital gains tax; so also do the United Kingdom and many other countries to various extents.

11. United States experience is often cited as evidence that a capital gains tax does not inhibit risk-taking, for Americans are reputed to be among the greatest risk-takers in the world. There is, of course, the point that development and capital accumulations in the U.S. had progressed much further than in Canada before income taxes became important.

12. Canada will soon be an island surrounded by capital gains taxes and since others are imposing them, it must be right and fair so we should impose them too.

42   The Taxation of Capital Gains *

The Royal Commission on Taxation

We have concluded that taxation at progressive rates of increments in economic power represents the fairest measure of ability to pay, and is the only means of achieving an equitable and neutral tax system. Gains realized on dispositions of property come within this concept naturally and logically. Such gains increase the taxpayer's economic power and thus enhance his ability to pay. We see no escape from the quandary in which the Canadian tax system finds itself except by the adoption of a concept under which the taxability of property gains is made clear and certain.

It appears to us, moreover, that property gains should be taxed in full as ordinary income. This proposal may seem extreme, particularly when in countries like the United States and the United Kingdom at least some such gains are taxed at reduced or preferential rates. However, we think that such preferential rates may be attributable in whole or in part to the existence of very high progressive rates of tax, or to the lack of comprehensive averaging provisions in the countries concerned. In addition, concern with the economic impact of taxation on investment may have been a major influence in the determiation of the level of taxation that should apply. Unquestionably, preferential rates and the arbitrary time periods which are sometimes used for the purpose of determining whether a particular gain should be taxed as income or on a preferential basis, can add greatly, as in the United States, to the complexity of the tax legislation and to the uncertainty of its application. Tax differentials can also produce a considerable distortion in the manner in which taxpayers organize and conduct their activities. Thus, preferential rates produce complexity and a lack of neutrality and moreover, as we discuss later, they are not necessarily the most efficient way to encourage investment and to relieve inequities. With an overall concept of income, it seems to us that it is neither feasible nor desirable to distinguish between types of increments to economic power.

We would anticipate some of the discussion that will arise regarding our proposal by pointing out the following:

1. We believe that our proposal for the integration of the corporate income tax with the individual income tax should eliminate the double taxation of corporate source income that could otherwise exist with the taxation of share gains.
2. Our proposed personal income tax schedule has a top marginal rate of 50 per cent, and the taxation in full of capital gains under such a schedule should not be considered in the same light as taxation under a schedule, such as is now applicable, with a top marginal rate of 80 per cent.

*Reprinted by permission from the Royal Commission on Taxation, *Report*, Queen's Printer, Ottawa, 1966, Vol. III.

3. We propose several averaging devices in respect of lump sum receipts of income that would also apply to the disposition of capital assets.

43   Capital Gains*

J. Harvey Perry

I have no hesitation in saying that long before the Royal Commission was ever appointed I was of the view that our position on so-called capital gains taxation was becoming increasingly untenable. You all know what the situation was and still is today. Those unhappy souls who are indiscreet enough to over-indulge in real estate trading are caught for full taxation at full rates, and those who conduct themselves by rules of such deviousness that even Lewis Carroll would have disbelieved them are home free. For trading in securities almost everyone is home free unless he is very close to the original point of issue. The intolerable aspect of the present situation is that the law, obscure as it may be, permits of no such invidious distinction as that now made between real estate and security trading. Indeed its proper administration would call for a complete reporting by the taxpayer of all transactions in capital assets each year, the tax authorities making up their own minds as to the taxability of those transactions on the basis of the trade or investment test.

To the extent that the present law is enforced it already results in the greater part of the damage foreseen by those who oppose a specific tax on capital gains. The serious capital gain — the capital gain that arises in the regular pursuit of an economic end, which all say must be encouraged, is already taxed, or should be under the law. The casual, gambling type gain is not taxed. The only reason for making any reservation in this statement is to recognize that the law is not always enforced, which is a very poor reason indeed for making any reservation. The law should be enforced.

We are therefore faced with one of the most unsavoury tax situations that could be imagined. Thousands of people each year being subjected to full taxation at full rates on capital gains because the law is being enforced to some extent, and thousands of others escaping with complete freedom because other gains are allowed to slip by. I should add that in saying this I do not cast blame on our friends from National Revenue. They are obviously acting with a general framework of government policy beyond their control.

---

*Reprinted by permission of author and publisher from J. Harvey Perry, "Anatomy of a Tax System", *November 1967 Conference of The Canadian Tax Foundation*, Canadian Tax Foundation, Toronto, 1968.

Surely to heavens it is time that we saw the so-called English concept of income for what it is — a scheme that ideally suited the selfish designs of the ruling classes of England a century and a half ago. It is self-evident to me that the trade or business concept of income was a neat trick for fobbing off most of the burden of the newly arrived income tax onto the commercial middle class and leaving inviolate the wealth of the ruling aristocracy. I ask now why we feel any obligation to retain this antiquated monstrosity and I find no answer. If this deplorable concept were honestly applied it would produce by far the most vicious type of capital gains tax that could be imagined, and in fact already has this result to a large extent.

Under the comprehensive tax base we propose abandoning this relic of our colonial inheritance and facing up to the reality that *any* capital gains represents just as significant an increment in one's command over the world's goods as any other form of gain.

The Rate Structure

Where the income tax base is defined only in a very partial sense — as in the present Income Tax Act — a highly progressive rate structure may contribute little to vertical equity and make little difference to revenue productivity. Where, on the other hand, the tax base is comprehensively defined — as in the Carter proposal — the rate structure is of great significance. Steep progressivity would then become meaningful in contributing to vertical equity, revenue productivity, and, through the increased responsiveness of a progressive rate structure, to changes in national income, to the built-in flexibility, and consequent stabilizing effectiveness, of the tax. The first of the following two extracts on tax rates compares the rate structure of the personal income tax in a group of countries, including Canada, in 1960. The second sets out the philosophy of the Carter Commission on a suitable rate structure, and indicates the modifications to progression which would be necessary under the comprehensive tax base.

44 Statistical Comparisons – Personal Income Taxes*

Marion Bryden

TABLE 1

PERCENTAGE OF BEFORE-TAX INCOME PAID IN DIRECT TAXES
BY STANDARD FAMILY IN SELECTED COUNTRIES, 1960[a]

Before-tax income in pounds sterling equivalent		Canada	United States	West Britain	Germany	Sweden	Norway	France	Italy	Belgium
£	$	%	%	%	%	%	%	%	%	%
500	1,705	- 3[a]	3	1	12	9	6	0	0	0
1,000	3,410	2	7	10	18	17	14	0	5	9
2,000	6,820	10	13	19	18	26	27	0	14	15
5,000	17,050	22	19	36	25	42	52	13	23	32
10,000	34,100	35	29	52	33	52	63	23	30	43
50,000	170,500	57	62	81	48	66	75	40	40	61

[a]Family allowances received are deducted from taxes paid in the calculation. This results in a negative figure for Canada at this income level.

TABLE 2

MARGINAL RATE OF TAX PAID BY STANDARD FAMILY
AT SIX INCOME LEVELS IN SELECTED COUNTRIES, 1960

Before-tax income in pounds sterling equivalent		Canada	United States	Britain	West Germany	Sweden
£	$	%	%	%	%	%
500	1,705	1[c]	3[d]	4	12	23
1,500	5,115	20	20	39	24	42
5,000	17,050	40	32	61	40	60
10,000	34,100	50	49	76	49	67
20,000	68,200	60	63	89	53	69
100,000	341,000	75	91	89	. 53	69

[c]Unemployment insurance contribution by employee.
[d]Social Security tax.

---

*Reprinted by permission of author and publisher from Canadian Tax Journal, Vol. XII, January-February 1964.

TABLE 3

EFFECTIVE PERSONAL INCOME TAX RATE ON
EACH QUINTILE OF INCOME IN THREE COUNTRIES, 1960[a]
TAXABLE RETURNS ONLY

Assessed or Gross Income Class	% of Taxpayers	% of Assessed Income	Effective Tax Rate-%
CANADA			
Under $ 3,199	39.4	20.5	5.31
$ 3,200- 4,299	24.4	21.6	6.62
4,300- 5,499	18.1	20.6	7.88
5,500- 7,999	12.2	18.5	9.93
8,000 and over	5.9	18.8	19.26
UNITED KINGDOM			
Under £ 599	39.1	22.1	4.72
£ 600- 799	24.6	20.8	6.33
800- 999	16.7	18.0	7.74
1,000- 1,499	14.1	20.0	11.28
1,500 and over	5.5	19.1	32.77
UNITED STATES			
Under $ 5,000	47.3	23.3	9.07
$ 5,000- 6,999	23.9	22.9	10.15
7,000- 8,999	13.8	17.6	11.73
9,000- 14,999	11.5	20.5	13.94
15,000 and over	3.5	15.7	24.93

[a]No state income taxes are included for the United States. For Canada there were no provincial income taxes in 1960 except in Quebec and the percentages relate to federal tax paid by each income class. They include Old Age Security income tax whereas the U.S. figures do not include Social Security tax which was 3% on income up to $4,800 in 1960.

Sources: Canada: *Taxation Statistics*, 1962, Department of National Revenue.
United Kingdom: *Report of the Commissioners of Her Majesty's Inland Revenue*, March 31, 1962.
United States: *Statistics of Income*, 1960. Individual Income Tax Returns. U.S. Treasury Department — Internal Revenue Service.

Notes on Tables:

[Table 1 shows the percentage of before-tax income paid in direct taxes in selected countries].

The percentages for all countries except Canada are based on calculations made by the National Institute of Economic and Social Research in Great Britain in 1961. Part of their results was published in the March 1961 issue of the National Institute Economic Review, and part in a paper by Professor Otto Eckstein to the National Tax Association Conference in 1962. The percentages for Canada were calculated by the Canadian Tax Foundation and are based on the same assumptions as the Institute study used. These assumptions were as follows:

1. The standard family is a husband and wife under 50 and two children under 10, with all their income from wages or salary. The only exemptions and deductions allotted to them are personal exemptions and the optional standard deduction in countries where it is allowed.

2. Direct taxes include personal income tax plus social security taxes paid by the employee (including unemployment insurance contributions by the employee), less family allowances received. State income taxes in the United States were not included, presumably because they vary from state to state and do not exist in 15 states. It appears that the Swedish percentages do include local income taxes, although these vary from one part of Sweden to another. The German percentages include income taxes allocated to the "Laender" (roughly the equivalent of provinces). In 1960 there were no provincial income taxes in Canada except in Quebec, so the Canadian percentages are based on federal taxes only.

3. Incomes in the various countries were converted into pounds sterling by the National Institute by using a cost-of-living exchange rate on a study of Milton Gilbert and Associates entitled *Comparative National Products and Price Levels, 1958* and other sources. The Institute considered comparisons based on official exchange rates meaningless. Its cost-of-living exchange rate enables the student to examine tax incidence on people at a similar standard of living in the various countries.

4. All the original calculations were done in pounds sterling, and Canada was not included. In preparing figures for Canada, we have applied the same cost-of-living exchange rate to the Canadian dollar as was used for the United States in the Institute study. Studies by price experts indicate that the cost of living in northern U.S. cities is less than 5% higher than in the major metropolitan areas of Canada. In 1960 — the year to which the table applies — the Canadian dollar was at a premium on the U.S. dollar of about 3%. It seemed reasonable, therefore, to assume that this would cancel out the slightly higher cost of living in the U.S. and make it feasible to use the same cost-of-living exchange rate for Canada as for the U.S.

The table shows that the burden of direct taxes as defined is relatively light in Canada, particularly at the lower income levels. It is heaviest in Sweden and Norway at the middle and upper income levels, but Britain exceeds Sweden at levels above $34,100.

[Table 2 indicates the marginal rates of tax paid at six income levels.] The [table] shows that Canada has the lowest marginal rate for the standard family at the lower income levels, but from $5,115 to $34,100 it exceeds the United Sttes; above that level it exceeds West Germany. It is particularly notable that the progression for three of the five countries shown cuts off at the $68,200 level. Only Canada and the United States continue progression beyond this point.

Table 3 shows for Canada, the United States and Britain, the effective personal income tax rate on each quintile of income in the country in 1960;

that is, it tells us what percentage of their income is paid by taxpayers who hold the bottom fifth, the middle fifth, the top fifth, or any other fifth of the total taxable income. It is another way of assessing the progressivity of the personal tax in each country, and it eliminates the problem of converting currencies in order to achieve comparability. It can be argued that each fifth is a comparable group of people in each country because they can claim one-fifth of the goods and services, and therefore they should be taxed at the same rate in each country if the tax burden is to be comparable.

The table shows that, of the three countries, Britain has the lowest tax on the bottom quintile and the heaviest on the top quintile. Canada is about the same as Britain in its burden on the second and third quintiles, but considerably lower than either Britain or the United States on the top quintile. The United States is highest in the percentage it takes from all quintiles except the top one. Of course, it can be argued that there is much greater taxable capacity in the U.S., since the bottom quintile's income goes up to $5,000 while the equivalent group in Canada stops at $3,200. The fourth quintile in Canada ranges from $5,500 to $8,000, while in the United States it goes from $9,000 to $15,000.

45   Criteria Governing the Selection of a Rate Schedule *

The Royal Commission on Taxation

In developing rate schedules we have been guided by several objectives and constraints. Our principal objective has been to allocate taxes among tax units in proportion to each unit's ability to pay. In addition, we believe that the rate schedule should be consistent with the realization of the following objectives:

1. Because sales taxes are, at best, proportionate to income, and property taxes are regressive, there should be compensatory reductions in the weight of income taxes on low income tax units to achieve the allocation of all taxes according to ability to pay.
2. The weight of taxes on middle income tax units should be reduced to narrow the unfavourable income tax differential between Canada and the United States.
3. The minimum rate of tax on any form of income should be no greater than 50 per cent, to minimize disincentive effects. Only the

*Reprinted by permission from the Royal Commission on Taxation, *Report*, Queen's Printer, Ottawa, 1966, Vol. III.

first objective in the list is concerned with ability to pay, but we believe that the others are of sufficient importance to be taken into account in developing the rate schedules we recommend.

Our selection of rate schedules has been subject to the following constraints.

1. In accordance with the Order in Council establishing this Commission, the tax system we recommend must raise approximately the same revenue as the present tax system.
2. Apart from the industries affected by eliminating inefficient concessions in the present tax law, the weight of taxation on equity investments should be no greater than at present, despite the widening of the tax base to include the full taxation of capital gains.

Were it not for the binding nature of the revenue constraint, it would be relatively easy to choose a rate schedule that was consistent with all of our objectives. There is no conflict among our objectives that could not be resolved by decreasing the revenue yield of the tax system. Because we are not able to reduce revenue, however, it is necessary to determine the emphasis that should be given to each objective. With some exceptions, primary emphasis has been placed on the first objective: making the income tax system equitable by allocating taxes in accordance with the ability to pay of tax units. In developing the rate schedules, several important assumptions have been made.

1. We assume that the first few dollars of a tax unit's income are not available for discretionary use. Below some limit, therefore, the marginal rate of tax should be zero. We have adopted a lower limit of $300 for single individuals and $700 for families. These limits, together with the other assumptions, determine the rate of progression of the marginal rates. The $300 and $700 limits would be appropriate if personal income taxes were the only taxes levied. However, these limits must be increased to compensate for sales and property taxes. Accordingly, in the rate schedules we recommend, the amounts subject to a zero rate of tax are higher than these limits.

2. We assume that all income in excess of some limit is available for discretionary use. Above some limit, therefore, the marginal rate of tax on additional income should be constant. Both in arriving at our "ideal" rate schedules and the recommended rate schedules, we have accepted $100,000 as the upper limit. This limit may be excessive, even though it is only one quarter of the present limit.

3. We assume that, between these limits, equal percentage differences in income are associated with equal differences in the fraction of additional income available for discretionary use. The income brackets should, ideally, encompass equal percentage differences in income. Marginal rates should rise by equal amounts from bracket to bracket.

4. Up to an income limit of $40,000 we assume that the fraction of income available for discretionary use is less for families than for individuals with the same income. Above this limit we assume that the fraction is the same for both. Consequently the rate schedule for individuals and families should merge at this point.

[Compensatory Adjustments for other Taxes]

Sales taxes are at best proportionate to income, and property taxes, where they are payable, decline as a proportion of income as income rises. Consequently, to allocate personal income taxes according to ability to pay, while ignoring sales and property taxes, would mean that low income tax units would be taxed too heavily relative to their ability to pay. To compensate for these non-income taxes we believe that the marginal income tax rates imposed on the first brackets should be reduced relative to what would be appropriate if personal income taxes were the only taxes.

To this end we recommend that, for unattached individuals, the first bracket should encompass the first $1,000 rather than the first $300 of income. We also recommend that this bracket should be subject to a zero rate of tax. This would be equivalent to maintaining the basic exemption of $1,000 for individuals. For families, we recommend a zero rate bracket that would encompass the first $2,100 of income. This would be slightly more generous than the present exemption for couples of $2,000.

[International Tax Comparisons]

To reduce the relative tax advantage enjoyed by residents of the United States, we have adopted as a third objective the establishment of a rate schedule that would result in roughly equal income taxes for middle income taxpayers in Canada and in the United States. Because of the lower average income of Canadians and the higher ratio of government spending to GNP, this objective cannot be achieved completely.

The Maximum Marginal Rate

If equity were the only consideration, the top personal rate of tax would be determined solely by revenue requirements. Given the size of the base and the assumed upper and lower limits between which marginal rates should vary, the top marginal rate would, in effect, be predetermined by revenue requirements.

We are persuaded that high marginal rates of tax have an adverse effect on the decision to work rather than enjoy leisure, on the decision to save rather than consume, and on the decision to hold assets that provide monetary returns rather than assets that provide benfits in kind. We think there would be great merit in adopting a top marginal rate no greater than 50 per cent. With such a maximum marginal rate, taxpayers would be assured that at least half of all gains would be theirs after taxes. We think there is a psychological barrier to greater effort, saving and profitable investment when the state can take more than one half of the potential gain.

The Taxation of Income from Equity Investments

We have made a number of recommendations that should enhance the attractiveness of equity investments independently of the tax rate applicable to them. These include provisions for the more neutral treatment of income from different sources, full write-off of losses on investments and accelerated capital cost allowances for new, small businesses. The provisions should reduce the risk of equity investments and so enhance their attractiveness.

[Revenue]

[Under the proposed new rate schedule], taxes would be reduced substantially below 1966 rates for a middle income married couple: by $61 at an income of $6,500; by $188 at an income of $10,000; and by $715 at an income of $15,000. *These reductions, of course, would apply only to taxpayers whose taxable income was unchanged by our recommendation.* For such taxpayers these tax cuts would be large enough to virtually eliminate the United States–Canadian differential for married couples.

Treatment of Dependents

We recommend the use of tax credits rather than separate rate schedules to allow for the non-discretionary expenses associated with dependent children. It might seem preferable to establish a separate rate schedule for each different family type that had different responsibilities and, therefore, different amounts of non-discretionary expenses. However, there are many differences between family responsibilities, such as the difference between families with dependent children and families with other dependants, the difference between either of these families and a tax unit supporting a student at a university or post-secondary vocational school, and the differences between otherwise similar families with school-age children where the wife is or is not working.

The difference between tax credits and exemptions is simple. A tax credit involves a reduction in taxes of a given amount, while an exemption grants a reduction in taxable income. The latter results in a tax reduction that increases with income. Because an exemption excludes from tax the last dollars of income received by a taxpayer, the value of an exemption depends upon the marginal rate applicable to the taxpayer. A tax credit, on the other hand, in effect exempts a given amount of the first dollars of a taxpayer's income. A tax credit thus affects all taxpayers in the same amount, while an exemption provides an allowance which increases in value as income increases. To put this in other terms, the revenue loss resulting from the use of exemptions is higher than from the use of credits, where credits and deductions achieve the same result for low income families.

We recommend the following credits: for the first child, $100; and for each additional child, $60. These credits would result in an average credit per child which decreased as the number of children increased. [Tax credits are also suggested to benefit families where both parents are working.]

The Unit of Taxation

One of the most important recommendations of the Carter Commission was to replace the 'American' principle of taxing the individual as the basic tax unit — presently used in Canada — by the 'British' principle of taxing the family as the basic unit. The extract below sets out the reasoning governing this recommendation.

46   The Family Unit*

The Royal Commission on Taxation

1. The present tax system treats the individual rather than the family as the basic unit for tax purposes. In our view this leads to inequities because we believe it is the ability of the family to pay, rather than of the individual members of the family, that should be taken into account in determining tax liabilities.

2. In our opinion a married couple should pay less tax than a single individual with the same aggregate income. However, we believe that at most income levels a married couple should pay higher taxes than two single individuals, each of whom has half the income of the couple, because of the economies that can be realized when two people live together. This result is not achieved with the present system.

3. The tax liabilities of married couples should be independent of the proportion of total income received by husband and wife. This result is not achieved under the present system, for the couple comprised of a husband and wife who have identical incomes pays a lower tax than a couple with the same income received by one of the spouses.

4. These problems could be eliminated by the aggregation of the income of husband and wife. By taxing the total income of the couple under a rate schedule that bears an appropriate relationship to the rate schedule applicable to individuals, a more equitable allocation of taxes between single individuals and couples could be achieved.

5. The aggregation of the income of husband and wife would have the important result that transactions between the two would have no tax consequences. In particular, *inter vivos* and testamentary transfers of property between spouses would not be subject to tax notwithstanding the general rule that gifts are included in the income of the donee tax unit.

6. Adopting the family as one of the basic units for tax purposes would have the advantage that the problems created by income splitting between

---

*Reprinted by permission from the Royal Commission on Taxation, *Report*, Queen's Printer, Ottawa, 1966, Vol. III.

husband and wife under the present approach would be largely eliminated. The restrictive sections of the Act that are now necessary to prevent income splitting have been sharply criticized as discriminatory and inconsistent. These restrictions could be abolished.

7. There are both advantages and disadvantages to the aggregation of the income of dependent children with family income. Except under unusual circumstances, compulsory aggregation of the income of dependent children with that of their parents would be preferable from an equity point of view, and the administrative problems would probably be less with aggregation. We therefore recommend compulsory aggregation of the income of dependent children with family income, with modifications that would provide the flexibility necessary to accommodate the diverse relationships that prevail between parents and their children and the unique character of the income sometimes received by dependent children.

Income Averaging for Tax Purposes

The present tax base in the personal income tax in Canada is defined over a one-year period. With a progressive rate schedule, two individuals with the same average tax base may pay, over a period of years, substantially different amounts in income tax if the annual income of one individual fluctuates more than that of the other. The greater the degree of fluctuation, the greater the degree of discrimination against the relatively unstable income. There is no reason why the tax base should be defined in terms of accretion over a one-year period, and the ideal solution, indeed the only complete solution to the problem of progressive tax rates and unstable incomes, would be lifetime averaging. Most averaging schemes, with the exception of Professor Vickrey's,[1] are more modest. The proposal by the Carter Commission for use in Canada is set out in the extract below.

47   Income Averaging *

The Royal Commission on Taxation

[Income fluctuation poses several problems]:

1. There is nothing sacrosanct about the measurement of income for tax purposes on an annual basis. The choice of the calendar year as the relevant time period is a matter of convention and convenience rather than principle. We can see no justification in equity for imposing substantially heavier taxes

[1]W. Vickrey, *Agenda for Progressive Taxation*, Ronald Press, New York, 1947.
*Reprinted by permission from the Royal Commission on Taxation, *Report*, Queen's Printer, Ottawa, 1966, Vol. III.

on those with fluctuating incomes, because there is no fundamental objection to the adoption of a longer time period and a longer time period would not produce this result. Some smoothing of income over a period of years would seem to us to be called for. We are not convinced, however, that equity demands income smoothing over a taxpayer's lifetime.

2. Without relief for irregular incomes the tax authorities would be drawn into an endless struggle to try to prevent taxpayers from manipulating the timing of their receipts or gains so as to minimize their tax liabilities. This struggle would produce ever greater complexities or arbitrariness in tax laws.

3. If there were no relieving provisions, those people who were able to manipulate the timing of their receipts or gains would, despite the efforts of the tax authorities, have an advantage relative to those who could not do so.

4. Unless there was some form of relief to those with irregular or fluctuating incomes, individuals might avoid occupations or businesses that were particularly subject to such variations.

These four points all seem to us to provide strong grounds for general relief from the tax consequences of lump sum or fluctuating incomes. In particular, the problem of taxpayer inequity is sufficient reason for providing relief even if it were possible to prevent the manipulation of income by taxpayers to avoid the full impact of progressive rates in each time period.

All measures of relief for fluctuating and irregular income are relatively complex and create compliance and administrative problems. Many forms of relief have to be rejected simply because they would not be understood by many taxpayers or would require too much record keeping. As in so many other areas of the tax structure, what is required is a compromise between the desirable and the practical.

Present Treatment

The present Canadian legislation recognizes the problem inherent in receipt by taxpayers of lump sum amounts or fluctuating income, and in some cases does attempt to provide alleviation. This is done through three distinct methods: the general averaging provision, restricted to income of farmers and fishermen; the special rates of tax applicable to income from exercising stock options and certain types of lump sum payments; and the spreading back of income over prior years, applicable to the income of authors from the sale of copyrights and to the income from recapture of depreciation or revaluation of inventory.

The present relief measures do not adequately meet the needs of the general body of Canadian taxpayers.

Alternatives to the Present Position

There are basically two approaches to the solution of the problem of lump sum and fluctuating income. First, there is the method of piecemeal relief, where the problem of fluctuating tax bases is, in effect, regarded as a series of separate problems, and specific and separate remedies are provided. This is the method now in effect in Canada. The second approach regards fluctuating and irregular incomes as a general problem to be solved by the application of a general remedy, applicable to all taxpayers. We favour the adoption of a combination of the two, with general but restricted provisions that would be available to all taxpayers, but with more generous provisions to deal with special hardship situations.

In our investigation of the alternative relieving provisions that might be introduced, we have placed great emphasis on the need for methods that had the following characteristics:

1. They should be made available on an optional basis.
2. They should be neutral among types of gains.
3. They should be administered with relative ease.
4. They should allow forward as well as backward averaging.

Block Averaging

In the belief that the problem of lump sum and fluctuating incomes is sufficiently widespread to require a more adequate method of granting relief than now exists, we recommend that a block averaging provision should be introduced that would be available to all taxpayers. However, to reduce the administrative problems that such a provision would entail, there should be restrictions, at least initially, based on both a minimum fluctuation in income and the minimum tax saving that would have to be obtained before the block averaging provision could be employed by a taxpayer.

The block averaging system has the advantage of already being an accepted part of Canadian tax legislation, and it appears to have operated to the reasonable satisfaction of both taxpayer and administrator.

Period of Averaging

It is necessary in a block averaging system to specify over what term or period of years income can be averaged. The period must be long enough to level effectively the peaks of income, but not so long as to create an impossible administrative task in recomputing tax on many returns for many earlier years. Three-year averaging would appear to be the minimum that would take care of most income fluctuations; five-year averaging is probably the maximum administratively feasible period. At present, farmers and fishermen are entitled to use a five-year block average. In order to avoid worsening the position of these two groups and because we think it is practical, given the methods of data storage and handling now available, to treat all taxpayers in the same way, we recommend that a five-year rather than a three-year averaging period should be adopted. Only consecutive years, with no years omitted, should be included in an averaging period. No overlapping of years in different averaging periods should be allowed except upon death or on giving up Canadian residence. . . . Only years in which the taxpayer has been resident in Canada should be included in an averaging period.

The five-year period should be treated as the maximum number of years that could be averaged. Taxpayers should be permitted to average over shorter periods if they wished to do so.

Restriction Related to the Size of the Tax Saving

To keep the administrative problems of a general averaging scheme within bounds, relief in respect of lump sum and fluctuating incomes should be provided, at least initially, only where fluctuations in the tax liabilities are substantial. Therefore we recommend that the right to average should only be available when the income in the lowest income year of the averaging period is less than 75 per cent of the income in the highest income year of the period. In addition, tax relief should be allowed only to the extent that the reduction in tax resulting from the averaging procedure exceeded $50. These restrictions would eliminate small claims and would restrict the use of the provision to those with material fluctuations in income.

Corporation Income Taxation

Most business activity in Canada is carried on under the corporate form of organization. Profits accrue directly to the corporation and may or may not be paid out currently to individual shareholders. The 'American' method of corporation income taxation has been to regard the corporation as a legal entity independent of individual shareholders, and correspondingly subject to taxation independent of the shareholders. The 'British' method, on the other hand, has been to recognize that corporate income, whether distributed or undistributed, accrues to shareholders, and to provide, accordingly, a measure of integration between personal and corporate income taxes. In 1965, however, the British adopted the American model. To date, the procedure in Canada has also followed the American model, though the whole issue has been opened for discussion by the Carter Commission's advocacy of full integration.

There are many other interesting aspects of corporation income taxation, such as its uncertain incidence, and its effect on savings and investment, but the extracts below will be addressed only to the integration controversy. The first extract sets out various methods of integration, and suggests that the only practicable and equitable method would be one of the partial integration proposals. The second extract presents in brief the Carter proposal for full integration.

48   Alternative Approaches To Integration*

J. R. Petrie

1. Repeal of the Corporate Income Tax

Outright repeal of the corporate income tax would eliminate the double taxation of distributed earnings, and would achieve the integration ideal of equal taxation of dividends and other types of personal income. But it would not meet the problem of undistributed earnings. Rather, it would accentuate it by permitting the accumulation of untaxed corporate earnings, and thus increase tax avoidance or tax postponement. Serious inequity would result if this plan were adopted without taxation of capital gains at the normal personal income tax rate. But even this would not solve the problem of tax postponement, or complete avoidance through the use of "wash sales". Furthermore, the loss of revenue entailed by the plan would necessitate serious adjustments in the national budget, transferring the tax load either to the personal income tax or to consumption taxes, or both.

2. Exemption of Dividends from Personal Income Tax

This plan would eliminate the double taxation of corporate income and dividends, and it would deal with undistributed profits as effectively as the present system. But it would be a grossly inequitable way of taxing distributed corporate earnings.

Dividend income would be removed from the progressive income tax and would pay tax at the going corporate rate. In the case of stockholders in the high personal rate brackets, the exemption of dividends would be a valuable concession, while it would be worthless in the case of stockholders in the lowest brackets. If rate progression on personal income is a sound principle, then it is violated by taxing dividends at a flat rate regardless of the other income of the shareholder.

3. The Partnership Approach

The proposal to tax corporate income in the same manner as the income of a partnership is taxed, i.e., by looking through the corporate form and taxing corporate income in the hands of the shareholders, whether distributed or not, is the most logical, direct, and uncompromising approach to the integration problem.

This plan has the important advantage of simplicity. There is no differentiation between corporate income and other business income. It solves once and for all the problem of undistributed earnings. It eliminates the need for a tax on capital gains to equalize the taxes on corporate income and other business income. Finally, it eliminates the long-standing controversy about the tax treatment of co-operatives.

*Reprinted by permission of author and publisher from J. R. Petrie, *The Taxation of Corporate Income in Canada*, University of Toronto Press, Toronto, 1952.

The objections to the plan are that it is based upon the false assumption that the receipt of earnings by a corporation represents the actual receipt of those earnings by the corporation's shareholders. It fails to recognize the fact that, while the shareholder has a beneficial interest in the corporation's retained earnings, he may have no voice in the company's dividend policy. The distribution or retention of earnings is the act of corporate management, which may be completely divorced from the corporate ownership.

Another defect in the general plan of taxing all corporate net income in the hands of shareholders involves the several administrative problems inherent in the plan. These problems fall into two groups, (1) those of determining to what classes of securities there should be an allocation of undistributed earnings in a given tax year, and (2) specific allocation problems arising after the classification of securities has been made.

4. The Dividends-Paid Credit Approach

The plan involves the retention of both the corporate income and the personal income taxes. Corporations, however, would be granted a deduction or credit for dividends actually paid, in addition to the deduction now allowed for bond interest paid.

This approach is in reality a tax on undistributed profits. It removes effectively the double taxation feature of the existing Canadian or United States system, it places a premium on the distribution of corporate earnings because no corporation tax is paid on distributed earnings, and it provides the same treatment for dividend income and other forms of personal income.

Inasmuch as this plan removes the double taxation of corporate income and dividends, it should provide a stimulus to investment in equity securities. From a tax viewpoint, shares and bonds would be placed on the same footing. Furthermore, there is no administrative problem connected with this approach.

But this method of integration has an important defect in that it tends to discriminate against small and expanding corporations. Large and well-established corporations having access to the capital market would be likely to distribute a large part of their earnings, thus avoiding the tax on distributed corporate income, and finance any further expansion through the sale of new shares or bonds. But most companies have at best a limited access to the capital market, and must rely upon retained earnings to provide funds for expansion.

From the Canadian viewpoint, there is a special problem attached to the dividends-paid credit approach, and that is the fairly heavy revenue loss that it would entail.

5. The Withholding Tax Approach

This plan involves the levy of a tax on all taxable corporate income, whether distributed or retained. The tax is regarded as being paid by the corporation on behalf of its shareholders. When dividends are distributed, individual shareholders include in their taxable personal incomes the cash dividends actually received plus the withholding tax paid on their behalf by the corporation. This is necessary because the tax paid by the corporation is used to meet part of the shareholders' tax liabilities. It is properly regarded, therefore, as part of the shareholders' income. After computing his personal income tax on this basis, the shareholder takes credit for the amount of tax withheld at the corporate level. This is the system used in Great Britain.

The withholding approach is designed to reduce or eliminate the double taxation of distributed profits by applying all or part of the tax paid by the corporation on such profits against the tax liability of the shareholders. For this reason, the shareholder is not required to pay a tax on his dividends, unless his individual tax liability exceeds the amount already paid by the corporation on his behalf.

[Objections to the Withholding Approach:]

(1) In theory the withholding approach eliminates the double taxation of corporate income and dividends, but because of the impracticability of equating the withholding rate with the highest personal income tax rate, the withholding approach would not equalize the taxation of distributed and undistributed profits. (2) The administrative complications involved in the necessity for refunds, in the treatment of dividends paid out of earnings retained before the utilization of the withholding approach, in the treatment of dividends paid out of tax-exempt income, in the treatment of dividends paid out of earnings accruing under a different rate structure, all would add unnecessarily to an already complicated tax structure. (3) The British system ignores conveniently changes in withholding rates, thus avoiding the problem arising from them. But it is doubtful if such a practice would be acceptable in Canada. (4) The withholding approach, while perhaps better in theory than the dividends-paid credit approach, has administrative difficulties attached to it which require most careful consideration in terms of achieving the kind of tax equity deemed desirable in an approach to integration.

6. The Dividends-Received Credit Approach

Under this approach a tax would be levied on corporate income, but an exemption (partial or total) or a tax credit would be applied to dividends when received by shareholders. While it is not a necessary feature of the plan, it is often contemplated that the corporate tax rate would be reduced to the level of the lowest personal income tax rate, and that dividends would be exempt from the first bracket rate of the individual tax rate.

The dividends-received credit approach resembles the withholding approach in some respects, but in several important respects it is quite different. It resembles withholding in that the reduction of the personal income tax on dividends is justified on the grounds that the corporate tax should be looked upon as a partial payment of the individual shareholder's tax liability in respect of his portion of the earnings. But it does not achieve equity among shareholders in different income brackets, as is done in the dividends-paid credit approach and the withholding approach.

49 Corporation Income Taxation*

The Royal Commission on Taxation

1. Taxes can be collected from organizations such as corporations but the burden is ultimately on people — customers, employees, suppliers or shareholders — whose power to consume is reduced by the tax on the organization. Corporations have the rights and obligations of persons under the law; management often makes corporate decisions without consulting the shareholders. These are valid but irrelevant propositions in considering who bears the corporation tax.

2. Equity and neutrality could best be achieved under a tax system where there were no taxes on organizations, and all individuals and families selling and holding interests in organizations were taxed on the realized and accrued net gains derived from these sales and holdings. The net gains from selling and holding interests in organizations would be treated in the same way as other kinds of net gains, and the net gains from selling and holding interests in all kinds of organizations would be taxed identically.

3. Unfortunately this ideal system cannot be recommended for two reasons:

   a) At the present time, valuation problems preclude the annual taxation of accrued net gains. In the absence of accrual taxation, and if there was no tax on the income of corporations, some individuals could postpone their personal income taxes on the income they wished to save.

   b) If the Canadian corporate source income of non-residents was taxed at lower rates than are now in effect, it would reduce the net benefit Canada derives from foreign direct investment in Canada. Because of existing tax treaties and the retaliation that would follow if these treaties were ignored, it would not be feasible to tax this income at the present level except by a corporation income tax like the tax now imposed at a rate of approximately 50 per cent.

4. Retaining the corporation income tax at a rate of approximately 50 per cent, but providing full integration of this tax with the personal income tax of residents, would solve the deferment problem, would maintain the net benefit from foreign direct investment in Canada and would achieve the greatest possible equity and neutrality.

The Proposed Integration System

5. The basic features of the full integration system we recommend are as follows:

   a) The income of corporations should be subject to tax at a flat rate of 50 per cent.

---

*Reprinted by permission from the Royal Commission on Taxation, *Report*, Vol. IV, Queen's Printer, Ottawa, 1966.

b) The income of individuals and families should be subject to progressive rates of tax with a top marginal rate of 50 per cent.

c) The corporation should be allowed to allocate after-tax corporate income to shareholders without having to pay cash dividends.

d) The tax base of the resident shareholder should include the corporate income paid or allocated to him, grossed-up for the corporation tax paid.

e) The resident shareholder should receive credit against his personal tax liability for the full amount of the corporation tax on after-tax corporate income paid or allocated to him, with a refund of the corporation tax if the credit exceeded the liability.

f) Realized gains and losses on corporate shares should be included in income and taxed at full progressive rates.

g) The cost basis of shares should be increased when the corporation allocated retained corporate earnings to shareholders and thereby created "allocated surplus", so that share gains resulting from the retention of earnings that had been taxed to the shareholder would not be taxed again to the shareholder when realized.

h) When dividends were paid out of allocated surplus they should not be included in the shareholder's income but should be deducted from his cost basis for the shares, because such dividends would represent a realization of funds already included in income and previously added to the cost basis of the shares.

i) A corporation with a small number of shareholders which met specified conditions should be entitled to elect to be taxed as a partnership in order to avoid the payment by the corporation of tax at 50 per cent and the claiming by the shareholders of refunds equal to the difference between that tax and tax calculated at their personal rates.

Advantages of Integration

6. The integration system has the following advantages relative to the present system:

a) The system would neither encourage nor discourage the retention of earnings by corporations.

b) Corporate cash retentions could be increased without worsening the cash position of most shareholders.

c) To the extent that the tax reduction was not passed on in the form of lower selling prices or higher purchasing prices, after-tax corporate income from Canadian equities would be increased for most resident shareholders with the result that share prices would rise, the cost of equity capital would fall, and the rate of capital formation by corporations would be increased until a new equilibrium was reached, that is, until rates of return declined toward their original levels.

   d) Non-residents holding shares in Canadian corporations would be encouraged to sell them to Canadians, and Canadian corporations wholly owned by non-residents would be encouraged to raise capital by issuing equities in Canada.

   e) Tax avoidance through surplus-stripping should no longer be a problem.

   f) Tax avoidance through the creation of associated corporations to take advantage of the dual rate would be removed.

   g) The tax treatment of corporations, trusts, and mutual organizations including co-operatives would be put on a similar basis.

   h) The allocation of resources would be improved with a resulting increase in the output of the goods and services that Canadians want.

   i) All corporate source income would be taxed at progressive rates of tax.

Taxation of Gratuitous Transfers

Present federal provisions for taxing testamentary transfers through estate tax are quite independent of provisions for taxing *inter vivos* transfers through gift tax. Present revenue from both taxes combined amounts to less than 2 per cent of total federal tax revenue. Inadequate revenue productivity suggests either abolition or reform. The present section focusses on reform, the more desirable alternative.

Several avenues of reform are possible. The major reason for the inadequacy of the present federal arrangements in terms of both revenue productivity and equity lies in the absence of integration of gift and estate taxes. The relatively low rates of gift tax encourage the partition of an estate prior to death and the final estate is taxed quite independently of all previous transfers made. The apparent solution here would be the integration of gift and estate taxes into one *cumulative transfer tax*, in which the estate would be regarded as the last of a series of gifts. On equity grounds, however, the problem remains that this arrangement takes no account of the proportion of the estate received by each legatee or the individual economic circumstances of the legatees.

A second path of reform takes account of the different proportions of the estate received by each legatee by taxing the individual proportions at progressive rates. The most sophisticated inheritance tax systems presently used are in West Germany and Sweden where a cumulative gift tax is integrated with the basic inheritance tax. This *inheritance tax* method, of which the provincial succession duties incorporate some features, does not solve the problem of gratuitous transfers from more than one donor, nor does it take into account the individual economic circumstances of each legatee. Moreover, an inheritance tax system would require very high tax rates to equal in revenue the cumulative transfer tax system outlined above.

The next step in reform lies in the so-called *cumulative accessions tax* method. This solves the problem of separately taxing transfers to one donee from different donors by aggregating for transfer tax purposes all gifts and bequests to a given donee from all donors. On revenue grounds this system is preferable to an inheritance tax system. Its only remaining problem is the equity issue — allowing for the other income which individual donees receive. In equity terms the ultimate step in sophistication is therefore to incorporate all gifts and bequests in a donee's cumulated income from all sources.

The remarkable aspect of the Carter proposal for reform of estate and gift taxation is that it approximates this optimal solution, differing from the optimum only in that it does not *require* cumulation of gifts received over time. The Carter proposal is set out in the first of two extracts below.

The provinces to date have not levied a tax on *inter vivos* gifts, and have employed methods of taxing testamentary transfers which have generally been of the inheritance tax variety, although several cases have combined features of both the estate tax and the inheritance tax approach. The Ontario Committee on taxation recommended the reform of provincial succession duties, while maintaining their predominantly inheritance tax form, and the introduction of a provincial gift tax. This approach is set out briefly in the second of the two extracts below.

50   Estate and Gift Taxation*

The Royal Commission on Taxation

Under the concept of a comprehensive tax base and a tax determined by ability to pay, the present gift taxes and estate taxes would be eliminated and gifts received from another tax unit would form part of the income of the tax unit receiving them. Gifts are by definition transfers of value for which no (or inadequate) payment or consideration is given. They include gifts made between living persons, that is, gifts *inter vivos*, and the passing of property on the death of the donor, that is, testamentary gifts or inheritances.

We also propose that where property has been given, either on death or during the lifetime of the donor, this should in general amount to a disposal of the property by the donor at its fair market value. Thus, any accrued property gain would be realized and would become taxable to the donor. However, a transfer to a member of the donor's family unit should be specifically excluded from being a disposition for tax purposes. This treatment would ensure that property gains, whether realized or unrealized, would be taxed not later than the date on which the family unit was terminated. It would also prevent the inequity that would arise if one person could give away property to a person who was not a member of his tax unit on which full tax had not been paid, because of an accrued gain, while another could only give away after-tax income.

One of the important features of our proposals is that property accumulated in a family unit should be freely transferable within that unit. In this way the

*Reprinted by permission from the Royal Commission on Taxation, *Report*, Vol. III, Queen's Printer, Ottawa, 1966.

estate which had been built up by a family unit could be used without restriction to support members of the family unit as long as it existed. This treatment would be applicable whether the transfer was made during the lifetime of the donor or on his death. However, a dependant child withdrawing from a unit would be required to include in his income, subject to a $5,000 lifetime exemption, the market value of property taken from the unit. This would be necessary so that if a dependent child received gifts from his parents in excess of that needed for consumption, the excess would be treated in the same way as gifts received by him after he has ceased to be a dependant.

One of the main reasons why people build up estates is to protect their families. The popularity of life insurance attests to this. The desirability of giving further relief to dependants of deceased heads of households was stressed constantly in briefs presented to the Commission. We agree with this objective and meet it with our recommendation concerning the family unit.

We also propose that each person should be entitled to certain exemptions, mainly for the sake of administrative simplicity. These would include the lifetime exemption of $5,000 for gifts received. In addition, we suggest annual exemptions of $250 for a person filing as a single individual, $250 for each spouse in a family unit, and $100 for each child in a family unit. Because of these exemptions it would be expected that most people will never pay any tax on gifts.

In many cases gifts will not be made directly to the donee but will be transferred so as to be held in trust. This may be either an *inter vivos* trust or a trust arising on death under the terms of a will. We do not regard a trust as a donee but rather as an intermediary. If the beneficiary of all the income from a trust or the prospective beneficiary of the corpus of the trust were a member of the family unit of the donor, the trust would receive the gift free of tax as if the gift had been made directly to the beneficiary. In other cases the trust would be subject to an initial tax on the gift in order to prevent avoidance of deferment of the tax. When the beneficiary eventually received the trust property he would include it in his income on a grossed-up basis and would receive credit for the initial tax paid by the trust.

Gifts That Should be Included in the Comprehensive Tax Base

We recommend that all property received from another tax unit by way of gift should be included in the tax base of the recipient. For this purpose the term "gift" should have an extended meaning and should include the following:

1. Gifts *inter vivos*.
2. Transfers of property for inadequate consideration, unless the transfer price was reached as a result of bona fide arm's length bargaining.
3. An extinguishment of debt, including non-enforcement by reason of limitation provisions, or the creation of an "artificial" debt, that is, where the parties were not dealing at arm's length and satisfactory terms of repayment had not been arranged.
4. Successions to property under intestate succession laws.

5. Succession under a will.
6. Receipt of property pursuant to laws for the relief of dependants.
7. Property accruing to the taxpayer by survivorship.
8. Receipt of a power of encroachment or a power of appointment which would permit the property to be used by or appointed to the taxpayer for his own use during his lifetime.
9. Receipt of property as a result of the exercise of a power of appointment.

51   The Taxation of Wealth *

The Ontario Committee on Taxation

Succession Duties vs. Estate Taxes

Death taxes as used today take two general forms. The first, used by Ontario, Quebec and British Columbia, is a tax on beneficiaries on the amounts that they receive by way of inheritance; this is a succession duty or inheritance tax. The second, now imposed by the federal government, under the name of an estate tax, is a levy on the estate of the deceased, which extracts a share of the assets before they are distributed to beneficiaries. The difference, then, lies in the taxpayer. The estate tax assessor looks upon the body of the deceased and in effect says "alas, my poor brother". The succession duty assessor looks upon the assembled heirs, murmuring "fortunate children".

In its pure form the estate tax is much simpler and undoubtedly easier to administer than a succession duty. To arrive at the estate tax, all that is required is to determine the total assets and taxable dispositions, then to deduct debts, funeral expenses, certain court costs and exemptions, and finally to apply the appropriate rate to the remainder. The tax is then collected from the executors or administrators of the estate and the remaining balance is distributed to, or held for, the beneficiaries. A succession duty is more complex, since the tax must be determined and collected on the value of each inheritance. Furthermore, the rates of duty may vary with the relationship of the beneficiary to the deceased and the size of the estate, as well as with the size of the bequest, making the rate schedules voluminous and complex.

In practice, however, the difference between the two is not as appears in theory. Estate taxes in most jurisdictions take into account the relationship of beneficiaries to the decedent. For example, the federal Estate Tax Act provides exemptions if the deceased had a widow or dependent children, which reduce the amount of tax that the estate would otherwise have to bear. Simi-

*Reprinted by permission from the Ontario Committee on Taxation, *Report*, Vol. III, Queen's Printer, Toronto, 1967.

larly, some succession duty Acts, such as the present Ontario statute, use the total value of the estate as one factor in determining the rate of tax.

Indeed, the distinction between the two forms is unlikely to be noticed by those who are legally liable for the tax. The Canadian Estate Tax Act requires the executors to pay the levy from the assets of the estate before distribution is made to the beneficiaries. The Ontario Succession Duty Act imposes the tax on the successors but prohibits executors from distributing inheritances without withholding the duty applicable to them. Any remaining differences are further diminished by the increasingly common practice of providing in wills that the executors shall pay all taxes out of the residue of the estate. Thus, although in theory the two forms of death tax are different, the effect on testators, beneficiaries, and executors is on the whole quite similar.

There is one factor that greatly limits the freedom of a Canadian province in choosing between these two forms of tax . . . . the British North America Act imposes certain limitations on the methods that provincial governments may use to raise revenue. The constraint of direct taxation prohibits a province from imposing a levy that is demanded of one person in the expectation that he will recover the payment from someone else. Thus Ontario is prevented by constitutional considerations from levying a tax on the estate of a deceased person before distribution to beneficiaries. To be direct, the courts have said, a death tax must be levied on the heirs.

This does not mean that the total size of an estate cannot be taken into account in computing the amount of tax due. In fact, under the present Ontario Act the rates of tax imposed on a beneficiary are in part based on the aggregate net value of the estate and in part on the amount by which he benefits from the estate and his relationship to the deceased.

In summary, although there is considerable latitude allowed in determining the method of calculation of the death duty, the provincial tax must be demanded directly of those benefiting from a distribution of assets. Ontario, must, therefore, levy a tax that takes the form of a succession duty.

[Gift Tax]

The federal gift tax was designed to discourage transfers of assets within a family that would have the effect of reducing the overall amount of income taxes paid by the family; hence its location in the Income Tax Act. There is considerable evidence that this provision has helped to preserve the income tax revenue. While a gift tax was imposed before the federal government entered the succession duty field in 1941, we nevertheless believe that it has proved to be even more important in preserving the base for death taxes. There is no doubt that a large proportion of gifts are made with a view to reducing death duties. It follows, then, that a gift tax should be levied by those jurisdictions that impose some form of death tax, and that the gift tax should be so constituted that is is complementary to the death tax. Accordingly, we are of the opinion that Ontario should enter the gift tax field with the objective not of raising revenue but of preserving the revenue from the succession duty.

As far as possible, Ontario's gift tax should parallel the provisions of the succession duty that we recommend. This means that the rates of tax and the method of calculation should be the same. It would also require the same methods of valuation. It must be recognized that this would increase substantially the taxes now applicable to gifts. On the other hand, an individual would still be able to distribute his assets over a period of years and attract less tax than under succession duty, simply because tax would be calculated annually at the comparatively lower rates applicable to the part of his estate that is disposed of in each year. This advantage to the taxpayer would be partially offset by the necessity of having to pay tax before it would otherwise have come due as a death duty. Gifts made within three years of death, together with the tax paid on them, would be brought into the aggregate net value of the estate, and a credit allowed against succession duty for the amount of provincial gift tax paid in respect of such gifts. This tax, then, may usefully be thought of as a discounted prepayment of succession duty.

Because the federal government is ideally situated to administer gift tax for the provinces as well as itself, we are loath to suggest the establishment by Ontario of a separate organization for this purpose. On the other hand, we would not expect the federal government to collect an Ontario gift tax unless it remained in the field and the base for the Ontario tax were identical with that of the federal tax. In the event that the federal government remains in the gift tax field, Ontario should try to persuade it to change the federal tax base to that which we propose. If this fails, Ontario must collect its own tax. In our view, the advantages to be gained by a provincial gift tax are sufficient to justify establishing a separate collection organization.

Taxes on Consumption and Services

Excise taxes and duties are not of great significance as a revenue source, and the Carter Commission has recommended the abolition of all excises except those on alcoholic and tobacco products. This section will not, therefore, deal with excise taxes or duties — which may in any event be seen as taxes on production rather than sales — but will focus on two areas; the various provincial sales taxes and proposals for reform, and the choice between a manufacturers' sales tax and a retail sales tax.

The first extract outlines the history of retail sales taxes in Canada. The second examines the sales tax in terms of its effect on equity and emphasizes the importance for equity of exempting food purchases. The third sets out the general economic effects of sales taxes.

An issue on which some unanimity appears to be emerging is that of extending retail sales taxes to services. The fourth and fifth extracts are a measure of this consensus, and set out the recommendations of the Ontario and Saskatchewan provincial tax commissions. It is also significant that the Carter proposal for a federal retail sales tax included services within the tax base.

The sixth extract sets out very briefly the case for a retail sales tax against a sales tax at the manufacturers' level, and the final extract presents the Carter argument for the abolition of the manufacturers' sales tax and its replacement by a retail sales tax.

The Ontario Committee on Taxation

The first retail sales tax in Canada was introduced by the City of Montreal on May 1, 1935, mainly to meet heavy relief payments which jeopardized the balanced budget required by statute. The rate of tax was 2 per cent, and it applied to all retail sales of tangible personal property except certain goods bought by manufacturers, and food.

The first provincial sales tax was introduced by Alberta on May 1, 1936, as a result of requests from municipalities for the Province to assume a larger share of education and social costs. The rate of tax was also 2 per cent, and was originally intended to apply to a very broad base, exempting only bread, milk and a few other necessities. Before the tax became effective, however, political pressures effected the exemption of drugs, most foods, meals, textbooks and sundry other items. The tax proved to be very unpopular and it was repealed on August 6, 1937. It has not subsequently been reintroduced.

Saskatchewan introduced a sales tax on August 2, 1937, as part of its effort to overcome a drastic decline in provincial revenues and a rapid increase in relief rolls occasioned by the catastrophic economic effects of both drought and depression. The rate was set at 2 per cent and applied to the sale of all goods, with the exception of certain foods, services and farm implements. The tax became a permanent addition to the revenue sources of the Province, with rate increases to 3 per cent in 1950 and 5 per cent in 1962 and a reduction to 4 per cent in 1965.

With the sales tax firmly established in one province, most of the other provinces followed a similar course, to help in the financing of their rising expenditures. Quebec was the second province to introduce a lasting retail sales tax; this became effective on July 1, 1940, at a rate of 2 per cent. The Montreal sales tax continued, but was administered by the Province. Numerous other Quebec municipalities introduced sales taxes of their own, also at the rate of 2 per cent. In 1961, the Quebec provincial rate was raised to 4 per cent, and in 1964 the Province took over the whole sales tax field, with the result that a uniform rate of 6 per cent now applies to the entire province, the municipalities receiving allocations from the Province. It was announced in the 1967 Budget that effective March 17, 1967, the rate would be increased to 8 per cent.

British Columbia entered the retail sales tax field on July 1, 1948, New Brunswick on June 1, 1950, and Newfoundland on November 15, 1950. These respective rates were 3 per cent, 4 per cent and 3 per cent. All three provinces have kept the sales tax as part of their revenue structures. British Columbia in 1954 increased its rate of tax from 3 per cent to 5 per cent, New Brunswick reduced its rate from 4 per cent to 3 per cent in 1954 but increased it to 6 per

---

*Reprinted by permission from the Ontario Committee on Taxation, *Report*, Vol. III, Queen's Printer, Toronto, 1967.

cent on January 1, 1967, and Newfoundland increased its rate in 1960 from 3 per cent to 5 per cent and in 1967 to 6 per cent.

In the wake of the national hospital insurance plan and the continuing rise of government expenditure, two more provinces, Nova Scotia and Prince Edward Island, imposed retail sales taxes at the close of the 1950's. Nova Scotia introduced a 3 per cent tax on January 1, 1959; Prince Edward Island followed with a 4 per cent tax on July 1, 1960. Both provinces have since raised their rates to 5 per cent.

That Ontario was able to defer the introduction of a sales tax until recently was due in part to the greater productivity of its other sources of revenue. But the rising costs of new hospital services and of the Province's responsibilities in education, coupled with the refusal of the federal government to grant greater income tax abatements requested by Ontario, led the Province to its decision to adopt a retail sales tax. The announcement was made by the Honourable James N. Allan, Treasurer of Ontario, on March 9, 1961, in the annual Budget Statement. The rate of tax was 3 per cent, effective from September 1, 1961. This rate was increased to 5 per cent on April 1, 1966.

On December 1, 1964, Manitoba introduced a selective 5 per cent sales tax called a "revenue tax". The tax was levied on fuel, coal and its derivatives, steam and hot water heating, electricity, local telephone charges, long distance telephone charges within the province, and natural and manufactured gas. This tax was thus a highly selective sales tax, unlike those of all the other provinces that utilize this source of revenue. It was announced on February 6, 1967, that a 5 per cent general retail sales tax on tangible personal property and services, with exemptions for food, children's clothing, manufacturers' goods, and a long list of other items, would be effective June 1, 1967. The only province that has avoided the introduction of a sales tax is Alberta.

53   Sales Tax and Equity*

The Ontario Committee on Taxation

On the basis of our theoretical analysis, we support the argument that the retail sales tax is borne by consumers. Therefore, although we recognize that the final retail price of every taxed commodity does not change by the full amount of any tax change, we believe that this is the best single assumption that can be made.

---

*Reprinted by permission from the Ontario Committee on Taxation, *Report*, Vol. III, Queen's Printer, Toronto, 1967.

Distribution of Burden Among Taxpayers

Having taken this position regarding the incidence of the sales tax, we can now examine the distribution of its burden among families, according to various income classes. Analysis is useful, in order to determine whether the tax bears more heavily on low-income classes and is as regressive as is often maintained. It is also useful in measuring the impact of the major exemptions on the distribution of the sales tax burden. Although non-residents of the province, largely tourists, bear some of the tax through their purchases, we estimate that about 91 per cent of the tax is borne by Ontario residents.

Table 29:1 is based on the highly simplified assumptions that consumers bear the tax in proportion to their purchases of taxable items and that consumers who are resident in Ontario bear 91 per cent of the total tax. The Table shows in A that the existing Ontario retail sales tax burden, in terms of family income distribution, is proportional over the first two family-income brackets, progressive between the second and third brackets, roughly proportional from the third bracket to the sixth bracket, and regressive to the final bracket for incomes of $10,000 and over. Our researches indicate that if the burden is computed by using expenditure rather than income as the base, the tax becomes more progressive.

We have heard suggestions that the removal of the exemption for food would simplify the administration of the tax and allow the current amount of revenue to be raised with a lower tax rate. If all food were subject to the levy, current revenues at the 5 per cent rate could be obtained with a tax rate of only 2.7 per cent. Taxing food would, as the Table shows in B, make the present sales tax regressive, the impact being particularly significant in the lowest income bracket where food is a large proportion of total family expenditure. It has been suggested that the regressiveness caused by the taxation of food could be offset if appropriate cash rebates were paid to families on a per-capita basis. In Ontario, we estimate that an annual rebate of $30 per person would return the total tax of over $200 million that would be paid on food if it were taxed at the 5 per cent rate. The figures in C of Table 29:1 indicate that such a rebate would make the tax much less regressive than in B, but the combined effect of taxing food and paying rebates changes the burden pattern only slightly from the existing tax which exempts food. This change from the current situation would come about because the rebate in the $2,000 to $3,999 income classes is greater than the amount of the sales tax that these families would pay on food. For the two highest income classes (those over $6,999), the reverse situation is true because the tax on food expenditures would exceed the rebates.

A fourth possibility, presented in D of Table 29:1, is to remove all exemptions and to tax services. In this case, the yield of the present tax could be obtained at a rate of 1.6 per cent. If this alternative were implemented, the Table indicates, the tax would be more regressive than in A and C and similar to B, except for the $10,000 and over class. When compared to A, the tax burden is higher on the $2,999 and under classes because expenditures on food and other exempt items form over 70 per cent of total expenditures incurred by

TABLE 29:1

BURDEN OF ONTARIO RETAIL SALES TAX EXPRESSED AS A PERCENTAGE OF FAMILY INCOME

	Under $2,000	$2,000 to $2,999	$3,000 to $3,999	$4,000 to $4,999	$5,000 to $6,999	$7,000 to $9,999	$10,000 and Over
A. Burden of present tax at 5% rate	1.55%	1.47%	2.03%	1.87%	1.96%	2.08%	1.54%
B. Burden if food is taxed and rate reduced from 5% to 2.7%	2.52	1.66	2.07	1.92	1.94	1.93	1.35
C. Burden if food is taxed, rate left at 5%, and annual per-capita rebate of $30 given	1.58	1.14	1.54	1.55	2.02	2.38	1.83
D. Burden if all goods and services taxed without exemptions and rate is reduced from 5% to 1.6%	2.41	1.66	2.01	1.96	2.01	1.89	1.72

Note: These calculations are based on 1961 statistics. They present the pattern of tax burden that would have resulted if the various sales tax plans had been in existence in 1961. In all four cases the yield from the tax would be the same.

this group. The burden is also higher on the $10,000 and over class because the effect of the lower rate is outweighed by the inclusion of services.

In summary, these examples indicate that the existing tax is more equitable than two of the alternatives and that it is slightly less equitable than the pattern obtained by taxing food and giving rebates to individuals. However, it is questionable whether the rebate plan would as effectively meet the social objective of removing the burden of tax on food as would the exemption method. This is because individuals may view the rebate as a windfall and use it for purposes other than the purchase of food. Moreover, because of whatever time lag might occur between the payment of the tax on food items and the subsequent rebate of the tax there is a cost which, while uniform for families of the same size, bears more heavily on those of low incomes. Finally, the administrative saving to be achieved by removing the exemption from food would in all likelihood be more than offset by the cost of administering the rebate system.

54   Economic Effects of Sales Taxes *

The Ontario Committee on Taxation

Revenue Yield

One obvious effect of the utilization of a retail sales tax is to increase the revenue yield of the provincial tax system where economic, political and constitutional limitations have restricted the amounts of revenue that can be raised from other sources. Furthermore, there are financial and economic limits within which the Province's program of deficit financing must be contained in any given period. In making possible a larger flow of funds to the provincial government, the extension of the sales tax increases the amount of government expenditure that can be undertaken.

Frictional Effects

All tax programs involve so-called "frictional" effects. These include changes in work effort, consumption and production patterns as well as administrative effects on firms and individuals. In general, it is viewed as a virtue if a tax has slight frictional effects. Although it is impossible to prove the superiority of one tax over another in this regard, some generalizations can be made about the retail sales tax. Where a tax is borne by individuals in proportion to their expenditures rather than to their incomes, their incomes

*Reprinted by permission from the Ontario Committee on Taxation, *Report*, Vol. III, Queen's Printer, Toronto, 1967.

from work effort are obviously not directly subject to the tax. There may well be an indirect encouraging effect on work effort, because the retail sales tax increases the cost of goods and products purchased, but this effect is likely to be small. In this respect, the retail sales tax is generally regarded as superior to the personal income tax because the latter directly lessens the income from work effort and does so at *progressive* rates. Income received from the extra or marginal work effort is taxed more heavily than average income.

A general retail sales tax will tend to be neutral with respect to the distribution of expenditures on the various kinds of goods and services. Where exemptions are granted to particular commodities, the effect is to increase expenditures on them. To the extent that it is socially desirable to increase these expenditures, exemptions will improve existing purchasing patterns. However, if there are no social benefits associated with greater expenditures on certain goods, the exemptions will distort the pattern of consumer purchases. The taxing of some producer goods and not others likewise distorts production processes away from the most efficient use of resources.

The retail sales tax is superior to the turnover tax, the value-added tax, or the federal manufacturers' sales tax, because it minimizes pyramiding and double taxation and its incidence is less uncertain.

While the government's administrative costs are low in relation to the yield of the retail sales tax, the use of such a tax does involve additional cost to retailers in determining and collecting the tax and keeping the books, records and documents prescribed in the Regulations. The cost of administering a sales tax at the retail level is obviously higher than for one at the manufacturing or wholesale level because of the greater number of business establishments involved in the process of tax collection. It is difficult to compare retail sales taxes and personal income taxes on this score, because each embraces many variations. But administrative costs to business firms and individuals, both as taxpayers and collectors or withholders of the tax, are likely to be similar for both taxes.

Effects on Saving and Consumption

It is generally argued that a sales tax will discourage consumption and encourage savings. This is because the tax is levied only on consumption and individuals will tend to substitute savings for consumption. This argument is valid if a comparison is made between an income tax and a sales tax or if the introduction of a sales tax is coupled with an expenditure program that allows individuals to maintain the pre-tax standard of living. However, if a comparison is made between pre-tax and post-tax situations, and if changes in government spending are not considered, the impact of a sales tax on consumption and saving is not clear. Many factors are relevant in analysing the effects of the tax, but we limit our discussion here to two of major importance. First, the tendency to increase saving and reduce consumption is much stronger if it is believed that the tax is temporary rather than permanent. If the tax is permanent, there is little to be gained by postponing expenditures. Second, the effect of the tax is different on different income groups. If the tax is expected to be permanent, the following effects are generally encountered. For low-income individuals who spend nearly all of their income and who do not save systematically, the sales tax likely increases the amount spent on consumption and reduces the amount saved. Many middle-income individuals have fixed savings commitments in the form of insurance and other savings plans. These individuals may increase, decrease or keep their levels of saving constant. Individuals with high incomes normally maintain their standard of consumption and their savings fall when a sales tax is imposed. However, the impact of the Ontario tax on consumption and saing is not as large as that of a general sales tax would be, because many items are exempt and consequently the prices of these items may not rise. Thus, the impact of a retail sales tax, and particularly the Ontario sales tax, on consumption and saving is likely to be small.

Effect on Economic Growth

It is often argued that with reference to the objective of sustained economic growth, the sales tax is to be preferred to a personal income tax. This assertion rests on the fact that the personal income tax is progressive and that most of the personal flow of investment funds is provided out of savings by individuals with high incomes. The desire and ability to provide funds for investment is believed to be much more greatly reduced by a personal income tax than by a sales tax. It is also argued that there will be a shift away from consumer goods and toward production goods because only consumer goods are taxable. Although this line of argument is valid if after the tax is imposed there is still adequate market demand for current production, it may not be completely correct when the return on new investment is inadequate as it may be during periods of low economic activity. The unemployment experienced during periods of low economic activity may make it at least as important to stimulate consumption as to provide funds for investment. Therefore, the argument for a sales tax on the ground that it will be more consistent with economic growth than an income tax is valid only if a shortage of investment funds is the chief problem. But the effect on economic growth of the two taxes is likely to be similar if the chief problem is inadequate demand for current production.

Effect on Inflation and Deflation

On the one hand, it is argued that sales taxes are deflationary because they tend to reduce consumption. On the other hand, sales taxes are sometimes thought of as being inflationary because of the price increases that they occasion. Not only do goods increase in price as a result of the tax, but many labour contracts in Canada are tied to the Consumer Price Index, and thus wages increase as a consequence of an increase in the tax. The combination of the inflationary and deflationary effects of the tax depends upon the economic conditions prevailing at the time the rate of tax is increased, but a rise in consumer prices is highly probable.

Relationship to the Business Cycle

The yield of the sales tax moves in the same direction as the business cycle because aggregate taxable purchases rise and fall with economic activity. However, the yield of the sales tax is not nearly as responsive to changes in economic activity as that of the personal income tax. The yield from personal income tax changes more than proportionately to changes in income. This is partly because the personal income tax is progressive, with the effect that individuals with increasing incomes generated by the expansionary phase of the business cycle move automatically into higher tax brackets. The income tax is also more responsive than the sales tax because national income fluctuations are greater than the fluctuations in expenditures.

Over time, the yield of the sales tax is likely to increase with increases in income. Although individuals in the higher income brackets spend a smaller proportion of their income than those with low incomes, the proportion of national income spent remains relatively constant. While the yield of the sales tax will not increase as much over time as that of the personal income tax, it will likely increase in proportion to income, particularly if expenditures on services are subject to tax. If services are not taxed, the expansion of revenue from the sales tax may fall behind the rate of growth of the economy because outlays for services represent a continuously rising proportion to total consumer expenditures.

55   The Inclusion of Services in the Tax Base I*

The Ontario Committee on Taxation

The present Ontario retail sales tax is a tax restricted to the consumption of tangible personal property. While the Act does not impose any tax on services as such, it does tax some services under the guise of tangible personal property. Telegraph and telephone services and long distance calls are taxed as these are included in the statutory definition of tangible personal property. Rentals of tangible personal property are taxed by definition as a "sale". Otherwise, no attempt has been made to sweep services into the ambit of the tax. Because service industries have in recent years accounted for an increasing percentage of Canada's gross national product, a consideration of the many arguments relating to the inclusion of services within the base of the sales tax is relevant to our task.

A sales tax is imposed on the assumption that a taxpayer's ability to pay

---

*Reprinted by permission from the Ontario Committee on **Taxation**, *Report*, Vol. III, Queen's Printer, Toronto, 1967.

can in part be measured by his expenditures on consumption. Consumer expenditures are made for both goods and services, and it seems somewhat artificial to levy tax on the basis of the consumption of goods, while ignoring the consumption of services. Moreover, it has been found that as income rises, expenditures on services tend to expand more rapidly than expenditures on goods, with the result that services represent an increasing share of total consumption. Often it is difficult to distinguish between a charge made for goods and a charge made for services. For example, a manufacturer may sell his product at a rate that includes installation of the product on the customer's premises.

As the stage at which a sales tax is levied comes closer to the point of ultimate consumption, the arguments in favour of a tax on services become stronger. Since the distribution of goods to consumers is essentially a service function, and the charges for distribution services are included in the final price of the article on which tax is paid, the costs of distribution are in effect subject to sales tax. If other services are not taxed, the sales tax discriminates not only as between goods and services but between one service industry and another.

Because many retail merchants deal in both goods and services (e.g. garages, appliance dealers, repair shops, etc.), it is frequently difficult to distinguish between the charge made for goods and the charge made for services. Thus a retail sales tax that is imposed only on tangible personal property obviously discriminates in favour of expenditures on services. In view of the strong argument in equity that favours the taxation of services, and of the revenues that could be obtained from such a tax, it is somewhat surprising that none of the Canadian provinces has yet attempted to levy a tax in this area. We note with interest that the Government of Manitoba proposes to do so, as of mid-1967.

One of the reasons for the reluctance of the provinces to tax services has undoubtedly been the administrative difficulties involved in such a tax. We believe that these difficulties have been overstated in the past and that, in spite of the large number of services enterprises that would need to be licensed and dealt with by the Branch, a sales tax on services is both feasible and desirable.

There are two broad approaches by which a tax on services might be imposed. The tax might be applied generally to all services, with specified exemptions, in the same way that the present tax applies generally to all goods, with specified exemptions. Alternatively, the tax may be applied only to specifically designated services. For reasons of administrative efficiency, the second form of taxation appears to us to be preferable. While we do not suggest taxing all services, the disadvantages and inequity associated with their blanket exemption should, we believe, be corrected. The taxation of services being desirable in principle, each broad class of service must be examined to determine whether or not it would be just to tax it under the principles that we have developed, and whether or not the tax could be collected without undue administrative difficulty.

To meet social objectives all medical, dental and health services, funeral services, public transportation services and adult education courses conducted by school boards, universities or other non-profit organizations should be exempt from sales tax. Services rendered to manufacturers or producers should likewise generally be exempt from tax, for the same reason as materials and machinery: to avoid double application of the tax.

If the tax is levied on all services, inevitable administrative problems arise in dealing with a large number of small service entrepreneurs. Further, serious conflicts arise as between the taxation of those types of services that can be rendered either by a service organization or by a single employee. For example, house-cleaning can be performed either by a service organization or by a domestic servant. Often, house-cleaning services are performed by one individual for a number of customers. It would thus be unrealistic administratively to attempt to collect tax on the services rendered by such a person. Consideration would also have to be given to the problem of services supplied through vending machines. Where such machines could not easily be adapted to collect small amounts of tax, the tax might become a burden of the business firms providing the services.

The determination of the particular services most appropriately subject to tax is a task best performed by government. We have developed, however, the following illustrative list of the types of services that we think should be taxed in addition to those already taxed as sales of tangible personal property:

(a) Installation, repair and maintenance of taxable tangible personal property;

(b) Personal services including those rendered by barbers, hair dressers, beauty parlours, dressmakers, steam and sauna baths, driving and dancing schools, dry cleaners and laundries;

(c) Hotel, motel and other transient accommodation (defined as provided by an establishment having four or more rooms to rent and for which rent is paid for continuous occupation for less than one month) ;

(d) Automobile parking services (excluding metered street parking) ;

(e) "Pay" television, radio and music program services, and television cable services provided to subscribers;

(f) Amusements, theatrical and other performances, sporting events and recreational facilities; and

(g) Services in respect of transactions in real estate, stocks, bonds and other securities rendered by brokers, dealers and agents.

The inclusion of amusements, theatrical and other performances, and sporting events in the list is consequential upon the recommendation that The Hospitals Tax Act be repealed and that expenditures now taxed under that Act be taxed under The Retail Sales Tax Act.

The Saskatchewan Royal Commission on Taxation (1965)

We would recommend extending the coverage of the retail sales tax to include purchases of services. Such purchases represent the acquisition of consumer satisfactions in precisely the same fashion as do purchases of commodities. The logic of our entire argument requires such an extension. We have contended that with this tax, as with any other, it is designed to fall upon individuals and be payable according to their means. The full measure of their means, insofar as consumer purchases are a valid indicator, must comprehend the whole of their purchases, and not simply a proportion (tangible non-exempt goods) which is not necessarily representative. We have indicated above that such an extension is necessary in the name of tax equity. The extension recommended would provide for a broader tax base and make it possible either to realize a greater return at existing rates or the same return at lower rates. In any event, it would spread the burden of payment more equitably among the tax-paying public. In the light of the prospective revenue needs of the province, we would recommend that the rate of the tax be lowered. At the rate provided for under the most recent legislation, we estimate that the extension of the tax base to include services should yield additional revenue in excess of three million dollars.

The term "services" should be interpreted broadly to include all consumer expenditure on intangibles. With respect to such purchases, all should be regarded as taxable except for categories of services where specific and valid reasons can be given for exception.

We would recommend that the following services or categories of services should be exempt from the operations of the retail sales tax:

(a) services related to food and food production;
(b) services related to the provision of health care;
(c) services related to the provision of educational opportunities;
(d) services of charitable and community service organizations, and in particular, memberships and donations in support of these services;
(e) financial services;
(f) services provided by municipally owned parking lots;
(g) transportation services.

In the light of what has been said previously, the reasoning behind most of these recommendations is readily apparent. In some instances, however, further comment is necessary. The exemption of financial services, even though on first glance such services may be regarded as fair game for the tax collector, is recommended on a number of grounds. The position of the province in levying and collecting a tax on bank services may, constitutionally,

*Reprinted by permission from the Saskatchewan Royal Commission on Taxation. *Report*, Queen's Printer, Regina, 1965.

be an ambiguous one since money, banking and interest are matters clearly left within the jurisdiction of the federal government under the B.N.A. Act. Apart from this, however, there are other aspects of the taxation of interest and other charges of financial institutions which make such taxation objectionable. A good deal of the charge, insofar as it would fall directly upon the consuming public, would be related to the costs of housing and to personal-loan borrowing to finance emergency expenditures (in all probability, expenditures on taxable commodities or services). Socially, as well as practically, we can see little reason for such taxation.

The reasons for the recommendation in respect of certain services related to the provision of permanent basic living accommodation may be clear as far as matters of principle are involved, but less so in the matter of application. By way of clarification, it should be said that we would include in this category of exemptions rentals, the services of rental and real estate agencies, and what may normally be transient living accommodation (such as hotel rooms) when occupied by the same tenant for a period in excess of 60 days. These suggested exemptions seem to us to be in keeping with a generally accepted social policy which recognizes the essential need for adequate shelter and accommodation. The field of transportation services has been recommended for exemption because of the prospective difficulties in administering a tax on such services in any equitable manner. Such taxation would discriminate against those using public transportation systems in favour of those moving themselves or their goods in their own vehicles. Insofar as businesses are concerned, a cost factor would be added with the usual results in price, and, ultimately in double taxation. The difficulties of enforcing the tax measure when arrangements and payment for much long-haul travel can be so easily arranged outside of the province are obvious.

Beyond this list of broad categories of service which we have recommended there may well be specific services which for one reason or another should be considered for inclusion within the exempt list. Such items as baby care and children's nurseries, and the services of such organizations as the Corps of Commissionaires might merit additional consideration. Then, too adminis-trative experience will undoubtedly yield information as to the feasibility of applying the tax to certain specific services — and the administrative reason may prove to be a good and sufficient one for exempting certain defined services. On the whole, however, and in keeping with our earlier contentions concerning the nature of the tax itself, we would urge that the list of exemptions be restricted and that such exemptions as there are be maintained insofar as it is possible within broad and clearly definable categories of service.

57 Merits of the Retail Tax*

J. F. Due

1. The retail tax avoids the inherent discrimination of the manufacturers' sales tax arising out of varying distribution channels. In order to minimize these disturbances, a number of adjustments have been made in the operation of the federal tax, involving notional prices and the "unlicensed wholesale branch" technique, which have greatly complicated the operation of the federal tax without fully solving the inherent discrimination. The retail tax, because it can be applied to the actual final selling price, avoids not only the discrimination, but also the complications introduced into the manufacturers' tax in order to lessen the discrimination. It is a far simpler tax for the vendor to understand.

2. The retail tax is directly related to consumer expenditures, since it applies to the retail selling price. With the manufacturers' tax the ratio of tax to consumption expenditures varies with the wholesale and retail margins on the different commodities. Uniformity of ratio of tax to taxable consumer expenditures is desirable if discrimination against consumers of some goods and possible re-allocation of consumer purchases are to be avoided.

3. The retail tax avoids the pyramiding which is inevitable under the manufacturers' tax as wholesalers and retailers apply percentage markups to purchase prices which include tax. While competitive forces reduce pyramiding over time, a certain element is inevitable.

4. The retail tax is directly evident to the consumer, whereas the manufacturers' tax is hidden in the price of the product. In the interests of logical decision-making on governmental expenditures and tax structures in a democracy, it is essential that individuals be aware of the tax they are bearing.

5. Maintenance of equality of tax treatment of imports and domestically produced goods, and elimination of tax on exports are much simpler with the retail tax, which applies to the final transaction through which the commodities pass. It is very difficult to maintain equality of tax treatment of imported and domestic goods when the sales tax is applied prior to the retail level.

6. The tax element introduced at a relatively early stage in the production-distribution channels has a generally disturbing influence on the whole pricing structure, and changes in the tax necessitate widespread price adjustments. On the other hand the retail tax is added to the selling price, or more correctly the customer's entire bill, and no price readjustments are required. Anticipated tax changes, while, as with other sales taxes, altering consumer buying, do not effect dealers' inventory policies, as does a manufacturers' sales tax. Anticipation of a reduction in the rate of a manufacturers' sales tax

---

*Reprinted by permission of author and publisher from J. F. Due, *Provincial Sales Taxes*, Canadian Tax Foundation, Toronto, 1964.

will cause dealers to reduce stock, and disturb the regularity of production in manufacturing.

The manufacturers' sales tax has only one significant advantage: the much smaller number of manufacturers than retailers. Almost solely on this ground did the federal government adopt and retain the manufacturers' form of sales tax. But in terms of the economy as a whole this advantage has been completely lost as the retail sales tax has developed. With a retail tax in use anyway, the fact that the manufacturers' tax is collected from fewer firms loses all significance.

58   A Federal Sales Tax*

The Royal Commission on Taxation

Manufacturers' Level: General Administrative Considerations

A Manufacturers' tax is relatively easy to administer. Compared with taxes at the wholesale and retail levels, the number of taxpayers is smaller, the typical taxpayer is larger, his records are probably more satisfactory, and evasion is minimal. The administrative inconveniences of refund procedures arising from the substantial movement of goods from the manufacturer to the wholesaler and on to another manufacturer may be reduced significantly by the widespread licensing of wholesalers.

With rising rates of tax, however, it is apparent that the increasing need for neutrality in the computation of the manufacturers' tax results in growing uncertainty and complexity. Attempts to improve the neutrality of the manufacturers' sales tax create valuation problems because of the complex and continuously changing production and distribution patterns. In a highly competitive economy, small differences between firms in the application of an 11 per cent tax to the costs of packaging, transportation, assembling, warehousing, sales promotion, servicing, installation, and to transactions not at arm's length or involving rights to goods being manufactured, are of great concern to the taxpayer. We found no generally satisfactory solution to the dilemma of choosing between measures which would achieve simplicity and certainty at the expense of neutrality, and measures which would achieve approximate neutrality at the expense of certainty and simplicity. Even the argument that cost of collection is low under a manufacturers' sales tax loses its validity in the broader federal-provincial context of duplicate administrative organization and taxpayer compliance responsibilities.

---

*Reprinted by permission from the Royal Commission on Taxation, *Report*, Queen's Printer, Ottawa, 1967.

Wholesale Level: Neutrality Considerations

A single-stage sales tax might be applied to the sale price of goods delivered to retailers, rather than to the sale price of goods delivered to wholesalers which would be the best base under a manufacturers' tax. We will call a tax applied to the sale price of goods delivered to retailers a wholesale tax.

A manufacturers' tax and a wholesale tax have a number of common characteristics: both are hidden taxes in the sense that the retailer buys tax-paid goods; both are incapable of achieving the neutrality of a retail tax; both stop short of entry into a sales tax field already occupied by the provinces; both can use the present administrative machinery; and both involve a limited number of taxpayers, generally with good record keeping.

Taking all factors into account, we anticipate that a wholesale tax would achieve greater certainty and simplicity than a manufacturers' tax, without any increase in the costs of administration.

Retail Level: Neutrality Considerations

If the federal government converted the manufacturers' tax into a tax at the retail level as we recommend, the fact that this type of tax is already used by eight of the ten provinces would have important consequences for both the method of administration and coverage of the tax. A sales tax should be "neutral" in its effect on the spending patterns of consumers, using as our practical measure of neutrality the tax to final selling price ratio.

[In the case of] the manufacturers' tax and the wholesale tax, we stated that the departures from a neutral tax, and the attendant complexities in endeavouring to achieve a rough measure of neutrality, would arise both from differences in the relative importance of different cost elements in different goods, and from differences in the stages of the distribution process at which these costs were incurred. Regardless of the distributional channels used, of who advertises, packages or imports, these cost elements that ultimately form part of the selling price of an article to the consumer converge at the point of imposition of a retail tax. At this tax level the goals of neutrality and simplicity would be achieved, for the tax would be a constant ratio of expenditures on taxable goods by all consumers.

There would be additional advantages in the retail tax. It would avoid the pyramiding effect, the marking-up of the tax element in the price of goods as they pass through the distributional stages, about which a number of participants have complained to this Commission. We believe, however, that this effect is frequently overstated. While various degrees of pyramiding can occur under a manufacturer's tax, and to a lesser extent under a wholesale tax, competitive conditions tend to reduce its impact over the long run.

Only a tax at the retail level could avoid the inequities that arise from the inclusion of tax in inventories at any other level. Examples of such inequities are the sale of obsolescent or damaged tax-paid goods, losses by breakage, and losses incurred when the tax is lowered or eliminated. A retail sales tax would provide the broadest base and so would require the lowest rate for a given revenue; and at this level there would be the greatest taxpayer awareness, because there would be full disclosure of the tax burden.

Novel Tax Devices — A Turnover Tax; A Value-Added Tax; A Selective Employment Tax; A Negative Income Tax

The use of the term "novel" in the title of this section does not imply that the devices discussed are necessarily recent in their theoretical conception, but simply that these devices are much in discussion, in some cases in use elsewhere, but to date have not been employed in Canada.

The Turnover Tax

A "Turnover" or "Cascade" form of transactions tax applies at a given rate to every transaction through which goods pass on their path from the first stage of production to final sale. For a variety of reasons, principally the problem of "pyramiding" and the built-in incentive to integration, most of the turnover taxes used widely until recently in Europe have been replaced by a tax on value-added. The extract below reflects the feelings of the Carter Commission on the use of a turnover tax in Canada.

59   Cumulative Turnover Tax*

The Royal Commission on Taxation

A turn-over tax has several merits. Because it may apply to all transactions at every stage of production and distribution, the extremely broad base would permit very considerable revenues to be raised at a low rate of tax. In contrast with a single-stage tax, a turn-over tax could avoid the administrative and compliance difficulties arising from the need to separate taxable from non-taxable transactions. In practice, however, the modifications usually introduced into turn-over taxes for the purpose of reducing the inherent inequities result in considerable administrative complications.

In our view, the defects of a turn-over tax outweigh its merits. It produces a variable tax element in final consumer prices. Because the tax "cascades" on each successive transaction as goods move through the production and distri-

---

*Reprinted by permission from the Royal Commission on Taxation, *Report*, Vol. V, Queen's Printer, Ottawa, 1967.

bution process, the proportion of tax in the final price to the consumer may vary widely from product to product. A commodity produced, and perhaps distributed, within an integrated firm may bear considerably less tax than a competing product that has passed through a considerable number of transactions on its way through the various production and distribution stages to the consumer. The resulting competitive inequities are self-evident.

Under a turn-over tax on all transactions, firms have a powerful incentive to eliminate as many independent transactions as possible. While vertical integration may not be economically harmful, indeed it may in some instances lead to increased efficiency, the encouragement of integration by the turn-over tax is improper. Certainly the tax would have the effect of discouraging specialization.

Furthermore, there would be difficulties in applying exemption to exports and in taxing imports, where products pass through a number of transactions before being exported, the tax would become buried in the price, and the refund to the exporter could not be made with precision. Any refund formula could be, at best, only an average of the tax in numerous transactions. Such an average would therefore be subject to the complaints of those exporters who believed that, in their case, the refund was inadequate; on the other hand, those exports which would benefit from the average might draw complaints of export subsidization. Similarly, it would be impossible to allocate precisely to imports a tax rate comparable with the tax borne by competitive, domestically produced goods because the latter would bear varying amounts of tax.

The significance of the above defects mounts as the rate of tax increases. We reject a cumulative turn-over tax as being an unsuitable form of sales taxation for Canada.

A Value-Added Tax

A tax on value-added might best be described as a sophisticated turn-over tax, where the cumulative tax factor is removed by taxing each transaction only in respect of the addition to sale value which has occurred in the stage immediately prior to the transaction in question. The tax base for any entrepreneur would then be the sale price of his output less the cost of materials and other inputs. The tax collected under the value-added approach would be identical to that collected under the retail sales tax approach, assuming the same rate of tax.

A value-added tax is generally thought of as an alternative to a retail sales tax. In general, since the anticipated revenue under a value-added tax would be the same as under a retail sales tax, the value-added approach seems simply to spread the direct impact of the tax over a larger number of firms, and therefore to add unnecessarily to the complexity of collecting a given amount of revenue — unless, as in the French case, it is not feasible to collect heavy taxes from retailers. The first extract below from the Carter Commission, reflects this view.

The Carter Commission did not consider a tax on value-added as an alternative to some other *direct* tax, such as the corporation income tax, and it is here that the value-added approach might bear considering for use in Canada. Under GATT regulations, exports may be freed only from the burden of indirect taxes. Suspension or refunding of direct taxes previously levied on goods and services at time of export is considered an export subsidy; such subsidies are disallowed by Article XVI of GATT. The point here is that a tax on value-added is considered an indirect tax; and countries, such as those in the European Common Market which rely heavily on indirect taxes, are placed at an export advantage relative to countries, such as Canada and the United States, which rely primarily on direct taxes. The second extract below rejects the argument that a value-added tax as a substitute for a corporation income tax would significantly increase the incentive to export in Canada, weighs the value-added tax in terms of equity, and suggests a final, very practical, argument for the introduction of a value-added tax — that the federal government must look for alternative sources of revenue.

60   Value-Added and Single-Stage Taxes: A Comparison*

The Royal Commission on Taxation

In taxing consumption both the value-added and the single-stage forms of tax collection would achieve a similar result; they would yield tax in an amount derived from the taxable value and the rate of the tax applied to it. The value-added form would yield this revenue in the form of "fractional payments" at each transaction stage, which would add up to the same amount as the "one-shot" yield under a single-stage tax.

Administrative Aspects

The elimination of the cumulative or "cascading" element in a transactions tax would be achieved under a value-added form because a taxpayer would deduct his purchases (or the tax thereon) from his sales (or the tax thereon). It would be necessary for each taxpayer to keep full records in respect of both purchases and sales in order to substantiate the deductions; and, in some cases, where a substantial proportion of exempt sales were made, for example, by exporters, the tax administration would have to process tax refund claims.

The accumulation of tax would be avoided under a single-stage tax by a technique generally described as "suspension". A manufacturer would be

*Reprinted by permission from the Royal Commission on Taxation, *Report*, Vol. V, Queen's Printer, Ottawa, 1967.

licensed to purchase his raw materials, parts, etc., exempt from tax, that is, in suspension and the cost of these materials in turn would enter into the selling price of his goods. Under a wholesale tax, these goods would then be sold tax free (in suspension) to a licensed wholesaler, who would account for tax on his sale price. This would mean that considerably fewer taxable transactions would be recorded by businesses than under a value-added tax, and, in the case of exports, no tax payments (or refunds) may be recorded at all. The tax administrators would then verify whether purchases made in suspension were legitimate over large areas of the purchasing field, for example, purchases of raw materials and partly manufactured goods. This would be a relatively simple task.

Where a government intends that there should be residual "double tax" elements in the tax structure, as, for example, is currently the case with production machinery in Canada, then under a value-added tax the administrators must check that no deductions have been taken on such purchases, and under single-stage suspension that no exemptions have been claimed upon purchase. The value-added procedure would, in our opinion, place a heavier record-keeping burden on the taxpayer, and a heavier administrative burden on the tax collector.

Exports

The value-added form would have no intrinsic advantages over the single-stage form in offering incentives or eliminating disincentives to exports. Under a single-stage tax, most exports would be made in suspension, the remainder being allowed a tax refund; any residual tax elements buried in the export price, for example, if producer goods were taxed, would be there because the law did not provide for their exemption. Under a value-added tax, with no change in the scope of the tax base, a similar exemption for exports could be achieved by deduction, and the same residual tax elements would remain in the export price. The single-stage form would involve less administrative inconvenience for refund claims than would occur under the value-added tax.

Evasion

A retail tax at rates in excess of 14 per cent might result in a significant evasion problem. Should this occur, the case for a value-added form of collection would be strengthened. Any consideration of its adoption must take into account the large number of taxpayers involved, the increased cost and complexity of administration, and the more onerous record-keeping burdens placed on taxpayers, particularly on retailers. We think that it would be unrealistic to consider instituting a value-added tax, rather than a federal retail tax, at a rate of 7 per cent to 8 per cent which would be equivalent to the present manufacturer's sales tax rate of 11 per cent, for in our opinion such a rate would not be high enough to encourage significant evasion of a retail tax. However, it must be assumed that the provinces would continue to levy their retail sales tax. Federal and provincial combined rates that totalled

14 per cent or more, and significant evasion at such rates, would constitute in our opinion the only circumstances in which a value-added form of collection could be justified for Canada.

If such evasion occurred, a federal value-added tax should be considered up to, and including, the retail level. This would collect the federal tax and at the same time safeguard the provinces' rights to their retail taxes on a single-stage "destination" basis. It would provide the enforcement mechanism of the federal value-added tax to the advantage of both levels of government.

Scope or Coverage

Exemptions or rate differentials introduce administrative difficulties into any tax structure, and the value-added tax is no exception to this rule. Indeed, a single-stage levy would be better suited to provide for the exemptions or rate differentials usually considered desirable on social grounds. The main appeal of the value-added form of taxation lies in its extremely broad base.

61   A Value-Added Tax for Canada? *

R. Malt

[This study argues] that, for both 1958 and 1960, repeal of the corporate income tax would have caused a significant increase in goods exports only when a very high price-elasticity of foreign demand acts in combination with a high degree of shifting and unshifting of the corporate income tax. Even the most optimistic sets of parameter values suggest an export incentive effect of between 6% and 7%. This is hardly a decisive argument in favour of an export-exempt value-added tax, particularly when it is remembered that there are relatively large costs in making the switch-over from income to value-added tax, and that the radical surgery of complete removal of the corporate income tax is itself highly unlikely. Reasonably optimistic parameter assumptions imply an export incentive effect of between $100 and $200 million increase in yearly exports, taking account of only short-run effects. Of course, a *decline* in export goods' value, after being freed of direct tax burden, is a possibility if price elasticity of foreign demand is very low (although recent Canadian experience with devaluation shows foreign demand does react favourably to an effective reduction in the price of Canadian goods).

*Reprinted by permission of editors and publisher from R. Malt, "Some Aspects of a Value-Added Tax for Canada", J. R. Allan and I. J. Goffman (eds.), *Queen's University Papers in Taxation and Public Finance*, Queen's University, Kingston.

If abolition of the corporation income tax does cause the quantity of goods exports to rise, the gain will tend to be wiped out by the familiar adjustment mechanism, through which "absorption" — imports and saving — increases until the balance of payments is again in equilibrium. As incomes increase, there will be a tendency for domestic prices to increase and with them, wages and costs. At the same time, imposition of the value-added tax itself may tend to push up the prices of goods and so militate against the very incentive which it was designed to produce. Nicholas Kaldor emphasized this point when discussing a possible value-added tax for Britain; he asserted that the lowering of industrial prices (in Britain) through withdrawal of taxes on business profits would be gradual, while a newly-imposed value-added tax might boost domestic prices at once. In the short run, results of this sort of scheme might be negative; over the long run, all benefits might be cancelled out. The Federation of British industries reached a similar conclusion, arguing that "the beneficial effect on exports of replacing direct taxes by indirect is likely to be no more than marginal, unless the shift towards indirect taxation is of considerable magnitude. We conclude, therefore, that the incentive to export goods offered by replacement of part or all of Canada's corporate income tax with an export-exempt value-added tax would not be significant, over either the short or the long run."

While this essay contends that an export-exempt value-added tax would probably not stimulate Canada's exports significantly, it may be noted that many countries, particularly in Western Europe, have either imposed a value-added tax or are studying it. In a decade or two, when Canadian exports have to compete in foreign markets with goods freed of all or most of their tax burden, through the value-added system, Canada may be forced to adopt the value-added tax simply in self-defence.

A Canadian value-added tax could serve as either a substitute for, or a complement to, existing taxes. As a substitute for part or all of the corporate income tax, the case for adoption of the value-added tax — and the rate at which it is to be applied — depends to a large extent on whether or not the corporate income tax is shifted forward. If it is shifted, then the corporate tax is merely a capricious form of sales tax, falling unevenly on goods and services according to the producers' profit margins; on welfare ground, replacement of the tax by a value-added tax is indicated. If the corporate income tax is not shifted, replacement of part or all of it by a tax on value added may have regressive redistributive effects. The question of corporate income tax shifting is very far from being resolved.

There is probably a much stronger case for using the value-added tax as a complement to existing taxes. Canada's federal government currently confronts a five-headed fiscal monster: (a) the share of the public sector in gross national expenditure is expanding; (b) provincial governments are pressing for a larger share of federal revenues, and for non-economic reasons, these claims are difficult to dismiss; (c) rates of personal income taxation cannot be raised much, partly because of political expediency, partly because rates in the U.S., whose tax policy has influence in Canada, are tending to fall; (d) taxing corporate profits at a rate exceeding those currently in force might produce serious disincentives to investment and risk-taking; and (c) revenue gained by plugging loopholes and wiping out exemptions in existing taxes is very limited.

The federal government may therefore be forced to turn to more extensive use of indirect taxes. One attractive proposal would be to convert the tax on manufacturers' sales into a value-added tax and extend it through the wholesale level, as in France. This could be followed — after consultation with the provinces — by a national value-added tax imposed up to and including the retail level, revenue being shared out among the provincial and federal governments. Such a plan would eliminate the present inconsistent provincial sales taxes under which eight provinces charge sales taxes ranging from 3% in Ontario to 6% in Quebec, and would be a major step toward unifying and simplifying Canada's tax structure.

By shifting control of retail-stage taxes from provincial treasuries to Ottawa, this would place a new and powerful weapon of fiscal policy in the federal government's armoury.

A Selective Employment Tax

Interest in a selective employment tax stems from the introduction of such a tax in the United Kingdom in 1966. The tax amounts to a selective payroll tax, and is a discriminatory tax on a selected group of employers of labour. Discrimination in the case of the British tax is against employers in the service sector; the tax is paid by all employers but is refunded to manufacturing establishments. In its present form the selective employment tax is subject to criticism, as the extract below points out, and the usefulness of such a tax in Canada might lie in a variation on the theme whereby the process of selection for tax liability is based on regional or locational factors. In this manner the tax might serve as a dirigistic device to influence the location of industries, and as an instrument of disaggregated stabilization policy. A subsequent extract argues in favour of disaggregated stabilization policy in Canada, and the selective employment or payroll tax would be a useful instrument to implement such a policy at the federal level.

62   The Selective Employment Tax in Britain*

James Cutt

Official Objectives

S.E.T. is officially designed to achieve two main objectives:

> First, it will improve the structure of the tax system by redressing the balance
> between services and manufacturing. Services, including distribution, have
> hitherto been lightly taxed as compared with manufactured products, which
> are subject to excise duties and the purchase tax . . . .

> Second, it will have a beneficial longer-term effect by encouraging economy in
> the use of labour in services and thereby making more labour available for the
> expansion of manufacturing industry.[1]

The revenue aspect of S.E.T. is thus not officially acknowledged as of
prime significance and the tax is, apparently, designed to attract rather odd
bedfellows — on the one hand liberals by its partial correction of the existing
discrimination against manufacturing, and, on the other, fiscal dirigists generally by its potential as a selective tax device.

Incidence

In the case of the taxed service industries S.E.T. may be considered not
to be shifted if it is incident in the short run on the income of the establishment. Alternatively, the tax may be shifted forward to consumers in the form
of higher prices and/or backwards to workers in the form of lower wages or
through dismissals. The "manpower economy and diversion" effect of S.E.T.
is predicated on the assumption of a substantial degree of backward shifting.
The stickiness of wages downward suggests that backward shifting is likely
to take the form of economy in the use of labour through dismissals, failure
to fill vacated positions, etc. The desired manpower effect is diminished to
the extent that the charge is simply passed along to consumers in the form
of higher prices for services.

Excluding significant price increases, the short-run distribution of the burden
of S.E.T. would seem likely to fall partially on labour, through dismissals,
etc., and partially on the income of service establishments and hence, for the
incorporated part of the service sector, on the recipients of dividends and
capital appreciation. In the long run the service industries are likely to adjust
fully to the tax and shift the entire burden to consumers in the form of
higher prices for services, and to labour in the service sector through the
slower growth of wages and employment opportunities.

---

*Reprinted by permission of publisher from J. Cutt, "The Selective Employment Tax in
Britain", *Canadian Tax Journal*, January-February 1967.

[1]Cmd. Paper 2986, *Selective Employment Tax*, Her Majesty's Stationery Office,
London, May 1966.

Growth

The case for S.E.T. in terms of growth may be seen in two parts, the first reflecting simply the direct subsidy to manufacturing, the second reflecting the change in relative labour costs between manufacturing and services. First, the case for subsidizing manufacturers is based on the "increasing returns to scale" argument that the potential for raising productivity in manufacturing is greater than in services, or, in other words, that manufacturers' cost curves fall relatively fast over time. Second, the relatively rapid rate of growth in manufacturing will result in a more rapid rate of growth of productivity, but not enough to obviate the need for a faster rate of growth of employment in manufacturing; hence the nature of S.E.T., which is both a direct subsidy to manufacturing and a means of diverting scarce manpower from the service sector where productivity increases are held to be less likely.

In appraising the likely overall effect of S.E.T. on growth, there are two aspects to be considered: first, whether in its role as a tax on services S.E.T. exercises an inhibitory effect on investment in the service sector; second, whether S.E.T. in its subsidy role is likely to make a significant positive contribution to growth.

In its tax role, the possibility of significant disincentive effects on investment in the service sector would seem unlikely. It has been argued that the final incidence of S.E.T. is likely to fall on labour through dismissals and the slower growth of wages and employment opportunities, and on consumers through higher prices for services. In either case, the tax would impinge much more heavily on consumption than on investment expenditure. Only to the extent that S.E.T. is borne by service sector income or profits would there be a possible reduction in investment in the service sector. An adverse effect on service sector investment may be considered particularly unlikely in the case of S.E.T., which increases labour costs in the service sector by between 3% — 5% and thus provides a direct incentive to substitute capital for labour.

With regard to the intended positive contribution of S.E.T. to growth, the tax-subsidy combination in its present form is subject to criticism on several counts. It may be argued that the subsidy to manufacturing is too small to have more than a slight effect. It would seem to amount to between 1.5% and 2% of manufacturers' wage bills. Given the possible rise in price of manufacturers' taxed service and construction inputs, the net reduction in manufacturers' input costs may not even amount to 1%.

Further, the division into manufacturing industries and service industries would seem to ignore the fact that there are large areas of the service sector, specifically retail distribution and catering, where standardization and mass production techniques have made possible significant economies of scale, and so should not be penalized equally with other service industries. In any event it is difficult to measure the real output of the service industries, and productivity comparisons between manufacturing and services are thus of limited value.

It is also arguable that to subsidize employment in manufacturing in general is to ignore areas within manufacturing which are stagnant or declining, where the appropriate growth-oriented tax policy should accelerate the release of scarce labour to the growing, dynamic sector of the economy. Paradoxically, S.E.T. might encourage the wasteful use and retention of labour in declining industries, and, by changing relative factor costs, provide a disincentive to mechanization and modernization; the labour-intensive shipbuilding industry is perhaps the best example. It has indeed been argued that one problem of British industry lies in over-manning rather than labour shortage, and that productivity can best be enhanced by an increase in capital equipment per worker.

Finally, the crude distinction between services and manufacturing effectively makes nonsense of regional planning.

The three previous points suggest that employment diversion in the interests of growth might better be accomplished by a reformed S.E.T. which was more selective between growing and declining industries and between growing and declining services, and which would also be selective in a general sense in a manner consistent with regional planning.

Exports

The subsidy on manufacturers' costs amounts to a cut in money wages in that sector or an indirect devaluation — neither of which, incidentally, conflicts with Britain's E.F.T.A. or G.A.T.T. obligations — and acts as a stimulus to exports and import substitution.

Again, however, criticism of S.E.T. in its present form seems appropriate. The export stimulus provided by the premium to manufacturing is far too small to have a significant effect, it has been argued that the total reduction in manufacturers' costs amounts to no more than 1%. Further, the broad distinction into services and manufacturing is, as in the growth argument, far too general. The subsidy accrues to manufacturers who export little or not at all and falls on service industries which are substantial exporters or import savers. The burden imposed on the British hotel and catering industry provides a major incentive to Britons to holiday abroad. Again the argument is for the abandonment of the Standard Industrial Classification as a basis for S.E.T. and for greater selectivity in the distribution of burdens and premiums.

Stabilization

The stabilizing effectiveness of S.E.T. depends on the extent to which it diminishes aggregate spending. The net reduction in aggregate spending as a result of S.E.T. in its first year of operation is expected to be £240 million, and is likely, as a result of shifting to be largely at the expense of consumer demand. This reduction is equivalent on the assumption of complete forward shifting to a tax of just over 1% on consumption expenditure, or, perhaps more accurately, of between 3% — 4% on consumer expenditure on services.

S.E.T. is a relatively minor addition to the stock of discretionary tax instruments — its revenue in the first year is a little higher than revenue from surtax or a little less than one third of purchase tax revenue — but has the merit that its effects are felt almost entirely on consumer spending, and thus have minimal adverse growth implications.

Given the suggested minimal responsiveness of S.E.T. revenue to changes in national income, and the relatively small size of S.E.T. revenue in relation to national income and changes in national income, the built-in flexibility of S.E.T. receipts is unlikely to be significant.

A change of S.E.T. into a proportional payroll tax would increase both the magnitude of tax revenue in relation to national income and the responsiveness of the tax base to changes in national income. The usefulness of S.E.T. as a discretionary and automatic stabilizing device would thus be substantially increased. Particularly interesting might be the establishment of reformed S.E.T. rates on the basis of formula flexibility, by which changes in tax rates are legislated in advance in relation to specified movements of economic indicators such as the wholesale price level. Further refinements might include regional selectivity, where a reformed S.E.T. offers a most useful means of coping with regional stabilization problems.

A Negative Income Tax

Dissatisfaction with present welfare measures in both the U.S.A. and Canada has led to a new concern for both building up the earning capacity of low-income groups and assuring every family an adequate standard of living regardless of its earning capacity. On the question of income maintenance, concern is now focused not only on income interruption, but also on the whole issue of income inadequacy or deficiency; a variety of devices have been suggested to provide a minimum income floor either for particular groups in society or on a universal basis.

Two approaches are much in vogue: the "selective" negative income tax approach whereby those whose income falls below a prescribed level receive a subsidy (negative tax) for all or part of the deficiency; and, the "universal" demogrant approach whereby everyone, regardless of need or means, receives a prescribed sum of money each year from the government. This sum may or may not be included in income for positive income tax purposes.

The negative income tax approach is the more practical of the two, largely because of its lower cost. It is also more desirable because its selectivity holds the promise of adequate payments to those really in need.

The extract below sets out briefly some negative income tax proposals for Canada, in the context of the Carter Commission Report.

63   Negative Income Taxation*

C. Green

The recent concern with poverty in the United States has generated interest in proposals to use the income tax system to transfer income to low income households. These proposals have been given various names, but "negative income taxes" still seems to be the most popular. Only one criterion determines eligibility for receipt of negative income tax payments: family income in relation to family size. In its simplest form negative income taxation would be confined to taxpaying units whose low income does not allow them to move above the existing zero tax rate brackets. Thus an early proposal suggested making payments to tax-filing units with unused exemptions and deductions. To avoid creating important potential incentives to reduce work effort the proposal called for payments of only a fraction, say 50%, of unused exemptions and deductions.

Negative income taxation would directly redistribute income to low income households and would put a floor under family income. Schemes of this sort have been supported — or defended — on the grounds that they (1) would provide and confine income transfers to households which really need economic assistance; (2) condition payments solely on the basis of family income and family size, thus achieving a degree of horizontal equity in the treatment of low income households not achieved by existing income transfer programs; (3) are more neutral with respect to resource allocation as a means of raising the income of earners whose productivity is very low; and (4) might stimulate incentives to work among populations at present subject to 100% "tax rates" in the public assistance programs.

The two tax schedules proposed in the Commission's *Report* use zero tax brackets instead of exemptions for heads of taxpaying units and their spouses. The *Report* also proposes tax credits for dependent children to replace the present exemptions for dependents. A negative income tax plan could be incorporated into the proposed tax schedules in a manner illustrated in Table 1. One approach, Plan A in Table 1, would be to let unattached individuals (U) receive 50% of the amount by which their taxable income falls short of $1,000. Married couples (C) with no children would receive 50% of the amount by which their income falls short of $2,100. Families with children (F) receive 50% of the amount by which their incomes fall short of $2,100 plus all of the unused tax credit allowed dependent children.

An alternative approach is indicated by Plan B in Table 1. A basic allowance is decided upon first. I have chosen $300 for unattached individuals, $700 for a married couple, and $700 plus the cash value of tax credits allowed children (a total of $860 for a family with two children). According to the *Report* these dollar values are the minimum levels of income below

*Reprinted by permission of author and publisher from C. Green, "Transfer Mechanisms Redistribution and Canada's Proposed Tax Reform", *Conference Report*, Canadian Tax Foundation, November 1967.

which households have no ability to pay (Vol. 3, p. 155)[1] Plan B, like Plan A, uses the tops of the zero rate brackets as the breakeven levels of income — $1,000 for unattached individuals and $2,100 for married couples. A tax rate is then chosen which reduces the $300 and $700 basic allowances to zero when taxable income reaches $1,000 and $2,100, respectively. These rates — and for simplicity flat rate schedules are adopted — are 30% and 33 1/3%, respectively.

Plans A and B — and any other guaranteed minimum income plan — are, in principle, alike. Each has three basic variables: (1) a minimum income guarantee when taxable income is zero; (2) a tax rate(s); and (3) a breakeven income level at which negative income tax payments are reduced to zero. Any two of these three basic variables determines the third. In plan A the choice of breakeven levels and a 50% negative income tax rate determine the minimum income guarantee. In plan B the choice of basic minimums and breakeven levels determine the level of the (average) negative tax rate.

Proponents of negative income taxation in the United States have had to wrestle with more problems than just those posed by the schedule of rates and the potential cost of the plan. The tax base is also important. A tax base riddled with as many deductions and exclusions as the U.S. personal income tax base would produce indefensible inequities if a negative income tax were introduced. Total income should be used in determining a tax unit's eligibility for and the level of its net negative income tax payments. Moreover, the relevant unit from the standpoint of welfare is the consumer unit and usually this is the family. Thus, at least for the purposes of determining eligibility for and the level of negative taxes, American proponents of negative income taxation have considered both broadening the definition of income beyond what is currently defined as "adjusted gross income" and redefining the tax unit. Canadian proponents of negative tax plans are more fortunate. If the main proposals of the *Report* are accepted Canada will have a comprehensive definition of income and a family tax unit. These proposals will make negative income taxation a good deal easier to implement if Canadians are inclined to adopt such a device.

---

[1]The Royal Commission on Taxation, *Report*, Queen's Printer, Ottawa, 1967.

TABLE 1

Taxable Income	Proposed Plan: Tax Payment at Bottom of Bracket			Proposed Plan + Negative Taxes: Negative Tax (−) or Positive Tax (+) at Bottom of Bracket					
				Plan A^a			Plan B^b		
	U	C	F^c	U	C	F^c	U	C	F^c
0- 500	0	0	0	−500	−1,050	−1,210	−300	−700	−860
500-1,000	0	0	0	−250	−800	−960	−150	−533	−693
1,000-1,500	0	0	0	0	−250	−710	0	−367	−527
1,500-2,000	60	0	0	+60	−300	−460	+60	−200	−360
2,000-2,100	135	0	0	+135	−50	−210	+135	−33	−193
2,100-2,500	152	0	0	+152	0	−160	+152	0	−160
2,500-3,000	+220	+52	0	+220	+52	−108	+220	+52	−108
3,000-4,000	+305	+117	0	+305	+117	−43	+305	+117	−43
4,000-5,000	+505	+277	+117	+505	+277	+117	+505	+277	+117

a Plan A: Negative tax payments are equal to 50% of this unused portion of zero bracket + 100% of unused tax credits allowed dependants.

b Plan B: Provides a *basic allowance* of $300 for unattached individuals, $700 for married couples, and $700 + value of tax credits allowed dependents for families with children. The tax rate of unattached individuals on income up to $1,000 (the breakeven level of income) is 30% while the rate for families is 33 1/3 % up to $2,100 — the breakeven level for a married couple without children. For income above $2,000 a family with dependents would receive any unused tax credits allowed its dependents. The breakeven level for a family with two children is about $3,270.

c Assumes a 4 person family including two dependant children.

Chapter Five
Municipal Finance

The previous chapters outlined the pattern of collective decision-making in a democracy. In the literature, the economic issues tend to be spelt out with the higher levels of government in mind, where the institutional simplicity enables the economic analysis to be more rigorous. Nevertheless, many of the same issues arise at the local levels of government. For example, the long-run economic objectives set out in Chapter One would be applicable to municipal as well as to higher levels of government. Some of these are: increased output in the "little economy" of the town or city; improved allocation of resources (for example, diversion of resources into public transport); satisfaction of collective needs (for example, education, public parks, cultural centres, public health); improvements in the distribution of income and wealth (for example, subsidized public housing); protection to particular industries (for example, tax holidays and other concessions to industries considered desirable for the municipality). Even balance of payments considerations are relevant to the municipality, as indicated by the well-known economic base theory of urban development.[1]

When economic policy is discussed at the higher levels of government, it is usually in the calm, detached atmosphere of government-to-government relations. At the municipal level, the same principles of policy are discussed, but the implementation of these principles is more directly related to the interests of individuals and small groups. This is reflected in the diversity of problems discussed and the intensity of the debates in the various municipal governments. Though questions discussed in municipal government are no less amenable to economic analysis than those at higher levels, municipal officials cannot avoid seeing the issues in terms of specific individuals and firms who will benefit or lose by the implementation of particular policies.

---

[1]The economic base theory of urban development "divides urban economic activity into two categories: exporting industry that brings money into the community from the outside world and non-exporting industries whose goods and services are sold within the community. The exporting industries are referred to as basic industries and the non-exporting industries are called service industries. It is also contended in discussions of the theory that the exporting or basic industries provide the sources of urban growth; they are 'city building' industries." Ralph W. Pfouts (ed.), *The Techniques of Urban Economic Analysis*, Chandler-Davis, West Trenton, N.J., 1961.

The reasons usually given for delegation of tax and expenditure authority to municipal governments are:

(a) It is considered an important part of a democratic social and institutional setup;

(b) In the case of a great many problems which have to be tackled on a collective basis, there is little need to carry out a standardized solution for the whole country, as needs and wishes may vary from one district to another. It is, of course, possible *per se* for a central authority to make decisions which do not involve standard norms for the whole country but instead meet local demands and wishes in various ways. On the other hand, the chances for local needs and desires to count are much greater if decisions are made locally. [On the question of decision-making, see Chapter Two, especially the essay by Buchanan and Tullock.]

(c) Finally, the administration of a great many projects can be carried out more cheaply and more effectively if one bases oneself on a decentralized system of authority and a decentralized administration than if complete centralization existed. It is not only possible to cut down on the number of channels through which various matters have to pass, but increased efficiency can also be achieved by utilizing knowledge of local conditions.[2]

Decentralization of decision-making at the operational level may therefore improve efficiency in the distribution of public goods. It may also improve equity in that the heterogeneous circumstances of particular individuals and firms can be considered on their merits rather than as undistinguishable units in a national mass. This also makes it possible for the interested citizen to participate in public decision-making in a manner that is open to only a few at the provincial or national level. However, this same characteristic is responsible also for one of the most acute problems of local government which hardly arises at higher levels of government, namely that the citizen who does not approve of the policies of his local government can move into a more congenial jurisdiction. It also means that an individual living in one jurisdiction can enjoy public services provided by a neighbouring jurisdiction without having to join with the residents in paying for them. This complaint is frequently heard from the governments of central cities in metropolitan areas, that rich people use the central city for work, for cultural activities and for shopping, but reside in the suburbs and so escape their share of costs, while the city becomes crowded with poor people whose tax capacity is low.[3]

There are various ways in which the problem can be handled. Charles M. Tiebout has developed a model in which individuals are assumed to choose among alternative residential locations in the same manner as they choose among other differentiated products in the market. "Instead of taking the people as given and trying to fit the non-national public goods pattern to them, offer a varied pattern of public goods and

---

[2]Leif Johansen, *Public Economics*, North-Holland Publishing Co., Amsterdam, 1965, p. 344.

[3]This argument is countered by "the suburban governments [who] argue that they must educate the boom baby crop of the commuter; they must protect his family and his property, but the lucrative tax base which should support these services — the factories and office buildings — are located in the central city". Julius Margolis, "Metropolitan Finance Problems: Territories, Functions and Growth", in J. M. Buchanan (ed.), *Public Finances: Needs, Sources, and Utilization*, Princeton Unviersity Press for the National Bureau of Economic Research, Princeton, N.J., 1961, p. 256.

make it possible for the people to move to suit their tastes. People who want good schools will then be able to move to communities where good schools are provided. To the extent that communities offer a varied pattern of public goods, each resident can, conceptually, choose the pattern which best satisfies his preferences. . . . That people with similar tastes move together is a first principle of fiscal federalism."[4] Tiebout's original article is reprinted in this chapter.

One of the advances introduced by Tiebout's model was that it showed that political fragmentation could have a rational economic base. "Product differentiation in local government, to retain the phrase borrowed from price theory, may originate in (a) a preference for private over public sources of supply, or the reverse, (b) differences in taste patterns for public services or (c) desire for intimate control over the processes of government. The fragmented metropolitan area may sort out citizens so as to bring together in a given municipality a group who would minimize the public sector in their everyday life, with a volunteer fire department, self-provision of garbage disposal and outdoor lighting of their own property, and dependence on personal libraries. Alternatively, another like-minded group of residents may prefer to substitute 'free' municipal swimming pools and golf courses for the more common 'free' paved streets (by retaining dirt roads). A third group may be less distinctive in matters of the quantity or mix of public services than in their desire to exercise close control over the local government that produces these services. This latter group may feel that 'bureaucracy' (diseconomies of scale in administration) more than offsets various economies of scale in production and finance, and so this might be an economy-in-government group. But more likely, this latter group wants *very* local government for its own sake; they want to feel important, as when they personally know their councilman, or they want to play politics for self-expression or just the fun of it, or otherwise personalize their local government. In this impersonal age of automation and the narrowest occupational specialization — this age of creative frustration for many people — the need for political participation may not be trivial and the trend may even be strongly upward."[5]

Tiebout's approach, as Musgrave points out, "means that a more homogenous pattern of preferences tends to be established within any one community, and the task of finding a satisfactory solution is simplified".[6] But between communities, social and economic differences will continue to exist. People with high incomes will associate with others with high incomes, and provide high levels of education, library services and recreation to their privileged children; lower income groups will also congregate in their separate suburbs, and their lower incomes and different preference patterns will result in an inferior level of many of these services. In the cities we know, the qualitative differences between the standards of well-to-do suburbs and crowded slums are very great, and to explain away these differences solely in terms of differences in preferences would be to assume that the state of income distribution is satisfactory, which most people would agree is not the case. The Tiebout model takes income distribution as given, and

---

[4]Charles M. Tiebout, "An Economic Theory of Fiscal Decentralization", in Buchanan, *op. cit.*, pp. 92-93.

[5]Wilbur R. Thompson, *A Preface to Urban Economics*, The Johns Hopkins Press for Resources for the Future, Inc., Baltimore, Md., 1965, p. 263.

[6]R. A. Musgrave, *The Theory of Public Finance*, McGraw-Hill, New York, 1959, p. 133.

provides a solution to the allocation problem through the price system. But as Samuelson, Musgrave and others[7] have made clear, the two cannot be separated. Actually, the major social problems of urban areas are a manifestation of inequalities in the distribution of income and wealth, and many of the merit wants that are most efficiently satisfied through the municipalities (such as public housing, public recreation facilities, public welfare), are specifically intended as measures of income redistribution. One way of avoiding the difficulty would be to assume that the task of redistributing income is the responsibility of a higher level of government, provincial or federal, so that the municipal problem may be treated as one of suboptimization. In fact, however, redistribution undertaken by higher levels of government has not done much to remove the income inequalities that underlie urban social and economic patterns, and the obligation that many municipal governments feel to supply merit wants has been a major factor in intensifying their financial troubles.

Of course, welfare expenditures and other forms of income transfer to less privileged people are not the only expenditures that are straining city finances. The rising population density in the cities is increasing the demand for public services such as police and fire protection, water supply and sanitation. Transportation requirements are increasing, requiring expenditures on traffic arteries, traffic control, parking for vehicles, and the development of mass transit facilities. At the same time the per capita property tax base of central cities is likely to decline because of the less intensive use of urban land (more parking facilities and open green spaces) and the transfer of high tax capacity manufacturing from the centre of the city to the periphery with its replacement by labour-intensive service industries. Moreover, the concentration of lower income groups in the city also tends to reduce the value per person of residential property.

The only solution may be the development of new sources of revenue for municipalities, as has been suggested by Harvey Brazer. He recommends that reliance on the property tax be consciously reduced, because though it may be a useful instrument to be used in rationalizing land-use patterns, "buildings generally and tangible personality of business are surely not subjects for taxation that are well designed to add equity to the distributional pattern of taxation, distribute the costs of city services in accordance with any other reasonable norm, or, perhaps most important, to alleviate those problems that now most trouble our central cities: congestion, obsolete plants, rapidly deteriorating housing in core areas, and so forth."[8] Brazer recommends an increase in provincial grants to cities, the size determined by population density and the number of non-residents served, plus the development of a sales tax, a personal income tax and a value-added tax on business at the city level, plus user charges for municipal services rendered.[9]

Another approach sees the urban problem arising out of a conflict of community objectives, and the only possible solution is to be found in trade-offs among them.

---

[7]Ibid., pp. 84-89.

[8]Harvey E. Brazer, "The Role of Major Metropolitan Centers in State and Local Finance", *American Economic Review*, Proceedings, Vol. XLVII, No. 2, May 1958, p. 315.

[9]Ibid., pp. 309-315.

The four key objectives as observed from the behaviour of citizen-voters, according to Wilbur Thompson, are:

1. Residential segregation by socioeconomic class, with income a simple, workable criterion for arranging "nice neighborhoods";
2. Small local government to achieve highly responsible government and the personal value of creative political participation as well — "political fragmentation";
3. Local fiscal autonomy, in the belief that government spending is most responsibly performed when the spender must impose the requisite taxes;
4. Minimum public service standards and redistribution of income in the name of both humanitarianism and equality of opportunity.[10]

In Thompson's formulation, no more than three of these objectives can be realized. Given the first three, "with fiscal capacity and public service needs highest in the poorer suburbs, minimum public service standards will be sacrificed". If the higher levels of government intervened to maintain standards, local fiscal autonomy would be lost. Local autonomy might be preserved if large-scale metropolitan government were instituted, but it would be at the expense of small local government, a course which has received little support from electors. Finally, the first three objectives might be achieved if the income-homogeneous communities were sacrificed, but "it is safe to say that a ground-swell of popular support for mixing income classes within small municipalities is not in the offing, certainly not in the suburbs — at any grain." The situation is that the citizen voter can achieve three of these objectives in reasonably full measure only by sacrificing the fourth, or he can trade off significant amounts of the most desired three objectives to achieve a minimal quantity of the fourth.

This short introduction does no more than indicate some of the issues that are being discussed in the field of public finance at the level of municipal government. The theoretical framework for the study of municipal government economics is rather untidy, since economists have only recently discovered the "little economy" of the city. Canadian economists have had very little to say about the economics of urbanism.[11] The following pieces, however, will indicate the main issues involved, and provide a basis upon which the reader will be able to follow the current discussions.

---

[10]Wilbur R. Thompson, "Toward an Urban Economics," in Leo F. Schnore and Henry Fagin (eds.), *Urban Research and Policy Planning*, Vol. I, Sage Publications, Inc., Beverly Hills, Calif., 1967, p. 151.

[11]A considerable amount of material on local government finances is available from the publications of the Canadian Tax Foundation, particularly the biennial *Provincial Finances* and the *Local Finance* series.

64   A Pure Theory of Local Expenditures, *

Charles M. Tiebout

One of the most important recent developments in the area of "applied economic theory" has been the work of Musgrave and Samuelson in public finance theory.[1] The two writers agree on what is probably the major point under investigation, namely, that no "market type" solution exists to determine the level of expenditures on public goods. Seemingly, we are faced with the problem of having a rather large portion of our national income allocated in a "non-optimal" way when compared with the private sector.

This discussion will show that the Musgrave-Samuelson analysis which is valid for federal expenditures, need not apply to local expenditures. The plan of the discussion is first to restate the assumptions made by Musgrave and Samuelson and the central problems with which they deal. After looking at a key difference between the federal versus local cases, I shall present a simple model. This model yields a solution for the level of expenditures for local public goods which reflects the preferences of the population more adequately than they can be reflected at the national level. The assumptions of the model will then be relaxed to see what implications are involved. Finally, policy considerations will be discussed.

The Theoretical Issue

Samuelson has defined public goods as *"collective consumption goods* $(X_{n+1}, \ldots, X_{n+m})$ which all enjoy in common in the sense that each individual's consumption of such a good leads to no subtraction from any other individual's consumption of that good, so that $X_{n+j} = X_{n}^{i}+_{j}$ simultaneously for each and every ith individual and each collective consumptive good."[2] While definitions are a matter of choice, it is worth noting that "consumption" has a much broader meaning here than in the usual sense of the term. Not only does it imply that the act of consumption by one person does not diminish the opportunities for consumption by another but it also allows this consumption to be in another form. For example, while the residents of a

---

*Reprinted by permission of publisher from *The Journal of Political Economy*, Vol. LXIV, October 1956, pp. 416-424.

I am grateful for the comments of my colleagues Karl de Schweinitz, Robert Eisner, and Robert Strotz, and those of Martin Bailey, of the University of Chicago.

[1]Richard A. Musgrave, "The Voluntary Exchange Theory of Public Economy", *Quarterly Journal of Economics*, Vol. LII, February 1939, pp. 213-217; "A Multiple Theory of the Budget", paper read at the Econometric Society annual meeting, December 1955 [subsequently published as "A Multiple Theory of Budget Determination", *Fianz-Archiv*, Vol. XVII, 1957, pp. 333-433]; [and his book, *The Theory of Public Finance*, McGraw-Hill, New York, 1959]; and Paul A. Samuelson, "The Pure Theory of Public Expenditures", *Review of Economics and Statistics*, Vol. XXXVI, No. 4, November 1954, pp. 387-389; and "Diagrammatic Exposition of a Pure Theory of Public Expenditures", *ibid.*, Vol. XXXVII, No. 4, November 1955, pp. 350-356.

[2]Samuelson, "The Pure Theory of Public Expenditures", *op. cit.*, p. 387.

new government housing project are made better off, benefits also accrue to other residents of the community in the form of the external economies of slum clearance.[3] Thus many goods that appear to lack the attributes of public goods may properly be considered public if consumption is defined to include these external economies.[4]

A definition alternative to Samuelson's might be. simply that a public good is one which should be produced, but for which there is no feasible method of charging the consumers. This is less elegant, but has the advantage that it allows for the objections of Enke and Margolis.[5] This definition, unfortunately, does not remove any of the problems faced by Musgrave and Samuelson.

The core problem with which both Musgrave and Samuelson deal concerns the mechanism by which consumer-voters register their preferences for public goods. The consumer is, in a sense, surrounded by a government whose objective it is to ascertain his wants for public goods and tax him accordingly. To use Alchian's term, the government's revenue-expenditure pattern for goods and services is expected to "adapt to" consumers' preferences.[6] Both Musgrave and Samuelson have shown that, in the vertically additive nature of voluntary demand curves, this problem has only a conceptual solution. If all consumer-voters could somehow be forced to reveal their true preferences for public goods, then the amount of such goods to be produced and the

---

[3]Samuelson allows for this when he states that "one man's circus may be another man's poison", referring, of course, to public goods. See Samuelson, "Diagrammatic Exposition of a Pure Theory of Public Expenditures", *op. cit.*, p. 351.

[4]There seems to be a problem connected with the external-economies aspect of public goods. Surely a radio broadcast, like national defense, has the attribute that A's enjoyment leaves B no worse off; yet this does not imply that broadcasting should, in a normative sense, be a public good (the arbitrary manner in which the level of radio programs is determined aside). The difference between defense and broadcasting is subtle but important. In both cases there is a problem of determining the optimal level of outputs and the corresponding level of benefits taxes. In the broadcasting case, however, A may be quite willing to pay more taxes than B, even if both have the same "ability to pay" (assuming that the benefits are determinate). Defense is another question. Here A is not content that B should pay less. A makes the *social judgment* that B's preference *should* be the same. A's preference, expressed as an annual defense expenditure such as $42.7 billion and representing the majority view, thus determines the level of defense. Here the A's may feel that the B's *should pay* the same amount of benefits tax.

If it is argued that this case is typical of public goods, then, once the level is somehow set, the voluntary exchange approach and the benefit theory associated with it do not make sense. If the preceding analysis is correct, we are now back in the area of equity in terms of ability to pay.

[5]They argue that, for most of the goods supplied by governments, increased use by some consumer-voters leaves less available for other consumer-voters. Crowded highways and schools, as contrasted with national defense, may be cited as examples. See Stephen Enke, "More on the Misuse of Mathematics in Economics: A Rejoinder", *Review of Economics and Statistics*, Vol. XXXVIII, May 1955, pp. 131-133 and Julius Margolis, "A Comment on the Pure Theory of Public Expenditure", *Review of Economics and Statistics*, Vol. XXXVII, November 1955, pp. 247-249.

[6] Armen A. Alchian, "Uncertainty, Evolution, and Economic Theory", *Journal of Political Economy*, Vol. LVIII, June 1950, pp. 211-221.

appropriate benefits tax could be determined.[7] As things now stand, there is no mechanism to force the consumer-voter to state his true preferences; in fact, the "rational" consumer will understate his preferences and hope to enjoy the goods while avoiding the tax.

The current method of solving this problem operates, unsatisfactorily, through the political mechanism. The expenditure wants of a "typical voter" are somehow pictured. This objective on the expenditure side is then combined with an ability-to-pay principle on the revenue side, giving us our current budget. Yet in terms of a satisfactory theory of public finance, it would be desirable (1) to force the voter to reveal his preferences; (2) to be able to satisfy them in the same sense that a private goods market does; and (3) to tax him accordingly. The question arises whether there is any set of social institutions by which this goal can be approximated.

Local Expenditures

Musgrave and Samuelson implicitly assume that expenditures are handled at the central government level. However, the provision of such governmental services as police and fire protection, education, hospitals and courts does not necessarily involve federal activity.[8] Many of these goods are provided by local governments. It is worthwhile to look briefly at the magnitude of these expenditures.[9]

Historically, local expenditures have exceeded those of the federal government. The thirties were the first peace-time years in which federal expenditures began to pull away from local expenditures. Even during the fiscal year 1954, federal expenditures on *goods and services exclusive of defense* amounted only to some 15 billions of dollars, while local expenditures during this same period amounted to some 17 billions of dollars. There is no need to quibble over which comparisons are relevant. The important point is that the often-neglected local expenditures are significant, and, when viewed in terms of expenditures on goods and services only, take on even more significance. Hence an important question arises whether at this level of government any mechanism operates to insure that expenditures on these public goods approximate the proper level.

Consider for a moment the case of the city resident about to move to the suburbs. What variables will influence his choice of a municipality? If he has

----

[7]The term "benefits tax" is used in contrast to the concept of taxation based on the "ability to pay", which really reduces to a notion that there is some "proper" distribution of income. Conceptually, this issue is separate from the problem of providing public goods and services. See Musgrave, "A Multiple Theory of the Budget", *op. cit.*

[8]The discussion that follows applies to local governments. It will be apparent as the argument proceeds that it also applies, with less force, to state governments.

[9]A question does arise as to just what are the proper expenditures to consider. Following Musgrave, I shall consider only expenditures on goods or services (his Branch I expenditures). Thus interest on the federal debt is not included. At the local level interest payments might be included, since they are considered payments for services currently used, such as those provided by roads and schools.

children, a high level of expenditures on schools may be important. Another person may prefer a community with a municipal golf course. The availability and quality of such facilities and services as beaches, parks, police protection, roads, and parking facilities will enter into the decision-making process. Of course, non-economic variables will also be considered, but this is of no concern at this point.

The consumer-voter may be viewed as picking that community which best satisfies his preference pattern for public goods. This is a major difference between central and local provision of public goods. At the central level the preferences of the consumer-voter are given, and the government tries to adjust to the pattern of these preferences, whereas at the local level various governments have their revenue and expenditure patterns more or less set.[10] Given these revenue and expenditure patterns, the consumer-voter moves to that community whose local government best satisfies his set of preferences. The greater the number of communities and the greater the variance among them, the closer the consumer will come to fully realizing his preference position.[11]

A Local Government Model

The implications of the preceding argument may be shown by postulating an extreme model. Here the following assumptions are made:

1. Consumer-voters are fully mobile and will move to that community where their preference patterns, which are set, are best satisfied.

2. Consumer-voters are assumed to have full knowledge of differences among revenue and expenditure patterns and to react to these differences.

3. There are a large number of communities in which the consumer-voters may choose to live.

4. Restrictions due to employment opportunities are not considered. It may be assumed that all persons are living on dividend income.

5. The public services supplied exhibit no external economics or diseconomies between communities.

Assumptions 6 and 7 to follow are less familiar and require brief explanations:

6. For every pattern of community services set by, say, a city manager who follows the preferences of the older residents of the community, there is an optimal community size. This optimum is defined in terms of the number of residents for which this bundle of services can be produced at the lowest average cost. This, of course, is closely analogous to the low point of a firm's average cost curve. Such a cost function implies that some factor or resource is fixed. If this were not so, there would be no logical reason to limit community size, given the preference patterns. In the same sense that the average cost

---

[10]This is an assumption about reality. In the extreme model that follows the patterns are assumed to be absolutely fixed.

[11]This is also true of many non-economic variables. Not only is the consumer-voter concerned with economic patterns, but he desires, for example, to associate with "nice" people. Again, the greater the number of communities, the closer he will come to satisfying his total preference function, which includes non-economic variables.

has a minimum for one firm but can be reproduced by another there is seemingly no reason why a duplicate community cannot exist. The assumption that some factor is fixed explains why it is not possible for the community in question to double its size by growth. The factor may be the limited land area of a suburban community, combined with a set of zoning laws against apartment buildings. It may be the local beach, whose capacity is limited. Anything of this nature will provide a restraint.

In order to see how this restraint works, let us consider the beach problem. Suppose the preference patterns of the community are such that the optimum size population is 13,000. Within this set of preferences there is a certain demand per family for beach space. This demand is such that at 13,000 population a 500 yard beach is required. If the actual length of the beach is, say, 600 yards, then it is not possible to realize this preference pattern with twice the optimum population, since there would be too little beach space by 400 yards.

The assumption of a fixed factor is necessary, as will be shown later, in order to get a determinate number of communities. It also has the advantage of introducing a realistic restraint into the model.

7. The last assumption is that communities below the optimum size seek to attract new residents to lower average costs. Those above optimum size do just the opposite. Those at an optimum try to keep their populations constant.

This assumption needs to be amplified. Clearly, communities below the optimum size, through chambers of commerce or other agencies, seek to attract new residents. This is best exemplified by the housing developments in some suburban areas, such as Park Forest in the Chicago area, and Levittown in the New York area, which need to reach an optimum size. The same is true of communities that try to attract manufacturing industries by setting up certain facilities and getting an optimum number of firms to move into the industrially zoned area.

The case of the city that is too large and tries to get rid of residents is more difficult to imagine. No alderman in his right political mind would ever admit that the city is too big. Nevertheless, economic forces are at work to push people out of it. Every resident who moved to the suburbs to find better schools, more parks, and so forth, is reacting, in part, against the pattern the city has to offer.

The case of the community which is at the optimum size and tries to remain so is not hard to visualize. Again proper zoning laws, implicit agreements among realtors, and the like are sufficient to keep the population stable.

Except when this system is in equilibrium, there will be a subset of consumer-voters who are discontented with the patterns of their community. Another set will be satisfied. Given the assumption about mobility and the other assumptions listed previously, movement will take place out of the communities of greater than optimal size into the communities of less than optimal size. The consumer-voter moves to the community that satisfies his preference pattern.

The act of moving or failing to move is crucial. Moving or failing to move replaces the usual market test of willingness to buy a good and reveals the consumer-voter's demand for public goods. Thus each locality has a revenue and expenditure pattern that reflects the desires of its residents. The next step is to see what this implies for the allocation of public goods at the local level.

Each city manager now has a certain demand for n local public goods. In supplying these goods, he and $m-1$ other city managers may be considered as going to a national market and bidding for the appropriate units of service of each kind: so many units of police for the ith community; twice that number for the jth community; and so on. The demand on the public goods market for each of the n commodities will be the sum of the demands of the m communities. In the limit, as shown in a less realistic model to be developed later, this total demand will approximate the demand that represents the true preferences of the consumer-voters — that is, the demand they would reveal, if they were forced, somehow, to state their true preferences.[12] In this model there is no attempt on the part of local governments to "adapt to" the preferences of consumer-voters. Instead, those local governments that attract the optimum number of residents may be viewed as being "adopted by" the economic system.[13]

A Comparison Model

It is interesting to contrast the results of the preceding model with those of an even more severe model in order to see how these results differ from the normal market result. It is convenient to look at this severe model by developing its private-market counterpart. First assume that there are no public goods, only private ones. The preferences for these goods can be expressed as one of n patterns. Let a law be passed that all persons living in any one of the communities shall spend their money in the particular pattern described for that community by law. Given our earlier assumptions 1 through 5, it follows that, if the consumers move to the community whose law happens to fit their preference pattern, they will be at their optimum. The n communities, in turn, will then send their buyers to market to purchase the goods for the consumer-voters in their community. Since this is simply a lumping together of all similar tastes for the purpose of making joint purchases, the allocation of resources will be the same as it would be if normal market forces operated. This conceptual experiment is the equivalent of substituting the city manager for the broker or middleman.

Now turn the argument around and consider only public goods. Assume with Musgrave that the costs of additional services are constant.[14] Further, assume that a doubling of the population means doubling the amount of services required. Let the number of communities be infinite and let each

---

[12]The word "approximate" is used in recognition of the limitations of this model, and of the more severe model to be developed shortly, with respect to the cost of mobility. This issue will be discussed later.

[13]See Alchian, *op. cit.*

[14]Musgrave, "The Voluntary Exchange Theory of Public Economy", *op. cit.*

announce a different pattern of expenditures on public goods. Define an empty community as one that fails to satisfy anybody's preference pattern. Given these assumptions, including the earlier assumptions 1 through 5, the consumer-voters will move to that community which *exactly* satisfies their preferences. This must be true, since a one-person community is allowed. The sum of the demands of the n communities reflects the demand for local public services. In this model the demand is exactly the same as it would be if it were determined by normal market forces.

However, this severe model does not make much sense. The number of communities is indeterminate. There is no reason why the number of communities will not be equal to the population, since each voter can find the one that exactly fits his preferences. Unless some sociological variable is introduced, this may reduce the solution of the problem of allocating public goods to the trite one of making each person his own municipal government. Hence this model is not even a first approximation of reality. It is presented to show the assumptions needed in a model of local government expenditures, which yields the same optimal allocation that a private market would.

The Local Government Model Re-Examined

The first model, described by the first five assumptions together with assumptions 6 and 7, falls short of this optimum. An example will serve to show why this is the case.

Let us return to the community with the 500-yard beach. By assumption, its optimum population was set at 13,000, given its preference patterns. Suppose that some people in addition to the optimal 13,000 would choose this community if it were available. Since they cannot move into this area, they must accept the next best substitute.[15] If a perfect substitute is found, no problem exists. If one is not found, then the failure to reach the optimal preference position and the substitution of a lower position becomes a matter of degree. In so far as there are a number of communities with similar revenue and expenditure patterns, the solution will approximate the ideal "market" solution.

Two related points need to be mentioned to show the allocative results of this model: (1) changes in the costs of one of the public services will cause changes in the quantity produced; (2) the costs of moving from community to community should be recognized. Both points can be illustrated in one example.

Suppose lifeguards throughout the country organize and succeed in raising their wages. Total taxes in communities with beaches will rise. Now residents who are largely indifferent to beaches will be forced to make a decision. Is the saving of this added tax worth the cost of moving to a community with little or no beach? Obviously, this decision depends on many factors, among which the availability of and proximity to a suitable substitute community is important. If enough people leave communities with beaches and move to

---

[15]In the constant cost model with an infinite number of communities this problem does not arise, since the number of beaches can be doubled or a person can find another community that is a duplicate of his now filled first choice.

communities without beaches, the total amount of lifeguard services used will fall. These models then, unlike their private-market counterpart, have mobility as a cost of registering demand. The higher this cost, *ceteris paribus*, the less optimal the allocation of resources.

This distinction should not be blown out of proportion. Actually, the cost of registering demand comes through the introduction of space into the economy. Yet space affects the allocation not only of resources supplied by local governments but of those supplied by the private market as well. Every time available resources or production techniques change, a new location becomes optimal for the firm. Indeed, the very concept of the shopping trip shows that the consumer does pay a cost to register his demand for private goods. In fact, Koopmans has stated that the nature of the assignment problem is such that in a space economy with transport costs there is *no* general equilibrium solution as set by market forces.[16]

Thus the problems stated by this model are not unique; they have their counterpart in the private market. We are maximizing within the framework of the resources available. If production functions show constant returns to scale with generally diminishing factor returns, and if indifference curves are regularly convex, an optimal solution is possible. On the production side it is assumed that communities are forced to keep production costs at a minimum through the efficiency of city managers or through competition from other communities.[17] Given this, on the demand side we may note with Samuelson that "each individual, in seeking as a competitive buyer to get to the highest level of indifference subject to given prices and *tax*, would be led as if by an Invisible Hand to the grand solution of the social maximum position".[18] Just as the consumer may be visualized as walking to a private market place to buy his goods, the prices of which are set, we place him in the position of walking to a community where the prices (taxes) of community services are set. Both trips take the consumer to market. There is no way in which the consumer can avoid revealing his preferences in a spatial economy. Spatial mobility provides the local public-goods counterpart to the private market's shopping trip.

External Economies and Mobility

Relaxing assumption 5 has some interesting implications. There are obvious external economies and diseconomies between communities. My community is better off if its neighbour sprays trees to prevent Dutch elm disease. On

---

[16]Tjalling Koopmans, "Mathematical Groundwork of Economic Optimization Theories", paper read at the annual meeting of the Econometric Society, December 1954.

[17]In this model and in reality, the city manager or elected official who is not able to keep his costs (taxes) low compared with those of similar communities will find himself out of a job. As an institutional observation, it may well be that city managers are under greater pressure to minimize costs than their private-market counterparts — firm managers. This follows from (1) the reluctance of the public to pay taxes and, what may be more important, (2) the fact that the costs of competitors — other communities — are a matter of public record and may easily be compared.

[18]Samuelson, "The Pure Theory of Public Expenditures", *op. cit.*, p. 388.

the other hand, my community is worse off if the neighbouring community has inadequate law enforcement.

In cases in which the external economies and diseconomies are of sufficient importance, some form of integration may be indicated.[19] Not all aspects of law enforcement are adequately handled at the local level. The function of the sheriff, state police, and the FBI — as contrasted with the local police — may be cited as resulting from a need for integration. In real life the diseconomies are minimized in so far as communities reflecting the same socio-economic preferences are contiguous. Suburban agglomerations such as Westchester, the North Shore and the Main Line are, in part, evidence of these external economies and diseconomies.

Assumptions 1 and 2 should be checked against reality. Consumer-voters do not have perfect knowledge and set preferences, nor are they perfectly mobile. The question is how do people actually react in choosing a community. There has been very little empirical study of the motivations of people in choosing a community. Such studies as have been undertaken seem to indicate a surprising awareness of differing revenue and expenditure patterns.[20] The general disdain with which proposals to integrate municipalities are met seems to reflect, in part, the fear that local revenue-expenditure patterns will be lost as communities are merged into a metropolitan area.

Policy Implications

The preceding analysis has policy implications for municipal integration, provision for mobility, and set local revenue and expenditure patterns. These implications are worth brief consideration.

On the usual economic welfare grounds, municipal integration is justified only if more of any service is forthcoming at the same total cost and without reduction of any other service. A general reduction of costs along with a reduction in one or more of the services provided cannot be justified on economic grounds unless the social welfare function is known. For example those who argue for a metropolitan police force instead of local police cannot prove their case on purely economic grounds.[21] If one of the communities were to receive less police protection after integration than it received before, integration could be objected to as a violation of consumers' choice.

Policies that promote residential mobility and increase the knowledge of the consumer-voter will improve the allocation of government expenditures in the same sense that mobility among jobs and knowledge relevant to the location of industry and labor improve the allocation of private resources.

Finally, we may raise the normative question whether local governments *should*, to the extent possible, have a fixed revenue-expenditure pattern. In a

---

19I am grateful to Stanley Long and Donald Markwalder for suggesting this point.

20See Wendell Bell, "Familism and Suburbanization: One Test of the Choice Hypothesis", a paper read at the annual meeting of the American Sociological Society, Washington, D.C., August 1955. [Published] in *Rural Sociology*, December, 1956.

21For example, in Cook County — the Chicago area — Sheriff Joseph Lohman argues for such a metropolitan police force.

large, dynamic metropolis this may be impossible. Perhaps it could more appropriately be considered by rural and suburban communities.

Conclusion

It is useful in closing to restate the problem as Samuelson sees it:

> However, no decentralized pricing system can serve to determine optimally these levels of collective consumption. Other kinds of "voting" or "signaling" would have to be tried. . . . Of course utopian voting and signaling schemes can be imagined. . . . The failure of market catallactics in no way denies the following truth: given sufficient knowledge the optimal decisions can always be found by scanning over all the attainable states of the world and selecting the one which according to the postulated ethical welfare function is best. The solution "exists"; the problem is how to "find" it.[22]

It is the contention of this article that, for a substantial portion of collective or public goods, this problem *does have* a conceptual solution. If consumer-voters are fully mobile, the appropriate local governments, whose revenue-expenditure patterns are set, are adopted by the consumer-voters. While the solution may not be perfect because of institutional rigidities, this does not invalidate its importance. The solution, like a general equilibrium solution for a private spatial economy, is the best that can be obtained given preferences and resource endowments.

Those who are tempted to compare this model with the competitive private model may be disappointed. Those who compare the reality described by this model with the reality of the competitive model — given the degree of monopoly, friction, and so forth — *may* find that local government represents a sector where the allocation of public goods (as a reflection of the preferences of the population) need not take a back seat to the private sector.

65   The Organization of Metropolitan Governments*

George F. Break

Few problems of political economy rival in complexity that of determining the best way to organize public affairs in the modern city. Sometimes there

---

[22]Samuelson, "The Pure Theory of Public Expenditures", *op. cit.*, pp. 388-389.
*Reprinted by permission of author and publisher from George F. Break, *Intergovernmental Fiscal Relations in the United States*, The Brookings Institution, Washington, D.C., 1967, pp. 174-180.

seems to be no one at all in effective charge, and matters drift on rather aim-lessly. At other times independent and powerful government agencies deter-minedly pursue their own ends, regardless of the effects on other agencies or on other parts of the metropolitan area. To describe the situation as "chaos loosely organized" is only a slight overstatement. In any case, the situation offers ample opportunities for private profit — one reason it has survived as long as it has — but only slight promise for rapid progress in the governmental sphere. Many U.S. [and Canadian] cities, it would appear, could benefit from a systematic reorganization of their public sectors. Of course, needs in this respect differ greatly from one place to another, but there are enough common threads in the urban fabric to warrant a brief discussion of problems and prospects.

The Allocation of Public Programs among Metropolitan Governments

The first problem concerns the level of government that should handle each public function or subfunction. Five criteria, of varying degrees of importance in specific instances, are usually thought to provide the basis for rational choice on this question. They are external benefits and costs, economies of scale, variety of consumer choice, political participation, and interprogram evalua-tions. The first three are primarily economic in nature, and the last two mainly political.

External Benefits and Costs.

In many respects metropolitan areas constitute a single economic entity but are serviced by a multiplicity of smaller governmental units. Therefore, the spillover problem with the inefficiencies and inequities that result . . . appears in its most intense form in city finance. One solution is to expand the geo-graphical scope of governmental units so as to convert external benefits and costs into internal ones. Another solution, which avoids some of the dis-advantages of highly centralized and unified government operations, is to make increased use of inter-governmental fiscal aids. Both are discussed in detail later.

Economies of Scale.

If education costs fall by $27 per pupil as the size of the school district is increased from 1,500 to 50,000 pupils in average daily attendance but increase by $10 per pupil if the size is extended to 80,000, as has recently been estimated by Nels W. Hanson,[1] the advantages of keeping school districts close to the 50,000 level are obvious. On the other hand, as already noted, Hirsch found economies of scale to be statistically insignificant in his 1951-55 study of St. Louis school districts ranging in size from 600 to 84,000 students.[2] Though his

---

[1]"Economy of Scale as a Cost Factor in Financing Public Schools", *National Tax Journal*, Vol. XVII, March 1964, pp. 92-95.

[2]Werner Z. Hirsch, "Determinants of Public Education Expenditures", *National Tax Journal*, Vol. XIII, March 1960, p. 36.

study had much less geographical scope than Hanson's, it did attempt to allow for quality variations in school services which must be held constant if economies and diseconomies of scale are to be measured accurately. Given the well-known difficulties involved in measuring educational quality, however, the question of what constitutes the optimal size of school district is likely to remain unresolved for some time. Nonetheless, since 26 per cent of metropolitan school districts still enroll fewer than 300 pupils,[3] much can still be done to increase school efficiency.

For other municipal services the problem of measuring quality seems less intractable, and various economic analyses can be drawn on to apply the economy-of-scale criterion. Though unit costs and size show little interrelationship for police and fire protection and for refuse collection,[4] significant scale economies appear to characterize such programs as water supply, sewage disposal, public health services and hospitals.[5] Others may be found in the table which classifies the most important municipal services by the presence or absence of economies of scale.

Finally, mention should be made of one important factor that affects the operation of all programs, though in varying degrees. Large governments, other things being equal, are better able to hire top-quality technical and professional personnel than are small governments, and they should, therefore, be able to provide better public services at a given cost.

This provides a strong argument either for consolidating small urban governments until they are large enough to be able to afford high quality officials or for making intergovernmental cooperative arrangements designed to attract the technical expertise needed for the more complex urban programs and to make it available to participating jurisdictions.

Variety of Consumer Choice.

Voters in federal elections frequently complain about the similarity of the economic programs offered by the two major parties. Too often, it has been said, they have "an echo not a choice". Consumers of metropolitan public services, however, are in a somewhat more favorable position. Different parts of the area are likely to offer different combinations of governmental services at different local tax rates, and the alert resident may seek out the specific package that is most appealing to him. Since individual tastes in this respect seem to be diverse, a city that offers a variety of local public programs should be a more attractive place to live than one that does not. One of the virtues of metropolitan decentralization, in other words, is the opportunity it gives

    [3] Advisory Commission on Intergovernmental Relations (ACIR), *Metropolitan Social and Economic Disparities: Implications for Intergovernmental Relations in Central Cities and Suburbs*, January 1965, p. 47.

    [4] Werner Z. Hirsch, "Expenditure Implications of Metropolitan Growth and Consolidation", *Review of Economics and Statistics*, Vol. XLI, August 1959, pp. 232-241, and "Cost Functions of an Urban Government Service: Refuse Collection", *ibid.*, Vol. XLVII, February 1965, pp. 87-92.

    [5] ACIR, *Performance of Urban Functions Local and Areawide*, September 1963, pp. 154-155, 168, and 200-203.

CLASSIFICATION OF PUBLIC PROGRAMS ACCORDING TO
ECONOMIES OF SCALE, BENEFIT SPILLOUTS, AND POLITICAL PROXIMITY

Program	Allocation Criterion			
	Economies of Scale	Benefit Spillouts	Political Proximity	Composite
Local Schools	+	+	0	=
Transportation	+	+	×	+
Public Welfare	0	+	0	=
Health and Hospitals	+	+	+	+
Police				
Basic Services	0	0	0	0
Special Services	+	+	0	+
Fire	0	0	0	0
Water Supply	+	+	+	+
Sewage Disposal	+	+	+	+
Refuse Collection	0	0	+	0
Refuse Disposal	+	+	+	+
Parks and Recreation	0	+	×	=
Public Housing	0	+	0	=
Urban Renewal	×	+	×	=
Libraries				
Basic	0	0	0	0
Special	+	+	+	+
Air and Water Pollution	+	+	+	+
Urban Planning	+	+	×	+

+ favors areawide control because economies of scale are important, or benefit spillouts are significant, or political proximity is unimportant

0 favors local control for the opposite reasons

= favors joint control

× indicates that the allocation criterion yields a debatable result

for a better adaptation of public goods to the desires of different groups of residents.[6]

In the nature of things, however, these opportunities are strictly limited. The system will work only for programs with benefits that flow mainly to the residents of a given area and that are financed by taxes with a strong benefits-received orientation. Two difficulties are immediately apparent. As may be seen in the table, many of the most important local programs generate benefits that spill over local boundaries, and some programs, public welfare being a prime example, cannot be financed by benefit levies at all. This means, for example, that local financing of welfare activities is likely to produce

---

[6]For a theoretical analysis of this question see Charles M. Tiebout, "A Pure Theory of Local Expenditures," *Journal of Political Economy*, Vol. LXIV, October 1956, pp. 416-424.

a flight of the affluent from above-average levels of public charity, either in the core city with its disadvantaged minorities or in residential suburbs with a high concentration of low-income residents. Though local financing of education by property taxation may produce a healthy competition among jurisdictions of approximately equal wealth per pupil, it also stimulates the use of zoning restrictions and other devices to create protected enclaves with relatively high tax capacities and low public service needs.

Vigorous competition among independent metropolitan governments, then, is likely to produce a mixture of good and bad effects. At its best it replaces sloth and inertia with an active search for better and more varied public services and for more efficient ways of providing them. At its worst, however, it enables some to enjoy high-quality services and low tax rates while others suffer from exactly the reverse. One of the most difficult problems facing the urban policy maker is how to achieve the former while avoiding the latter. To solve this he will need, among other things, to experiment with new kinds of intergovernmental relations.

Political Participation.

Essential though it is to effective democracy, active citizen participation in political decision-making is no guarantee of success in government. Under the right circumstances, it results in programs that are well adapted to voter wishes and that are operated without waste or graft. Under less favorable circumstances, however, it can produce divisive debate and stalemate instead of action or, as is sometimes worse, it can produce actions that exacerbate rather than solve the problems at hand. There is no need at this point to discuss the various organizational devices that can be used to increase the chances of good results.[7] People-to-government proximity is generally regarded as one of them and it is a quality that tends to flourish in small jurisdictions.[8] Participation that is not rewarded with tangible results, however, is not likely to continue long, and local governments can be too small to cope with many urban problems entirely on their own. Nor is the nearness of the voter to his government equally important for all local programs, and attempts to distinguish those, such as local libraries, that are likely to benefit most from a high degree of accessibility, from those, such as air and water pollution control, that are likely to benefit least.

---

[7]In the words of the ACIR these features include "the number and nature of elective officials, the manner of their election (by district or at large), their terms, the distribution of powers among them and the appointive personnel, provisions for notice and hearings on proposed policy changes, administrative provisions for receiving and acting on complaints, provisions for initiative and referendum, and recourse to the courts". *Alternative Approaches to Governmental Reorganization in Metropolitan Areas,* June 1962, p. 13.

[8]For a discussion of ways of strengthening neighborhood government in large urban areas see Luther H. Gulick, *The Metropolitan Problem and American Ideas,* Knopf, New York, 1962, pp. 107-113. In Gulick's opinion one reason that broad metropolitan institutions have so far failed to achieve a high degree of acceptability in this country is that reformers have concentrated on areawide decision-making processes and have neglected ways of preserving legitimate local interests.

Interprogram Evaluations.

In principle, each use of public funds should be compared with every other use and only the most valuable ones chosen. Whereas in the private sector of the economy the impersonal forces of the money market are relied upon for this purpose, in the public sector it is the highly personal budgeting process that must produce the answers desired. Ideally, this means either that all urban programs should be managed by one multipurpose governnment,[9] or if separate governmental units are to exist for other reasons, that their activities should be subject to review at some higher level. In practice, however, the provision of areawide services often depends on the cooperative efforts of independent governmental units. In such cases, it is essential to have some reasonably objective basis for allocating costs to specific jurisdictions, and it is here that benefit-cost analysis . . . has an important role to play.

It will be noted that the five criteria just discussed point, as criteria often do, in opposing directions. Whereas the first, second, and fifth all favor relatively large governmental units, the other two definitely throw their lots in with the small jurisdictions. How one makes the choice in practice, therefore, will depend on the importance he accords the different criteria. Diversity of opinion on this score is inevitable, but as a basis for further discussion, the tabulation below presents one considered choice, which has been guided particularly by the work of the Advisory Commission on Intergovernmental Relations (ACIR) and Werner Hirsch.[10] The tabulation shows the allocation of program responsibilities among metropolitan governments.

Primarily Local	Joint	Primarily Areawide
Fire	Elementary and	Planning
Basic Police Services	Secondary Schools	Health and Hospitals
Basic Libraries	Transportation	Water Supply
Local Parks	Public Housing	Sewage and Sanitation
Refuse Collection	Urban Renewal	Air and Water Pollution
	Public Welfare	Refuse Disposal
		Special Police Services
		Special Libraries
		Regional Parks

If this classification is realistic, some solution intermediate between complete local control and complete metropolitan centralization is needed. In its simplest form it would be a two-level federal system, the base being formed by a number of independent municipalities dealing with all programs that generate purely local benefits and large enough to take advantage of most of the economies

---

[9]For a discussion of the advantages and limitations of general government see *ibid.*, pp. 81-89.

[10]In addition to the studies already cited see Werner Z. Hirsch, "Local Versus Areawide Urban Government Services", *National Tax Journal*, Vol. XVII, December 1964, pp. 331-339.

of scale inherent in such programs — 50,000 to 100,000 people is a commonly suggested size. On the second level would be a single metropolitan government which, in addition to having jurisdiction over the areawide programs listed above, would assist the municipalities both by making grants to them for whatever external benefits their activities yield and by setting uniform revenue-raising rules, to be discussed later, designed to strengthen local taxing powers.

The present hodgepodge of metropolitan governments will not be converted overnight into some simple, functional system. The mere magnitude of the task is imposing enough, to say nothing of the distrust with which many people view big city governments,[11] or of the inertia and vested interests that always oppose basic reforms.

66   Financial Implications of Urban Growth *

The Economic Council of Canada

The concentration of population in urban centres, and particularly in the large centres, brings greatly increased demands for collective services and social capital. These have fallen at least initially on municipal governments but the growth in the responsibilities of these governments has not been matched by corresponding increases in their financial powers. Many municipalities have been caught in a "squeeze", with revenues from their own sources — still largely the real property tax — lagging behind expenditure requirements. Their accounts have been balanced in recent years by larger grants from senior governments and an increased absolute volume of borrowing and, over the longer run, by some shift of functions to the senior governments. But, there is considerable evidence to suggest that the *terms* on which the accounting balance has been attained — particularly in respect of the quality of urban services — are less than satisfactory from the viewpoint of either the contribution of urban development to growth or the participation of the urban resident in the fruits of the growth process.

With a strong trend towards further urban concentration of Canada's population in the future, especially in the larger centres, it is important to give much greater attention to the financial development of our urban municipal

---

[11] According to the ACIR, "distrust of the central city and its motives with respect to regional approaches is found in suburbia across the land". *Intergovernmental Responsibilities for Water Supply and Sewage Disposal in Metropolitan Areas*, October 1962, p. 50. See also ACIR, *Factors Affecting Voter Reactions to Governmental Reorganization in Metropolitan Areas*, May 1962.

*Reprinted by permission from Economic Council of Canada, *Fourth Annual Review: The Canadian Economy from the 1960's to the 1970's*, Queen's Printer, Ottawa, 1967, pp. 215-225.

governments. The Economic Council of Canada has only begun to work in this area and many of our conclusions at this time must of necessity be tentative — partly because of the great difficulty in obtaining adequate comparative data on individual municipalities. But the urgent nature of the problem must, we feel, be brought under public scrutiny without delay.

Examination of the historical record suggests that the financial structure of Canadian municipalities was reasonably well adapted to the requirements of the late nineteenth century. But modernization of this nineteenth century machinery has failed to keep pace with the needs of accentuated urbanization in this century.

At Confederation the real property tax provided a substantial proportion of provincial-municipal revenue and the provinces in fact looked to expanding municipal organization and property tax revenue to finance a growing proportion of provincial-municipal responsibilities. This was consistent with the view then held that the functions of government left with the provincial-municipal jurisdiction — civil government, local public works, the administration of justice, education and social welfare — would show only slow growth. In fact, with increasing urbanization, some of these services and notably education, social welfare and transportation facilities, grew very rapidly. Despite some shift in responsibilities to senior governments during the 1930's and 1940's, particularly in respect of health and welfare services, many municipalities faced increasing pressure on their finances in the renewed upsurge of expenditure after the Second World War.

The prolonged expansion in municipal expenditures since 1945 has been basd on a combination of factors including the backlog of projects deferred during the Depression and the war, rising average incomes and the particularly rapid growth in the population classes requiring the largest proportion of municipally supported services, notably school age children.

Clearly the increase in education expenditures was the dominant feature of the municipal financial scene throughout the period (Table 1). Gross spending on local schools, which includes provincial grants, accounted for half of the total increase in spending at the municipal level over the decade 1953 to 1963 and its importance increased in the later years of the period. Since provincial grants to local school authorities rose sharply also, the increase in education spending which the municipalities had to finance from their own revenue sources (net general expenditure) was somewhat less though it still comprised, by a very considerable margin, the largest part of the increase in their budgets. From 1945 to 1958, expenditures on transportation accounted for the second largest proportion of the increase in spending financed from the municipalities' own sources but in more recent years this function appears to have been compressed to make way for increased school costs, the rising level of debt charges and more protective services. Total expenditures accelerated from 1963 to 1966, but the functional expenditure data available for this period (incomplete as they are) suggest that the distribution of spending has not changed greatly since the early 1960's. The proportion of spending on local schools which is financed from municipal sources varies somewhat from prov-

TABLE 1
MUNICIPAL GOVERNMENT EXPENDITURES

	1953	1963	Change 1953-63	Percentage Composition of Total Change 1953-63
		(Millions of dollars)		
GROSS GENERAL EXPENDITURE				
Education[1]	536	1,677	1,141	49
Transportation	195	532	337	15
Debt charges	66	201	135	6
Protection	116	300	184	8
Sanitation	64	188	124	5
All other	270	663	393	17
Total	1,247	3,561	2,314	100
Less:				
GRANTS-IN-AID				
Education	156	789	633	80
Transportation	41	128	87	11
Protection	5	1	- 4	- 1
Sanitation	—	5	5	1
All other	13	85	72	9
Total	215	1,008	793	100
Debt Charge Adjustment	20	—	- 20	
Equals:				
NET GENERAL EXPENDITURE				
Education	380	888	508	33
Transportation	154	404	250	16
Debt charges	46	201	155	10
Protection	111	299	188	12
Sanitation	64	183	119	8
All other	257	578	321	21
Total	1,012	2,553	1,541	100

[1]Includes federal and provincial grants to local school authorities.
Source: Based on data from Dominion Bureau of Statistics.

ince to province and has fallen considerably in recent years. However, for the country as a whole, local municipal governments continued to contribute more than half of the total cost of primary and secondary education in 1963.

Revenue from the municipalities' own sources failed to keep pace with increased expenditures over the period 1953 to 1963 and the gap was filled more and more by transfers from the provincial governments (Table 2). The proportion of the total to be financed by borrowing (or liquidation of financial assets), on the other hand, has apparently not varied a great deal, taking all municipalities together, although it has risen substantially in absolute terms. Moreover, municipal general and school debt net of sinking funds rose much more rapidly than the general debt of federal and provincial governments from 1953 to 1963.

TABLE 2

MUNICIPAL EXPENDITURES AND FINANCING

	1953		1963	
	(Millions of dollars)		(Millions of dollars)	
EXPENDITURES:				
Net general expenditure	1,012		2,553	
Add:				
Federal and provincial grants to local schools	156		789	
Other grants-in-aid	79[1]		219	
Equals:				
Gross general expenditure including local schools	1,247		3,561	
	(Percentage Distribution)		(Percentage Distribution)	
FINANCING:				
Federal and provincial grants:				
To local schools	156	13	789	22
Other grants-in-aid	79[1]	6	219	6
Unconditional grants	33	3	112	3
Revenue from own sources				
Real property tax	655	53	1,674	47
All other	165	13	307	9
Remainder: to be financed by net change in financial assets	159	13	460	13
Total financing	1,247	100	3,561	100

[1]Includes also a $20 million adjustment to debt charges.
Source: Based on data from Dominion Bureau of Statistics.

Real property taxes continued to account for more than three quarters of the total revenue from the municipalities' own sources over the period 1953 to 1963 and it is worth noting that they rose more than one and a half times as rapidly as personal income. Despite this very considerable response, the operation of this tax source continues to provide a sharp contrast with the more dynamic revenue sources open to senior governments. The personal income tax, for example, automatically produces substantially higher revenues at unchanged tax rates in a growing economy because of the fairly rapid expansion in taxable income. Data on the real property tax base are at present most inadequate, but our preliminary investigation suggests that on average the base has risen at only about the same rate as personal income, or perhaps very slightly faster. But since municipal expenditures were rising considerably faster than personal income, many municipalities have for some time faced upward trends in the rates which they must apply to the property tax base. In some cities this upward trend in rates has accelerated in the last several years. The necessity of facing annual decisions to raise the tax base (reassessment) or to increase tax rates obviously has decided advantages for budget restraint and municipal taxpayers' interests. At the same time, it may create some built-in discrimination against services performed at the municipal level no matter how important they may be in relation to growth or to the general welfare.

Prospects for the Larger Urban Areas

Aggregate municipal figures may obscure as much as they reveal. The scattered evidence already available shows considerable variation among municipalities in property tax burdens, standards of service and general financial position. With close to two thirds of Canada's total population expected to be living in major urban areas by 1980, it is essential to look behind the national aggregates and focus attention upon the prospective financial problems of these larger centres.

Surprisingly, however, despite the fact that the annual budgets of some cities exceed those of several provincial governments, no uniform financial data have yet been established in Canada to permit nation-wide comparisons and analyses of the operations of even the largest of our cities. The Dominion Bureau of Statistics has done a great deal of useful work on municipal financial statistics but the lowest level of disaggregation for which uniform data are available is the consolidated total of municipalities in each province. In the United States, despite the far greater number of municipalities, a considerable amount of comparable data has been published on individual cities across the country.

We have attempted a very modest beginning towards filling this gap. Rough estimates of total revenues and expenditures (current and capital) for the larger urban centres have been constructed on the basis of a sample of cities and metropolitan areas for which some data are available. The data derived from the sample cities show that on a per capita basis both tax levies and expenditures are higher for the large cities taken together than for the smaller cities.[1] These per capita data from the sample have been used in conjunction with the estimated total population in cities of 100,000 and over to project a rough idea of the dimensions of the future financial requirements of large urban areas (Table 3).

On the basis of these calculations it is clear that unless further action is taken to alleviate the situation, Canada's large cities are likely to face a rapidly widening gap between revenues and expenditures or a substantial reduction in the quality of municipal services between now and 1980. Part of the gap will, of course, continue to be filled by borrowing; but the constraint on borrowing implied by the slower growth in revenue from the municipalities' own

---

[1]This association appears to be due more to other characteristics of large urban areas, particularly higher average income levels, rather than population size itself.

sources suggests that considerable assistance will have to be made available from other sources.

TABLE 3

ESTIMATED REVENUES AND EXPENDITURES OF MUNICIPALITIES
WITH POPULATIONS OF 100,000 AND OVER

	1966	1980
	(Billions of dollars)	
Revenue from own sources	1.6	4.7
Transfers from senior governments	0.5	1.5
Total revenue	2.1	6.2
Gross expenditure[1]	2.6	8.6
Revenue less expenditure	- 0.5	- 2.4

[1]Because of data limitations, expenditures are gross of debt retirement but net of provincial operating grants to local schools. The latter grants have also been eliminated from the transfers from senior governments.
Source: Based on estimates by Economic Council of Canada.

For the purposes of these calculations, per capita expenditures were projected at three quarters of the rate of increase over the period 1954 to 1964. Underlying the estimates are assumptions providing for some continued increase in both the quality and price of urban services, with some easing in the expansion of requirements for education, and increased emphasis on such services as transportation, urban renewal and low-income housing and pollution abatement. On the basis of such considerations as the long-run national potential for a more rapid increase in personal income per capita and the present inadequate quality of some urban services, these expenditure estimates to 1980 are likely to be conservative.

For revenue from own sources, the projections allow for revenue per capita to rise at roughly the same rate of increase that would occur in personal income per capita if the economy remains close to its potential output. For these cities, this implies a more rapid rise in revenues than could be produced only by an expanding tax base at present tax levels; that is, the trend implies some property tax rate increase or greater exploitation of other revenue sources. Transfers from senior governments were assumed to continue to support the same proportion of gross municipal expenditure (excluding operating expenditures of local school boards) as in recent years.

These figures clearly indicate that some action to obtain additional revenues will have to be taken even to prevent a decrease in the quality of our urban services. Commendable efforts are already being made in several provinces to reform the property tax through, for example, better assessment practices. These need to be extended rapidly in all parts of the country. In addition, the possibility of greater returns from other municipal revenue services, such as utility charges, need to be explored more thoroughly. But it is highly doubtful that the municipal revenue base, even with improvement, would be sufficient to support the growing needs of many of our large communities as their populations expand. It is not a question of whether further assistance is required from the senior governments, but rather what forms should such assistance take.

This question has concerned all of the Royal Commissions or committees which have looked at the problems of municipal finance in recent years, and a general consensus appears to be emerging. The broad principle to be followed, difficult though its application may be in practice, is this: services whose benefits accrue to areas wider than the individual municipality should in part be the responsibility of a wider government jurisdiction. In an economy where people are increasingly mobile, this principle can be translated into a case for the broader jurisdiction, particularly jurisdictions with access to the more dynamic tax sources, supporting a substantial part of *services* to *people* while allocating local expenditures more to *services* to *property*. For this reason, several of the recent Commissions have recommended a larger share of financial support from senior governments for education. The Council supports this conclusion. There are cogent reasons for retaining a substantial local interest and responsibility in schooling; but the present variation across the country in the proportion of local schooling supported by municipalities suggests that there are many areas where the average municipal share could be lowered without undue harm to local responsibility and autonomy. Other areas of responsibility, such as transportation, may be less clear-cut than education. Nevertheless, we feel strongly that further research into the causal factors behind rapidly increasing city expenditure would help to suggest guidelines for a more appropriate division of costs and burdens in these areas as well. It must be recognized, however, that any shifts of financial responsibility to senior levels of government involve an increased revenue requirement at these levels. The total tax burden may well be redistributed as between areas and income groups, but it cannot be reduced except by a restriction of expenditure programmes or through greater efficiency in public spending.

In the past, the problems of our urban areas have been approached by senior governments more from a viewpoint of maintaining financial integrity and financial control than from that of planning for growth. It is becoming more and more clear, however, that many aspects of Canadian economic growth and of policies at all levels of government, as well as of private decision-making, are being increasingly affected by the financial problems of urban governments, particularly of the larger cities. These problems must be attacked on a broad front within the framework of the Canadian constitution.

To this end, the Council strongly commends the suggestion of a special study of urban development which was made in the May 1967 federal Speech from the Throne. Specifically, we would hope that the provincial governments in conjunction with the federal government would join to examine the future requirements of growing urban centres and the methods of financing them — in other words, an extension of, or a counterpart to, the work of the federal-provincial Tax Structure Committee focusing on urban development. This should be conducted as an operational project rather than an academic research exercise, and it should examine the possibility of taking more adequate account of municipal tax burdens and the requirements of basic urban services in federal-provincial fiscal arrangements.

Any such arrangements would, of course, call for substantial improvement and co-ordination of assessment practices, but bearing in mind the recent tendency of the provinces to incorporate measures of fiscal capacity in their local government grants, these suggestions are consistent with developing trends. The project should also attempt to provide intermunicipal comparisons of the costs of performing various services in individual cities across the nation. Such comparisons are, we believe, fundamental to progress in this area and they would, as municipal financial experts have pointed out,[2] provide useful guidelines for decision-makers and administrators in evaluating the efficient use of the resources devoted to enlarging municipal services.

The central features of past urban growth in Canada are unmistakable. Traced over a period of more than a hundred years, its population and economic activity have increasingly been concentrated in urban areas and particularly the larger cities. The trend of rapid urbanization, moreover, has been inextricably meshed with the evolution of the economy from a specialized producer of primary products to a ranking industrial nation. The trends which are now apparent indicate that the population distribution in Canada still provides a significant margin for continued concentration in urban centres. Consequently, the pace and magnitude of urban growth is likely to persist, with further population increase taking place entirely in the cities. By 1980, according to our projections, over 80 per cent of the total population will be urban, while 60 per cent will be concentrated in some 29 metropolises and large city complexes of 100,000 population and over. This implies that the pace of urbanization in Canada will continue to be the highest among the major industrial countries in the world. The economic benefits to be derived from urban concentration will thus continue to be an important factor in the longer-run rise of per capita output and income.

Urban growth in Canada, however, has been accompanied by numerous problems of growing intensity, and with certain adverse effects upon the quality of urban living. These problems and disadvantages will be greatly accentuated by further rapid urbanization, unless the development of the major city complexes across the country can be carried out in such a way as to meet the mounting collective requirements of the expanded urban population. The dimensions of this challenge — of the need to provide adequately for urban housing, balanced transport systems, water supply and waste disposal, parks and recreation, the control of air pollution and many other urban services, all within a framework of efficient, orderly growth and an environment of improving quality — undoubtedly call for new and imaginative public policies

---

[2]See, for example, Elswood F. Bole, "The Development and Use of Program and Performance Budgeting for Municipalities", an address at the Conference on Municipal Finance Statistics, Queen's University, May 1966.

involving all three levels of government, including new priorities in the allocation of resources.

It is clear, in this context, that the benefits of urban agglomeration and proximity have to be set off against the costs of congestion and overtaxed facilities. The need to balance these opposing forces raises the question as to whether attempts should be made to limit the expansion of the largest centres by deliberate policies of decentralization to smaller cities and towns or by the creation of entirely new urban communities. This involves the difficult concept of the "optimum size" for the modern industrial city — that level where benefits from larger size are counterbalanced by the increase in costs. No one who has lived in one of the truly giant metropolises of the world — New York, Tokyo, London or Paris — fails to have some feeling that these centres may well have passed a desirable upper limit. As a concept, the "city of optimum size" is undoubtedly attractive, but given the present state of our knowledge, it provides little in the way of practical policy guides. Objective criteria for defining this "optimum" are lacking in the face of the problems of measuring the magnitude of both private and public benefits and costs associated with living and working in an urban environment and their distribution among the residents of the community. It will be necessary to achieve a thorough understanding of the dynamic forces underlying the growth of cities, to specify social choices among alternative city sizes and forms, and to devise acceptable means for influencing the location of economic activity among centres before the concept of optimum size can be applied. Under present circumstances, therefore, current policy can best be directed towards orderly growth and an improved environment within Canada's presently expanding urban centres.

Finally, it will be noted that our discussion has made only incidental reference to a broad range of social questions requiring attention in the continued growth of our large cities. Many of these are closely related to the physical character of the big city and the adequacy of its services. Obvious among them are those of poverty and low income, of poor health and family breakdown, and of crime and delinquency, all of which are so frequently associated with low levels of education, bad housing, inadequate sanitation and general urban decay. More broadly, there are in our cities growing problems of divisive social segregation and stratification, of pressures upon the individual from the hurried pace of urban living, of conflicting conformity in the comfortable suburbs, and of anonymity and lack of identification in the face of the immensity of the big city. In all these further respects, the continued rapid expansion of large centres re-emphasizes a complex of challenges if the quality of human life is to be improved, if the fruits of economic progress are to be equitably shared, and if the human resources and human potential of an urban, industrial society are to be fully developed.

Chapter Six
Fiscal Policy
for Stabilization and Growth

The budgetary objective of stabilization is concerned with the maintenance of a high level of resource utilization and a stable value of money. In effect, it is a primary function of fiscal policy to hold within prescribed limits departures from full employment and price stability, whether these departures represent merely short-run fluctuations or secular maladjustments. In the event of unemployment, fiscal policy should act to adjust the level of aggregate demand upward to the value of potential output at full employment. Conversely, in the event of inflation, fiscal policy should adjust the level of aggregate demand downward to the value of full employment output measured in current rather than rising prices. Finally, a dynamic fiscal policy should in circumstances of both full employment and price stability maintain a *rising* level of aggregate demand so as to match increasing capacity to produce over time.

Full employment is taken to mean a socially tolerable rate of unemployment. This rate varies from one nation to another, but may be considered to be between 3 per cent and 4 per cent in Canada. Price stability equally does not mean price rigidity. It is indeed desirable in a growing economy that prices rise in dynamic expanding sectors of the economy in order to attract resources to these areas. Theoretically, these price increases would be matched by price falls in declining sectors. Relative price stability would thus imply an overall stable price level, consistent with changing prices in particular sectors. In fact, prices tend to sticky downward and relative price stability is likely to imply upward pressure on the general price level. The problem is to distinguish such general pressure on the price level — what might be termed "functional" price increases — from inflationary price increases. Perhaps the simplest distinction is that an inflationary rise in prices is both cumulative and pervasive in nature.

The thorny issue of conflict and trade-off between the joint stabilization objectives of full employment and price stability has been dealt with at some length in the section on policy objectives.

Stabilization measures to affect aggregate demand may be either automatic or discretionary. Automatic policy covers those changes in revenue and expenditure which are built into the system; obvious examples are the automatic drop in income tax revenue as incomes drop in a situation of unemployment, and the associated increase in government transfer payments to the unemployed, both changes operating to moderate the down-turn. Discretionary policy measures, on the other hand, represent *ad hoc* budgetary changes, i.e., changes geared to the exigencies of a particular situation. The role of both discretionary and automatic fiscal policy in Canada is set out in the first extract below, which also considers a third alternative lying between discretionary and automatic measures — formula flexibility. Under formula flexibility changes in budgetary policy are legislated *ex ante* to take effect in the event of specified movements of economic variables; for example, an increase in income tax rates of a specified magnitude might be provided for *ex ante* in relation to specified changes in the index of wholesale prices. The major advantage of formula flexibility lies in the avoidance of a variety of time lags between the development of the stabilization problem and the implementation of policy measures to deal with the problem. These time lags are dealt with specifically in the second extract below. The limitations of formula flexibility are examined in both the first and second extracts.

The first extract includes an appraisal of Canadian fiscal policy from 1953 to 1963 using the concept of the full employment budget surplus. This is a concept which has been developed in the U.S.A. to facilitate the evaluation of discretionary fiscal policy. The problem is that the actual budget surplus or deficit may provide a misleading impression of the extent to which that surplus or deficit actually represents contractionary or expansionary policy, respectively, since it reflects the impact of built-in automatic factors as well as the effect of discretionary policy changes. Thus a large budget deficit which on the face of it seems expansionary may simply represent a slowdown in the rate of economic growth and increasing unemployment. Likewise, a budget surplus which appears to be restrictive may simply represent an inflationary rise in money incomes.

The concept of the full employment budget surplus has been developed to abstract from the effects of automatic stabilizers by setting up in national accounts terms the actual surplus which would be generated by a *given* budget programme at full employment at the prevailing level of prices, thus isolating the extent to which that given budget programme is contractionary or expansionary.

It has been generally assumed, even in federal states, that the sole responsibility for stabilization policy rests with the federal government, and that it must simply be hoped that the lower levels of government will refrain from introducing perverse policies. This thesis is challenged in the third extract below, where the case is made for an integral role for the provincial governments in Canada in stabilization policy. The major argument against such a development is, of course, concerned with the leakage between provinces which might vitiate the stabilization policy of any one province, and the argument developed as a consequence is for a co-ordinated federal-provincial stabilization policy in Canada — one which would reflect the particular and often conflicting needs of various parts of the country, but which would also avoid perversity and competitive provincial fiscal policies.

The final extract is what might best be termed an overview article on the tax side of the budget which examines, in the light of the various problems of fiscal policy, the most effective tax policy for stabilization purposes.

As suggested above, a dynamic stabilization policy must provide for a rising level of aggregate demand to match increasing capacity to produce over time, i.e., ensure a stable growth path. In this sense the growth objective may be subsumed under the stabilization objective. Generally, however, the growth objective is not only stated in this implicit manner, but is stated quite explicitly. In its examination of budgetary objectives, the Carter Commission stated the growth objective as follows: budget policy must "maximize the current and future output of goods and services desired by Canadians".

There are three aspects of the explicit growth role which may be played by fiscal policy. The first refers to the direct growth effects of government expenditure in the economy. Government investment by definition provides for the growth of national income, and much of what is arbitrarily classified as government consumption is growth-promoting in nature. Implicit in this effect is the condition that tax means employed to finance all or part of this expenditure be devised so as to exercise a minimal adverse effect on private sector growth. In this sense taxation must clearly be of a sort which does not have serious implications for private incentives to work, save and invest.

The second aspect takes as its initial premise the condition that the raising of tax revenue should have minimal *unintended* disincentive effects on the private sector, and would then go on to suggest a policy of fiscal dirigism — that fiscal policy be so designed as to provide a whole series of incentive and disincentive effects in the private sector, the purpose of this structure of fiscal concessions and penalties being the shaping of the rate and pattern of the growth path in a way consistent with overall national objectives. In this way the *quality* or nature of the growth path as distinct from the purely quantitative notion of a rate of economic growth becomes an objective of fiscal policy. Such a direct explicit involvement by government in determining the nature and pace of economic growth was, with a few qualifications, rejected by the Carter Commission, which viewed the role of fiscal policy in relation to economic growth in a much more indirect way.

The third aspect of the growth role reflects this indirect role. The initial premise of this role is that the proper rate of growth is that determined by a fully employed and efficient private sector. Given the elimination of unemployment, which causes the actual growth rate to fall below the potential growth rate, and measures to ensure the efficient operation of the private sector (typical difficulties here would be such matters as industries operating under decreasing cost conditions, and the occurrence of external economies and diseconomies), fiscal policy must unharness the "invisible hand" by being essentially neutral in nature, thus permitting resources to flow according to market forces.

Only one extract is included on the relationship of fiscal policy and the growth objective. There is obviously much literature available, but the Carter Commission survey of the effect of the present, and the likely effect of a reformed, tax system on the three major determinants of economic growth — labour supply, technical change, and capital formation — is so manifestly the most thorough and comprehensive that it has been included solely and at length.

67 Fiscal Policy for Stability*

The Royal Commission on Taxation

We define full employment to exist when the unemployment rate is 3.5 per cent. We also [contend] that with good management we expect the consumer price index to increase at an annual rate of between 1.5 per cent and 2.0 per cent and domestic wholesale prices to be virtually constant if this unemployment rate is maintained, unless the structure of the economy is changed or the rate of change of foreign prices differs from that of the past. For purposes of this discussion we shall define this 1.5 per cent to 2.0 per cent per annum rate of price increase as relative price stability.

The Existing Fiscal Policy Weapons

The most important federal tax weapons for countering economic instability are the personal income tax and the corporate income tax. The most important transfer payment programme for stabilization purposes is the unemployment insurance system, although the existence of other transfer programmes and subsidies increases the inherent stability of the system. All these measures, together with the general expenditure programmes of the government, are important for stabilization policy; some are most effective as automatic stabilizers, others are useful for discretionary policy as well.

Built-in Stability

The characteristics of the tax-expenditure system tend to reduce the impact on the economic system of fluctuations in demand. This reaction of the system to changes in the demand for output is known as built-in stability. When autonomous demand declines, incomes will decline. This income decline in turn will lead to declines in consumer purchases and the accumulation of inventories that further lower income. A chain of income declines is therefore set in process by the initial decline in demand. Each successive decline will diminish in strength, however, because some portion of the decline in income results in a decline in saving, in reduced tax payments, or in reduced imports rather than in reduced demand for domestic goods. These three leakages limit the process, which is known as a multiplier process. The response of incomes to an initial increase in demand will be subject to a similar multiplier process. The extent to which an initial change in autonomous demand is multiplied through its effects on consumption and income will depend on these leakages. If the leakages are large, the multiplier will be low and the economic system will have a great deal of resistance to changes in demand; that is, the built-in stability of the economy will be high. If the leakages are low, the multiplier will be high, because a given change in income will lead to a larger change in consumer expenditures on domestic output.

*Reprinted by permission from the Royal Commission on Taxation, *Report*, Queen's Printer, Ottawa, 1966.

The Canadian economy has a high degree of built-in stability for three reasons:

1. Because imports are important to both consumers and business, changes in income and expenditure lead to a relatively large change in imports. For a one-dollar change in consumer expenditure the import leakage accounts for about $0.20. For a one-dollar change in fixed capital formation of businesses the import leakage accounts for about $0.30.

2. Because corporations tend to maintain stable dividend payments, swings in corporate income affect corporate retained earnings (net business savings) rather than dividends. Because corporate income is more volatile than other forms of income, this saving leakage is particularly important. It is estimated that at least $0.10 of a one-dollar change in gross national product (GNP) is absorbed by changes in after-tax corporate retained earnings.

3. The tax-expenditure system absorbs a large portion of income changes. This is due to the overwhelming importance of those taxes that vary with changes in income and expenditure, and the relative unimportance of other taxes. In addition, the unemployment insurance system automatically increases government disbursements and reduces government receipts if the income reduction leads to the unemployment of workers. It is estimated that $0.31 of a one-dollar change in GNP is absorbed by the tax-expenditure system.

Changes in government expenditures can, of course, initiate the multiplier process; changes in tax rates, by changing private expenditures, will also do so.

As a result of these leakages the multiplier is relatively low for Canada, the precise value depending upon the particular type of tax or expenditure change that initiates the process and also the time period over which the impact is considered.

The automatic fiscal stabilizers effectively reduce fluctuations in the economy; but they are not an unmixed blessing. They have the following important characteristics:

1. They will cushion, but they cannot by themselves reverse, a deviation. Once the economy has deviated in either direction from full employment, discretionary changes in taxes or expenditures are required to return to full employment unless there is an offsetting change in private demand.

2. The more effective the automatic stabilizers, the less effective discretionary policies will be. The automatic stabilizers do not discriminate between income changes that are destabilizing and those that are the result of stabilization policy. Discretionary policies must therefore be stronger the greater the built-in stability of the system.

3. Most of the built-in stabilizers tend to stabilize income at a fixed level rather than around the rising trend of full-employment output that is characteristic of a growing economy. This means that they tend to reduce the rate of increase of money income that accompanies a rapidly rising price level when the economy has excess demand; they are therefore a bulwark against inflation. However, the more effective the automatic stabilizers are in preventing increases in income, the more difficult it will be for the output of the economy to grow.

Here too, the stabilizers act as an indiscriminate brake on the increasing income, whether the increase in income is the result of increasing prices that should be suppressed or of increasing output that should be encouraged.

4. Unless offset by discretionary tax changes, the built-in stabilizers will tend to produce larger and larger revenues at full employment. This characteristic of a tax system is termed revenue drag. Unless government expenditures rise to match these additional revenues, or taxes are cut, aggregate demand will be reduced by the tax system. Unless the contribution of other sectors to aggregate demand is growing at a rate sufficiently above the rate of growth of potential output, the resulting revenue drag will repress the growth of actual output below that of potential output, with under-employment and under-utilization of capacity as a result.

Therefore, there is clearly a need for discretionary changes in the fiscal system to supplement and offset the built-in behaviour of the tax structure. What instruments are best suited for this purpose?

Discretionary Policy

After weighing the evidence and assessing the political as well as the economic problems involved in the use of stabilizing fiscal policy, we have reached the conclusion that changes in personal income tax rates or credits are beyond question the most effective single tool for discretionary stabilization policy. This does not mean that the other tools can be discarded; in some situations the imposition of taxes on capital expenditures, changes in the capital cost allowance rates, and changes in sales or excise taxes might be useful. But, by and large, situations of deficient or excess demand that threaten to move the economy toward extreme unemployment or excessive rates of price increase should be counted primarily by changes in the personal income tax. We discuss below alternative discretionary tax changes and the reasons why the personal income tax is superior as a general instrument of fiscal policy.

Changes in Sales and Excise Taxes

Frequent use of changes in sales or excise taxes will lead to speculative antici-pation of such actions. For example, if people expect sales taxes to be cut during a recession, they may postpone purchases of durable goods in order to wait for the lower prices resulting from the tax cut. Needless to say, this postponement will contribute to any recessionary tendencies. The reverse situation of antici-pating a tax increase would contribute to any inflationary tendencies. In addition, the use of increases in these taxes to fight inflation exerts two opposite effects on the price level. On the one hand, the increase in taxes reduces demand, and hence helps to eliminate inflationary pressure. On the other hand, the increase in taxes exerts an upward cost pressure on prices.

Changes in Corporate Income Tax

Changes in corporate income taxes are likely to have a delayed impact on the investment spending of corporations and the lag is probably highly variable. The following factors also must be taken into account:

1. A tax rate change that is known to be temporary will not affect significantly the expected rate of return on planned capital-intensive projects.

2. During a period of rising unemployment when corporations have excess capacity, it will be difficult to induce them to make additions to capacity by reducing the rate of corporate income tax, especially in the short run. The only sure way of inducing them to expand capacity is by increasing the demand for their output.

3. For corporations that have already accumulated the funds to finance an addition to capacity, and whose directors are convinced that they will be unable to meet future demand unless steps are taken immediately to put additional capacity in place, raising corporate taxes on a temporary basis is unlikely to deter the expenditure.

4. Many capital-intensive projects have a long gestation period so that, once begun, they are difficult to turn off, regardless of what is done to the rate of corporate income tax.

5. A substantial proportion of Canadian dividends flows to non-resident direct investors who obtain credit for Canadian corporate taxes and withholding taxes against their domestic tax liabilities. Reducing Canadian corporate taxes in these cases will not change the after-tax position of the parent company but will only increase the revenues of foreign governments.

The corporate income tax modifications introduced in the 1966 Budget, deferred depreciation, and the temporary refundable tax on cash flow, represent imaginative attempts to use the corporate income tax for the stabilization of investment. However, we believe a temporary tax on investment spending would be a simpler and more effective way of achieving this end.

Changes in Personal Income Tax

The impact of a change in personal income tax upon the take-home pay of workers is quick. There are, moreover, no serious technical obstacles to the rapid translation of changes in personal tax rates into new rates of withholding tax. However, the full response of consumer expenditures to a tax change will take some time, both because consumers do not immediately adjust their expenditures fully to a change in income, and because changes in consumer expenditures themselves affect income with some delay, that is, the working out of the multiplier process itself takes some time. The evidence indicates that consumers make a fairly substantial adjustment to a change in disposable income within one quarter — with 60 per cent of the ultimate response being achieved. A substantial fraction of the initial response represents durable goods purchases, which is in accord with *a priori* expectations. Furthermore, the evidence indicates that the reaction of consumers to tax-induced changes in income is similar to their reaction to other changes in income.

The precise speed of reaction of production to a change in final demand is more difficult to measure. For the service industries, the lag is obviously zero, since production and consumption are synchronous events. For purchases of goods, there is likely to be some lag, because producers can sell goods out of inventories. The lag in production is probably longer for most durable goods than for most non-durable goods. Evidence in the United States indicates that even for durable goods the response is reasonably rapid — with 60 per cent of the response of production to a given change in sales taking place within one quarter, and over 80 per cent after two quarters have elapsed.

However, a portion of the eventual change in value added is produced in industries one or more steps removed from the ultimate consumer (for example, auto firms will order steel). Consequently, the lags may be longer than suggested above. On the other hand, to the extent that producers anticipate expected changes in sales in their order-placing and inventory-stocking behaviour, the lags will be reduced.

We have estimated the time pattern of GNP responses to a given tax change on the reasonably conservative assumptions that the production response lagged one quarter behind the change in final demand, that is, that any change in demand is reflected in inventories in the first quarter, and that producers expand production the following quarter to match the increase in sales. The pattern we obtained indicated that 40 per cent of the GNP response was achieved by the end of two quarters, and 66 per cent within the year. If some allowance is made for inventory responses, 70 per cent of the adjustment is achieved within one year.

This result, which suggests that the response of the system to changes in tax rates is reasonably rapid, is confirmed by an analysis of the recent United States tax cut, and by the evidence provided by a quarterly econometric model in the United States.

Finally, personal tax changes can be designed to affect all income groups, or primarily those at particular income levels, depending upon the desired impact on expenditures. A greater impact would result if the tax change were directed solely toward those in the lower income groups; this follows because those with low incomes tend to spend nearly all of a change in income. The tax change would therefore be almost completely reflected in the change in consumer expenditures. But while it would be easy to lower the taxes of those with low income when a stimulus was required, it would be difficult to place the full burden of tax increases upon this group when it became necessary to reduce excess demand. If the change is to be reversible we believe an equal percentage change in the tax burden of all taxpayers is probably the most politically feasible technique.

Changes in Government Expenditures

In the past, the time required to plan and institute new expenditure programmes has reduced their usefulness for stabilization purposes. Plans conceived and executed in haste are likely to be of a non-productive or vote-buying nature. Such expenditures tend to discredit stabilization policy.

The institution of special expenditure programmes to help cure recessions under the existing budgetary process should be avoided unless the recession is particularly severe. For the present, therefore, we recommend that accelerating or slowing down expenditure increases on existing programmes only be used for stabilization purposes.

The development of longer term budgeting, particularly for capital expenditures, would permit much more effective use of government expenditures for stabilization purposes.

General Versus Specific Policies

We have recommended that discretionary fiscal policy should place heavy reliance upon changes in the personal income tax. Across-the-board cuts or increases in this tax are an excellent example of a general stabilization weapon. By affecting the disposable income of consumers in all income groups in every region of the country, such changes will have very widespread effects upon consumer demand for goods and services. Furthermore, the variations in consumer demand will, through their impact upon sales and capacity utilization, affect producers' investment plans.

This is not to argue that each region or each industry will be equally affected by the change in tax. The short-run response of consumers' spending on durable goods is greater than that of their spending on services; the demand for food is unlikely to be affected as much as the demand for automobiles.

This uneven, but general, impact is quite desirable, however. Those industries and regions that will reap the greatest benefit from a tax cut, for example, will also be those most affected by the recession; auto workers are frequently laid off in recessions, farm workers usually are not. Similarly, the locus of inflation has typically been in those sectors with the greatest cyclical responses to increases in incomes. These are precisely the sectors that would feel the bite of an anti-inflationary tax increase. In addition to the discretionary use of the personal income tax as a stabilizer, specific temporary excise taxes should be levied in those instances where severe bottlenecks are creating inflationary pressure in the durable goods and construction sectors of the economy.

Evaluation of Federal Fiscal Policy 1953-63

When government revenues exceed expenditures, a surplus is created. The surplus means that the reduction in private demand brought about by taxes has not been offset by public demand. Conversely, when the government runs a deficit, the government is adding to aggregate demand. Changes in the surplus over time therefore usually indicate the direction of impact of the tax-expenditure system on aggregate demand.

However, an examination of changes in the actual surplus or deficit is not very helpful in the evaluation of discretionary fiscal policy because the changes in the actual surplus are the net result of the changes in revenues and expenditures brought about both by the built-in stability of the system and by discretionary policy. One method of isolating the effects of discretionary policy is to abstract from the automatic changes in revenues and expenditures by reconstructing the government accounts on the assumption that full employment was continuously maintained. Changes in the estimated surplus at full employment show whether the discretionary fiscal policy was expansionary or contractionary. Revenues will expand each year as GNP grows at the full-employment rate. Discretionary policies are neutral if these increases in revenues are exactly matched by tax cuts or offset by increased expenditures. Discretionary policies are contractionary if these revenues are not offset by tax cuts or by higher expenditures. An expansionary policy would require either tax cuts, or expenditure increases, or a combination of the two, *larger* than the normal revenue increase. An examination of the changes in the full-employment surplus over time thus focuses attention on the crucial fact that, because of the strong income elasticity of the tax system, failure to reduce taxes or raise expenditures year after year will mean that the tax-expenditure system imposes an increasing drag on the expansion of GNP.

Basically, we want to estimate the net impact of the government's fiscal policy at the full-employment level of income. This is the full-employment surplus. The difference between the full-employment surplus and the actual surplus reflects the operation of automatic fiscal policy or built-in stability.

The method used to estimate the full-employment surplus can be described briefly.

1. Estimates were made of the additional revenues that would have been forthcoming from each source had the gap between actual and potential GNP been closed. This involved adjusting the revenue from each source by the percentage gap plus an adjustment for the elasticity of revenues from that source to changes in GNP.
2. Only one adjustment was made to actual expenditures to estimate what they would have been had full employment been maintained. Actual expenditures were adjusted to take into account the fact that with full employment, unemployment insurance benefits would have been less. None of the other federal expenditures seemed sufficiently sensitive to the level of unemployment to warrant adjustment.
3. The difference between 1 and 2 is defined as the full-employment surplus.

The estimates clearly show that, had there been full employment, only the years 1953 and 1958 would have shown a deficit rather than the seven years when deficits actually occurred. The differences would have been very large. In 1961, for example, there was an actual deficit of $455 million. With full employment and the existing tax-expenditure system, the estimates show that a surplus of $574 million would have prevailed, a difference of $1,029 million.

The year-to-year changes in the actual surplus reflect both the changes in the level of GNP and changes in discretionary policy. Because the full-employment surplus estimates abstract from most of the fluctuations in the rate of increase of GNP, they are less variable than the changes in the actual surplus.

In Table 3-4 estimates of the discretionary fiscal policy changes are shown, together with the revenue drag. The revenue drag should be looked upon as the increase in revenues produced by the growth of potential GNP in the absence of any discretionary tax and abatement changes. The discretionary changes in taxes, abatements and expenditures are then either added to or offset against the drag to give the estimated change in the full-employment surplus.

Had full employment been maintained in 1957 and 1958, to use these years as an example, it is estimated that in the absence of any discretionary fiscal policies revenues would have risen by $377 million. The tax system would have reduced aggregate demand to that extent. In fact, however, the government adopted four discretionary measures that more than offset this automatic tightening. The provinces received tax abatements of $52 million. Tax rates or bases were changed so that tax revenue was reduced by $288 million, and the federal government increased its transfers to the provinces by $135 million. The federal government itself increased its expenditures by $446 million. All of these discretionary measures more than offset the revenue drag, and the net addition to demand amounted to about $550 million.

TABLE 3-4

THE IMPACT OF DISCRETIONARY FISCAL POLICY ON THE
FULL-EMPLOYMENT SURPLUS
1954-63
(millions of dollars)

Year-to-Year Changes	Discretionary Fiscal Policy [a]					Change in the Full-Employment Surplus [c]
		Tax Policy		Expenditure Policy		
	Revenue [b] Drag	Abatements to Provinces	Rate and Base Changes	Change in Transfers to Provinces	Change in Other Federal Expenditures	
	(1)	(2)	(3)	(4)	(5)	(6)
1953-54	241	—13	—129	—19	—20	60
1954-55	506	—14	—145	—15	—131	201
1955-56	629	0	—82	—33	—292	222
1956-57	355	—125	—39	—29	—198	—36
1957-58	377	—52	—288	—135	—446	—544
1958-59	571	0	+235	—216	—142	448
1959-60	497	0	+98	—106	—116	373
1960-61	424	0	—109	—133	—315	—133
1961-62	351	—333	—11	+5	—364	—352
1962-63	532	—44	—123	—27	—57	281

[a] Minus signs indicate policy changes that reduced the surplus.

[b] Changes in revenues, had full-employment GNP been maintained each year, if there had been no change in tax rates, tax bases or abatements. Fiscal drag varies from year to year as a direct result of variations in the growth of potential GNP. These variations are primarily the result of fluctuations in the growth of the labour force and fluctuations in agricultural output.

[c] The change in full-employment surplus is equal to Column (1) plus the sum of Column (2) to (5).

Note: The estimates of fiscal drag provided in this table are obtained residually, i.e., by substracting the estimates of discretionary changes in revenue from the estimated changes in full-employment revenues. The revenue drag estimates therefore contain the estimation errors in both these series — in particular, changes in minor taxes are wholly allocated to the drag, whereas a portion of changes in these taxes may in fact be due to discretionary rate changes. An alternative estimate is provided in the supporting appendix.

In the following year, just the opposite occurred. The estimated revenue drag was large; and it was increased by a large increase in tax rates or tax bases. The additional revenue from the tax increase just about offset the increased transfer to the provinces. On balance, the tax-expenditure system depressed aggregate demand, for the full-employment surplus rose by an estimated $448 million.

We have categorized discretionary fiscal policies as neutral if they offset the revenue drag, restrictive if they did not offset the drag, and expansionary if they more than offset the drag so that year-to-year reductions in the full-employment surplus occurred.

The record may be briefly summarized on a year-by-year basis:

1954

The unemployment rate rose to 4.6 per cent. This would have justified an expansionary budget. The mildly contractionary fiscal policy adopted probably was not particularly harmful. Certainly the inflationary boom that followed provided some justification, in retrospect, for the restraint shown in 1954.

1955-56

The unemployment rate in 1956 fell to 3.4 per cent, approximately our target level. Consumer prices rose sharply in 1956 because of the speed with which the gap was closed. The price level in Canada rose slightly more rapidly than in the United States. In 1955 and 1956 tax rates were cut, and there was a larger increase in government expenditures in the latter year. On balance, the discretionary policies were neutral, when the impact of inflation on revenues is taken into account. The unprecedented investment boom that was approaching its peak in 1956 should have been restrained by restrictive discretionary policies. The outlook at the time was for continued expansion, and there was no conflict between the full-employment and price stability objectives. The restrictive discretionary policies in 1955 were about right; 1956 was a year of policy failure because much more restrictive fiscal measures should have been adopted.

1957

Unemployment increased markedly and Canadian prices continued to rise, but at a slower rate than they had in the previous year. It was therefore a year when there was conflict between the unemployment and price stability objectives. Forecasts at the time did not reflect the severity or persistence of the decline in employment. With the information available at the time, the optimum policy probably would have been one of neutrality or mild restraint, depending upon the relative importance attached to the inflation and unemployment objectives. In retrospect, a policy of fiscal ease would have been optimum. The basic problem with fiscal policy in 1957 was the faulty diagnosis on which it was based.

1958

The 1958 discretionary changes were strongly expansionary. Given the sharp increase in unemployment and the sharp decline in the rate of increase of prices, this was clearly the appropriate policy to adopt. There was a large cut in taxes, a large increase in expenditures, and there were large transfers to the provinces. Had there not been a diagnostic error because the persistence of the unemployment problem had not been recognized, the policy would have been even more expansionary than it was.

1959

In retrospect, fiscal policy in 1959 can only be described as completely inappropriate. Although for the three months prior to the budget, unemployment had averaged about 6.8 per cent on a seasonally adjusted basis, most analysts at the time expected a much more dramatic expansion of GNP than in fact occurred. This forecast error partly explains the quick "about face" in discretionary fiscal policy that included a substantial increase in taxes virtually offsetting the tax cut of the previous year, and a drastic reduction in the rate of increase of government expenditures. Although forecasting errors were important, an exaggerated fear of inflation was also responsible for the policy failure of 1959. This fear arose because of the persistent increase in prices after the 1956 boom came to an end and the large increases in the money supply that had accompanied the conversion loan in 1958. The only expansionary policy was the much higher transfers to the provinces; but these were not undertaken as a stimulus to the economy. There were diagnostic errors and too great an emphasis on the price stability goal, but the policies adopted were too extreme even if allowance is made for these extenuating circumstances.

1960

Fiscal policy was even less appropriate in 1960. At budget time, the employment outlook was bleak, and the unemployment rate was already about 6.3 per cent. Consumer prices had risen much less rapidly in 1959 than they had in the two preceding years. Despite the strong indications that an expansionary budget would be appropriate, taxes were raised and the rate of increase of government expenditures reduced even further. The only expansionary change was the increase in the transfers to the provinces. With a flexible exchange rate, the balance of payments did not impose any limitation on the budget in 1960. The restraint imposed in 1960 was probably the result of the mistaken view that the economy had to be kept under restraint to reduce the capital inflow which was largely induced by high interest rates. The policy failure in 1960 can therefore be attributed partly to the lack of emphasis placed on the full-employment objective and partly to diagnostic errors.

1961

After two years of fiscal restraint despite substantial unemployment, the policy adopted in 1961 was appropriate in direction if not in magnitude. Taxes were cut and federal expenditures increased, as were the abatements and transfers to the provinces. Prices had been remarkably stable, and the rate of unemployment was extremely high. It was in June of that year that the government both advocated and promised a substantial devaluation of the Canadian dollar. This led to the adoption of the fixed exchange rate a year later. The exchange rate problem was transformed from one of trying to push the value of the Canadian dollar down to a problem of trying to maintain its value. In the last half of 1961, the government may have wanted to curtail aggregate demand in order to maintain the value of the Canadian dollar, but the rate was not fixed and there was no need for the government to attempt to hold it. With unemployment at 7.1 per cent, there was clearly no need to be concerned about excess demand. The inadequate stimulus of the 1961 budget may be accounted for by exchange rate considerations but, if so, they were not necessary considerations.

1962

Fiscal policy in 1962 was more expansionary mainly because of the larger federal tax abatement to the provinces and the substantial increase in other federal expenditures. The informal adoption of a fixed exchange rate in the first half of the year and its formal adoption in the second half may have explained the relatively modest expansionary fiscal policies adopted, for prices had been virtually stable in 1961 and unemployment was still high. The devaluation was itself a major stimulus to the economy. The aftermath of the exchange rate crisis, which was of Canada's own making, probably forced a more restrictive domestic policy than otherwise would have been necessary.

1963

A restrictive fiscal policy was adopted again in 1963. Tax rates were raised and the rate of increase of government expenditures was cut. Because of the delayed impact of a number of the changes, the effect of tax-expenditure policy in 1963 was to reduce the full-employment surplus, but by a much smaller amount than the increase resulting from revenue drag. Thus, the net effect was restrictive. Although unemployment had been dropping, it was still well above the full-employment level and prices had risen only modestly. The premature return to fiscal restraint may have been attributable to the mistaken idea that a balanced budget was desirable for its own sake; or it may have been thought necessary to restore confidence following the exchange crisis. One might question that foreign confidence was the main reason, before the Budget in June 1963, the Bank of Canada had been able to abandon its tight money policy, which it had been forced to introduce right after the fixed exchange rate was adopted in the previous year. On the other hand, the budgetary measures may have been a necessary prerequisite for the latter measure. Unless one puts great weight on this external stability objective, it is difficult to justify the fiscal restrictiveness of the Budget brought down in 1963.

Our assessment of the fiscal policy record may be briefly summarized as follows:

Year	Tone of Discre-tionary Fiscal Policy Actually Adopted	Recommended Tone in Retrospect
1954	neutral	mildly expansionary
1955	mildly restrictive	neutral
1956	neutral	restrictive
1957	mildly expansionary	as adopted
1958	strongly expansionary	as adopted
1959	strongly restrictive	strongly expansionary
1960	strongly restrictive	strongly expansionary
1961	mildly expansionary	strongly expansionary
1962	expansionary	strongly expansionary
1963	restrictive	expansionary

In our view, fiscal policy was approximately in the right direction and of the right magnitude about half the time. In three of the ten years, 1959, 1960 and 1963, we would judge discretionary fiscal policy to be perverse, and especially so in 1959 and 1960.

Looked at in broad terms, fiscal policy in the period under consideration was too expansionary in 1956 and too restrictive thereafter. In very few years was there a real problem of choosing between conflicting objectives, although faulty forecasts and other errors of diagnosis led policy makers to think and act as though they were faced with such conflicts. From 1959 and 1961, we believe the price stability objective was given inordinate weight; in 1962 and 1963 the external stability objective may have been over-emphasized. But most of the time the problem was not that there was undue emphasis on one objective relative to others, but rather that policy was inefficient in the sense that frequently it would have been possible to realize one or more objectives to a greater degree without sacrificing others. We could have had less unemployment without more rapid increases in prices or more un-stable international economic relations.

The Need for Federal Budgetary Flexibility

A period of time must necessarily elapse between the emergence of a need for discretionary policy measures and the full impact of those measures upon the level of economic activity. Four distinct causes of this overall lag can be distinguished:

1. The recognition of the need for a change in policy: a period of time usually will elapse between the need for a policy change, in terms of the

objectives of policy, and the recognition of the need. The time lag involved depends upon both the speed with which relevant current statistics are compiled and the state of the art of economic forecasting.

2. The achievement of a consensus among policy makers on what needs to be done: this lag may be long if current statistics and forecasts diverge. The time involved in this process may reflect differences of opinion among policy makers about the relative importance of the different objectives. A clear definition of targets would help to reduce this source of delay.

3. The execution of the policy decided upon: this time lag may be long if the policy makers attempt to act within the constraints of the annual budget process. In addition, personal income tax changes enacted in the past have usually been delayed to permit preparation of new withholding schedules.

The above three constitute what are called the "inside lags" of fiscal policy.

4. The delay in the impact of a policy change upon the spending behaviour of households and firms: this is the so-called "outside lag" of fiscal policy which, because it is rooted in the behavioural responses of individuals, cannot be readily reduced by changes in government procedures.

A reduction in the overall policy lag would greatly increase the power of fiscal policy. Infrequent but timely moves would forestall or abort recessions and inflations, and effective stabilization policies would increase public confidence in them. This would itself tend to stabilize private spending decisions. Let us now examine what can be done. We will consider the outside lag first.

The full impact of changes in personal income taxes upon private spending is felt only after several months have elapsed. However, as we have shown earlier, there is a substantial impact upon consumer spending, particularly for durable goods, in the quarter following the change. Moreover, to the extent that producers anticipate the ultimate response of consumer demand in placing their orders and in their inventory-stocking behaviour, the lag between tax changes and output and employment changes will be reduced. As Canada's performance on the stabilization front is improved, we are confident that such anticipatory behaviour will become more prevalent and that the outside lag will decline.

We also believe that some of the inside lags can be reduced and that high priority should be given to measures that will shorten them. The following recommendations, if adopted, should be effective:

1. The economic statistics available to policy makers should be improved. Additional data are urgently required in the following fields: quarterly intentions data for consumers and business, money flows data, capacity utilization data, and data on new orders and contracts let. Substantial reductions in the time required to collect, compile and circulate information on the current economic situation would be possible if additonal resources were devoted to the task.

Analogous recommendations have been made repeatedly by other Royal Commissions. We shall simply state that the situation cries out for improvement. The data collection and processing agencies must be given more resources in order that they may meet their expanding responsibilities. Modern technology makes possible dramatic improvements in both data collection and processing. The costs of obtaining this information are minor in comparison with the costs of policy failures that result from a lack of complete, consistent and current economic data.

2. A method must be found that makes it easier for the government to make changes in tax-expenditure policy promptly for stabilization purposes. Furthermore, we require a method that makes it difficult for governments to procrastinate. We have examined a number of methods of speeding up the making of changes and rejected all of them except one, that would require the government to make policy statements of its intentions whenever there was firm evidence that economic goals were not being met.

A suggestion that has been made in the past is for what is called "formula flexibility", which involves linking changes in fiscal policy to measures of performance in relation to the objectives of policy. For example, a cut in personal income taxes could be automatically put into effect if the national unemployment rate exceeded 4.5 per cent for three months in a row, and an additional cut could be automatic if the national unemployment rate exceeded 5 per cent for three months. Conversely, if both the wholesale price index and the consumer price index rose at an annual rate in excess of 3 per cent a year for three months in a row, a tax increase would automatically go into effect.

Formula flexibility *per se* has three disadvantages. First, because the indicators occasionally move erratically, and because the appropriateness of policy in any case cannot be determined by one or two indicators alone, the formula may trigger policy moves that are either inadequate or destabilizing. Second, no formula can be designed to handle effectively situations where the goals of stabilization policy are in conflict. Third, formula flexibility, like built-in stability, is an adjunct to, not a substitute for, discretionary fiscal policy. If the tax cuts affected by the formula are rescinded by the formula as the economy responds to them, the removal of the stimulus may lead to an aborted recovery.

In view of these disadvantages, we believe formula flexibility by itself is undesirable. The main advantage of a formula is that it commits the government to timely action; but this advantage can be obtained without the disadvantages if a modified scheme is adopted.

Therefore, we recommend that the government of the day should be required to make a policy statement as to what it was doing or planned to do about unemployment or inflation when statistical measures, such as the ones we have already described, indicate that the economic objectives were not being met. These policy statements could be used as an occasion for the government to announce changes in fiscal policy outside the regular annual budget. Parliament would be given an opportunity to debate the government's policy statement. This procedure would focus attention on the stability policy objectives, would help to prevent government procrastination, and would avoid the timing rigidities of the annual budget as "the" appropriate time to announce fiscal policy changes.

3. When the statistical measures reveal that the economy has failed to meet the objectives, the government should have the power to change specific tax rates within specified limits subject to subsequent approval by Parliament.

Annual budgeting is an important part of the democratic process; but it can place limitations on the use of tax changes for economic stabilization. Although tax changes have been introduced outside the annual budget, for example, in September 1950 and December 1960, the infrequency with which this has been done in the past suggests that the need must reach crisis proportions before the step is taken.

4. The lag that elapses between the announcement of a tax change whether in the annual budget or not, and the time at which new tax rates or allowances result in lower or higher collections should be reduced. This time lag, which is long in the case of some taxes, is important because taxpayers as spenders are affected at the time higher or lower taxes come into effect, rather than at the time a tax change is announced or a change in tax liability is incurred.

For the personal income tax, at least, we believe that a flexible fiscal policy requires that tax collections respond quickly to a change in rates and allowances. With planning, this lag could be reduced substantially. For example, all withholding tables could specify a number of alternatives so that a change in personal tax rates could be made effective almost immediately by simply announcing which of the general tables in the hands of those withholding tax should be applied in the future. Alternatively, across-the-board percentage tax cuts can be quickly implemented using the existing tables.

68 The Time Lags of Fiscal Policy*

R. M. Will

1. Introduction

I have decided to restrict the scope of my paper to a consideration of fiscal time lags, or of the time that elapses between a change in economic conditions requiring discretionary fiscal action and the time a change in policy can be put into effect and its impact felt on the level of economic activity. The flexibility or lack of flexibility of monetary, debt management and credit policies is of no less importance in judging the efficacy of stabilization policy and the place of full employment and price stability among the goals of economic policy. For example, the mix of these policies that will be employed to maintain economic stability or to offset an unstable economic situation depends to a very significant degree on the relative speed with which the different types or arms of stabilization policy can be implemented once the need for a change in policy exists.

Most research on the time lags of fiscal policy has, until recently, been concerned with the flexibility of public works as an instrument of stabilization policy and then only with the time required to get on-site activity under way and public works projects completed after a decision to increase expenditures on public works had been taken. Studies dealing specifically with the time lags associated with public works expenditure have paid little or no attention to what Professor Friedman refers to as the "recognition lag" of stabilization policy — the time that elapses between the need for stabilizing action and the taking of action — or to the lag that exists between the time action is taken and the time its effects are felt. The need for a flexible tax policy as well as expenditure policy has, of course, always been recognized, but until a recent study by Albert Ando and E. Cary Brown for the Commission on Money and Credit, efforts to measure or quantitatively determine the time lags associated with tax changes have been few. Proposals for granting stand-by powers to the government to vary tax rates within specified limits without prior legislative approval, for triggering automatically tax changes as soon as a predetermined set of conditions is known to exist, and for setting up emergency votes or appropriations to finance public works in the case of a sudden downturn in economic conditions, all reflect a view widely held among economists that discretionary fiscal changes, considered within the context of the annual budget and the budgetary process as we know it, are too unwieldy and inflexible to be used effectively as an economic stabilizer.

The fear has been expressed that efforts to pursue an active stabilization policy may actually result in greater rather than less instability if time lags are long and if a particular policy, once put into effect, cannot be terminated or reversed quickly. While the possibility of perverse effects on economic

*Reprinted by permission from R. M. Will in Economic Council of Canada, *Conference on Stabilization Policies*, Queen's Printer, Ottawa, 1966.

activity and the level of prices cannot be dismissed, it appears that some of the concern that has been shown in this regard rests on, or is the product of, a misunderstanding of the nature of economic instability and the role stabilization policy must play in combatting it. I refer specifically to the tendency to view stabilization policy as an offset to the business or reference cycle, with a reversal in the direction of policy being required each time the economy passes a cyclical turning point. This view of stabilization policy, often more implicit than explicit in the literature, suggests that the economy is in a constant state of instability and that the government must at all times be engaged actively in either braking or stimulating the economy. Given the fact that post-war recessions have averaged less than a year in duration, it is easy to understand why this view of the stabilization process might give rise to serious concern about spill-over or the carry-over of the effects of a policy change appropriate for one phase of the cycle into the following phase.

There are good reasons for rejecting cyclical turning points, whether of the business cycle or of certain economic time series, as signalling the need for a change or reversal in stabilization policy. The peaks and troughs of the business cycle, while reliable indicators of changes in the direction of economic activity or output, tell us little about the economy's performance in relation to such specific goals of stabilization policy as price stability and full employment. Rising prices can occur during downswings of the cycle as well as during upswings, as evidenced by the increase in consumer prices that followed the cyclical peak of 1957. Unemployment, although it follows fairly closely movements of the business cycle, increasing during downswings and declining during periods of cyclical expansion, may not disappear during the upward phase of the cycle, but may persist, as the experience since 1957 has proven, over the course of one or more complete cycles. Stabilization policy, it is clear, cannot be geared to the ups and downs of the business cycle. Instead, the government's stabilizing efforts should be related to the economy's performance in terms of specific target variables, e.g. the unemployment rate accepted as constituting full employment and the maximum per annum increase in the general price level considered to be consistent with price stability as a policy goal. A change in policy is called for, or should be given careful consideration by policy-makers, whenever a departure from a target variable occurs or is threatened.

These target variables must be known if the length of the recognition lag of stabilization policy is to be estimated. Failure on the part of monetary and fiscal authorities to respond quickly and decisively to an increase in unemployment need not necessarily suggest a long recognition lag, or a delay in introducing a policy change once the need for it is recognized. It may mean little more than that full employment, as a policy goal, has not been accorded high priority. The problem of determining when a change in stabilization policy is needed is even more difficult in cases where conflict between policy goals exists. Immediate steps may not be taken to cope with a deteriorating employment situation, not because policy-makers are unaware of a rising unemployment rate, but because they fear that the type of policy change required to stimulate output and employment would result in inflation. Ideally, a system of weights or priorities should be assigned to the target variables or goals of stabilization policy that would clearly indicate one policy or another as being appropriate whenever such a conflict exists. How these weights or priorities might be established is, of course, a big question.

2. The Inside Lags of Fiscal Policy

The inside lags of fiscal policy, in contrast to the time required for the effects of a change in policy to be felt in the economy, consist of the recognition lag and a combination of lags which I shall call, for lack of a better name, the action lag. Included in the latter time lag are the rigidities imposed on fiscal policy by the convention of annual budgeting, the time required to put new tax rates into effect once approved by Parliament, and the delays that are likely to be encountered in accelerating government spending on public works because of a lack of advance planning of projects, the time needed to award new contracts, etc. Some of these lags or delays in implementing changes in fiscal policy defy precise measurement, if for no other reason than that they are apt to vary, depending on the date or time of year at which the need for taking action is recognized. A tax reduction, the need for which is recognized a few weeks before the annual budget is brought down, can clearly be implemented more quickly than a tax reduction that the government decides is needed immediately or shortly after the budget is brought down. A large part of this paper is devoted to suggesting means of reducing the inside lags of fiscal policy, whatever their lengths may be.

A. The Recognition Lag

One of the difficulties encountered in determining quantitatively this policy lag has already been mentioned, namely a lack of sufficient knowledge about the target variables that are considered to be important by policy-makers, and hence about the type of economic condition or situation in the past that has required that stabilizing action be taken. There is the further problem of telling with any certainty when or at what date the authorities recognize that a change in fiscal policy is needed and agree upon a specific course of action. The situation here is quite different than in the case of monetary policy, where it is reasonable to assume that action is taken immediately or fairly soon after the need for it is recognized, since policy changes can be introduced at almost anytime and also, possibly, because the time required by monetary authorities to agree upon the type of action to be taken is relatively short. Recognition of the need for a change in discretionary fiscal policy, on the other hand, may not be translated into action until several months later — until the next budget is presented to Parliament or, in the case of a change in the level of government expenditures, until the next estimates are prepared.

The recognition lag can be shortened and the potential of fiscal policy as an economic stabilizer can be enhanced by (1) improvement in the type and quality of economic intelligence and reporting available to the policy-maker and (2) reduction in the time presently required to collect, compile and circulate information on the current economic situation and short-term outlook. The quick assessment of changing economic conditions that is an integral part of a successful policy of economic stabilization requires a comprehensive and fully integrated system of economic statistics providing accurate and up-to-date information on all aspects of the country's economic performance. The electronic computer has reduced significantly the time required to assemble and prepare economic data and has provided, as well, valuable new techniques for analyzing the current economic situation and making short-term economic forecasts. Even with this advance in technology, the time presently consumed in preparing many of the principal economic indicators is long in relation to the requirements of a flexible stabilization policy. Between five and six weeks are now taken to prepare advance-preliminary estimates of quarterly GNP, and in the case of a few other important indicators such as quarterly corporation profits and average hours worked per week, as long as eight weeks transpire between the end of the reporting period and the time an advance or preliminary estimate is available for circulation within the government. While there are clearly limits to what can be done to reduce the lag in reporting a change in economic conditions or in some key economic variable, much of the economic data required in the formulation of stabilization policy could be made available sooner than is presently the case, if greater resources were provided for the preparation of economic statistics within the federal government and if higher priority, generally, were given to improving the calibre of economic intelligence available to the policy-maker.

In the area of new data, mention should be made of the need for additional and improved pre-flow data, e.g. new orders, contracts and commitments, that precede the actual flow of goods and activity, and for anticipations data relating to the expectations and plans of consumers, investors and other decision-makers. For example, we do not have in Canada information on either the expenditure plans of consumers or the inventory and sales expectations of manufacturing concerns. We also lack quarterly (and semi-annual) data on investment intentions.

Economic Forecasting

Because the economy is never static but is constantly undergoing change and changing tempo, it is inevitable that some prediction of the future course of economic events should form part of any analysis of the current economic situation. To a degree, analysis of present conditions and short-term economic forecasting are inseparable. The economy's current position or state cannot be appraised satisfactorily without some reference to where it is going or is likely to be at a given time in the future. The economic forecaster, on the other hand, relies heavily on knowledge of where the economy stands currently and of economic conditions in the recent past.

The question is not whether economic forecasting should play a role in the formulation of stabilization policy, but what precisely is the role to be. Should economic forecasting be accepted as a *basis* for policy-making, or should it serve only as a *guide* to policy-making — as an interpretative framework within which data pertaining to the current situation can be assessed and policy decisions made? Given the present state of development of forecasting techniques, it is difficult to believe that anyone would be prepared to argue seriously that major changes in stabilization policy, that is, the type of change that establishes the emphasis and direction of stabilization policy, can or should be based upon an economic forecast. Major policy changes must rest upon something firmer than a prediction that an economic disturbance or event is likely to occur six, nine or twelve months hence. The role of economic forecasting is, instead, that of assisting the policy-maker in the interpretation and analysis of current economic data. In this way the economic forecaster can help reduce the length of the recognition lag, although he is unable to eliminate it completely. Elimination of the recognition lag could presumably be achieved only with a hundred-per-cent-sure system of economic forecasting.

Economic forecasting within the Canadian government appears to be on a par with forecasting in the United States, the United Kingdom and those West European countries where it is regarded, as in Canada, as an interpretative background against which policy formulation takes place rather than as part of an official economic plan or projection aimed at achieving stated policy goals or targets.

B. The Action Lag

Before anything can be said about the length of this portion of the inside lag of fiscal policy, it is necessary to define what is meant by, or what constitutes, government action in response to the need for a change in stabilization policy. For example, has the government acted when a change in the personal income tax is announced in the annual budget, or does fiscal action is this case not occur until a new tax schedule or exemption level results in a higher or lower level of tax collections? Tax changes contained in a spring budget customarily do not become effective until July 1, a date which, in addition to being administratively convenient (it divides the taxation year in two), provides the government with sufficient time to prepare and distribute new deduction tables for use by employers who collect income tax at source. I think we would all agree that disposable (after tax) income is the relevant variable in considering the impact of a tax change on consumer spending and, therefore, that fiscal action in this case should be regarded as occurring at the time disposable income is changed. Fiscal action in the form of a change in the level of government spending poses a similar problem. Clearly, action precedes a change in actual outlay by the government in the case of a higher or reduced level of spending on public works and on goods produced to order on government account (e.g. military hardware, communications equipment, etc.). For the purpose of measuring the inside lag of fiscal policy, it is assumed that an increase in this type of government spending occurs at the time contracts are awarded and orders are placed.

So defined, the action lag of fiscal policy consists of more than a policy lag. It is also an administrative lag in so far as its length depends on the time required to implement or put into effect a policy change once decided upon and announced by the government. Policy flexibility achieved by means of overcoming the rigidity imposed on fiscal policy by the convention of annual budgeting is not sufficient to reduce the action lag to a tolerable length. Steps must also be taken to reduce or eliminate the administrative part of this lag. Tax collections must respond quickly to changes in rates, exemption levels, etc., while on the expenditure side, contracts must be let and orders placed as soon as, or shortly after, a decision to accelerate government spending is made.

The Budgetary Process

Budgeting as a decision-making process within the federal government has been described by authorities on the subject. Our concern here is only with the timing of budgetary decisions in relation to the needs of a flexible stabilization policy. On the assumption that supplementary estimates cover only expenditure items unforseen at the time the main estimates are prepared, the broad outline of the government's spending programme for the fiscal year beginning April 1 is determined in the previous autumn. Customarily, the Minister of Finance provides in September, at the time departments and agencies are requested to submit estimates, a rough indication of what the government believes to be an appropriate level of spending for the ensuing fiscal year. For example, if the short-term outlook were for continued economic expansion and increasing inflationary pressure in the construction and capital goods industries, the Minister might indicate at this time that capital spending by the government in the next fiscal year should be kept at a minimum. The government's final opportunity to relate the main estimates to the needs of stabilization policy comes in November and December when the estimates submitted by the various departments and agencies are reviewed by the Treasury Board. These estimates, when assembled, normally exceed the level of spending finally approved by the Board by several hundred million dollars. By deciding which items in a department's or agency's estimates are to be left in and which should be excluded, the government can make any last-minute adjustment in the over-all level of the estimates that economic conditions may warrant.

With respect to revenues, the budgetary process is only slightly less inflexible. For a budget presented late in March or early in April, all major decisions affecting the main pattern or impact of the budget will normally have been made by early or mid-February. I am told that the latest possible date for incorporating substantive tax changes into the budget is two weeks prior to its presentation to Parliament. A more likely expedient than a last-minute, hastily contrived, tax change as a means of adjusting the budget to a sudden change in economic conditions would be to delay delivery of the budget. If the economic climate is clouded and the outlook uncertain at the time crucial budgetary decisions are normally made, the possibility of the late-spring budget always exists and should be seriously considered by the government.

From the foregoing it is apparent that the time lag associated with the budgetary process is variable, depending on the time of the year the need for a change in policy is perceived. It may be as short as a few weeks in the case of a tax change decided upon just before the budget is brought down, or as long as 13 to 14 months in the case where the need for a higher or lower level of taxation is recognized immediately after final budgetary decisions have been reached. For expenditures, the time lag can even be longer. If, for example, a change in economic conditions should occur late in December or early in January that calls for a higher level of government spending than contained in the recently approved estimates, government spending would not be able to be increased significantly — save by use of supplementary estimates for this purpose — until a year the following April.

If fiscal policy is to make an important contribution to economic stability, it is clear that some form of inter-budget flexibility is needed. Fiscal authorities must be given at least some freedom to vary the major parameters of fiscal policy as soon as the need for stabilizing action is recognized. Moreover, such flexibility must be sought in ways that do not abrogate Parliament's constitutional authority over taxation and at the same time preserve the institutions that are essential to the efficient and prudent exercise of this authority.

Supplementary Budgets

In theory, the Minister of Finance can introduce a supplementary budget or issue a financial statement proposing tax changes any time Parliament is in session. Tax changes have been introduced outside the annual budget on three occasions since World War II — in September 1950 and December 1957, when tax changes were announced in a financial statement, and in December 1960, when a supplementary or "baby" budget was brought down. Supplementary estimates may also be tabled any time Parliament is in session. The supplementary budget and financial statement, as a means of introducing inter-budget tax changes, have an advantage over most other expedients for achieving a greater degree of budgetary flexibility in so far as political opposition to them is likely to be less. An obvious disadvantage of the supplementary budget, compared to formula flexibility and the granting of stand-by powers to the government to vary taxes between budgets, is that it provides flexibility only when Parliament is sitting.

Greater use should be made of the supplementary budget when needed to increase the flexibility of fiscal policy. The argument that tax changes introduced by supplementary budget are likely to be piecemeal and unrelated to the over-all tax structure is not so much a criticism of supplementary budgets as of all tax changes for stabilization purposes, whether introduced within or outside the framework of the annual budget.

Formula Flexibility

The great appeal of formula flexibility is that it eliminates, or is supposed to eliminate, the time that elapses between recognition of the need for a change in discretionary fiscal policy and the taking of action. By automatically triggering taxes or government spending whenever a particular index (e.g. unemployment rate, consumer price index) reaches a critical level or continues to move in the same direction for a specified period of time, it also guards against the possibility that no action may be taken, either because policy-makers fail to agree to the need for action, or because policy-makers, although in agreement as to need, are unable to concur with respect to the type of action to be taken. Formula flexibility extends to the area of discretionary fiscal policy some of the automatic features of the built-in stabilizers.

At best, formula flexibility is a poor automatic pilot, absolving the policy-maker of the responsibility for taking discretionary action. First, there is the difficulty of designing a formula that will trigger policy as soon as an unsatisfactory economic situation develops, yet will not be so sensitive as to result in unnecessary, and possibly destabilizing, action being taken. A formula capable of distinguishing between legitimate and false signals, i.e. between situations requiring a policy change and those that do not, may be so insensitive as to bring about a change in policy too late for it to serve as an effective stabilizer.

A second criticism of formula flexibility is that it is based on the assumption that stabilizing action can be prescribed in advance of need. It assumes, moreover, a sameness of economic disturbances in respect of both their nature and magnitude that does not in fact exist.

The limitations of formula flexibility are perhaps greatest in situations where conflict exists among the goals of stabilization policy — where pursuit of a policy needed to achieve one of the goals of economic stability seriously jeopardizes the chances of attaining another goal.

Stand-By Authority

Both the United Kingdom and the United States governments have recently shown interest in this means of achieving greater budgetary flexibility. The precise form which any arrangement granting the cabinet or executive authority to introduce fiscal changes without prior legislative approval can vary greatly, depending on the type of government, i.e. whether parliamentary or presidential, and what is politically feasible. Political considerations, reflecting the legislature's ultimate right to levy taxes, are likely to dictate (1) that stand-by authority be fairly specific with respect to both the type and maximum amount of fiscal change allowable under it and (2) that any fiscal change implemented under stand-by arrangements receive legislative approval within a specified period of time or else be discontinued. The terms under which stand-by powers are granted may also specify some signal level of economic activity or set of conditions that has to be met before action can be taken, in which case stand-by authority differs little from formula flexibility.

The great advantage of stand-by authority over formula flexibility is the element of discretion it retains over changes in fiscal policy. Whereas the choice of policy instrument that can be used under it is often narrowly restricted, if a choice exists at all, stand-by authority is likely to provide the policy-maker with some opportunity to relate the size of a fiscal change to the need for it. Even more important, stand-by arrangements give the policy-maker the option of taking no action, if the fiscal change or changes authorized under them are not considered to be appropriate.

Achieving a Flexible Expenditure Policy

Some of the rigidity imposed on government spending by the convention of annual budgeting can be overcome by use of the contingency or emergency appropriation. The idea of a vote of funds to be spent only in the event of a decline in economic conditions is not new in Canada. Machinery set up at the close of World War II to combat depression included a recon-struction vote which, in addition to providing funds for the advance planning of public works projects, could be used at the discretion of the Treasury Board to finance public works projects needed for stabilization purposes but not included in the main annual estimates. Political considerations, however, are likely to require that emergency appropriations of a size capable of in-creasing significantly the level of government spending be for the financing of specific projects or, at least, projects which have received the prior ap-proval of Parliament.

Both Sweden and Austria have experimented with means of increasing the flexibility of government expenditures within the framework of the annual budget.

The question may well be asked whether the advance planning of public works is feasible, given the specialized nature of most types of public con-struction and the need to keep abreast of the latest improvements in materials and technology, and in the design of buildings, harbour facilities etc. A shelf or reserve of fully planned projects, to be drawn upon only in time of recession, must clearly be limited to standard plan projects, i.e. projects which, once planned, do not become quickly obsolete. This type of public works project is likely to be small and involve comparatively little expenditure. For the greater part of public works spending, advance planning is possible only within the context of a long-range capital expenditure programme. Ideally, the capital expenditure programme of each department engaged in public works spending should consist of projects at all stages of planning, in-cluding an adequate number of projects in the final planning stage to permit tenders to be called immediately, or shortly after, a decision to accelerate capital spending is made.

3. The Outside Lags of Fiscal Policy

The effectiveness of a change in taxes or government spending as an eco-nomic stabilizer depends on both the size of the impact that the change has on the level of economic activity and the speed with which this impact is felt in the economy. The former refers to the so-called multiplier effects of a fiscal change — the latter to the outside lags associated with such a change. Fiscal flexibility requires that these lags, as well as the inside lags of fiscal policy, be short.

The limitations of time and space necessitate restricting the discussion here to the outside lags associated with a change in the personal income tax. The personal income tax is, in my opinion, the fiscal policy variable that is most important for stabilization purposes in terms of the impact or leverage that can be expected from it. Whatever is concluded about the over-all flexibility of fiscal policy will therefore depend heavily on how quickly the private sector responds to a change in this tax. The outside lags of a change in the personal income tax consist of two distinct lags: (1) the lag in consumer response to a change in tax and (2) the lag in the response of production to a change in consumer spending. The two lags will be looked at in turn.

Consumer Response to a Tax Change

Until a decade ago, economists would have agreed almost without exception that this response lag was short. This view, based largely on intuition and the most naive type of Keynesian consumption function, lent support to the policy conclusion, also generally accepted, that fiscal policy constituted both a powerful and rapid means of influencing the level of economic activity and hence of maintaining economic stability. Income groups with allegedly high propensities to spend were assumed by some economists to be also especially fast reactors — hence the traditional prescription for anti-recessionary fiscal policy that ran in terms of tax cuts and increased transfer payments for low-income groups, particularly when the latter take the form of relief payments and unemployment compensation.

A number of theoretical considerations have been put forth in recent years that require careful examination in view of the implications they may have for the efficacy of tax changes as an instrument of stabilization policy. For example, the belief that consumption is determined not only by current income, but also by the highest level of income attained in the past, or that habit persistence is an important factor influencing consumption pretty much invalidates the notion of a reversible consumption function and the idea that tax changes produce symmetrical results on either side of a given level of disposable income. These two distinct yet related contributions to consumption theory cannot be reconciled with the view that consumer expenditure adjusts quickly and simply to a change in disposable or after-tax income.

The distinction made by Milton Friedman between permanent and transient income, and his suggestion that consumption is related only to the permanent component of an individual's income, cast further doubts on the nature of the consumption-income relationship and on the possibility of finding out more about this relationship by statistical and econometric methods. The implications of the Friedman hypothesis for a stability-oriented tax policy are clear and serious. An increase (decrease) in disposable cash income brought about by a tax cut (increase) may or may not result in an increase (decrease) in consumption, depending on whether the change in income is deemed by the consumer to be permanent or transient. Transitory changes in income, according to Friedman, have no effect on consumer spending.

Closely related to the Friedman view of consumer behaviour is a group of hypotheses that stresses the relation between a consumer's or family's standard of living — a standard that is assumed to change only gradually — and the total resources available for this purpose. According to this latter view, it is the consumer's stock of assets or accumulated wealth, actual or desired, rather than his flow of cash income, that is the important determinant of consumer spending. Short-run or temporary variations in cash income, this group of hypotheses suggests, are unlikely to have much, if any, effect on consumption.

No completely satisfactory means exists for determining quantitatively the length of the response lags associated with a change in the personal income tax. Ando and Brown, in their study of fiscal time lags, made extensive use of what is known as the distributed-lag technique. This statistical tool, which was first applied to this type of problem by L. M. Koyck and Robert M. Solo, consists essentially of estimating an infinite distributed-lag relationship by regressing, by the simple least-squares method, a dependent variable against the current value of the independent variable and lagged values of the dependent variable.

Using this technique, it was estimated that only about 40 per cent of the effect on consumer expenditure of a given change in income will have taken place after a lag of one quarter, 54 per cent after a lag of two quarters, and 72 per cent after a lag of four quarters or one year. Transmission of the full effect of a change in income on consumer expenditure, it is evident, is a lengthy and drawn-out process. About 10 per cent of the effect is still to be felt at the end of two years (eight quarters). Very similar results were obtained using constant-dollar values for the period 1952-64; nor did the distributed-lag relation between consumer expenditure and disposable income prove to be significantly different when the period covered was extended to include the early post-war years.

Viewed in light of the requirements of a flexible stabilization policy, a response lag of the order of magnitude indicated would appear to be troublesomely, if not prohibitively, long. It is possible to argue that the inside lags associated with a tax change do not in themselves preclude the use of the personal income tax for stabilization purposes, but that if changes in this tax are to serve effectively as an economic stabilizer, consumers must be assumed to react quickly to variations in after-tax income. A slow or sluggish consumer response, when added to the recognition and action lags, may well mean that changes in the personal income tax are relatively ineffective in coping with many or most instances of economic instability.

Response of Production to a Change in Consumer Spending

The lag between a change in consumer spending and a resultant change in production is probably short in so far as producers can be expected to respond quickly to new demand conditions once they become known. Even before the rate of output of consumer-goods industries is adjusted, a higher or lower level of consumer spending may be reflected in inventories of goods in process and in orders placed for raw materials and intermediate goods. The possibility of a serious lag would appear to exist only in the case of a delay between the time a change in consumer spending occurs and the time this change is known to producers. Speculation about the length of this lag, as well as work aimed at determining the lag quantitatively, is hampered by a lack of information concerning the manner or process by which producers become aware of a change in demand conditions. If the assumption is made that producers adjust the rate of output to changes in new orders which, in turn, are geared to the level of retail sales, there is the possibility of a recognition lag on the part of both distributors and producers, i.e. they may be unable to distinguish immediately a change in demand from random or seasonal fluctuations in sales and new orders. Given this process of transmitting changes in demand from consumer to producer, there is also the possibility that distributors — retailers and wholesalers — may take the occasion afforded by an initial increase in sales to bring inventories into line with current and expected sales, in which case new orders placed with producers may increase only if the higher level of sales persist. Some justification exists for the view that the relation between consumer purchases and production depends on the complexity of distribution channels and on the type of inventory policies followed by distributors and producers.

A strong argument can be made that producers short-circuit the transmission process just referred to by keeping a close eye on retail sales and the state of the economy, generally. By anticipating the effect a tax change will have on consumer spending, producers may reduce the outside lag to the point where at least some of the effects of a tax change may be felt actually *before* there has been time for consumer spending to adjust to a new level of after-tax income. The emphasis that many of our large corporations place on market analysis and forecasts suggests that something not far short of simultaneity of movement of sales and production may exist in some industries.

The problem of measuring the outside lag of fiscal policy is complicated by the fact that producers' behaviour is influenced by expectations about future sales as well as by changes in actual sales. What producers expect sales to be following a tax change or any other type of fiscal change could depend on how successful they feel the government will be in achieving its stability goal. If, for example, they believe that the stabilizing action taken is inadequate to prevent a deterioration in economic conditions, their reaction to an increase in sales and new orders is likely to be cautious. They may follow a "wait and see" policy, in which case the lag between an increase in sales or new orders and any subsequent change in production will be long or, should production not be adjusted at all, infinite. Strong anti-recessionary action of the type that is likely to instill confidence in the government's ability and resolve to prevent a serious decline in economic activity, on the other hand, is likely to produce quite a different response on the part of producers. When the consensus is that the economy is about to expand, the response of production to a policy-induced increase in sales or new orders will probably be both great and quick. It is when producers' expectations are that economic activity will decline, despite any stabilizing action that may be taken by the government, that the proverbial string may defy being pushed.

69   The Theory of Fiscal Policy from the Point of View of the Province*

C. L. Barber

In their discussions of fiscal policy economists have usually had the central government of the country in mind. While they have often recognized that in a federal country the provinces or states may have important functions within their control, they have not expected them to follow a conscious fiscal policy aimed at maintaining low levels of unemployment, stable prices, and a reasonable rate of economic growth. Indeed, local governments have frequently been accused of following a perverse fiscal policy, thus offsetting some of the benefits that might otherwise have been obtained from the fiscal policy pursued by the federal government. Yet it is not entirely clear why state and provincial governments should not pursue a conscious fiscal policy. Let us consider this question in some detail. In what respects is the position of a province different from that of the federal government? And do these differences rule out or make impossible a deliberate fiscal policy at the provincial level? Further, assuming provincial policy is feasible, is it also desirable?

It is clear, to begin with, that the size of the income or population that comes under provincial control does not rule out the possibility of a fiscal policy. For although Canada as a whole is much larger than any individual province, the large provinces compare favourably in size with many independent countries. Thus, whether the comparison is made in terms of national income or population the province of Ontario is as large as or larger than half a dozen important industrial countries. To a lesser extent the same is true of Quebec. Even British Columbia has a national income which is larger than that of Ireland and almost as large as that of New Zealand. No one would suggest that Austria or Denmark or Sweden should not pursue an independent fiscal policy. On grounds of size, then, one would

---

*Reprinted by permission from the Ontario Committee on Taxation, *Report*, Queen's Printer, Toronto, 1967.

suppose that Ontario, Quebec, and British Columbia ought equally to pursue such a policy. To a lesser extent, the same would be true of the other Canadian provinces.

Moreover, the volume of revenues and expenditures that now come under provincial and municipal control also argue for the importance of a positive provincial fiscal policy. As of 1963 the combined expenditures of provincial and municipal governments exceeded those of the federal government by more than $1 billion. Similarly, the revenues at the disposal of provincial and municipal governments, after federal transfers, exceeded those at the disposal of the federal government by roughly the same amount. Thus, within any one province, the volume of revenue and expenditure coming under the control of the province and its municipalities will usually be slightly higher than those under federal control. Moreover, in the important area of government capital expenditures in recent years, provincial and municipal expenditures have exceeded those of the federal government by a ratio of almost 3 to 1.

Perhaps the major difference that most economists see between the position of the federal government and that of a province is in respect to the monetary power of the fiscal government. The government in Ottawa can use its control over the Bank of Canada to support the price of its bonds when it wishes to pursue a policy of deficit finance in a period of declining income. The provincial government does not have this alternative available. However, it would be easy to exaggerate the importance of this difference. If, as is true at present, Canada has a fixed exchange rate, monetary policy will have to be closely geared to the requirements of the balance of payments. This means that an increase in the size of the federal deficit, due say to a tax cut or an increase in government expenditure, might require a tighter monetary policy. For rising incomes within Canada would lead to higher imports and might thus cause Canada's balance-of-payments position to worsen. On the other hand, if the Bank of Canada were pursuing a policy of active monetary ease to offset the effects of a recession, the provincial government would benefit from this equally with the federal government. Only in circumstances where there was serious unemployment in one part of Canada at a time when the rest of the country was prosperous is there any likelihood that the monetary policy suited to the needs of the federal government would differ from that desired by a province. Moreover, it will be argued below that the debt limits which a province faces do not differ essentially from those faced by the federal government. Thus, the absence of control over monetary policy cannot be taken seriously as an argument against the possibility of an active fiscal policy at the provincial governmental level. The province will not be free, as the federal government well may be, to choose the particular mix of monetary and fiscal policy it desires. It will simply have to adjust its fiscal policy to the monetary policy determined at the federal level. But again, this does not argue against the ability of a province to pursue an independent fiscal policy.

A province also differs from the federal government in not having any control over the exchange rate. But this, too, is not a bar against an active and effectual provincial fiscal policy. When Canada had a flexible exchange rate, it is true, the federal government was able through its monetary policy to influence the level of the exchange rate and thus exercise an important policy influence on the economy. But even in these circumstances, it seems likely that federal monetary and exchange-rate policy, if correctly conceived, would normally be complementary to both federal and provincial fiscal policy. Moreover, now that Canada has returned to a fixed exchange rate, a position most other countries find themselves in and the normal requirement of the International Monetary Fund, any changes in the exchange rate will occur very infrequently and only when it can be justified on the grounds that Canada's price and cost level relative to those of other countries is out of line at the existing exchange rate. Furthermore, there is reason to believe that when a country is on a fixed exchange rate fiscal policy is much more effective than monetary policy. And to the degree that fiscal policy involves the maintenance of a reasonable degree of price stability there is a greater need for fiscal policy under a fixed exchange rate. For in these circumstances the maintenance of a competitive price and cost position may be the key to successful competition in world markets.

A province also differs from the federal government in respect to immigration policy. But again the differences are those of degree rather than of kind. Depending on the buoyancy of the labour market and the level of unemployment the federal government can either encourage or discourage immigration. In contrast, a province cannot directly restrict the movement of either Canadians from other parts of Canada or of new Canadians across its borders. Moreover, if a province succeeds, through the use of vigorous fiscal measures, in reducing unemployment within its borders to comparatively low levels, there will be an increased inflow of workers from other parts of Canada. To some degree, this is also true of Canada as a whole. Immigration increases in periods when the demand for labour is growing rapidly and falls off in periods of slack and high levels of unemployment. Thus, inability to control the volume of immigration does not prevent a province from having an active fiscal policy.

Another major difference between Canada and an individual province is the much larger leakages that will occur in the case of provincial fiscal policy measures. In other words, while an increase in provincial spending or a reduction in provincial taxes will lead to some increase in the demand for goods and services produced within the province, a substantial proportion of the increased expenditure may be for goods produced in other provinces or outside of Canada entirely. In the case of national policy measures, the leakage through imports is confined to the expenditures on the goods and services of other countries. However, to the degree that fiscal policy measures are being carried out by a number of provinces at the same time offsetting effects will occur. Moreover, this is again a difference in degree rather than kind. Many small countries may have import leakages which are as large as those of Ontario or Quebec. In some degree, a province is in a position to minimize these leakages in respect to the first round of additional expenditures, for a wide range of public works expenditures comes under its jurisdiction and these often have a large local employment content. However, it must be recognized that this does seriously limit the effectiveness of provincial fiscal policy unless all or a number of provinces act in parallel fashion. The limitation will be especially serious for the smaller provinces.

Perhaps the key factor in determining whether a province can pursue an independent fiscal policy is the nature of the province's borrowing capacity and the extent to which it can increase its debt. It is usually argued that the provinces and municipalities are in a very much inferior position in this respect to that of the federal or central government. And yet it is not entirely clear why this should be so. In part, it reflects the fact that the central government can always use its control over the central bank to increase the money supply and thereby support the value of its securities. Such an opportunity is not open to junior levels of government. But it would be a mistake to assess the ultimate borrowing capacity of different levels of government on the basis of what happened during the Great Depression, even though that experience may still condition the lending practices of investment institutions. For it is virtually certain that in any future period of cyclical decline, the central bank will pursue a policy of monetary ease and this will benefit junior levels of government as well as the central government.

Ultimately, borrowing capacity depends on the willingness and ability of the government to service the debt incurred and for this reason the reputation and taxable capacity of the government has a key bearing on its credit rating. It is clear that the federal government, with its access to all forms of taxation and its present control of a dominant share of the taxes which have the highest growth potential, the personal and corporate income tax, will have the largest borrowing capacity. Similarly, local governments, which are heavily dependent on the property tax or on grants from senior levels of government, are in the weakest position. Nevertheless, most of the provinces are at present in a comparatively strong credit position. Not only are their net debt charges much lower in relation to income than was true in earlier years but they now also have a very substantial guaranteed floor under the revenues they receive from the federal government.

There is also reason to believe that, for the larger provinces at least, under some circumstances a moderate increase in the size of their outstanding debt might improve rather than weaken their credit rating. To some degree the preferred status of federal government securities is due to the fact that they are available in larger quantities and in a wider range of maturities, and are more actively traded.

In evaluating the ability of the provinces to pursue an independent countercyclical policy much depends on the severity of the cyclical fluctuations which are anticipated. On the basis of the post-war years to date, there is reason to believe that the typical cycle will consist mainly of a reduction or cessation in the normal rate of growth and perhaps occasionally a small and short-lived decline in gross national product. In cycles of such moderate amplitude almost all of the Canadian provinces have ample power to pursue counter-cyclical fiscal policies. The only provinces that might have difficulty would be the Atlantic provinces. These provinces already have a net interest burden which is more than twice as high relative to provincial income as that in any other province.

If a more severe cyclical contraction were to occur there would be more risk of provincial debt limits' being tested, particularly if the decline proved protracted. But if, as seems likely, the federal government pursues a vigorous fiscal and monetary policy in such a period it is very unlikely that such a test would arise.

To sum up, while in certain respects a province is not in as strong a position to pursue an independent fiscal policy as the federal government, the differences are mainly of degree rather than kind and even where the province lacks certain powers that reside in the federal sphere this will not prevent the use of fiscal policy by a province.

Having concluded that a provincial fiscal policy is possible, let us next consider the question of whether, in fact, there is any need for an active provincial fiscal policy. Several considerations support the desirability of an active fiscal policy on the part of the province.

First, there is the practical matter that control over many areas of expenditure has been given to the provinces under the terms of the British North America Act. If the federal government wishes to pursue fiscal policy measures in these areas it can do so only with the agreement of or in co-operation with the provinces. For example, while housing expenditure has been an active tool of fiscal policy at the federal level, strictly speaking, control over this area belongs to the provinces. Again price stability may require or make desirable policy measures affecting wage negotiations and this lies largely in the provincial sphere of jurisdiction. Still again, both the rate of economic growth and the avoidance of structural unemployment may require important educational measures. And this area too, except for vocational and agricultural education where there is joint jurisdiction, comes under provincial control.

Further, there may often be substantial regional variation in the need for government policy measures. Yet many federal measures tend to affect all parts of the country equally. In contrast, the provinces are in a better position to take measures that will affect employment in one particular part of the country. The federal government could scarcely cut taxes in one area and leave them unchanged elsewhere. Yet the area of capital expenditures under federal control may be too limited to make a regional fiscal policy effective.

What Should be the Objectives of Provincial Fiscal Policy?

In respect to unemployment, and within limits, the objectives of provincial fiscal policy should be the same as those of the federal government, that is, a low level of unemployment. The level of unemployment selected as a goal might well vary depending on the degree to which a particular province is affected by seasonal and structural unemployment and the success it achieves in reducing or minimizing this type of unemployment. Thus, in Ontario, where seasonal and structural unemployment has been moderate, the goal might well be 2.5 per cent of the labour force or lower. In contrast where, as is true of the Atlantic area, unemployment has never fallen below 4 per cent throughout the post-war period, a goal of from 4 to 5 per cent would be more appropriate.

As a practical guide to policy let each province adopt the following goal. Just as a suitable goal for federal policy is to keep the level of Canada's gross national product moving up the path of potential full employment gross national product, so also a similar goal can be adopted by each province. Let each province attempt to keep its provincial gross national product moving up the path of potential full employment provincial G.N.P.

But how do we decide on whether federal or provincial action is needed, and what is the relative magnitude of the role each should play? There appears to be no simple answer to this question. To the degree that the federal government succeeds through the use of monetary, fiscal, exchange-rate, and other policy measures in keeping unemployment at low or moderate levels without any substantial rise in prices there may be little need for provincial fiscal measures. Only to the extent that national measures or cyclical fluctuations have an unequal impact on different parts of the country would there be room for supplementary provincial measures. Even here provincial fiscal policy might well make a significant contribution. The federal government would feel freer to pursue an expansive fiscal policy if it felt confident that its possible inflationary effects in some areas of the country would be offset by counter-measures on the part of the provincial governments in these areas. Further, there may be circumstances when the most appropriate expansionary measures are those that fall under the control of the provincial government. Thus, highway expenditures may often be the form of social capital expenditure that can be expanded most quickly in periods of economic slack. Similarly, on social and other grounds it may be considered desirable in such periods to increase expenditures on public low-rent housing and urban renewal. All of these expenditures come under provincial jurisdiction.

In respect to frictional, structural, and seasonal unemployment the provincial government's goal should be very similar to that of the federal government. A province should be particularly interested in reducing seasonal and frictional unemployment because this is essentially a local or intra-provincial problem. In respect to structural unemployment its responsibility will vary depending on whether the solution to the problem requires a movement within the area or a movement to other areas. It seems appropriate to expect the federal government to take more responsibility for facilitating interregional movements of labour. Where the solution to the problem involves additional education or training the province has a special responsibility, for education falls primarily within its jurisdiction.

Up to the present time provincial governments have not given much indication that they regard the achievement of reasonable price stability as, in part, their responsibility. And yet one aspect of price stability, the achievement of non-inflationary wage settlements in the collective bargaining process, is an area for which they bear a primary responsibility. Then too, the provinces' control over marketing arrangements for farm products and their control over public utility rates have some implications for price stability. Thus, it seems clear that price stability should be one of the provinces' fiscal policy goals.

In respect to the third major goal of economic policy, a reasonable rate of economic growth, it has recently become clear that many provinces now recognize and accept some major responsibility. Thus, in his budget address on February 7, 1963, the Honourable James N. Allan, Provincial Treasurer of Ontario, stated: "The government has long considered the promotion of economic growth and development to be one of its major responsibilities." Similar statements have been made by the officials of other provincial governments and almost all of them have been increasingly active in this field in recent years.

70   Taxation for Stabilization*

S. Surrey

My remarks will start from two premises: the first is that it would be desirable to use rapid tax changes for economic stabilization purposes, when such changes are needed. The second premise is that by one arrangement or another the legislative processes will permit such temporary tax increases and decreases to be undertaken with sufficient speed to meet stabilization requirements.

General Criteria

Starting with general criteria, *the essence of the kind of countercyclical tax action we are here concerned with is speed.* As we all know inflation and deflation tend to become cumulative, feeding upon themselves and becoming harder and harder to stem or reverse as they follow their course. Yet while great improvements have been made in our economic forecasting methods, they cannot tell us — and given the dynamic world we live in I doubt that in the foreseeable future they will be able to tell us — what action is needed much in advance of the time when that action must be taken. We cannot therefore afford to be slow in taking action once it becomes clear that action is needed. Moreover, the action we take must make its effects felt very promptly. This need for speed and flexibility in stabilization policy points to three basic criteria for assessing specific countercyclical tax measures.

*Reprinted by permission of author and publisher from *Canadian Tax Journal*, Vol. XIV, May-June 1966.

One is simplicity. To meet this requirement the method of tax change should entail a minimum modification of the normal tax collection and payments process. The tax change should be easy for the taxpayer to comply with and easy for him to understand. And, of course, it should be easy for the Internal Revenue Service to put into effect.

A second important criterion for judging the merits of alternative temporary tax changes is the immediacy and certainty of their economic effects. As I have already observed, there will not be much time to waste once a determination of the need for action is made. Tax action which is delayed in its economic effects even though taken promptly, may well fail in its purpose. In fact, given the speed with which the economic situation can sometimes change there is risk that action of such nature may even be perverse in the timing of its effects and actually aggravate rather than diminish instability.

I believe that this criterion has an important bearing on the question of the extent to which short range tax changes should aim at influencing investment or consumption. It is true that investment is the more volatile sector in our economy and it would be desirable to try to mitigate sharp fluctuations in the investment sector. On the other hand, evidence appears to indicate that the time lags between tax changes and expenditure change are substantially less and the effects are more certain for consumption than for investment. Consequently, for countercyclical tax policy it is probably advisable to aim at both consumption and investment but to place primary reliance on influencing consumption.

As a third general criterion to apply to the choice of temporary tax changes, the design of countercyclical changes should be such that the changes can be assured of ready and therefore speedy general acceptance. Proposals that provoke controversy, or that, because of their novelty or complexity, require considerable study to understand and appraise must inevitably cause delay in taking action and therefore cannot really be fitted into a policy of temporary countercyclical tax changes.

Closely related to acceptability is the criterion of symmetry. If legislation is to be rapidly enacted, the Congress and the public must be assured that the legislation does not involve making long run permanent rate changes in the tax system. This consideration requires that the changes be temporary. If after a year or so the change is no longer needed, it should come off in the same way that it went on. If on the other hand it develops that the increase or decrease in revenue needs will be permanent — as far as anything can be "permanent" in a tax system — it should be understood that the temporary change itself will expire and be replaced by a long-run tax change developed in the usual way and including whatever structural changes the Congress might think appropriate.

Even temporary changes, however, still involve the problem that different types of change are available and a voter is apt to choose among them on the ground of which one affects him most favourably. But it may be that a type of change that is relatively favourable to a group of taxpayers when an increase is required will become relatively unfavourable when tax reduction is called for.

It has therefore been suggested that the prospects for general agreement on the available types of change might be improved if a further principle of symmetry is advanced that countercyclical tax decreases should be the mirror opposite of tax increases. Under this principle, tax changes may work to the relative advantage of some people in some stages of the economic cycle but not at others, and the tendency would thus be neither to favour nor disfavour any group over the full course of upswings and downswings. However, in view of the many considerations that enter into the formulation of fair and effective tax changes there is a question as to just how much weight to give to this version of the symmetry principle. Perhaps a more flexible interpretation that permits the inflationary and deflationary phases to be treated somewhat differently might prove more realistic and useful. At least, I would leave this particular aspect of symmetry as an open one to be considered after we have learned more about the entire process of these stabilization tax changes, rather than regard it as a governing concept.

Structural Changes Unsuitable

If these criteria can be considered valid guides for the choice of counter-cyclical tax measures, it seems clear that proposals which involve structural changes in our tax system are usually of doubtful appropriateness. Or, to put the matter another way, only those structural changes which are readily and generally acceptable, whose effects are immediate and predictable, and which are relatively simple to implement, ought to be considered in connection with short-run stabilizing tax policy. This presumably renders ineligible many of the long standing and thus usually controversial proposals for tax reforms.

I think it also precludes adding to our existing structure in such a process a new type of tax, whether the tax is to provide additional revenue or to permit reduction in yield from existing sources. A new tax always involves a number of basic policy questions which are far more numerous than is usually perceived or recognized when the tax is proposed, and which cannot properly be considered at the same time that attention is being given to temporary stabilizing tax changes.

This should not be construed to preclude consideration at appropriate times of possible modifications of the present structure that would make it more amenable to implementing a flexible tax policy. For the present, however, I think it advisable to focus on what can be done within the existing structure.

Let me now turn to some of the technical issues that would be involved in temporary changes of specific taxes within our existing structure.

Individual Income Tax

On the basis of the criteria of immediacy and certainty of economic effect the individual income tax is probably the most suitable for implementing temporary changes in tax rates. Due to the withholding feature of the tax, a very quick impact on the disposable income of individuals can be achieved. Indeed the sensitivity of this withholding procedure has been increased through the recent adoption of a graduated withholding system. In turn, the influence of changes in current disposable income on consumer expenditures is probably the most prompt and most reliable influence on aggregate demand that fiscal policy has to work with, whether for short-run changes up and down or for longer range changes in the level of demand.

There are numerous ways by which temporary changes in the individual income tax can be produced. One approach suggested by the criteria of simplicity and ready acceptability is to devise a "neutral" type of short range tax change. By "neutrality" is meant a tax change that does not attempt to alter the general progressivity of the tax as it exists before the change.

"Neutral" Changes

Neutrality is itself subject to alternative interpretations. One interpretation appealing as a theoretical matter to some economists calls for a tax change equal to a *uniform per cent of the "disposable income"* of taxpayers — that is, the income they have available to spend on goods and services or to save. This approach would leave the relative position of taxpayers measured by their disposable income unchanged. That is, if one individual had 50% more disposable income than another before the tax change, he would still have 50% more after the tax change.

There are some important practical difficulties with this method, however, which preclude its use for countercyclical purposes.

There are two other simpler methods of implementing individual income tax changes that may also be interpreted as "neutral".

One of these is a *uniform point change in tax rates* in each bracket. This method may be considered "neutral" since the tax change amounts to a uniform percentage of everyone's taxable income. That is, if all the existing bracket rates were increased by one point, an individual with $2,000 of taxable income would pay $20, and an individual with $10,000 of taxable income would pay $100. Also, since all brackets would be increased by one point, the differences from one bracket to another would remain the same as before the tax change.

Another "neutral" method of changing taxes is by means of a *uniform percentage change in tax liabilities*. Under this method the *relative* amount of tax paid by each individual is the same after the tax change as before the change. Thus, under an increase, if one individual's tax liability is 10% higher than another's before the change, it will still be 10% higher after the change. (Illustrations based on U.S. tax rates have been omitted).

At incomes (of $3,000 and under) where no tax is imposed under present law, neither the *uniform percentage of tax liability* nor the *uniform point change in rates* methods would, of course, cause any change in tax liability up or down; the *uniform percentage of disposable income* method would produce tax changes for these incomes. Beyond this level, the *uniform percentage of tax liability* method would impose larger tax increases on higher incomes and smaller tax increases on lower incomes than either of the other two methods. Symmetrically, this method would provide larger tax reductions for higher incomes and smaller tax reductions for lower incomes than either of the other two methods. Under the *uniform point change in rates* method, the differential increases and decreases as between higher and lower incomes fall in between those for the other two methods.

To put either the *uniform percentage of tax liabilities change* or *uniform point change in tax rates* into effect, new withholding percentage formulas and new withholding wage bracket tables would be needed. This can be done accurately, since either method can be translated into increased tax rates.

In general — and this is the significant point in all this technical discussion of "neutral" methods — one should really not exaggerate what amounts to fine points of difference between the *uniform percentage change in tax liability* method and the method providing a *uniform point change in tax rates*. Each is simple to express in the tax return and to understand. Each therefore seems appropriate as a method for countercyclical change in the individual income tax.

Capital Gains

With regard to capital gains, the question is whether or not the tax rate should go up or down with personal income tax rates. Capital gains which are not taxed at the ceiling rate of 25% are taxed at a rate which is in effect 50% of the marginal income tax rate. It seems reasonable to continue the 50% inclusion rule through a temporary tax change which would make the gains subject to tax increase or decrease that was proportional to the tax change on other income.

As to whether the alternative ceiling rate on capital gains should be changed, one could raise the question whether the occurrence of a temporary increase or decrease might cause investors to speed up or slow down sales that they would have made in the near future. On balance changes of a point or two in the ceiling rate seem unlikely to have this effect. This issue might well be decided on the basis of the general attitude toward the fairness of including the ceiling capital gains rate in a program of temporary changes in the individual income tax.

Corporate Income Tax

There are a number of reasons — both economic and equity — for considering the corporate income tax in a balanced package of contracyclical income tax changes. Broad neutrality as between individuals and business, which is predominantly corporate, is probably desirable. Moreover, individual income tax rate changes would apply to unincorporated businesses. Appreciable disparities in the treatment of corporate and non-corporate enterprise would affect the choice between the corporate and non-corporate form of business organization in the important area of small and medium-sized businesses. Furthermore, most observers — including both expert and non-expert opinion — believe that if *higher* burdens are placed on individuals in response to economic conditions, even though the emphasis may be on curtailing consumption, corporate business should be called on also to make some contribution. Changes in corporate tax payments may influence both dividend payments and investment outlays. This belief probably does not apply with the same force to tax decreases during a downswing. Still, reduction in the corporate tax paralleling that in individual taxes may be appropriate to maintain a simple symmetry over the cycle and also because of its economic effects.

Changes in corporate tax can be made in a manner more or less parallel to the changes discussed for the individual income tax. A simple change in the tax applying to all corporations could be achieved on either the point change method or the percentage of tax liability method. In the case of a *point change*, the normal tax rate, which is now 22%, could be changed by the desired number of points.

As an alternative, a uniform *percentage change in corporate tax liabilities* might be used. The percentage comparable to a uniform one point change would be a 2⅓ percentage change in tax liabilities. As compared to the one point change in the normal rate, this method would produce a larger increase and a larger decrease in tax liabilities of large corporations, and a smaller increase or decrease in the liabilities of smaller corporations.

Use of Excise Taxes for Countercyclical Purposes

An attempt to include excise tax changes as part of a countercyclical tax program would give rise to a number of problems and difficulties.

A major problem would arise from the fact that the federal excise system as of now is made up almost entirely of three groups of taxes., (1) the sumptuary taxes on liquor and tobacco; (2) user charges and dedicated taxes; and (3) regulatory taxes.

This threefold classification of the excise system severely limits the adjustments that could be made to the existing excise taxes for countercyclical purposes. The regulatory taxes raise little revenue and do not lend themselves to adjustments for revenue purposes. Those taxes that are levied as user charges or whose revenues are dedicated to special purposes also do not readily lend themselves to anticyclical adjustments. The taxes are designed to charge users with the cost of certain public expenditure programs, and their use in a countercyclical manner might be considered discriminatory and inequitable. To raise charges above user cost levels in an inflationary period would be a form of discriminatory penalty tax on the users of the services; a reduction below user cost levels would in effect be a subsidy of the users of the service. It is questionable if public policy would be well served by alternatively penalizing and subsidizing, for example, users of the federal airways system and thus air transportation.

It would be possible to revise liquor and tobacco taxes up and down according to cyclical revenue policy (the British have done this a number of times), but there are constraints on how much could be done. Taxation of liquor and tobacco is supported by the public for sumptuary as well as revenue reasons. At the same time, the policy has been to avoid severely depressing these industries. If the desired fiscal policy called for a reduction in federal tax rates, sumptuary conditions might argue against a drastic reduction in alcohol and tobacco taxes. On the other hand, while fiscal considerations might warrant substantially higher tax rates in general, the effect on the alcohol and tobacco industries might lead to little or no tax increase on their products.

Finally, taxes that affect prices always incur the danger of setting up perverse expectation effects. If consumers anticipated that prices were going to rise as a result of an increase in the tax, they would accelerate their purchases, thereby aggravating inflationary pressures. On the downside, they may hold back purchases in anticipation of tax reduction, thereby aggravating the decline at least in the early stages before the decrease in tax was actually in effect.

In view of the structure of the present excise system then, it would be difficult to utilize existing excises as much of a countercyclical measure. Nor would it be at all desirable to impose new selective excises or reinstitute those that have been repealed.

71   Fiscal Policy for Growth *

The Royal Commission on Taxation

There are many alternative concepts of economic growth, and when they are used indiscriminately confusion is inevitable. In particular, the term is often used to describe increases in actual gross national product (GNP). This tends to result in confusion because it does not distinguish between the changes in GNP brought about by changes in the utilization of the capacity to produce on the one hand, and changes in the capacity to produce on the other. Controlling the degree of utilization is the problem of economic stability which we have just considered. Changing the capacity (potential) to produce is the subject matter of this chapter.

We define an increase in potential GNP as economic growth. Potential GNP measures the capacity to produce in a given year if all resources were employed in that year. Because the supply of labour and capital will be increased if full employment is continuously maintained, the growth of potential GNP depends in part upon the success or failure of stabilization policy in the past.

We briefly consider the relative importance of the major determinants of the rate of growth: the quantity and quality of labour and capital, and a

*Reprinted by permission from the Royal Commission on Taxation, *Report*, Queen's Printer, Ottawa, 1967, Vol. II.

group of factors we have called "technical change". We then discuss what can be done through the tax system to increase the rate of growth by influencing each of the determinants of growth.

The Relative Importance of Various Factors in Growth

The growth rate of potential private non-farm output is defined as equal to the sum of the growth rate of technical change plus the growth rates of the capital stock and of labour hours, each weighted by the marginal contributions to output of changes in capital and labour.

The relative importance of technical change, capital and labour is then found by dividing the product of its own growth rate and its marginal contribution to output by the growth rate of potential private non-farm output.

The results for the period 1926-63 indicate that potential private non-farm output grew at an average rate in excess of 4 per cent a year over the period. The estimates show that 46 per cent of this growth was the result of technical change, 31 per cent resulted from the increase in the imput of labour, and 23 per cent arose from the increase in the input of capital.

The Supply of Labour

The examination of the record of Canadian growth indicated that about 30 per cent of the private non-farm growth rate has been the result of the growth of labour input.

The growth of labour input depends on two basic processes: demographic change and the choices made by the population with respect to work and leisure.

Demographic Factors

Among the demographic factors we may distinguish natural increase and net migration. It was found that economic variables, and in particular tax variables, do not play a significant role in the determination of natural increase. While there is a specific tax exemption for dependent children in Canada, together with a system of family allowances, these provisions have not had any observed effect on the birth rate and therefore on natural increase.

Turning to migration, it was found that since the 1920's net migration has contributed about 13 per cent of the total increase in the Canadian population; since World War II the contribution has been twice this amount. Furthermore, these proportions understate the share of migration in total population increase because they omit the children born to immigrants in Canada.

The past record of immigration into Canada shows that the volume of immigration expands and contracts as the Canadian economy achieves or falls short of full employment. This reflects both the direct demand-pull on immigrants and the fact that barriers against persons wanting to come to Canada are raised and lowered according to the government's estimation of labour requirements which is itself strongly influenced by the tightness of the labour market. The investigation revealed that taxes probably do not affect the pattern of immigrant flows. The fact that the Canadian standard of living is substantially above the standards in the home countries of most immigrants probably means that taxes have little influence.

Net migration is also determined by the outflow of population from Canada. The United States is the most important destination of emigrants from Canada, and attention was concentrated on the flow to that country. The findings revealed that once again the extent to which resources are unemployed in Canada is apparently the most important determinant of this outflow. The underlying process appears to be one where the higher standard of living in the United States continually attracts Canadians. As long as the Canadian economy successfully maintains full employment there is sufficient resistance to this magnetism. During periods of rising unemployment, falling income will loosen the ties that keep workers here, and emigration to the United States will speed up. It was found that changes in the Canadian personal income tax rates apparently had relatively little effect on total emigration of Canadians to the United States, but may have had some effect on the emigration of Canadian skilled workers to that country.

An examination was made of the occupations of Canadian emigrants to the United States. It was found that the proportion of skilled persons among emigrants to the United States from Canada was higher than the proportion of the same skills in the Canadian labour force. This suggests that there has been a concentration of skilled workers among Canadian emigrants, the group for whom the United States–Canadian income tax differentials are least favourable to Canada.

Higher wages and salaries for comparable work, better research facilities, a greater diversity of employment opportunities for professionals, and the interconnection between firms in the two countries have probably exerted a much greater influence than tax differentials. Nevertheless, it would be desirable to reduce these differentials so that the tax system would not provide an additional impetus to emigration from Canada to the United States.

The Decision to Work

The second major process in the growth of labour input is the willingness of the population to work. This includes both their decisions to participate in the labour force and the number of hours a year they are prepared to work.

Since 1921 between 53 per cent and 55 per cent of the population has been in the labour force. However, the constancy of this overall participation rate conceals a number of significant developments. As would be expected, the participation rate for males aged 20 to 64 years, the group forming the bulk of the labour force, has been very high and steady over time. It is in the other groups, the aged, the young, and the females that there have been significant changes.

The participation rates for both males and females over 65 years of age have declined. In the case of males the decline has been substantial and steady; for females it has been less marked. These movements have been the result of a sharp decline in the proportion of the labour force in agriculture that has traditionally provided employment for the aged, the extension of compulsory retirement, the growth of private and public pension plans, and forms of assistance to the elderly. It is possible that the tax system has affected the willingness of the elderly to work by reducing their incentives when they are presumably already low. However, given the low income brackets of the majority of the aged, we believe that taxes have played a negligible role.

The participation rate for males under the age of 19 has declined. Although it has increased for females in this age group, it is still less than the rate for males. The overriding factor here has been the extension of school-leaving age. Males are staying in school longer; and while females are to some extent doing likewise, they are also finding that there are more opportunities for gainful employment. It is clear that it is school and not taxes that explains the overall reduction in labour force participation by the young.

The participation rate for females between the ages of 20 and 64 has also increased. There are many factors that can be adduced to account for the change. On the supply side, mechanization in the home has meant more spare time for housewives; the average size of families has decreased; more people are living in urban areas close to employment opportunities; increasing education has made women better suited to employment, and the decline of employment in agriculture has released females from an activity that used to absorb, although generally as unpaid family workers, substantial numbers of women. On the demand side, the growth of the service industries and the increased relative importance of non-production workers in manufacturing have opened opportunities for women that did not exist before.

If United States experience is an indication of what can be expected in Canada, these trends should continue. It is reasonable to expect that changes in the personal tax burden would have an effect upon the participation rate of females. When the personal tax burden is increased, the family can maintain its previous level of disposable income if the wife takes a job. On the other hand, an increase in taxes would mean that her earnings would be taxed more heavily. The evidence put before us suggests that there may be a negative relationship between changes in personal tax rates and changes in female participation rates.

While there is, of course, a point where equity is violated by lower taxes on the incomes of working wives (we expressly mean wives and not all women), we have considered in our recommendations provisions that would remove some of the tax disincentives to working wives. We recommend a tax credit for working women with young children.

Turning to the question of how many hours the labour force is prepared to work, we observe that over the years, Canada, along with all other industrial economies, has witnessed a substantial reduction in the work-week. The major sources of the downward trend are shifts from industries, such as agriculture, that have always required a much longer work-week, and a general decline within all industries. The latter development is complicated because it is not clear what proportion of the decline in hours has been due to the voluntary pursuit of more leisure by workers. On the contrary, leisure may be imposed on them through a reduced demand for labour, either from technical change which substitutes capital for labour, or through periods of involuntary unemployment which similarly lead to a non-reversible reduction in the hours worked per man as a way of sharing the work. While it is likely that these developments are highly interdependent, the evidence suggests that periods of rising unemployment have been associated with rapid reductions in hours worked. In addition, it appears that these declines in hours are rarely fully reversed in periods of expansion. This would account for the observed decline in hours over a long period. The evidence did not indicate that taxes have had a significant effect on average hours worked.

It has been argued that this decline in hours has been partially offset by the increase in the amount of labour expended per hour. Even for wage and salary workers, who form the majority of the labour force and who work a given number of hours per week, there is room for variation in effort, depending on motivation and managerial ability. Studies of professional workers in the United States who have the opportunity to vary their effort indicate that their efforts have not been substantially reduced during the recent period of high taxation. This is due in part to the tax-free benefits of their occupations, together with a number of special pressures. It is dangerous, however, to infer from the behaviour of this unique group the effect of taxes on the labour effort of all wage and salary workers.

Although we have no evidence to support our contention, we are convinced that high marginal personal rates of tax do have a negative effect on labour, managerial and professional effort. In arriving at our recommendations we have therefore proposed rate schedules in which they are reduced.

Technical Change

Technical change is defined to include changes in the quality of labour and capital, and changes in the inter-industry distribution of inputs and outputs.

The finding that technical change accounted for almost one half the growth of private non-farm output, and somewhat more for the total economy, agrees with a number of studies made in Canada, in the United States, and in other countries which indicate that the most important source of growth in a modern economy is this residual component.

It is not possible to explain the whole of technical change for many of its determinants are unknown, while others, such as the importance of the scale of operation and the size of the market, are particularly difficult to measure. We shall concentrate on three components only: structural change, research and development, and improvements in the quality of the factors of production.

Structural Change: Industrial and Regional Mix

The tax structure has had little if any effect on the shift of labour from agriculture to industry. If anything, it probably delayed the shift because farmers have been generously treated under the Income Tax Act. The tax structure has not been neutral between industries and regions, but until recently there was no *explicit* attempt to use the tax system to alter the allocation of resources among either industries or regions. Whatever the intention, in our view the tax system probably has affected the allocation of resources among industries and regions to a significant extent. In order to make the discussion more concrete, the following two important provisions are considered briefly here:

1. The incentives to the oil and mining industries provided by the depletion allowances and the three-year exemption for new mines.
2. The exemption of services from federal (and provincial) sales taxes.

The incentives to the two resource industries can be presumed to have increased investment in these industries relative to what it otherwise would have been. Because both industries are highly specific geographically, there is a presumption that the income tax system shifted factors of production to the regions where the basic resources were located. The exemption of services from sales taxes presumably increased the growth of the service industries relative to other industries; because the industry is not geographically specific, the exemption has probably not had any effect on regional allocation.

The effects of these and similar features of the tax system on the output of the economy depends essentially upon the answers to four questions:

1. Did the tax system change the allocation of resources to the industry relative to a neutral tax system?
2. If so, in what direction and to what extent?
3. Would the market have efficiently allocated resources among industries and regions had the tax system been reasonably neutral?
4. If not, did the tax system compensate for the market imperfection or compound the imperfection?

If the market would have worked well in the absence of the special tax provision for an industry, and if that provision had an effect on the allocation of resources, the tax provision must have brought about a misallocation of resources. If the market would not have worked well, and if the provision had an effect that compounded rather than compensated for the imperfection, the provision must have brought about a misallocation of resources. Only if the tax provision had no effect, or had an effect that compensated for a market imperfection, can the provision be given a clean bill of health from an efficiency point of view. It may, of course, still be unacceptable from an equity point of view. On the other hand, changes that have undesirable economic effects may still be justified if the improvement in equity was thought to be overriding.

To be more specific, if all product and capital markets worked perfectly, and if there were no other interferences with the allocation of the market, the Canadian tax treatment of oil, mining and service industries would distort the allocation of resources. This would come about because the tax treatment would induce more resources to flow to these industries relative to other industries. The value of the additional output in the favoured industries would be less than the value of the forgone output in other industries.

Unfortunately there is no method of determining in a completely objective, and hence incontrovertible, way how well product and factor markets work or the precise impact of particular features of the tax system on the allocation of resources.

A large part of the service industry is characterized by a multitude of highly labour-intensive and competitive small firms. There is no reason to believe that the market discriminates against the service industry. The marginal value productivity of labour in this industry is relatively low. This leads us to the conclusion that the failure to tax services in the past has probably distorted the allocation of resources. We have no hesitation, therefore, in recommending that services should be taxed to remove the discrimination against goods.

The situation with respect to the oil and mining industries is more complicated. The available evidence suggests to us that the market may, to a limited extent, discriminate against investment in the resource industries because of the risks involved in some aspects of those activities. Some tax incentives therefore seem justified; but we have concluded that the present incentives are too liberal in relation to the imperfection they are intended to offset and extremely inefficient. They bonus investments that would have taken place in the absence of the tax concessions. We are of the opinion that they induce too much investment in this sector relative to other sectors. Furthermore, the present incentives do nothing to meet the greatest risk of all, loss of the original capital put into a risky venture. We intend to meet this problem, to the extent that a tax system can legitimately do so, through our proposed treatment of losses. We shall therefore recommend that depletion allowances and the three-year exemption for new mines should be removed. However, we will also discuss a number of means of providing more efficient incentives to these industries where this is warranted.

In addition to section 71A and the accelerated depreciation provisions for investment in designated areas added to the *Income Tax Act* in 1963, the government introduced in 1965 the *Area Development Incentives Act*. Under the latter Act the Minister of Industry is empowered to make subsidies to firms establishing new facilities or expanding existing facilities in designated areas. The subsidies are established by a formula based on the approved capital cost of the facility. A subsidy under this Act is not taxable to the firm.

We commend this change from tax concessions to subsidies. We believe that investment credits (subsidies) are at least as efficient as accelerated depreciation and, per dollar of revenue forgone, more efficient than the three-year exemption of income for new businesses. The fact that the costs of the

subsidy can be readily determined is also a desirable feature, for it en-
courages the comparison of costs and benefits. Because the present tax incentives allow a business to postpone the deduction of any capital cost
allowances until after the three-year exempt period has expired, they provide
a much larger concession than is immediately apparent. It is not possible
to say how great the resulting tax concession may be. We do not think
this feature of the present measure is desirable.

Although we cannot be certain how effective the area development incentives will prove to be, we are reasonably certain that they will be more
efficient than the present tax incentives. Because the former will be more
useful, and because our recommendation for accelerated capital cost allowances for new businesses, regardless of location, should assist in meeting the
financing problems of such businesses, there seems no reason to keep the
depressed area tax incentives; we believe they would be redundant. It is
our recommendation that they be removed from the Act, but, of course,
not in such a manner as to remove the incentive to those businesses
now availing themselves of the provisions.

Research and Development

Recent findings on the importance of technical change for economic growth
have brought about increasing enthusiasm for research and development.
This enthusiasm is reflected in the spate of speeches and articles on the
subject and in the introduction of new governmnet programmes to encourage
research. The federal government now has four subsidy-type programmes and
a tax incentive designed to encourage research by business. The four expenditure programmes are: the Industrial Research Assistance Program administered
by the Defence Research Board; and the Defence Development Assistance
Program and the Program for the Advancement of Industrial Technology,
both administered by the Department of Industry. The National Research
Council programme, and the Program for the Advancement of Industrial
Technology which was enacted in June 1965, are the most important.

The combined effect of sections 72 and 72A of the *Income Tax Act* is
to grant not only an immediate write-off of current and capital expenditures
but also an extra deduction from income of 50 per cent of the increase
in these expenditures over those in the year ended prior to April 11, 1962.
Scientific research includes expenses incurred in the development of a pro-
totype.

In the 1965 Budget the Minister announced his intention to modify the
present incentive when it expires in 1966. These proposed modifications include: (a) a cash grant or credit against tax liabilities of 25 per cent of
research expenditures that will provide an equal incentive to all businesses
regardless of their tax position; (b) application of the incentive to all capital
expenditures and to current research expenditures in excess of the preceding
three-year average; (c) administration by the Department of Industry; and
(d) review by that Department of expenditures of over $50,000 a year to
ensure that the expenditures would be likely to benefit Canada.

The new system proposed by the Minister would remedy many of the defects in the existing provisions. The suggested use of grants rather than tax concessions is to be commended; the extension of the base period from one to three years would make the scheme less capricious; the allowance of all capital expenditures seems sensible (presumably capital expenditures are additions) the insistence that the Department of Industry approve large expenditures will ensure that the Department responsible for justifying the expenditures to Parliament will also be responsible for approving them. The basic question in our minds is whether or not this scheme is necessary at all given the National Research Council programme and the Program for the Advancement of Industrial Technology.

What is urgently needed is an appraisal of the returns that are likely to result from different kinds of research and development expenditures. We recognize that this appraisal will be exceedingly difficult to make because, by their very nature, the returns to research are most uncertain. The indirect returns may well exceed the direct returns. Nevertheless, unless some view is taken of the returns to "basic" research versus "development" research and of research undertaken by institutions relative to private industrial research, there can be substantial waste and confusion. The establishment of a Secretariat within the Privy Council Office to co-ordinate federal research programmes is obviously a move in the right direction, although it will also be necessary to undertake research on research if the co-ordination is to accomplish more than consistency. Consistent error is no improvement over confusion.

As was the case with respect to regional development incentives, we doubt whether broad incentives that apply without qualification to something as vague as "research and development" can be effective. Per dollar of revenue forgone or cost incurred, we have little doubt that the National Research Council programme and the new Program for the Advancement of Industrial Technology are a great deal more efficient than general tax incentives. Under the former, the qualifications and work of those engaged in research are under review by persons knowledgeable in the field. Under the latter, applicants for grants have to satisfy the Department of Industry that the projects would constitute a substantial advance having commercial potential, and would not merely be a minor variation of an old theme. Because it is a requirement of the Program for the Advancement of Industrial Technology that successful developments must be exploited in Canada, there is at least some possibility that Canadian market and production conditions will be taken into account. We recommend that consideration should be given to placing more reliance on the National Research Council programme and the Program for the Advancement of Industrial Technology, and to dropping both the tax concession in section 72A of the *Income Tax Act* for research and development and the proposed general grant programme for research and development announced in the 1965 Budget, unless a careful evaluation of the effectiveness of these general forms of encouragement suggests that they would be relatively more efficient. However, one aspect of the current tax encouragement should be retained as part of an overall, more generous approach to capital expenditures. We recommend that expenditures on research and product development, even if they are of a long-term or capital nature, should be explicitly permitted as a current deduction in determining income.

Improved Quality of the Factors of Production

The increased supplies of labour and capital, which were estimated by our research staff to account for over one half the growth rate of private non-farm output, were assumed to be of homogeneous quality over the entire period. It is likely that this assumption is not valid and that the estimates consequently understate the contribution of these factors. The argument that new capital embodies ever-improved quality appears to be eminently reasonable. However, probably because of the inadequacies of the date, this hypothesis has not been substantiated for Canada, although it is reasonable to assume that increases in the constant dollar value of the capital stock understate the real additions to productive capacity.

There are two basic sources of change in the quality of the labour force: changes in its age and sex composition, and changes in the ability of workers as a result of education and on-the-job training. The first source is well known, and many analyses of economic growth take this factor into account by standardizing the labour supply for differentials in age and sex. In Canada there has been a very slight decline in the overall quality of labour force as a result of changes in its age and sex composition.

An attempt was made by our research staff to follow several of the fascinating beginnings that have been made in measuring the impact of changes in the skill of those in the labour force. The one aspect of skill that it has proved feasible to measure is formal education. In contrast to the findings in the United States, the research suggests that in Canada formal education has improved labour's quality only by a very small amount over the past four decades. The disparity between the findings in the two countries is largely explained by the very significant lag in Canada in educating large numbers of its population. Because this lag has only recently been reduced, the impact will no doubt be felt in future decades and will give an added boost to Canada's potential growth rate. Our recommendations have sought to provide a measure of encouragement to the post-secondary education of Canadians to assist in this quality improvement. An evaluation of the role played by other forms of investment in "human capital", such as on-the-job training and health improvements, was not possible, either because of conceptual difficulties or because the data required are not yet available in Canada.

Capital Formation

The Rate of Investment

In determining the factors that influence capital formation, two salient findings emerged.

1. Capital requirements, as measured by the relationship of actual to potential output, are key determinants of the level of fixed investment.
2. Gross business saving, defined as the sum of depreciation allowances and retained earnings, has a statistically significant and quantitatively important impact upon fixed investment.

These findings indicate that fiscal policy can influence the level of investment, and hence the rate of growth of potential GNP. Fiscal policy is a major tool available for influencing aggregate demand and will affect investment in two ways: avoidance of excess capacity will provide a direct stimulus to private investment; increased levels of utilization tend to raise business income and hence gross business saving, providing a further stimulus to investment. The maintenance of full employment will therefore yield additional benefits through a more rapid rate of capital formation.

The retardation of capital formation caused by the Great Depression and World War II held the annual average growth rate of long-run potential GNP over the 1926-63 period down by about 0.3 percentage points, despite the high rates of capital formation during the postwar years. Milder depressions will, of course, not retard capital formation to the same extent; but, their effect upon capital formation and growth can be quite substantial. Over the next six years the private non-farm capital stock is expected to grow at a rate of about 5 per cent a year, if there is no gap between actual and potential output. If actual output falls short of potential output by 5 per cent, this capital stock will grow at a rate of about 4 per cent a year.

Once a full-employment path is achieved, further increases in the rate of growth may be obtained by increasing the rate of growth of capital, labour input, or productivity.

The significance of our second statistical finding is now apparent. If capital formation depended solely upon capital requirements, tax structure policy, as distinct from stabilization policy, could not affect the rate of investment and hence the rate of growth. However, because investment is partly determined by gross business saving, changes in the tax structure which change the level of gross business saving at a given level of output will probably affect the level of investment, on the assumption that tax-induced changes in corporate retentions have the same effect as other changes.

The two major statutory provisions within the present tax structure that have a substantial impact upon the level of after-tax corporate income are the schedule of corporate income tax rates and the allowable capital consumption rates. For changes in these tax variables to affect the level of gross business saving at full employment, two conditions must hold:

1. The corporate income tax rate change must not be fully shifted to consumers and wage earners.
2. Changes in after-tax corporate income resulting from the tax rate change must not be offset by changes in dividend payments.

The evidence we have examined suggests that both these conditions hold in Canada.

Shifting

A detailed study was made by our research staff of the behaviour of individual industries in response to the tax increases that occurred in the early 1950's. It was found that firms with market power, that is, those possessing the ability to shift corporate income taxes through price increases, shifted changes in these taxes only partially. When the fact that firms without market power probably cannot shift the tax at all is taken into account, these detailed results indicate that, on the average, manufacturing firms probably shifted about one third of the tax within two to five years. This finding was confirmed by a more aggregative analysis of the shares of GNP going to labour and capital for the postwar period as a whole.

Under the system we propose of fully integrating personal and corporate income taxes for resident shareholders, by giving them full credit against their personal income tax liabilities for the corporate tax paid with respect to corporate income allocated to them, there would be a reduction in taxes on corporate source income for most Canadian shareholders. However, because the credit would be confined to resident shareholders, there would be no change in the tax position of the wholly owned subsidiaries operating in Canada.

Dividend Behaviour

The evidence on dividend behaviour indicates that changes in corporate and personal income tax rates have not affected the proportion of after-tax profits paid out. This means that taxation has affected dividend payments only through its effect upon after-tax profits, and, in so far as after-tax profits are affected, dividends have borne a proportionate share of the tax burden. Therefore, changes in capital cost allowance provisions will probably have a larger impact upon gross business saving than changes in tax rates, that is, a tax reduction through liberalizing capital cost allowances will tend to increase gross business saving more than a tax rate reduction of equivalent value.

Under our proposal for integration of corporate and personal income tax, resident shareholders will receive full credit for corporate taxes on all corporate income *allotted* to them whether the allocations took the form of cash dividends, stock dividends, or other capitalization of surplus. Because we suggest a top personal income tax rate of 50 per cent and a flat corporate income tax rate of 50 per cent, most shareholders will receive a credit for or a rebate of corporate income taxes with respect to corporate income allocated to them. This means that the corporation would be able to reduce its cash distribution without reducing the cash flow to shareholders, for the tax credit or rebate would augment the lower cash dividend. It is our expectation that this change in the tax system would, on balance, increase gross business saving.

The Rate of Return and the Cost of Capital

Economic theory would suggest that increases in the marginal rate of return will stimulate investment, whereas increases in the cost of capital, which is often associated with reduced availability of funds, should reduce it. Unfortunately, it is difficult to obtain quantitative estimates of the significance of these effects. The expected marginal rate of return is difficult to measure, and the average realized rate of return is probably an inadequate substitute for it. Even if measures of the expected rate of return were available, it would be extremely difficult to assess the impact upon it of tax changes in the past. Drawing inferences about the impact of future tax changes upon the expected rate of return is hazardous. Nevertheless, we accept the view that tax changes that increase the expected after-tax rate of return on investments will increase the demand for new securities and reduce the cost of funds, thereby stimulating the rate of investment in fixed capital.

The Rate of Saving

There are a variety of fiscal means available for increasing the rate of domestic saving. The most important and perhaps the most effective way is for the government to achieve a surplus of revenues over expenditures. Positive net saving by the government will permit an excess of total investment over private saving without creating inflationary pressures. Such a policy has the virtue that it can generate a large increase in domestic saving, if that is required, and that the increase can be achieved without harmful side effects upon the goals of horizontal and vertical equity.

Some policy recommendations that have achieved currency do not share this virtue. We refer in particular to proposals to change the tax mix by increasing the burden of sales and excise taxes and reducing the burden of income taxes, and to proposals to reduce or eliminate progression in the personal income tax rates. The adoption of such measures would increase the tax burden upon those with low incomes and hence would conflict with the goal of vertical equity.

The increase in personal saving that would result from a reduction in the progressiveness of the income tax would likely be quite moderate, if those with incomes over $8,000 save 25 per cent of their after-tax income, and the remaining taxpayers save 5 per cent of their after-tax income, the elimination of any progressiveness in the rates on taxable income, while preserving the same total personal tax burden, would yield an annual increase in personal saving of about $40 million. This would involve shifting some $350 million of tax burden from the upper income to the low and middle income groups. Because the same amount of aggregate domestic saving could be achieved by an across-the-board tax increase of $80 to $90 million, we conclude that reducing progression is an inefficient means of stimulating saving.

Changing the tax mix by increasing sales taxes and by an across-the-board reduction in personal income taxes may affect personal savings in two ways. First, such a change would reduce the overall progressiveness of the tax system. However, the above illustration leads us to doubt whether such a reduction in progressiveness would increase saving significantly. Second, because sales taxes fall on consumption today, and on saving only some time in the future (when the assets are liquidated and spent), a switch to sales taxes reduces the tax burden on the saved portion of current income. Presumably, if the effect of the greater emphasis on sales taxes were important, a combination of increased sales taxes, reduced average personal income tax burden, and increased progression of the personal income tax rate structure to maintain the overall progressiveness of the system might be a package that would stimulate saving without reducing progressiveness. However, the stimulus to saving so provided would not be great. Moving from personal income taxes to sales taxes is equivalent, from the standpoint of the typical saver, to a rise in the rate of interest earned on his saving. Because the available evidence suggests that personal saving is quite unresponsive to changes in interest rates, it follows that the rate of saving is unlikely to respond dramatically to changes in the tax mix.

If a substantial reduction of the tax burden on saving were desired, it could be achieved most effectively by allowing taxpayers to deduct from their income for tax purposes some or all of their saving; the revenue could be maintained through higher taxes on income. Under the present system taxpayers may deduct certain contributions to pension plans and registered retirement savings plans in determining their taxable incomes. We will propose a system that deals with all contractual saving in a roughly similar manner. By raising or lowering the limits to the allowable deductions for registered retirement saving, and giving more or less generous tax treatment to the current earnings on the assets acquired, it might be possible to change the level of private saving. However, the extent to which increases in contractual saving would be offset by reductions in other forms of saving is uncertain.

We should also point out that the above comparison referred to a change in emphasis from taxes on income to taxes on consumer expenditure. If a sales tax falls on capital goods as well, as is now the case with respect to the manufacturer's sales tax, the change will reduce rather than stimulate *real* saving. The removal of the sales tax from capital goods, which is desirable on grounds of allocative efficiency, would also be a desirable change in the tax mix from the growth standpoint because the capital goods purchasing power of each dollar saved would be increased. If the revenue now raised by the sales tax on capital goods were raised instead through the personal income tax, vertical equity as well as saving and investment would be enhanced because, in the long run, a significant share of the burden of the sales tax on capital goods, like that of all sales taxes, is likely to be shifted forward to consumers.

These findings that changes in the tax mix within a given overall tax yield would do little to stimulate personal saving are neither surprising nor disheartening. Personal saving accounts for only a small share of total saving, being overwhelmed by gross business saving. In addition, a large portion of personal saving finances increases in residential housing rather than increases in business fixed capital. Year-to-year changes in personal saving are even less important. In contrast to business, foreign, and government saving, which fluctuate greatly from year to year, personal saving is remarkably stable. Despite the large changes in both the tax burden and the relative importance of different taxes, personal saving today bears about the same relationship to personal disposable income as it did in the 1920's.

The remarkable stability of the relationship between personal saving and disposable income, together with the stability of the relationship between dividends and net profits, suggest that reductions in the effective corporate income tax rate, offset by increases in either personal income taxes or indirect taxes, could be used to increase private saving. We have already stated that the available evidence does not suggest that changes in corporate income tax rates are fully shifted. Therefore, a reduction in Canadian corporate income tax rates would probably lead to increases in after-tax corporate income. Because corporations save (retain) about one half of their after-tax income, while individuals save only 5 per cent to 10 per cent on average, about one half of a corporate income tax cut would be saved, but an equivalent increase in personal income taxes would reduce personal saving by only about 10 per cent of the additional tax. Such an increase in saving could be achieved without reducing vertical equity if the offsetting increase in the personal income tax were concentrated in the higher income groups. For while this group saves more than 10 per cent of its after-tax income, it is unlikely to save as much as corporations. The existence of a differential rate of saving between corporations and upper income individuals means that an increase in saving could be achieved by moving taxes from corporations to upper income individuals.

Our proposal for integrating personal and corporate taxes would, however, achieve an increase in saving without some of the unfortunate side effects of the switch from corporate to personal income taxes we have just discussed.

There are two methods that can be used to increase corporate saving without reducing the corporate income tax rate: investment credits and accelerated capital cost allowances.

Investment credits involve providing the corporation with a tax reduction equal to a percentage of its capital expenditures during a specified period in excess of a prescribed capital expenditure base. In effect, if the corporation increased its capital expenditures, it would be given credit for having paid taxes that it had not paid. This would reduce the net tax liabilities of the corporation and, under our integration proposal, would put greater tax rebates or credits in the hands of resident shareholders when earnings were allocated to them. Investment credits would improve the cash position of corporations, increase the rate of return on capital-intensive projects, and directly increase rates of return to resident shareholders.

With accelerated capital cost allowances, the corporation receives the equivalent of an interest-free loan from the government because corporate income tax is postponed. Because the corporate income tax is postponed and not forgiven, as in the case of a credit, this procedure is less expensive to the revenue. Accelerated capital cost allowances also improve the cash flow of the corporation, increase the rate of return on capital-intensive investment projects, and increase the rate of return to resident shareholders through the reduction in the cost of capital to the corporation.

The Allocation of Saving

In addition to stimulating the aggregate amount of saving and investment, measures may be taken to improve the efficiency with which available saving is allocated to alternative investment uses. The most efficient allocation of saving is achieved when the expected marginal social rate of return is equal in each alternative investment use.

There are reasons why the most efficient allocation of resources would not be achieved even in the absence of taxation or with a completely neutral tax system. First, the expected social rate of return may differ from the rate of return that can be attained by private investors. Second, expected private rates of return will not be equated at the margin because private investors probably prefer safe to risky ventures, and attach liquidity premiums to readily marketable assets. Third, the present tax system itself has a number of features which tend to distort the allocation of saving. The more important of these are discussed in the following pages.

Treatment of Losses

The present tax system severely restricts the deduction of losses from other income. Because capital gains are not taxed, capital losses are not deductible. Business losses cannot be transferred except under very special circumstances, and they cannot be used to offset other income except in the year in which they occur. They can be carried back only one year and forward for five years against business income. The limitations on the deductibility of losses increase the after-tax return that would have to be expected on a risky venture before it becomes comparable to the after-tax return expected on a venture with low risk. This harmful feature reinforces the discrimination against risky ventures that would occur in any case.

We have concluded that this bias created by restrictions on the deductibility of business losses under the present system should be removed. Also, we have framed our recommendations so as to avoid creating a bias through taxing capital gains without adequate provision for capital losses. To this end we recommend later that capital losses should be fully deductible against other income in any year with but very few restrictions. We also recommend that the carry-back and carry-forward periods for business losses should be extended and that business losses should be deductible from other income in any year. However, we have not gone so far as to recommend refunds of tax with respect to losses, or the unlimited transferability of business losses.

Risky Ventures

At least with the present state of knowledge, economic markets are a more efficient means of allocating resources than direct governmental planning and direction. This is not to say that there is no need for government intervention to achieve socially desirable ends, or that there is no need for government regulation to impose some constraints on the freedom of action of individual entrepreneurs, for such is of course one of the purposes of government. But the aims of government can for the most part be achieved most efficiently by subsidies, specific expenditure programmes, and other types of direct action. Where possible they should be achieved in this fashion rather than indirectly and inefficiently through manipulation of the tax system.

The incorporation of special incentives into the tax system consequently requires justification. We believe that there are several considerations which justify the inclusion of special tax incentives to encourage investment in risky ventures. First, the capital markets are by no means "perfect" in the efficiency of their allocation of resources to highly risky ventures, particularly because such ventures are generally new, small enterprises. Second, while there is need for direct governmental action in assisting new firms to obtain financing, we have concluded that incentives built into the tax system can provide an efficient means both of making risky investments more profitable and of reducing their need for external funds.

Our general approach is in favour of a treatment which is not an exemption from tax but rather a postponement of the payment of taxes ordinarily due, the postponement being realized by permitting immediate full write-off of the cost of depreciable assets acquired. The postponement is in effect an interest-free loan repayable to the government out of income subsequently earned. It therefore does not reduce the long-term tax liability, but it does decrease the amount of funds required to finance the investment and, in so doing, increases the investment's profitability. We believe that this is the approach that is most consistent with equity and with the nature of the risks that deserve to be recognized in a tax system.

The Dual Corporate Tax Rate

Another problem that exists under the present system is the discriminatory treatment of income earned through the corporate form compared with other forms of organization, and the discrimination between corporations with large and small profits. These differences in tax treatment mean that projects with the same expected before-tax rate of return have different expected after-tax rates of return depending on the organization which undertakes the project. This leads to an inefficient allocation of resources, for all kinds of projects cannot be undertaken by all forms of organization.

The lower rate of corporate income tax on income below $35,000 is one of the features of the present system which contributes most to this result. The low income company is not necessarily a small company in terms of assets nor is it necessarily owned by low income shareholders. The lower corporate rate is therefore a most inefficient method of compensating for the riskiness of new, small businesses. The dual corporate rate can create gross inequities because high income shareholders can pay low rates of corporate tax and arrange that the company retain the earnings. These undistributed earnings have in the past frequently been realized by the shareholder by a variety of techniques that encountered little or no personal income tax.

We recommend that the dual rate of corporate tax be abolished in the interest of improving the allocation of resources and of increasing equity.

Capital Gains

The absence of a tax on capital gains has undoubtedly had the effect of encouraging an inefficient allocation of resources. Two ventures with the same expected before-tax rate of return will have very different expected after-tax rates of return if one return is taxable and the other is not.

The taxation of capital gains can be considered only in the light of the treatment of capital and other losses, the integration of personal and corporate income taxes, the averaging provisions that we propose, and our proposed marginal rates of personal income tax. We can conclude that the exclusion of capital gains has the effect of distorting the allocation of saving. It has also created great uncertainty and placed a high premium on the form rather than the substance of transactions. For these reasons, and because the exclusion is grossly inequitable, we recommend the inclusion of these gains in income and the deduction of capital losses from income with further compensating changes in other features of the system that would, we are convinced, compensate for the negative effects on investment and saving of taxing capital gains.

Capital Cost Allowances

If it is reasonable to assume that in most cases the depreciation charged by businesses on their financial statements reflects the management's best estimate of the "true" rate of depreciation, the present capital cost allowance provisions are exceedingly generous in the earlier years of the life of the asset. Based on a survey of large corporations conducted by our research staff it is estimated that Canadian corporations had, in the eight-year period ending in 1962, deferred their taxable incomes by over $2 billion, relative to their incomes as reported in their financial statements, as a result of the high capital cost allowance rates. The tax deferred on these incomes would therefore be about $1 billion.

The ideal method, that is, one that is neutral with respect to investment in assets with different lives or expected rates of return, would allow the firm to deduct the reduction in the estimated market value of the asset that occurs during the year. Needless to say, this method would be administratively impractical, because well-functioning markets do not exist for many types of used assets.

The preference of business firms for the straight-line method for their own internal planning is some indication that, among the feasible accounting methods available, this one is accepted as a more satisfactory approximation to the ideal than other alternatives.

Earnings Retention

We think that the objective should be the development of a tax system that does not discriminate in either direction with respect to cash retentions. It would be unwise to develop a tax system that forced cash distributions for the result would be to penalize growing firms that were ploughing back earnings. We doubt whether such firms would be adequately served by the capital markets, particularly if they are engaged in ventures of high risk. Favourable tax treatment of cash retentions, on the other hand, constricts the growth and development of capital markets and makes it even more difficult for new firms, which have no past income to draw on, to obtain funds.

The recommendations we make with respect to the integration of corporate and personal income taxes would put pressure on corporations to allocate their profits to shareholders, but would be neutral with respect to the *form* of distribution: cash dividends, stock dividends, or other capitalization of corporate surplus would have the same status for tax purposes. Because the overall tax burden on income flowing through corporations would be reduced, however, corporations would be able to increase both their cash retentions and the cash put in the hands of the shareholders. We also recommend the continuation of the present liberal capital cost allowance provisions, which we expect will continue to provide the major source of funds for business investment. If the internal funds available to firms were still deemed to be inadequate, we would recommend either more generous capital cost allowances, or the adoption of investment tax credits, both of which link the provision of funds to capital expenditure, rather than a return to the discriminatory treatment of dividends relative to the retention of earnings.

Selected Bibliography

Chapter One

The Objectives of Economic Policy

T. E. H. Reid, *Economic Planning in a Democratic Society?*, University of Toronto Press, Toronto, 1963.

W. A. Johr and H. W. Singer, *The Role of the Economist as Official Advisor*, especially Part I, George Allen & Unwin, London, 1955.

Robert Solo (ed.), *Economics and the Public Interest*, Rutgers University Press, New Brunswick, N.J., 1955.

Richard A. Musgrave, *The Theory of Public Finance*, Part I, McGraw-Hill, New York, 1959.

The Economic Council of Canada, *First, Second, Third & Fourth Annual Reviews*, Queen's Printer, Ottawa.

W. J. Baumol, *Welfare Economics and the Theory of the State*, second ed., Harvard University Press, Cambridge, Mass., 1965.

The Royal Commission on National Development in the Arts, Letters and Sciences, 1949-1951, *Report* (The Massey Report), King's Printer, Ottawa, 1951.

Harry G. Johnson, *The Canadian Quandary*, McGraw-Hill, Toronto, 1963.

William C. Birdsall, "A Study of the Demand for Public Goods", in R. A. Musgrave (ed.), *Essays in Fiscal Federalism*, The Brookings Institution, Washington, 1965.

Kenneth J. Arrow, *Social Choice and Individual Values*, Wiley, New York, 1951.

Chapter Two

Government Expenditures

Francis M. Bator, *The Question of Government Spending*, Collier, New York, 1962.

Anthony Downs, *An Economic Theory of Democracy*, Harper & Row, New York, 1957.

P. A. Samuelson, "The Pure Theory of Public Expenditure", *Review of Economics and Statistics*, Vol. XXXVI, November 1954, pp. 387-389.

P. A. Samuelson, "Diagrammatic Exposition of a Theory of Public Expenditure", *Review of Economics and Statistics*, Vol. XXXVIII, November 1955, pp. 350-356.

P. A. Samuelson, "Aspects of Public Expenditures Theories", *Review of Economics and Statistics*, Vol. XL, November 1958, pp. 332-338.

Gerhard Colm, "Comments on Samuelson's Theory of Public Finance", *Review of Economics and Statistics*, Vol. XXXVIII, November 1956, pp. 408-412.

Julius Margolis, "A Comment on the Pure Theory of Public Expenditure", *Review of Economics and Statistics*, Vol. XXXVII, November 1955, pp. 347-349.

Richard A. Musgrave, *The Theory of Public Finance*, McGraw-Hill, New York, 1959, Ch. 1, 2, 3, 4, 7, 11.

J. G. Head, "Public Goods and Public Policy", *Public Finance*, Vol. XVII, No. 3, 1962, pp. 197-219.

Robert Dorfman (ed.), *Measuring Benefits of Government Investments*, The Brookings Institution, Washington, 1965.

James M. Buchanan, *Public Finance: Needs, Sources and Utilization*, Princeton University Press for The National Bureau of Economic Research, Princeton, N.J., 1961, pp. 295-420 and pp. 439-504.

Roland N. McKean, *Public Spending*, McGraw-Hill, New York, 1968.

A. T. Peacock and J. Wiseman, *The Growth of Public Expenditures in the U.K.*, Princeton University Press, Princeton, N.J., 1961.

C. Hitch and R. N. McKean, *The Economics of Defense in the Nuclear Age*, Harvard University Press, Cambridge, Mass., 1965.

A. R. Prest and R. Turney, "Cost-Benefit Analysis: A Survey", *Economic Journal*, Vol. LXXV, December 1965, pp. 683-735.

S. B. Chase, Jr. (ed.), *Problems in Public Expenditure Analysis*, The Brookings Institution, Washington, 1968.

Maffeo Pantaleoni, "Contribution to the Theory of the Distribution of Public Expenditure", in R. A. Musgrave and A. T. Peacock (eds.), *Classics in the Theory of Public Finance*, Macmillan, London, 1958 and St. Martin's Press, New York, 1967, pp. 16-27.

Roland N. McKean, "Evaluating Alternative Expenditure Programs", in James M. Buchanan (ed.), *Public Finance: Needs, Sources and Utilization*. Princeton University Press for The National Bureau of Economic Research, Princeton, N.J., 1961, pp. 337-364.

Otto Eckstein, "A Survey of the Theory of Public Expenditure Criteria", in James M. Buchanan (ed.), *Public Finance: Needs, Sources and Utilization*, Princeton University Press for the National Bureau of Economic Research, Princeton, N.J., 1961, pp. 439-504.

Chapter Three

Federal-Provincial Relations

George F. Break, *Intergovernmental Fiscal Relations in the U.S.*, The Brookings Institution, Washington, 1967.

James M. Buchanan, "Federalism and Fiscal Equity", *American Economic Review*, Vol. XL, No. 4, September 1950, reprinted in R. A. Musgrave and C. S. Shoup (eds.), *Readings in the Economics of Taxation*, Richard D. Irwin, Homewood, Ill., 1959, pp. 93-109.

Richard A. Musgrave (ed.), *Essays in Fiscal Federalism*, The Brookings Institution, Washington, 1965.

Richard A. Musgrave, *The Theory of Public Finance*, McGraw-Hill, New York, 1959, Ch. 8.

Richard A. Musgrave, "Approaches to Fiscal Theory of Political Federalism",
    in James M. Buchanan (ed.), *Public Finance: Needs, Sources and Utiliza-*
    tion, Princeton University Press for The National Bureau of Economic
    Research, Princeton, N.J., 1961.
Milton A. Moore, J. Harvey Perry, and Donald I. Beach, *The Financing of*
    Canadian Federation, The Canadian Tax Foundation, Toronto, 1966.
G. V. LaForest, *The Allocation of Taxing Power under the Canadian Consti-*
    tution, The Canadian Tax Foundation, Toronto, 1967.

Chapter Four

Taxation in Canada

J. Harvey Perry, *Taxation in Canada*, third ed., University of Toronto Press,
    Toronto, 1961.
R. A. Musgrave, *The Theory of Public Finance*, McGraw-Hill, New York,
    1959.
J. M. Buchanan, *The Public Finances*, Irwin, Homewood, Ill., 1965.
J. F. Due, *Government Finance: The Economics of the Public Sector*, fourth
    ed., Irwin, Homewood, Ill., 1967.
R. A. Musgrave and A. T. Peacock (eds.), *Classics in the Theory of Public*
    Finance, Macmillan, London, 1958, and St. Martin's Press, New York,
    1967.
The Canadian Tax Foundation, *Report of the November 1967 Conference*,
    Toronto, 1968.
The Canadian Tax Foundation, *Provincial Finances, 1967*, Toronto, 1968.
The Canadian Tax Foundation, *National Finances 1967-1968*, Toronto, 1968.
The Ontario Committee on Taxation, *Report*, Queen's Printer, Toronto, 1967.
The Royal Commission on Taxation, *Report*, Queen's Printer, Ottawa, 1966-
    1967.
The Saskatchewan Royal Commission on Taxation, *Report*, Queen's Printer,
    Regina, 1965.
J. R. Petrie, *The Taxation of Corporate Income in Canada*, University of
    Toronto Press, Toronto, 1952.

Chapter Five

Municipal Finance

Julius Margolis, "Metropolitan Finance Problems: Territories, Functions and
    Growth", in James M. Buchanan (ed.), *Public Finance: Needs, Sources*
    and Utilization, Princeton University Press for The National Bureau of
    Economic Research, Princeton, N.J., 1961, pp. 229-294.
Richard A. Musgrave (ed.), *Essays in Fiscal Federalism*, The Brookings Insti-
    tution, Washington, 1965, pp. 63-121, and pp. 187-234.

James A. Maxwell, *Financing State and Local Governments*, The Brookings Institution, Washington, 1965.

Wilbur R. Thompson, *A Preface to Urban Economics*, The Johns Hopkins Press for Resources for the Future, Baltimore, 1965.

The Canadian Tax Foundation, *The Local Finances*, Toronto, various issues.

Leroy O. Stone, *Urban Development in Canada*, Dominion Bureau of Statistics, Ottawa, 1967.

Ralph W. Pfouts, *The Techniques of Urban Economic Analysis*, Chandler-Davis, West Trenton, N.J., 1960.

Chapter Six

Fiscal Policy for Stabilization and Growth

E. S. Phelps, *Fiscal Neutrality Toward Economic Growth*, McGraw-Hill, New York, 1965.

J. F. Due, *Government Finance: The Economics of the Public Sector*, fourth ed., Irwin, Homewood, Ill., 1967.

R. A. Musgrave, *The Theory of Public Finance*, McGraw-Hill, New York, 1959.

The Royal Commission on Taxation, *Report*, Queen's Printer, Ottawa, 1966-1967.

The Economic Council of Canada, *Conference on Stabilization Policies*, Queen's Printer, Ottawa, 1966.

The Ontario Committee on Taxation, *Report*, Queen's Printer, Toronto, 1967.

Index

Balance of payments, 8, 18
Benefit-cost analysis, 77, 81, 83, 84
Block averaging, 215
British North America Act, 1867, 88, 90, 103
Budget, government, 74
Budget policy, objectives of, 14, 16
Budgetary flexibility, 301
Built-in stability, economic, 290
Buoyant economy, inflationary, 35
Burden of Ontario Retail Sales Tax, 231

Canadian federation, objectives of, 109-116
Capital gains, taxation of, 198, 199, 204
Carter Commission (*see* Royal Commission on Taxation, 1967)
Classification of Public Programs, 274
Collective needs, 8
Commodity taxes, 181
Conditional and Unconditional Grants, 119
Constitution: Canadian, amendment of, 95, 97; provincial, 93 (*see also* British North America Act, 1867)
Constitutional custom, 90
Constitutional laws of federal government, 89, 90-103
Corporation Income Tax, 179
Corporate tax, dual rate of, 345
Corporate profits tax, 168
Court decisions, effect of, on economy, 97
Customs, 169, 182

Democracy, economic theory of, 50
Discrimination, in taxation, 165
Dividend behaviour, and fiscal policy, 340

Earnings retention, and fiscal policy, 347
Economic base theory of urban development, 257
Economic decision-making, technique for, 70-72
Economic grants, policy objectives of, 8, 15, 17, 30-33, 38
Economic growth and equity, conflict between, 37, 38, 39
Economic objectives: for Canada, 20-22; critiques of, 22; and individual liberties, 20; long-term, 8; national, priority of, 22; and rate of increase of productivity, 20; short-term, 8
Economic policy: and improvement of factors of production, 8; instruments of, 7; objectives of, 1, 44-48; and price stability, 8; and production expansion, 8
Economics, external, 269-274
Education, expenditure for, 278, 283
Effective Total Tax Incidence for the Total Tax Structure, 171
Equity, 15, 23-27, 28, 29, 30, 37, 38, 72, 132 (*see also* Fiscal equity)
Estate tax, 169, 179, 180, 223, 225, 226
Estimated Revenues and Expenditures of Municipalities, 282
Essential supplies, security of, 8
European Common Market, 245
Excise duties, uses of, 181, 328, 329
Expenditure: evaluation of government, 74-84; by local government, 264, 279, 280
Exports, tax incentives for, 246

Fads, in economics, 44-48
Federal finance, principles in Canada, 125
Federal government: defined, 88; constitutional laws of, 89, 90-103; economists' attitude toward, 86; and provincial relations, 21
Federal system, and unitary system compared, 86
Federal Tax Revenue, 175
Fiscal equity, 132; and optimum resource allocation, 139
Fiscal policy: and budgetary process, 310; and corporate income tax, 292, 293; and economic instability, 290; evaluation of, 295-301; and expenditure by government, 294; federal budgetary, 301-304; flexibility of, 313; formula for, 312; general and specific, compared, 295; for growth, 329-347; and personal income tax, 293; provincial objectives of, 321, 323; provincial view-point of, 317-323; and sales and excise taxes, 292; and stand-by authority, 312; and supplementary budgets, 312
Fiscal policy lags: action, 309-313; inside, 307-313; outside, 313-317; recognition, 307-309

Fiscal residuum, 133-134
Full employment, and budget surplus, 296; as policy objective, 8, 17, 34

Gift tax, 180, 223, 224, 226
Grants: conditional and unconditional, 116-121; federal to provinces, 94, 95, 116, 125, 149-152
Gratuitous transfers, taxation of, 222, 223
Growth: and allocation of saving, 344, 345; capital formation of, 338, 341; and corporate tax rate, 345-347; and dividend behaviour, 340, 341; factors, importance of, 330; of labour supply, 330-333; and rate of saving, 341-344; research and development, 336-338; and structural change, 334-336; and technical change, 333; urban, 277-289.

Hospital insurance premiums, 169

Impact of Discretionary Fiscal Policy on Full-Employment Surplus, 297
Import duties, 169, 182
Income: averaging of, 213-216; concept of, American, 193, Canadian, 194, English, 193, general, 192; definition of, 192, 195-198; distribution of, 8, 16, 18, 59, as policy objective, 8, 15, 16, 18, 20; measurables, 72
Income tax: alternative approach to, 217, 218, 219; assumptions regarding, 167; corporate, 177, 216-223, integration of, with personal, 217; personal, 167, 173-176, 192, statistical comparison of, 205-208, on equity investments, 210, maximum marginal rate of, 210, rates of, 205ff, and treatment of dependents, 211
Inflation, 34
Interests, government, 53

Labour conventions, and powers of federal government, 98
Local costs, 72
Local expenditures, theory of, 262, 263-267
Local government, differentiation of products of, 259

Majority rule, 60
Metropolitan governments, organization of, 271-275
Monetary policy, 35
Municipal Expenditures and Financing, 280
Municipal finance, 257-261
Municipal Government Expenditures, 279
Municipal revenue, 279, 280
Municipalities: conflict of objectives of; 260-261; decentralization of, 285

Need, and equity, 135
Negative Personal Income Tax, 256
Net Tax Revenue, Provinces, 184
Net Tax Revenue of All Governments, 174

Official commissions, decision making by, 57
Old Age Security, 175, 182
Ontario, and federation, 111-113

Performance budget, meaning of, 74, 75
Personal Income Tax, 178
Personal Income Tax, Statistical Comparison, 205, 206
Policy objectives, non-economic, 11, 13-14
Political action, economic theory of, 51
Population, and economic policy, 8
Post war period, problems of, 35
Power: delegation of, 95; economic, of provinces, 89-91; of federations and provinces, 93-95
Price, external influence on, 35
Price fluctuation, prevention of, as goal, 20
Price stability, and economic policy, 8, 15
Principal Taxes Levied by Provinces, 186-187, 188-189, 190-191
Private consumption, economic policy for, 8
Private enterprise mechanism, 31
Product differentiation, in local government, 259
Productivity maximization, as goal, 20
Program budget, 73, 74-83; management approach to, 73, 74, 75
Project evaluation, benefit-cost analysis approach to, 77-80
Protection and priorities, economic policy for, 8

Public expenditure: constitutional basis for, 90-95; powers of, 90-95; theory of, 144-149
Public goods, 55, 262, 263, 267, 271

Quebec, and federation, 113-116

Rate schedule, selection of, 208, 211
Redistribution, of wealth, 29
Residential locations, choice of, 258
Revenue: functions of and rearrangement of, 115; sharing between governments, 154-156
Rowell-Sirois Report (*see* Royal Commission on Federal-Provincial Relations)
Royal Commission on Federal-Provincial Relations, 87, 103-107, 127
Royal Commission on Taxation, 1967, 87; goals of, 17-20; and tax policy, 107

Sales tax: and business cycle, 235; in Canada, 228-229; and consumption, 233; and deflation, 234; economic effect of, 232-235; and economic growth, 234; equity of, 229-232; federal, 241-243; general, 168; and inflation, 234; on manufactures and material, 240; merits of, 240; and saving, 233; on services, 235-237
Selective employment tax, 253
Selective factor tax, 169
Shadow prices, use of, 71
Social contract, meaning of, 63
Social opportunity costs, 72
Social Security, 98
Spending power, nature of, 101
Stabilization of economy, 287
Stabilization policy, discretionary, 292-295
Standard of living, in Canada, 38
Succession duties (*see* Estate tax)

Tax: evasion of, 246; exemption of churches, 165; treatment of loss of, 344
Tax base, comprehensive, 196, 198
Tax burden, distribution of, 230
Tax changes, suitability of, 323-325

Tax incidence, 166-170; empirical result of, 169
Tax principles: conflict of, 165; and social policy, 160-165, 166
Tax revenue: in Canada, 173; provincial, 183
Tax systems: dividend-paid credit approach to, 218; dividend-received credit approach to, 219; neutral, 41
Taxation: advantages of integration of, 221, 222; of alcohol, 165; of consumption and services, 227-243; injustice of, 20-28; simplicity of, 162; of tobacco, 165; unit of, 212
Taxation for stabilization: capital gains, 327; corporate income, 327; criteria for, 223-225; excise, 328
Taxes: cumulative turnover, 243-245; gift, 180, 226; negative income, 253-256; non-resident withholding, 180; property, 168, 260, 278, 280; sales (*see* Sales tax); selective employment, 249-253; selective factor, 169; value-added, 245, 249-256
Total Tax Payments, 1961, 167
Trade-off, 33-37
Trade-Off Zone, 36
Transportation, municipal expenditures on, 278

Unemployment, and trade-off, 34, 35
Unemployment Insurance legislation, 99
United Nations, Department of Economic and Social Affairs, 74, 75
Urban development, economic base theory of, 257
Urban growth, Economic Council of Canada, 277

Value-added tax, 245
Vertical equity, 42
Value judgments, 2

Wealth, taxation of, 225, 226, 227
Welfare, economic, 12, 13
Welfare expenditure, urban financing of, 260
Withholding tax system, effect of, 218, 219